Integrative and eclectic therapy: a handbook

Open University Press
Psychotherapy Handbooks Series
Series editor: Windy Dryden

Integrative and eclectic therapy: a handbook

Edited by
WINDY DRYDEN

Open University Press
Buckingham · Philadelphia

Open University Press
Celtic Court
22 Ballmoor
Buckingham
MK18 1XW

and
1900 Frost Road, Suite 101
Bristol, PA 19007, USA

First published 1992

A catalogue record of this book is available from the British Library

Library of Congress Cataloging-in-Publication Data

Integrative and eclectic therapy: a handbook/edited by Windy Dryden.
      p.   cm.—(Psychotherapy handbooks series)
    Includes index.
    ISBN 0-335-09337-X (pb)   ISBN 0-335-09338-8 (hb.)
    1. Eclectic psychotherapy. I. Dryden, Windy. II. Series.
    [DNLM: 1. Counseling—methods. 2. Psychotherapy—methods. WM
420 I598]
RC489.E24I54 1992
616.89′14—dc20
DNLM/DLC
for Library of Congress   92-1063
                                                              CIP

Typeset by Colset Private Limited, Singapore
Printed in Great Britain by Biddles Limited, Guildford and Kings Lynn

Contents

Contributors

HAL ARKOWITZ, Department of Psychology, University of Arizona, USA

MICHAEL BARKHAM, MRC/ESRC Social and Applied Psychology Unit, University of Sheffield

PETRŪSKA CLARKSON, *metanoia* Psychotherapy Training Institute, London

PAULINE COWMEADOW, United Medical and Dental Schools, Guy's Hospital, London

MICHAEL CROWE, Marital and Sex Therapy Clinic, Maudsley Hospital, London

SUE CULLEY, Independent Counsellor, Trainer and Consultant, London

ROY ESKAPA, London Centre for Multimodal Therapy; London Enuresis Clinic

WAGUIH R. GUIRGUIS, Psychosexual Clinic, St Clement's Hospital, Ipswich

PHIL LAPWORTH, *metanoia* Psychotherapy Training Institute, London

JOHN C. NORCROSS, Department of Psychology, University of Scranton, USA

JANE RIDLEY, Marital and Sex Therapy Clinic, Maudsley Hospital, London

JOHN ROWAN, Independent Consultant, London

ANTHONY RYLE, Senior Fellow, United Medical and Dental Schools of Guys and St Thomas's Hospitals, London

ANDY TREACHER, Department of Clinical and Community Psychology, Heavitree, Exeter

Introduction

In 1984, I edited a book entitled *Individual Therapy in Britain* (Dryden 1984a). My purpose in publishing that text was to encourage British practitioners and students of counselling and psychotherapy to use a text with British contributors and which was prepared for the British market. While most of the approaches that were covered in that text were 'pure forms', there was sufficient evidence that British practitioners were interested in eclectic/integrative approaches to therapy to justify the inclusion of three chapters on that topic – one that considered pertinent issues (Dryden 1984b) and two that documented specific approaches to eclectic/integrative therapy (Inskipp and Johns 1984; Murgatroyd and Apter 1984).

Since that time, British interest in integrative/eclectic approaches to therapy has burgeoned. First, there is now a UK branch of the Society for the Exploration of Psychotherapy Integration (SEPI), an international organization which held its annual conference in London in July 1991 (the first time it has taken place outside the United States). Second, the number of articles with an integrative or eclectic focus appearing in British journals by British authors has mushroomed in recent years (see Appendix). Finally, there is now a British Institute of Integrative Psychotherapy (BIIP).

Given this increase in interest in integrative and eclectic therapy in Britain, I decided to include a separate volume on this theme in the Psychotherapy Handbooks series. This volume, then, contains the best of current British work in this field. In order to place this work in an international context, I invited two leading American figures in the psychotherapy integration movement to contribute the opening chapter to the volume. Here, John Norcross and Hal Arkowitz present a state of the art review of this field and seek to locate the chapters that follow within it.

In these chapters, leading contributors to integrative and eclectic therapy in Britain discuss their work. In Chapters 2 to 5, Petrūska Clarkson, Anthony Ryle and Pauline Cowmeadow, Roy Eskapa and Sue Culley outline specific integrative/eclectic approaches that have gained prominence in Britain. The first two have pioneered their own approaches while the latter are British representatives of the work of American pioneers (namely Arnold Lazarus and Gerard Egan, respectively). In Chapters 6 to 9, integrative and eclectic work is presented with special reference to specific therapeutic arenas or modalities. Thus, in Chapter 6, Jane Ridley and Michael Crowe discuss their pioneering work in couple therapy, Waguih Guirguis outlines his 'Ipswich' model of sex therapy in Chapter 7, while in Chapters 8 and 9, Andy Treacher and John Rowan present their highly individualistic, yet innovative approaches to family therapy and group therapy, respectively.

In Chapter 10, Michael Barkham reviews the research literature on integrative and eclectic therapy, highlighting work emanating from Britain, while in Chapter 11, Petrūska Clarkson discusses the training of integrative therapists, an issue that is particularly timely, since the registration of psychotherapists in Britain is now rapidly becoming a reality. The book ends with an appendix in which British authored articles with an integrative or eclectic theme or focus and published in British journals are presented as a resource for those wishing to study British developments in integrative and eclectic therapy in its historical context.

References

Dryden, W. (ed.) (1984a) *Individual Therapy in Britain*, Milton Keynes: Open University Press.
—— (1984b) Issues in the eclectic practice of individual therapy, in W. Dryden (ed.) *Individual Therapy in Britain*, Milton Keynes: Open University Press.
Inskipp, F. and Johns, H. (1984) Developmental eclecticism: Egan's skills model of helping, in W. Dryden (ed.) *Individual Therapy in Britain*, Milton Keynes: Open University Press.
Murgatroyd, S. and Apter, M.J. (1984) Eclectic psychotherapy: a structural–phenomenological approach, in W. Dryden (ed.) *Individual Therapy in Britain*, Milton Keynes: Open University Press.

The evolution and current status of psychotherapy integration

JOHN C. NORCROSS AND HAL ARKOWITZ

Psychotherapy integration has a long history, but it was not until the late 1970s that it crystallized into a strong and coherent force on the psychotherapy scene. While various labels are applied to this movement – eclecticism, integration, convergence, pluralism, rapprochement, unification, prescriptionism – their goals are indeed similar. Psychotherapy integration is characterized by a dissatisfaction with single-school approaches and a concomitant desire to look across and beyond school boundaries to see what can be learned from other ways of thinking about psychotherapy and behaviour change.

Psychotherapy integration has experienced dramatic growth in the past decade, leading some observers (Moultrup 1986; London 1988) to label it a metamorphosis in mental health. Eclecticism, or the increasingly favoured term 'integration' (Norcross and Prochaska 1988), remains the modal theoretical orientation of both American (Norcross *et al.* 1989) and British (Norcross, Dryden and Brust 1992) psychotherapists, and the prevalence may be rising (Jensen *et al.* 1990). Leading counselling textbooks increasingly identify their theoretical persuasion as eclectic (Brabeck and Welfel 1985), and an integrative or eclectic chapter is routinely included in compendia of various treatment approaches. The publication of books which synthesize various therapeutic concepts and methods continues unabated, and the field has matured to a point where entire handbooks, such as this volume and that of Norcross and Goldfried (1992), are deemed necessary. Reflecting and engendering the burgeoning field has been the establishment of interdisciplinary psychotherapy organizations devoted to integration – notably the Society for the Exploration of Psychotherapy Integration (SEPI) – and of international publications, including SEPI's *Journal of Psychotherapy Integration*. The surge of integrative fervour will also apparently persist well into the 1990s: a recent panel of psychotherapy experts portended its increasing popularity throughout this decade (Norcross, Alford and DeMichele 1992).

A spirit of open enquiry and lively debate pervades the field, as evidenced by the appearance of several series of articles in different journals. The journals include: *Behavior Therapy* (Garfield 1982; Goldfried 1982b; Kendall 1982; Wachtel

1982a); the *British Journal of Clinical Psychology* (Davis 1983; Messer 1983; Murray 1983; Wachtel 1983; Yates 1983); the *British Journal of Guidance and Counselling* (Beitman 1989; Dryden and Norcross 1989; Lazarus 1989b; Messer 1989; Norcross and Grencavage 1989); and *Psychiatric Annals* (Babcock 1988; Birk 1988; London and Palmer 1988; Powell 1988; Rhoads 1988). A major article on psychotherapy integration appeared in the *American Journal of Psychiatry* (Beitman *et al.* 1989). In addition, theoretical integration was prominently reviewed in the recent *Annual Review of Psychology* chapter on individual psychotherapy (Goldfried *et al.* 1990).

In this introductory chapter, we will begin by considering multiple reasons for the recent growth of psychotherapy integration. The bulk of the chapter will then review the four main contemporary thrusts of integration, and outline what we consider the limitations and obstacles of psychotherapy integration in general. Finally, we will consider the impact integrative thinking has already had – and will likely have – on the field of psychotherapy.

Why integration now?

Integration as a point of view has probably existed as long as philosophy and psychotherapy. In philosophy, the third-century biographer, Diogenes Laertius, referred to an eclectic school which flourished in Alexandria in the second century AD (Lunde 1974). In psychotherapy, Freud consciously struggled with the selection and integration of diverse methods (Frances 1988). More formal ideas on synthesizing the psychotherapies appeared in the literature as early as the 1930s (French 1933).

Although the notion of integrating various therapeutic approaches has intrigued mental health professionals for some time (Goldfried and Newman 1992), it has been only within the past 15 years that integration has developed into a clearly delineated area of interest. The last decade, in particular, has witnessed both a general decline in ideological struggles and the stirrings of rapprochement. The debates across theoretical systems appear to be less polemical, or at least more issue-specific.

A confluence of scientific, professional and socio-economic circumstances has produced the recent preoccupation with psychotherapy integration. Several intertwined, mutually reinforcing factors have fostered the movement in the past decade (see London 1983, 1988; Norcross and Grencavage 1989; Arkowitz 1992).

Psychotherapy integration has, in part, *been a response to the improved quality of psychotherapy outcome research during this period, and to the lack of strong evidence to support differential outcomes among existing therapies.* Prior to the late 1970s, there were few well-designed studies on the outcome of psychotherapy. Since then, the number of such studies has increased dramatically (e.g. see review by Lambert *et al.* 1986), and meta-analytic procedures (e.g. Smith *et al.* 1980) have provided more objective ways to summarize and compare the results of different studies. These studies have revealed surprisingly few differences in outcome among different therapies, and there is little evidence that one empirically evaluated psychotherapy is consistently superior to another (e.g. Elkin *et al.* 1989; Beckham 1990; Barkham, Chapter 10, this volume). While we need to be cautious in accepting the null hypothesis, and while there are many possible interpretations of such findings (e.g. Stiles *et al.* 1986), they very likely served as a catalyst for many who began to consider integrative interpretations of these results. Luborsky *et al.* (1975), borrowing a phrase from the Dodo bird in *Alice in Wonderland*, concluded that 'everybody has won and all must have prizes'. Or in the words of London (1988: 7), 'Meta-analytic research shows charity for all treatments and malice towards none.'

A corollary of the equivalence paradox – no differential efficacy despite technical diversity – has been the *growing consensus that no one approach is clinically adequate for all problems, patients and situations*. Psychotherapy has entered a period of intense self-examination in which the failures of our pet theories are reappraised and their limitations realized. The grand-systems era has been undermined by a wave of scepticism in which leading figures of each school have criticized their own theories and assumptions. Omer and London (1988) trace scepticism within psychoanalysis (e.g. implausibility of truly 'free associations', doubts about Freud's archaeology metaphor), behaviour therapy (e.g. questions on presumed derivation from learning theory, over-reliance on observed behaviours), and cognitive therapy (e.g. doubts on the precedence of cognition over affect and behaviour, difficulty of dispelling dysfunctional thinking). Obviously, no clinical theory has a monopoly on truth or utility; clinical realities have come to demand a pluralistic, if not integrative, perspective.

Another contributing factor has been *the proliferation of the number of specific therapies*. Paralleling the growth of interest in psychotherapy integration has been a sharp increase in the number of different therapies (Karasu 1986), and in the number of variations within each of the major psychotherapies. This increasing diversity has had two effects. One was to make available a greater range of theories and techniques, from which an integration could be crafted. A second has been to alert therapists to the almost infinite number of possible variations in technique. The latter may have discouraged the search for further variations and encouraged therapists to seek more creative ways to utilize existing therapies.

The field has been staggered by over-choice and fragmented by future shock. Which of 400 plus therapies should be studied, taught or bought? No single theory has been able to corner the market on validity or utility. London (1988: 5–6) wryly observed that the hyperinflation of brand name therapies has produced narcissistic fatigue: 'With so many brand names around that no one can recognize, let alone remember, and so many competitors doing psychotherapy, it is becoming too arduous to launch still another new brand.'

Along with the proliferation of 'brand name' therapies has been a trend towards *more specific and operational descriptions of psychotherapy practice*. There were relatively few specific and operational descriptions of psychotherapeutic techniques prior to 1970. From the late 1970s onwards, a number of specific treatment manuals appeared (e.g. Beck *et al.* 1979; Luborsky 1984; Strupp and Binder 1984), often growing out of research on the disparate therapies. In fact, Luborsky and DeRubeis (1984) referred to this manualization of therapy as a 'small revolution'. The availability of more clearly described therapy procedures has permitted more accurate comparisons and contrasts among them, providing further impetus for various approaches to psychotherapy integration.

Escalating interest in short-term psychotherapies during the past 20 years (Budman 1981) has also contributed to the growing interest in integration. An interest in short-term therapies was accompanied by the development of more problem-focused therapies. A common emphasis on a problem focus (although there is still divergence in how to define the term 'problem') has brought therapies that were formerly very different somewhat closer together, and has created variations of different therapies that were more compatible with each other.

A trend towards increasing interactions among professionals of different therapy orientations in specialized clinics for the treatment of specific disorders, particularly in North America, may also have had an effect on the development of psychotherapy integration (London and Palmer 1988). Since the 1970s, there has been a movement towards such specialized clinics for a variety of problems, including sexual dysfunctions, agoraphobia, obsessive-compulsive disorders, depression and eating disorders, to name just a few. These clinics are often staffed by professionals of diverse theoretical orientations, with greater emphasis on their expertise about the clinical problem than on their theoretical orientation *per se*. This diversity stood in contrast to the earlier emphasis on institutes devoted to specific therapies. At the very least, the exposure to other theories and therapies in such clinics may have stimulated some to consider other orientations more seriously.

An additional reason for integrating the psychotherapies *is a matrix of socio-economic influences*. The total therapy industry continues to grow: invasion of non-doctoral and non-medical counsellors, the boom in professional practice, the mushrooming of training institutes and the outpouring of third-party funding in the United States (London 1988).

Meanwhile, pressures for accountability are mounting in the USA from insurance companies, government policy-makers, consumer groups and judicial officials. Third parties and the public are demanding crisp and informative answers regarding the quality, durability and efficiency of psychosocial treatments (Parloff 1979). Until recently the field has had the luxury of functioning within a culture of individual professional freedom. However, the shrinking job market, increased competition and diminishing public support portend a future which is discontinuous with our expansive past (Fishman and Neigher 1982).

Without some change from the field, psychotherapists stand to lose prestige, customers and money. These socio-economic considerations increasingly have psychotherapists pulling together rather than apart. Mental health professionals report that the impact of political and economic changes have led them to work harder, to be more creative and to adjust their treatments to meet the needs of their clients (Brown 1983). Intertheoretical co-operation and a more unified psychotherapy community represent attempts to respond to these socio-political forces.

The development of a professional network has been both a consequence and a cause of the interest in psychotherapy integration. Before 1970 the strands for psychotherapy integration were available, but they did not yet form a connected and unified body of thought. In 1983, the Society for the Exploration of Psychotherapy

Integration (SEPI) was formed (see the description by Goldfried and Newman 1992) to bring together those who were interested in various forms of rapprochement among the psychotherapies. Even at the outset, there was strong interest expressed in this group by many professionals from a variety of orientations and backgrounds. The organization has brought together those interested in integration through a newsletter, annual conferences and a journal.

Four directions for integration

There are numerous pathways towards the integration of the psychotherapies (Mahrer 1989). The three most popular routes at present are technical eclecticism, theoretical integration and common factors (Arkowitz 1989). In addition, there is a newly emerging fourth direction that integrates psychotherapy theory and practice with theory and research from the broader fields of psychology and psychiatry (Arkowitz 1991a, b; 1992).

All four directions are guided by the general assumption that we have much to learn by looking beyond the confines of single theories or the techniques traditionally associated with those theories. However, they do so in rather different ways and at different levels.

Technical eclecticism is the least theoretical of the four. Technical eclectics seek to improve our ability to select the best treatment for the person and problem. This search is guided primarily by data on what has worked best for others in the past with similar problems and similar characteristics. In contrast to the other three directions, technical eclecticism pays significantly less attention to 'why' these techniques work, and instead focuses on predicting for whom they will work. The foundation for technical eclecticism is primarily actuarial rather than theoretical. The work of Beutler (1983; Beutler and Clarkin 1990) and Lazarus (1976, 1981) are illustrations of this form of integration.

The meaning of eclecticism parallels the dictionary definition: 'Choosing what is best from diverse sources, styles, and systems'; 'using techniques and rationales based on more than one orientation to meet the needs of the individual case'; 'the systematic use of a variety of therapeutic interventions in the treatment of a single patient'; and 'the pragmatics of selecting a variety of procedures and wider interventions for specific problems'. The common thread is that technical eclecticism is relatively atheoretical, pragmatic and empirical.

The *common factors* approach attempts to look across diverse therapies to search for elements that they may share in common. This view is based on the belief that these factors may be at least as important in accounting for therapy outcome as the unique factors that differentiate among them. The common factors identified may then become the basis for more parsimonious theory and more efficacious treatment. The work of Frank (1961, 1982) and Goldfried (1980, 1991) has been among the most important contributions to this approach.

One way of determining common therapeutic principles is by focusing on a level of abstraction somewhere between theory and technique. This intermediate level of abstraction, known as a clinical strategy or a change process, may be thought of as a heuristic that implicitly guides the efforts of experienced therapists. Goldfried (1980: 996) argues:

> To the extent that clinicians of varying orientations are able to arrive at a common set of strategies, it is likely that what emerges will consist of robust phenomena, as they have managed to survive the distortions imposed by the therapists' varying theoretical biases.

Common factors may, in fact, be the curative factors.

Renewed interest in common factors has been sparked by well-controlled therapy outcomes which attest to lack of differential outcome. Reviews by Beutler *et al.* (1989a) and Lambert (1989), for example, suggested that techniques accounted for less than 15 per cent of the outcome variance in psychotherapy. This conclusion provides further impetus to look towards common factors and away from the techniques uniquely associated with the different therapies.

In *theoretical integration*, two or more therapies are integrated in the hope that the result will be better than the individual therapies on which they were based. As the name implies, there is an emphasis on integrating the underlying *theories* of psychotherapy (what London (1986) has eloquently labelled 'theory smushing') along with the integration of therapy techniques from each (what London has called 'technique melding'). The various proposals to integrate psychoanalytic and behavioural theories best illustrate this direction, most notably the work of Wachtel (1977, 1987). Other writers have focused on different integrations (e.g. Thoresen 1973; Appelbaum 1976; Wandersman *et al.* 1976; Gurman 1981; Feldman and Pinsof 1982; Segraves 1982; LeBow 1984; Wachtel and Wachtel 1986).

Theoretical integration refers to a commitment to a conceptual or theoretical creation beyond a technical blend of methods. The goal is to create a conceptual framework that synthesizes the best elements of two or more approaches to therapy. Theoretical integration aspires to more than a simple combination. Instead, it seeks an emergent theory that is more than the sum of its parts, and that leads to new directions for practice and research.

Theoretical integration may be most sharply contrasted with technical eclecticism. The primary distinction is that between empirical pragmatism and theoretical flexibility. Or to take John Davis's culinary metaphor (cited in Norcross and Napolitano 1986: 253): 'The eclectic selects among several dishes to constitute a meal, the integrationist creates new dishes by combining different ingredients.' Despite this sharp contrast, Arkowitz (1989) has suggested that technical eclecticism and theoretical integration are more complementary than antagonistic. (Readers interested in the relative merits of theoretical integration versus technical eclecticism are directed to the debates of Goldfried and Wachtel (1987), Arkowitz (1989), Beitman (1989), Beutler (1989b) and Lazarus (1989b).)

More recently, there has been the emergence of interest in a fourth type of integration in which *psychotherapy theory and practice are integrated with basic theory and research in psychology and psychiatry*. This type of integration aspires to enhance our knowledge of change processes by turning to basic theory and research on cognition, affect, behaviour, biological substrates and interpersonal influences.

This direction is illustrated by the work of Arkowitz (1991b), Goldstein *et al.* (1966), Greenberg and Safran (1987), Horowitz (1988, 1991), Schwartz (1991), Stein (1992) and Wolfe (1992). It may be considered to be a form of theoretical integration, but the theories to which this approach turns are not psychotherapy theories *per se*, and any empirically supported theory would serve to elucidate aspects of the change process.

In clinical work, the distinctions among these four directions for psychotherapy integration are not so apparent. The distinctions may, in therapy practice, be largely semantic and conceptual, and not particularly functional. Few clients experiencing an 'integrative' therapy would be able to distinguish among them.

Moreover, we hasten to add that the strategies are not so distinct or mutually exclusive. No technical eclectic can totally disregard theory, and no theoretical integrationist can ignore technique. Without some commonalities among different schools of therapy, theoretical integration would be impossible. And even the most ardent proponent of common factors cannot practise 'non-specifically' or 'commonly'; specific techniques and strategies must be applied.

In the sections which follow, we will briefly trace the early origins of each of these thrusts of psychotherapy integration, review some American proposals exemplifying each, and present some British contributions to them emanating from this volume. Some more recent developments in each will then be traced. More comprehensive histories of psychotherapy integration can be found in Goldfried and Newman (1992) and Arkowitz (1992).

Technical eclecticism

Eclecticism is an integration strategy that selects what seems best from a variety of alternatives. Eclectic psychotherapists choose from among available therapy techniques on the basis of what they think will work best for the particular person and problem. Different techniques from different therapies may be applied to the same person, or different techniques may be used with different patients and problems.

In eclecticism, the basis for treatment selection is more actuarial than theoretical. The main criterion used by eclectics to select treatments is what has worked best for similar people with similar problems in the past. Theory is not viewed as a particularly important basis for treatment selection. This relative de-emphasis on theory distinguishes eclecticism from both theoretical integration and the common factors approach.

Early stirrings

An eclectic approach was not really feasible until around the 1970s. Prior to that time, the field of psychotherapy was, to a large extent, dominated by monolithic theories that were uniformly applied to all people and all problems. In none of these therapies were there many specific and clearly described techniques from which therapists could choose to form an eclectic approach.

Various surveys since the early 1960s have demonstrated that a large percentage of practising therapists endorsed some form of eclecticism to describe their approach (e.g. Kelly 1961; Garfield and Kurtz 1976). This suggests that the realities of practice were leading clinicians towards some form of eclecticism, and that psychotherapy theories were not reflecting this fact. Nonetheless, prior to 1980, eclecticism was often little more than an idiosyncratic mixture of techniques selected on no clearly discernible conceptual basis. The term conveyed little information about how therapists practised and how techniques were selected and combined. This chaotic situation led Eysenck (1970) to describe eclecticism as 'a mish-mash of theories, a hugger-mugger of procedures, a gallimaufry of therapies' (p. 145). Eysenck strongly criticized eclectics for lacking an acceptable rationale and empirical evaluation of their approach.

In 1967, Lazarus formally introduced the concept of *technical eclecticism*, using procedures drawn from different sources without necessarily subscribing to their underlying theories. For Lazarus, no necessary connection exists between meta-beliefs and techniques. It is not necessary to build a composite from divergent theories, on the one hand, nor to accept divergent conceptions, on the other, in order to utilize their technical procedures:

> To attempt a theoretical rapprochement is as futile as trying to picture the edge of the universe. But to read through the vast amount of literature on psychotherapy, *in search of techniques, can be clinically enriching and therapeutically rewarding.*
>
> (Lazarus 1967: 416)

In 1969, Paul posed a question for behaviour therapy that was later to guide psychotherapy research more generally. Paul asked: 'What treatment, by whom, is most effective for this individual with that specific problem, under which set of circumstances, and how does it come about?' (Paul 1969: 44). This question directed the attention of therapists and researchers to the many variables that could possibly influence the outcome of psychotherapy. It also pointed to the possibility of maximizing treatment outcome by an optimal selection and matching of particular therapies with particular people and problems. Paul's question became the cornerstone of later eclectic approaches to psychotherapy.

Lazarus's multimodal therapy

Arnold Lazarus (1967, 1971, 1973, 1976, 1981, 1986b; Lazarus and Messer 1988, 1991) has broadened the potential base of eclecticism from behaviour therapy to techniques associated with other therapy systems. Originally Lazarus referred to his eclectic approach as 'multimodal behaviour therapy' (Lazarus 1973, 1976), and later as 'multimodal therapy' (Lazarus 1981, 1986b). He pointed to the importance of assessment and intervention in the various modalities that characterize human functioning including behaviour, affect, sensation, imagery, cognition, interpersonal relationships and biology. Consistent with other modern eclectics, Lazarus emphasizes treatment specificity, the matching of techniques to persons and problems, and selecting treatments based on empirical evidence for their effectiveness.

Despite his relative de-emphasis on theory as a basis for selecting techniques, Lazarus (1986b) acknowledged that every practitioner uses at least some theory to guide his or her choices. Multimodal therapy rests primarily on social learning theory, drawing also from general systems theory and communications theory. Indeed, an inspection of the techniques that Lazarus (1986b) lists as part of multimodal therapy reveals that it draws heavily from behavioural and cognitive therapies, and minimally from psychodynamic and other therapies. Lazarus's eclectic approach appears to fall somewhere between a broadened version of cognitive-behaviour therapy and an eclectic strategy that can choose from among *any* therapy system. Beutler's (1983, 1986) systematic eclecticism takes us closer to a comprehensive eclecticism, and it is to this approach that we turn next.

Beutler's systematic eclecticism

Larry Beutler's systematic eclectic psychotherapy shares several features in common with Lazarus's technical eclecticism: an emphasis on treatment specificity; the matching of technique to person and problem; an emphasis on empirical data to determine choice of therapy; and a relative de-emphasis on the role of theory to guide the choice of therapy (Beutler 1983, 1986). Unlike Lazarus's technical eclecticism, which is still strongly rooted in cognitive and behaviour therapies, Beutler's approach draws from the entire range of psychotherapy approaches.

Beutler *et al.* (1991) have argued that there are data to suggest that most of the variance in outcome in psychotherapy is due to variables other than specific techniques. Systematic eclecticism directs attention to the matching of a broad array of patient variables, treatment variables and patient–treatment interactions that are most likely to maximize therapy outcome. Instead of focusing primarily on the match between problem and technique, Beutler also includes such variables as therapist characteristics (e.g. experience, attitudes, beliefs), patient characteristics (e.g. symptom complexity, coping style, resistance to influence), technique variables, and interactions among these variables. According to Beutler, it is only within this broad context that we should seek the best match between problems and techniques.

As Beutler *et al.* (1991) correctly point out, the number of variables potentially involved in such a matrix are limitless. Further, there is little to guide us in the selection of variables that might be most productive or relevant. It is here that Beutler turns to theory to help guide these choices. Beutler (1986) suggests that a *functional* theory must be developed that encourages and dictates the utilization of these approaches. Such a functional approach would be highly actuarial in nature, emphasizing what has worked best in the past in similar matches among variables. In addition, Beutler bases his work on social psychological theories of persuasion and influence to understand some of the possible interactions of patient and treatment characteristics.

In a recent extension of the systematic eclectic approach, Beutler and Clarkin (1990) tried to identify empirically the patient qualities that hold most promise for enhancing the fit between specific patients and treatments. These dimensions included level of motivating distress, problem severity, coping style and the propensity to resist interpersonal influence. Beutler (1989a) found that the average amount of outcome variance accounted for by such variables was substantially higher than the amount of variance that could be accounted for by techniques alone. Beutler *et al.* (1991) reviewed research on patient coping style and reactance levels as predictors of different rates of response to different procedures and present some preliminary data from prospective studies in which some of these variables were used to predict therapy outcome. Thus, Beutler's systematic eclecticism continues to evolve and has begun to stimulate empirical research as well.

Emerging directions

Eclecticism in practice and integration in aspiration is an accurate description of what most in the integrative movement do much of the time (Wachtel 1991). The future will bring greater efforts to specify what operations are performed with various clients, and the means by which those operations are selected. As London (1964: 33) observed:

> However interesting, plausible, and appealing a theory may be, it is techniques, not theories, that are actually used on people. Study of the effects of psychotherapy, therefore, is always the study of the effectiveness of techniques.

An emerging direction in eclecticism is that psychological therapies will be increasingly matched to client variables other than diagnosis (Lazarus *et al.* 1992). While there will be a continued movement towards specific treatments for different diagnostic groupings of patients, diagnosis is limited as a basis for developing psychosocial interventions (Beutler 1989a). Diagnostic systems not only change with the shifts of political winds, but their descriptive nature also make them better suited for use as outcome variables than for determiners of different treatments. Psychosocial treatments are seldom so specific (nor would we want them to be) that they can effect a change in major depression but not in anxiety, interpersonal relationships, thought patterns and situational stressors.

This is not to say that the effect of a given psychotherapy procedure is or will be found to be uniform in all cases. Indeed, there are wide variations in outcomes for all interventions and this variation is likely to be demonstrated to be as wide within diagnostic groups as it is between them. The challenge of technical eclecticism is to discover patient characteristics which predispose the effective use of different procedures irrespective of the patient's formal diagnosis.

Furthermore, the meaning of technical eclecticism will be broadened to denote not only specific clinical procedures but also therapist relationship stances (Lazarus *et al.* 1992). Psychotherapy will never be so technical as to overshadow the power of a given therapist's ability to form a therapeutic relationship. Yet the predictors and contributors to these human influences are not beyond the scope of psychological science. Regrettably, the historical emphasis of technical eclecticism on systematic synthesis of techniques has led to a relative neglect of tailoring interpersonal stances to fit particular clients' needs. This lacuna is all the more serious in that, with most disorders, the therapeutic relationship accounts for far more psychotherapy outcome variance than does technical intervention (Lambert and DeJulio 1978). As a result, the scope of technical eclecticism will be enlarged to include the prescriptive use of the therapeutic relationship. One way to conceptualize the issue, paralleling the notion of 'treatment of choice' in terms of techniques, is how clinicians determine the 'relationship of choice' in terms of their interpersonal stances for individual clients (Norcross 1991).

The challenge will be to articulate and operationalize the grounds on which eclectics tailor their interpersonal styles and stimulus value to different clients. Beutler's systematic eclecticism, for one, advocates that therapists adjust several interpersonal dimensions to fit various client presentations. The dimensions of therapeutic style that might be influenced by client presentations include (a) the degree to which the therapist engages in a process of confronting the client with feared objects, ideas and images; (b) the degree to which the therapist focuses on altering internal or external experiences and behaviours; (c) the degree to which the therapist draws attention to in-therapy or extra-therapy activities; and (d) the amount to which the therapist directs therapeutic tasks and initiates topics of discussion. Similarly, noting that even empathy and warmth are not universally indicated psychotherapist behaviours for all clients, Lazarus has adapted Howard *et al.*'s (1987) taxonomy of therapist styles to adjust multimodal therapy in terms of level of support and direction to specific clients.

These and other schemes for relational 'match-making in psychotherapy' (Talley *et al.* 1990) will empirically examine the commonly shared perception among therapists of feeling oneself to be better suited to deal with some patients rather than others. The accumulating empirical literature may then be able to generate prescriptive matching decisions for use of technical as well as interpersonal interventions in specific circumstances.

Common factors

The common factors approach has been a search for the basic ingredients that different therapies may share in common. The common factors approach seeks to abstract *similarities* across different therapies. These similarities may be at the level of theory or clinical practice. Those interested in common factors believe that apparent differences in theoretical constructs or clinical techniques are more superficial than real, and may mask some basic underlying similarities. Implicit in the commonalities search has been the promise that they can not only help us build better theories of change, but also more effective therapies.

Early stirrings

In many ways, the history of the common factors approach parallels that of theoretical integration. Early proposals appeared as far back as the 1930s.

One of the earliest papers on therapeutic commonalities was by Rosenzweig (1936). In it, he pointed to several factors that he believed might account for the effectiveness of different therapies. These included the therapist's ability to inspire hope, the importance of providing the patient with alternative, and more plausible, ways of viewing the self and the world.

Results from a series of studies by Fiedler (1950a, b) also focused on the relationship as a source of common factors in psychotherapy, and provided a fascinating, although indirect examination of some of these factors. Fiedler (1950a, b) asked therapists of different experience levels and orientations to describe what they considered to be the components of the ideal therapeutic relationship. He found that expert therapists of different schools agreed more with each other than they did with novices from their own school. In a companion study using ratings of actual therapy sessions, Fiedler found a similar pattern of findings using actual ratings of the therapy sessions. The experts from different schools were more similar to each other than to novices within their own school in the characteristics of the relationship they actually developed with their clients. Although Fiedler did not examine the outcome of these therapies, his results provide some indirect support for the common factors notion in suggesting that experience may shape therapists to behave in some basically similar ways, at least with respect to the type of relationship they establish.

Jerome Frank's common factors

One of the most influential early writings on commonalities was a book by Jerome Frank (1961) entitled *Persuasion and Healing*. Frank argued that psychotherapy was an influencing process, and that we may learn about what accounts for change by looking at other influencing processes. He examined basic similarities among psychotherapy, placebo effects in medicine, brainwashing and faith-healing both in our own culture and others. Based upon his review, he suggested that some of the basic ingredients in all psychotherapies include: arousing hope, emotional arousal, encouraging changed activity outside of the session, and encouraging new ways of understanding oneself and one's problems through interpretations and corrective emotional experiences.

Frank posited that all psychotherapeutic methods are elaborations and variations of age-old procedures of psychological healing. The features that distinguish psychotherapies from each other, however, receive special emphasis in our pluralistic and competitive society. Since the prestige and financial security of clinicians hinge on their particular approach being more successful than that of their rivals, little attention has traditionally been accorded to the identification of shared components.

Frank (1973, 1974, 1982) continued to modify and develop his common factors model, and has more recently focused on the restoration of morale as a significant common factor. Frank hypothesized that all therapies address a common problem – a 'demoralization', consisting of a loss of self-esteem, subjective feelings of incompetence, alienation, hopelessness and helplessness. He suggested that all therapies may be equally effective in restoring morale, despite the different ways in which they do so. He has also further suggested the following as therapeutic components shared by different psychotherapies: an emotionally charged confiding relationship with a helping person; a healing setting; a conceptual scheme or myth to explain symptoms; and a ritual to help resolve symptoms (Frank 1982).

Some of the central themes of common factors thinking were already apparent during this time. There was a strong emphasis on the commonalities in the therapy relationship, and various attempts to conceptualize these relationship factors. Many proposals also included corrective emotional experiences in therapy and the disconfirmation of dysfunctional expectancies, the arousal of hope and positive expectancies, changes in self-perceptions, persuasion and attitude change, and restoration of morale.

Prochaska's trans-theoretical approach

James Prochaska and his associates (Prochaska 1984, 1991; Prochaska and DiClemente 1986) have focused on commonalities in the process of change, across different problems and different methods of change. Prochaska pointed to *stages of change* (e.g. precontemplation, contemplation, action and maintenance), *levels of change* (e.g. problematic behaviours, maladaptive cognitions, interpersonal conflicts, family/systems conflicts, intrapersonal conflicts) and *change processes* (e.g. consciousness-raising, stimulus control, self re-evaluation, environmental re-evaluation). The trans-theoretical model is one of the best examples of the common factors approach. It abstracts factors that do indeed appear to be common to various types of psychotherapy. Even more important is the fact that this model is stated in a form that lends itself to hypothesis-testing with empirical research, an area that is sadly lacking in some other forms of integration. The model has already generated considerable research. For example, Prochaska and his associates have demonstrated that it is possible to measure these stages, levels and processes of change, and have published several studies that have demonstrated interesting interactions among them in people trying to change (Prochaska 1984; Prochaska and DiClemente 1986; Prochaska *et al.* 1991). Prochaska's model is one of the few integrative proposals that goes beyond interesting theoretical speculation and moves us towards an empirical basis for integrative common factors models of therapy.

Emerging directions

In the past decade, there has been a sharp increase in interest in the common factors approach, with perhaps more books and papers appearing on the topic during these years than in all previous years combined (e.g. Brady *et al.* 1980; Garfield 1980; Goldfried 1980, 1982a; Beutler 1983; Cornsweet 1983; Prochaska 1984; Haaga 1986; Karasu 1986; Lambert 1986; Orlinsky and Howard 1987; Jones *et al.* 1988; Arkowitz and Hannah 1989; Grencavage and Norcross 1990). The proposals have become more specific and there was more discussion about the locus of the common factors (e.g. in patient, in therapist, in relationship, in techniques, and so on). One of the most promising signs is that empirical studies growing out of a common factors perspective have begun to appear (e.g. Prochaska 1984; Prochaska and DiClemente 1986; Goldfried 1991; Prochaska *et al.* 1991). Such studies attempt to measure common factors, test hypotheses about them, and determine the correlations of different possible common factors with therapy outcome.

Empirical work points to the importance of *both* common and unique factors in diverse systems of psychotherapy. In one study, Goldfried (1991) found that both cognitive-behaviour therapists and psychodynamic-interpersonal therapists tended to focus more on feedback about interpersonal than intrapersonal themes, despite theoretical differences that might lead one to think otherwise. Some differences between the two did emerge. Cognitive-behaviour therapists focused more on patients' actions, while psychodynamic-interpersonal therapists focused more on emotions and expectations. One particularly provocative finding was that, although the two therapies did not differ in their emphasis on interpersonal feedback, this type of feedback was more strongly associated with outcome in the psychodynamic than cognitive-behavioural therapy. In addition, feedback relating to 'transference' themes had a stronger relationship to outcome for psychodynamic than for cognitive-behaviour therapy. Thus, a commonality may have a different impact in the context of different patients, therapies and therapy relationships. This suggests the possibility that our conceptualization of common factors may be too unitary and simplistic, and that we may need to examine contextual factors as well (cf. Jones *et al.* 1988).

In a recent paper, Grencavage and Norcross (1990) took the rather unique approach of looking for the commonalities among common factors suggested in the writings of 50 different authors. They grouped the various proposals into categories and presented the most frequent ones within each. Under *client characteristics*, they found that positive expectations, hope and faith were by far the most frequent. For *therapist qualities*, they found a general category of positive descriptors, followed by cultivation of hope and positive expectancies, as well as factors relating to warmth, positive regard and empathic understanding. The largest number of different factors related to *change processes*. These included catharsis, acquisition and practice of new behaviours, provision of rationale, fostering insight/awareness, and emotional and interpersonal learning. *Treatment structures* that were frequently suggested included use of techniques/rituals, focus on inner world and exploration of emotional issues, adherence to theory, and a healing setting. Under *relationship elements*, there was a rather general factor, endorsed by a large majority of the writers, that they described as the development of the alliance/relationship. In addition to trying to extract what common wisdom there may be among those proposing common factors, this paper also draws our attention to possible locus of the various common factors. Clearly, they are all interrelated (e.g. the relationship and change processes), but there are still questions to be explored about the best places to look for the most potent commonalities.

How can the identification of what is already there create something better than what we started with? The concept of *bootstrapping* may be useful here. The dictionary defines bootstrapping as a procedure that creates something better without external aid. In statistical terms, bootstrapping tries to improve our ability to predict by reducing the bias and measurement error that is associated with each of the individual predictors (see examples by Dawes 1971). In the case of psychotherapy integration, those individual predictors are the different therapies. The bias and measurement errors relate to those sources of error that are uniquely associated with each therapy that may obscure the 'true' factors that may be the causal agents for change in all therapies.

Crucial to the bootstrapping process is the relationship of the identified factors to some important criterion. One goal of the common factors approach is to discover the profile of factors *that are most strongly associated with positive therapeutic outcome*. Once identified, such factors may be used as starting points for the development of improved theories and therapies. It is even conceivable that such bootstrapping can yield a weighting of different factors for different clinical problems.

Theoretical integration

Early stirrings

The history of theoretical integration is largely the history of attempts to combine psychoanalytic and behavioural approaches to psychotherapy. Several early papers attempted to demonstrate that concepts from psychoanalysis could be translated into the language of learning theory (e.g. Kubie 1934; Sears 1944; Shoben 1949).

In what may represent one of the earliest attempts at theoretical integration, French delivered an address at the 1932 meeting of the American Psychiatric Association in which he drew certain parallels between psychoanalysis and Pavlovian conditioning. Acknowledging the wide discrepancy between these two approaches, French discussed the similarities between the psychoanalytic concept of repression and Pavlovian concepts of extinction and inhibition. Trying to tie sublimation to learning principles, he invoked the principle of differentiation, suggesting that some sort of discrimination training had probably taken place to differentiate the unacceptable from the more socially accepted manifestations of certain impulses (Goldfried and Newman 1992).

The following year the text of French's presentation was published, together with comments by members of the original audience (French 1933). As one might expect, French's presentation resulted in mixed audience reaction. As one of the most unabashedly negative responses by a member of the audience, Myerson, acknowledged:

> I was tempted to call for a bell-boy and ask him to page John B. Watson, Ivan Pavlov, and Sigmund Freud, while Dr. French was reading his paper. I think Pavlov would have exploded; and what would have happened to Watson is scandalous to contemplate, since the whole of his behavioristic school is founded on the conditioned reflex . . . Freud . . . would be scandalized by such a rapprochement made by one of his pupils, reading a paper of this kind.
>
> (in French 1933: 1202)

Meyer was not nearly as unsympathetic. Although he stated that the field should encourage separate lines of enquiry and should not attempt to substitute any one for another too prematurely, Meyer nonetheless suggested that one should 'enjoy the convergences which show in such discussions as we have had this morning' (French 1933: 1201).

Dollard and Miller's translation and synthesis

A significant event in the history of theoretical integration occurred in 1950 with the publication of Dollard and Miller's book, *Personality and Psychotherapy: An Analysis in Terms of Learning, Thinking, and Culture*. This book went far beyond its description as a simple attempt to translate psychoanalytic concepts into behavioural language. Rather, it was an attempt to synthesize and integrate ideas about neurosis and psychotherapy from these two perspectives in order to provide a unifying theory for the field. In the opening of their book, Dollard and Miller (1950: 3) wrote:

> The ultimate goal is to combine the vitality of psychoanalysis, the rigor of the natural science laboratory, and the facts of culture. We believe that a psychology of this kind should occupy a fundamental position in the social sciences and humanities – making it unnecessary for each of them to invent its own special assumptions about human nature and personality.

What Dollard and Miller achieved was no less than an integrative theory of neurotic behaviour based on anxiety and conflict, and new suggestions for psychotherapy that grew out of their integration. Granted, some of their work was an attempt to translate the concepts of psychoanalysis into the language of learning theory (e.g. they attempted to explain the pleasure principle in terms of reinforcement and repression in terms of the inhibition of cue-producing responses that mediate thinking). However, they also presented a rather sophisticated formulation of the dynamics of conflict and anxiety in neurosis, drawing from concepts in both learning theory and psychoanalysis. They also suggested procedures for overcoming repression, and proposed the use of modelling, self-control strategies and homework assignments in therapy. Many of these techniques have since been 'rediscovered' and are now a basic part of several modern-day therapies.

While their theory of anxiety and conflict caught the attention of researchers in learning (see review by Heilizer 1977), their integration did not have much direct influence on the field of psychotherapy. The influence has been more indirect, serving as a reminder of the possibility and potentials of integration during times when integrative thinking was not a part of the *Zeitgeist*. Now that psychotherapy integration is more established as a field, perhaps their work will be rediscovered as it deserves to be.

Wachtel's cyclical psychodynamics

In 1977, Paul Wachtel published his book, *Psychoanalysis and Behavior Therapy: Toward an Integration*. It remains the most comprehensive and successful attempt to integrate behavioural and psychodynamic approaches, and one of the most influential books in the entire field of psychotherapy integration. Wachtel did his graduate work at Yale when both John Dollard and Neal Miller were on the faculty. In fact, Dollard was one of his first therapy supervisors. Wachtel (1987) notes that he was quite impressed with their attempt to build a theoretical bridge between the concepts of psychoanalysis and learning theory. He noted that any attempt to integrate behavioural and psychoanalytic approaches needs to appreciate the diversity within both and must be specific about the components of such an integration (Wachtel 1977).

Which behaviour therapy and which psychoanalytic therapy shall be integrated? Some may be more compatible than others: for example, orthodox Freudian psychoanalysis and operant behavioural therapies are probably so incompatible that an integration between the two is unlikely. By contrast, Wachtel pursued an integration that incorporated a behaviour therapy emphasizing anxiety reduction and changes in interpersonal behaviour, with interpersonal psychoanalytic approaches (Erikson, Horney and Sullivan) that emphasized the current interpersonal context of the individual and encouraged greater therapist activity than many other psychoanalytic approaches.

The goal of Wachtel's work was to build a framework that could incorporate selected elements of interpersonal psychodynamic approaches and behavioural approaches. It is important to note that his goal was *not* a fixed superordinate theory (or therapy) that would be a hybrid of two sub-approaches. Instead, Wachtel sought to include what he believed were some of the virtues of both in an evolving framework that could incorporate elements of each in a logical and internally consistent way, benefiting from what he saw as their complementary strengths (Wachtel 1984). This framework, which might change with further developments in each theory, could show how concepts from each of the therapies interacted with each other in ways that might suggest new theory for understanding the causes of psychopathology and new clinical strategies for change. From the psychodynamic perspective, he emphasized unconscious processes and conflict, and the importance of meanings and fantasies that influenced our interactions with the world. From the behavioural side, the elements included the use of active-intervention techniques, a concern with the environmental context of behaviour, a focus on the patient's goals in therapy, and a respect for empirical evidence (Wachtel 1977, 1987).

In understanding the origins of psychopathology, Wachtel paid considerable attention to the importance of early experience. He adopted the psychoanalytic view that ways of feeling, acting and behaving that reflect unresolved conflicts will persist into our later life, continuing to influence us even outside of our awareness. Had he stopped here, he would have remained a primarily psychodynamic theorist. However, based on learning and interpersonal orientations, he also saw the importance of present interpersonal influences. He wrote (1977: 52–3):

> Thus, from this perspective, the early pattern persists, not in spite of changing conditions but because the person's pattern of experiencing and interacting with others tends continually to recreate the old conditions again and again.

In this view, our past experiences skew our present environment, and often lead us to create the very conditions that perpetuate our problems in a kind of vicious circle. For example, the people we choose and the relationships we form may confirm the dysfunctional views that we carry forward from our past and that are at the heart of many of our problems. Wachtel later called this approach 'cyclical psychodynamics' (Wachtel 1987). The view of causality in this theory is circular and reciprocal, rather than the linear causal views of behavioural and psychoanalytic theories.

Wachtel also explored the implications of this integration for the practice of psychotherapy. It follows from cyclical psychodynamic theory that intervening into the factors currently maintaining the problem will be an important aid to change. In addition, active behavioural interventions may also serve as a source of new insights (Wachtel 1975) and insights can promote changes in behaviour (Wachtel 1982a), with the two working synergistically.

Emerging directions

The debate about theoretical integration is now dealing with important and substantive issues in psychotherapy theory and practice. Interest in a psycho-dynamic–behavioural integration has continued to grow and remains a strong force in psychotherapy integration. In the 1980s three books were published that reprinted classic papers relating to theoretical integration (Marmor and Woods 1980; Goldfried 1982a; Wachtel 1987). There seems to be an interest in reading and rereading earlier contributions, now that they can be understood in the con-text of a growing body of thought on psychotherapy integration. A number of books and papers continue to develop clinical strategies and to debate issues relating to psychodynamic–behavioural integration (Wachtel 1977, 1987, 1991; Papajohn 1982; Segraves 1982; Fensterheim 1983; Rhoads 1984; Arkowitz 1985, 1989; Wachtel and Wachtel 1986; Lazarus and Messer 1988, 1991; Beutler 1989a; Fitzpatrick and Weber 1989; Wolfe 1989).

There has also been an increasing interest in theoretical integration other than the psychodynamic–behavioural. Some papers have discussed the possibility of an integration between humanistic and behavioural therapies (e.g. Thoresen 1973; Wandersman et al. 1976). In addition, a number of writers from the family therapy area have been exploring various clinical and theoretical integrations between family/systems therapies and others (e.g. Gurman 1981; Feldman and Pinsof 1982; Segraves 1982; Pinsof 1983; Lebow 1984; Wachtel and Wachtel 1986). A small but growing literature on incorporating interpersonal factors into an integrative model has also appeared (e.g. Safran and Segal 1990; Andrews 1991a, b).

Different writers have often referred to theoretical integration at different levels or units of analysis – for example, integrations have been addressed to theories, assumptions about human nature, methods of verification, or combina-tions of these. Schacht (1984) suggested that some of the conflict and confusion that characterized previous discussions may have resulted from ambiguity about the units and levels that were being discussed. Integration may also take various forms or models. Schacht (1984) sees the most elementary one as a simple *transla-tion* of concepts, as was part of Dollard and Miller's mission. In a *complementary model*, each approach is seen as appropriate for dealing with different problems in the same patient (e.g. systematic desensitization for a phobia and psycho-analytic therapy for identity problems). A third model is a *synergistic* one in which the two therapies may be applied to the same problem and are expected to interact in the patient to produce clinical results superior to what might be obtained by either therapy alone. The techniques of each therapy remain unchanged, but the locus of their integration lies in their effects on the patient. In the *emergent* model, the different therapies merge to produce a novel hybrid approach with new characteristics not contained by either therapy alone. This is exemplified by Feather and Rhoads's (1972a, b) psychodynamic behaviour therapy involving the application of desensitization to inferred underlying fantasies and conflicts. Finally, according to Schacht, the most challenging level is *theoretical integration* in which there is an integration of theories and metapsychologies, with the hope for an emergent model of human behaviour. Wachtel's work best illustrates this approach.

Recent research demonstrates an emerging preference for both the term 'integration' and the practice of theoretical integration, as opposed to technical eclecticism. Results of studies (Norcross and Prochaska 1982; Norcross and Napolitano 1986) show clinicians preferring the self-identification of integrative over eclectic by almost a two-to-one margin. That is, they like the ring of 'integrative' better than 'eclectic'. In similar fashion, when instructed to select the type of integration they practise, the majority of eclectics – 61 per cent and 65 per cent – chose theoretical integration.

The preference for integration over eclecticism probably represents a historical shift. In a 1975 investigation (Garfield and Kurtz 1977), most clinicians favoured eclecticism; in a 1986 study (Norcross and Prochaska 1988), most favoured integration. This may reflect a theoretical progression analogous to a social pro-gression: one that proceeds from segregation to desegregation to integration. Eclecticism has represented desegregation, in which ideas, methods and people from diverse theoretical backgrounds mix and intermingle. Currently we appear to be in transition from desegregation to integration, with increasing efforts directed at discovering viable integrative principles for assimilating and accom-modating the best that different systems have to offer.

Integration with basic psychological theory and research

Recently, there has been increasing interest in a relatively new direction for psychotherapy integration that seeks even broader frameworks than the specific integration of two or more existing theories of psychotherapy. In this form of integration, there is an attempt to look *outside* of (rather than *across*) existing psychotherapy theories for ways to further our understanding of change. In this approach, many are beginning to look to basic theory and research in other areas that may elucidate the processes of change in ways that may improve our ability to help people change. As one example, many have looked for a framework that can potentially incorporate systemic interactions among cognitive, affective, behavioural and interpersonal aspects of human functioning (e.g. Goldfried and Safran 1986; Greenberg and Safran 1987; Horowitz 1988, 1991; Beckham 1990; Safran and Segal 1990; Andrews 1991a and b; Schwartz 1991).

Some are even questioning the existence of sharp distinctions among these response systems, suggesting that such a distinction may be artificial (Schwartz 1984, 1991; Barlow 1988). A recent paper by Beckham (1990) illustrates this trend. After reviewing the outcome research on depression, Beckham (1990: 211) suggested that:

> Depression may be viewed as a homeostatic system to the extent that it involves many different components of a patient's life and consists of feedback loops of reciprocal maintaining processes between these components. According to this model, the effect of psychotherapy in altering one element of the depressive homeostasis quickly spreads to other elements in the depressive system.

Beckham suggested that the elements in this homeostasis are cognitive, affective, interpersonal and biological. Further, he argued that different therapies for depression may be equally effective because they all disturb this homeostatic balance by intervening through one part of the system.

In the area of anxiety, Barlow (1988) has built an impressive theory of anxiety along with implications for treatment based on the construct of anxious apprehension. He defines anxious apprehension as a diffuse cognitive-affective structure.

In addition to these larger-scale systemic integrations, there has also been a growing interest in the cognitive sciences in general, and the construct of schema in particular, as areas for integration with our therapies and theories of change. Stein (1992) has discussed the increasing interest of many psychotherapies including cognitive-behavioural (e.g. Beck and Weishaar 1989), as well as psychodynamic theorists (e.g. Horowitz 1988, 1991) in the construct of schema. Stein also elaborated the utility of the construct for understanding a range of phenomena in psychotherapy and change.

Wolfe (1989, 1992) has developed an integrative theory and therapy for anxiety disorders that draws heavily on schema theory. Wolfe elaborated on some aspects of schema theory and integrates these concepts into some new ways of dealing with anxiety disorders. Arkowitz (1991b) has drawn from schema theory, social psychology and Gestalt psychotherapy to develop an integrative model of resistance to change, along with implications for treatment and some preliminary data to support this model.

Social psychology has been another source of integration with psychotherapy. As early as 1966, Goldstein *et al.* (1966) conceptualized psychotherapy as a process of persuasion and attitude change, and looked to basic research and theory that might enhance our ability to achieve attitude change in psychotherapy. In their book, they made some innovative suggestions for psychotherapy that are still worth considering today. A recent book by their students has updated and expanded these earlier proposals (Higginbotham *et al.* 1988).

In the general strategy for integration discussed in this section, the hope is that basic psychological knowledge can inform our understanding of psychopathology and change, and even suggest new ways to approach psychotherapy. In addition, there is also the hope that observations from the 'laboratory' of psychotherapy can inform basic theory and research. This direction of psychotherapy integration holds a great deal of promise for theory and practice in psychotherapy, although the clinical implications are still somewhat remote. The greatest potential of this new direction is for strengthening the empirical base of psychotherapy integration, since links would be made with theory and constructs that are already rooted in supporting research.

British contributions

British interest in psychotherapy integration is not new (Dryden 1984). More than 25 years ago, for example, Marks and Gelder (1966) were among the first to discuss areas of similarity and complementarity between behavioural and psychodynamic therapies. The chapters in this book reflect the diversity and vitality of the current British interest in psychotherapy integration. We will use our framework of the four directions for psychotherapy integration to place each of these chapters in some perspective. Many of the chapters draw heavily on all four approaches, but in different ways. For ease of communication, we will use the phrase 'combined theoretical integration' to refer to approaches that seem to combine theoretical integration, common factors and integration with other areas. A few chapters may best be described as attempts to develop a combined theoretical framework that to some extent endeavours to integrate two or more theories, to some extent looks at commonalities among therapies, and to some extent looks outside of theories of therapy to other areas of theory. A few chapters then use this framework as a basis for selecting treatments for people and thus also have elements of technical eclecticism. Examples of this blend can be found in the work of Clarkson (Chapter 2) and Culley (Chapter 5, both in this volume). Clarkson's approach draws from systems, psychoanalytic, behavioural and humanistic thinking, as well as common factors and other theories. This proposed framework is then used to guide the selection of treatment. Clarkson's proposal is one of the few to employ systems theory concepts, an interesting choice since systems theory seems especially well-suited to integrative thinking.

The framework proposed by Culley is grounded in the Rogerian client-centred approach and cognitive-behaviour therapy. Within this conceptual framework, it appears to be more of a technically eclectic approach. Culley presents a stage model of counselling in which there are different aims, different strategies to accomplish them and different skills that are required at different stages of therapy. However, like the stage theory approach of Prochaska and his associates discussed earlier, Culley's is one of the few proposals to address the need for different approaches at different stages of change.

Rowan's proposal (Chapter 9, this volume) may be considered to fit the category of combined theoretical integration, but elements of technical eclecticism are not as clear as they are with Clarkson and Culley. Rowan attempts to blend past approaches, like those of psychoanalytic therapy, with those that are more present-oriented like existential therapies, with those that are more future-oriented like transpersonal therapies. He proposes this integration for group work. Rowan's proposal may be categorized as a combined form of theoretical integration with some hints of a technical eclecticism to match clients to treatments.

The chapters by Ryle and Cowmeadow (Chapter 3), Ridley and Crowe (Chapter 6) and Guirguis (Chapter 7, all in this volume) fit most closely the category of theoretical integration in which two or more theories or therapies are synthesized. Ryle and Cowmeadow describe the former's cognitive-analytic therapy as an attempt to incorporate concepts from both cognitive-behaviour therapy and psychoanalytic therapy. Both Ryle and Cowmeadow, and Barkham (Chapter 10, this volume) discuss recent research that cognitive-analytic therapy has generated. This is particularly noteworthy in view of the relative lack of such research in theoretical integration.

Ridley and Crowe's behavioural-systems couple therapy takes its origins from behavioural marital therapy and family systems work. It is more than a simple combination of these two, but an attempt to integrate these views and come up with new approaches from such an integration. In this way, it has some elements of theoretical integration. Within this general framework, it also has elements of technical eclecticism, emphasizing as it does the alternative levels of intervention (ALI) hierarchy to help choose the particular approach for particular couples at particular points in therapy.

Guirguis describes the need for a comprehensive and integrative model of sexual dysfunction that pays attention to the role of physical as well as psychological factors. The clinical approach and underlying rationale described by Guirguis may best be described as a theoretical integration between behavioural and psychodynamic approaches. The approach begins as a largely behavioural programme to break the cycle of performance anxiety and deficit. However, when resistances, obstacles or lack of progress are encountered, it looks primarily (but not exclusively) to psychodynamic perspectives to help understand and deal with the issues that emerge.

Eskapa (Chapter 4, this volume) presents a summary and update of multimodal therapy, originally developed by Arnold Lazarus. As discussed earlier, this therapy clearly falls within the category of technical eclecticism. Eskapa notes that British and European students seem less aware of multimodal therapy than their American counterparts, and his chapter is an attempt to bridge that gap.

Treacher's (Chapter 8, this volume) approach may be broadly categorized as eclectic, but not precisely as 'technically eclectic'. Treacher finds something of value in most approaches, but diverges from technical eclectics in his relative de-emphasis on technique. It appears that Treacher is advocating the virtues of experienced clinical judgement as the basis for matching what we do to our clients and their needs, but the specific bases for such judgements are not clearly articulated.

Clarkson (Chapter 11, this volume) discusses some important issues relating to training for psychotherapy integration. The basis for the chapter and the recommended training programme is systemic integrative therapy as described by Clarkson in her other chapter in this Handbook. Clarkson suggests that training in psychotherapy integration can occur either from the beginning of one's psychotherapy training, or after the student has completed training in one or more pure forms of therapy. She advocates both models for training in psycho-therapy integration.

Clarkson presents details of a carefully thought-out training programme in systemic eclectic therapy at a training institute. While the systemic integrative psychotherapy is a rather broadly integrative model, it is still only *one* model of integration. We believe there are real risks to the formation of institutes for train-ing in particular types of integration, and in the granting of credentials for integrative therapists. While Clarkson seems to be aware of several of these prob-lems, we remain concerned that the exploration of psychotherapy integration may revert to a more narrow training in a fixed 'school' of integration. In closing her chapter, Clarkson cites a paragraph from Norcross. In coming full circle, and in sharing Clarkson's concern, we will cite Clarkson citing Norcross:

> . . . it is premature to advance any one integrative system . . . I urge students, in the integrative spirit, to take the 'best' from each model and to discern converging themes for themselves.

Barkham (Chapter 10, this volume) presents an overview of research on integrative-eclectic therapy in general, and research on integrative-eclectic therapy in Britain. He observes that there has been considerably more written on theoretical and clinical issues relating to integration than there has been on research. This is true for Britain as well as other parts of the world. None-theless, Barkham reviews some interesting research on a variety of topics relevant to integration. These include: group designs and case-studies on integrative therapies, including cognitive-analytic therapy; studies of common factors as perceived by clients; the Sheffield programme of research on sequencing of con-trasting therapeutic orientations; and experience in using the assimilation model to match clients to treatments. Clearly, a number of different research directions are beginning to emerge in psychotherapy integration research in Britain, and we find that a positive and exciting indication.

Obstacles and trade-offs

The accelerated development of eclectic and integrative psychotherapies has not been paralleled by serious consideration of their potential limitations and trade-offs (Arkowitz and Messer 1984; Dryden 1986). If we are to avoid uncritical growth or fleeting interest in psychotherapy integration, then some honest recog-nition of the barriers we are likely to encounter is sorely needed (Goldfried and Safran 1986). Caught up in the excitement and possibilities of the movement, we have neglected the problems – the 'X-rated topics' of integration. Healthy maturation, be it for individuals or for movements, requires self awareness and constructive criticism.

What's stopping psychotherapy integration now? Norcross and Thomas (1988) conducted a survey of the SEPI membership to answer this question. Fifty-eight prominent integrationists rated, in terms of severity, twelve potential obstacles using a five-point, Likert-type scale (where 1 = not an obstacle, 3 = moderate

Table 1.1 Obstacles to psychotherapy integration

Obstacle	Severity rating Mean	Rank
Intrinsic investment of individuals in their private perceptions and theories	3.97	1
Inadequate commitment to training in more than one psychotherapy system	3.74	2
Approaches have divergent assumptions about psychopathology and health	3.67	3
Inadequate empirical research on the integration of psychotherapies	3.58	4
Absence of a 'common' language for psychotherapists	3.47	5

obstacle, and 5 = severe obstacle). The top five obstacles and their mean scores are presented in Table 1.1.

The most severely rated obstruction centred around the partisan zealotry and territorial interests of 'pure'-form psychotherapists. Representative responses were: 'egocentric, self-centred colleagues'; 'the institutionalization of schools'; and 'ideological warfare, factional rivalry'. In examining the history of different therapy methods, Goldfried (1980: 991) notes that, traditionally, therapists have been guided by a particular theoretical framework, 'often to the point of being completely blind to alternative conceptualizations and potentially effective intervention procedures'.

Unfortunately, professional reputations are made by emphasizing the new and different, not the basic and similar. In the field of psychotherapy, as well as in other scientific disciplines, the ownership of ideas secures far too much emphasis. Although the idea of naturally occurring, co-operative efforts among professionals is engaging, their behaviour may realistically be expected to reflect the competition so characteristic of our society at large (Goldfried 1980).

Inadequate training in eclectic/integrative therapy was the second-ranked impediment. The reasons are multiple and explicable. Training students to competence in multiple theories and interventions is unprecedented in the history of psychotherapy. Understandable in the light of its exacting and novel nature, the acquisition of integrative perspectives has occurred quite idiosyncratically and perhaps serendipitously to date.

The critical training question is how to facilitate adequate knowledge of and competence in the various psychotherapeutic systems. On the one hand, intense concentration on a single theoretical system, though possibly myopic and misleading, is often secure and complete. On the other hand, cursory exposure to multiple therapeutic systems leaves students with a few clichés and disunited techniques, though it does encourage integration (Norcross 1986b; Robertson 1986). Several special sections addressed integrative training and supervision (Norcross et al. 1986; Beutler et al. 1987; Halgin 1988).

The third-ranked obstacle concerned differences in ontological and epistemological issues. These entail basic and sometimes contradictory assumptions about human nature, determinants of personality development and the origins of psychopathology. For instance, are people innately good, evil, both, neither? Do phobias represent learned maladaptive habits or intrapsychic conflicts? But it may be precisely these diverse world views that make psychotherapy integration interesting, in that it brings together the individual strengths of these complementary orientations (Beitman *et al.* 1988).

We have not conducted sufficient research on psychotherapy integration – the fourth obstacle to be addressed here. Comparative outcome research has been a limited source of direction with regard to selection of method and articulation of prescriptive guidelines (Lambert 1986; Barkham, Chapter 10, this volume). If our empirical research has little to say, and if collective clinical experience has divergent things to say, then why should we do A, not B? We may again be guided by selective perception and personal preference, a situation the integrative movement seeks to avoid.

The models of psychotherapy integration are more like general frameworks than formal theories. It is often difficult to derive testable hypotheses from them that allow us to accept or reject their ideas. They may be good general ideas, but they are still far from good theory. In addition, those proposals that call for an integration of two existing therapy theories have yet to demonstrate that they can lead to predictions other than those generated by each theory separately. The paucity of good theory in psychotherapy integration may be one of the reasons why it has as yet been so hard to generate much new research. The new direction for integration involving basic psychological research and theory holds some promise for improving theory and stimulating more research.

We are convinced that the largest challenge facing psychotherapy integration is to find ways to generate and test hypotheses from these new points of view. Without such data, integrative theories may become either extinct or a part of a large body of unsubstantiated clinical lore.

Another obstacle to the establishment of clinically sophisticated and consensually validated integrative psychotherapies is the absence of a common language (Norcross 1987). This was rated the fifth most serious impediment to progress. Each psychotherapeutic tradition has its own jargon, a clinical shorthand among its adherents, which widens the precipice across differing orientations.

The 'language problem', as it has become known, confounds understanding of each other's constructs and, in some cases, leads to active avoidance of those constructs. Many a behaviourist's mind has wandered when case discussions turn to 'transference issues' and 'warded-off conflicts'. Similarly, psychodynamic therapists typically tune out buzz words like 'conditioning procedures' and 'discriminative stimuli'. Isolated language systems encourage clinicians to wrap themselves in semantic cocoons from which they cannot escape and which others cannot penetrate. As Lazarus (1986a: 241) concluded: 'Basically, integration or rapprochement is impossible when a person speaks and understands only Chinese and another converses only in Greek!'

A common language thus offers the promise of increased communication between clinicians and researchers, on the one hand, and among practitioners of diverse persuasions, on the other. Meaningful trans-theoretical dialogue may allow us to enrich each other's clinical practices, access the empirical literature, and discover robust therapeutic phenomena cutting across varying orientations (Norcross 1987).

The purpose of a common language is to facilitate communication, comprehension and research; it is not intended to establish consensus. Before an agreement or disagreement can be reached on a given matter, it is necessary to ensure that the same phenomenon is in fact being discussed. Punitive super-ego, negative self-statements and poor self-image may indeed be similar phenomena, but that cannot be known with certainty until the constructs are defined operationally and consensually (Stricker 1986).

To be sure, this is a demanding task (Messer 1987). In the short run, using the vernacular – descriptive, ordinary, natural language – might suffice (Driscoll 1987). In the long run, a common language may profit from being linked to a superordinate theory of personality or derived from an empirical data base (e.g. Ryle 1987; Strong 1987).

We would nominate two additional concerns pertaining to the maturation of psychotherapy integration. First, it is disappointing indeed that many eclectic and integrative authors are under-aware of each other's work. In addressing this surprising and troubling trend, Dryden (1986: 374) writes that,

> It is important that the pioneers of eclectic psychotherapy demonstrate an eclectic attitude (i.e. willingness to draw upon diverse sources) among their own ranks. Otherwise they will act as poor role models and increase the chances that schools of eclectic therapy will proliferate in the future. If this happens, the nettle will not have been grasped!

Integrative compendiums on the order of this volume may serve a corrective function in this respect.

Our second concern relates to a potential contradiction in the synthesis of two or more psychotherapy systems: the integration of today may become the single-school approach of tomorrow (Arkowitz 1992). Integrative therapies may, ironically, become the rigid and institutionalized perspectives which integration has attempted to counter in the first place. As we discussed earlier, the formation of institutes for integrative psychotherapy and the accreditation of integrative clinicians could potentially contribute to such an unfortunate rigidifying of a field that should be characterized by openness and exploration. It is ironic that integration itself must avoid becoming another 'school' of psychotherapy.

Wachtel's original vision can serve as a template. He sought an 'evolving framework' for integration rather than a fixed, static synthesis. What does the concept of evolving framework imply? We may be moving towards what Schwartz (1991) and others have described as an 'open system' model that consists not only of the interaction of its existing components, but one which allows for new elements to be introduced and old ones to be abandoned. There is some internal cohesiveness to the system – not all elements can enter readily into it. Some elements fit more readily into the existing system than others. Other elements, are either unable to enter into the system or must change in order to do so.

Moreover, change in one element potentially changes the entire system. For example, a psychodynamic–behavioural integration may be an overall framework that encourages attempts to introduce a number of different elements from an evolving behaviour therapy, and to introduce them at different times, to see how they interact with elements that are also introduced from an evolving body of psychodynamic theory and therapy. Different elements can be introduced and different resulting systems can be explored. This view of integration is quite different from a fixed synthesis of static entities. The open system framework is one which can generate different models at different times that may lead to new theories, new variations of clinical therapy and new research.

Contributions and promises

At present, psychotherapy integration has probably had its strongest impact in desegregating the field of psychotherapy, rather than in truly integrating it. Integrative perspectives have been catalytic in the search for new ways of conceptualizing and conducting psychotherapy that go beyond the confines of single-school theories. They have encouraged practitioners and researchers to examine what other theories and therapies have to offer. The spirit of integration also encouraged new ways of thinking about psychotherapy and change. The historical 'dogma eat dogma' ambience of psychotherapy is gradually abating.

To date, psychotherapy integration has been most successful in engendering an informed pluralism and nascent convergence. Clinical experience and research findings alike lead us to the conclusion that each therapeutic orientation has its share of failures, and that none is consistently superior to any other. These observations have stimulated many workers in the field to suggest that contributions from orientations other than their own might be fruitfully employed. The weakness of any one perspective might be complemented by another's strength. Pinsof (1983: 20), for example, describes his integrative problem-centred therapy as one that

> rests upon the twin assumptions that each modality and orientation has its particular domain of expertise, and that these domains can be interrelated to maximize their assets and minimize their deficits.

This, then, is the important first step: to view rival systems not as an adversary, but as a healthy diversity (Landsman 1974); not as contradictory, but as complementary (Norcross 1986b). We have begun to build, rather than burn, the bridges which span chasms separating theories. At long last, we can temper our splitting propensities and reject the puerile claims of 'We are good – they are bad' (Miller 1985) and proudly exclaim 'We are good – they are also good' (Norcross 1988).

There is a pernicious misconception in our field that certain processes and outcomes are the exclusive property of particular therapy systems. Norcross (1988) has labelled this fallacy the 'exclusivity myth'. Cases in point are the behaviourist's contention of exclusive ownership of behaviour change, the experientialist's presumed monopoly on intense affective expression and the psychoanalyst's assertion of unique genetic insights. The exclusivity myth is part and parcel of the hostile, ideological cold war. Psychotherapy integration has brought many of these warring factions to the negotiation table for peace talks.

Many observers (Karasu 1977; Marmor and Woods 1980; Goldfried 1982a; Messer 1986b) have noted increasing confluence of attitudes and practices amongst the psychotherapies. Recent studies of clinical practitioners point to many areas of convergence as well as remaining points of contention. In one study (Mahoney *et al.* 1989), 486 psychologists representing five major theoretical orientations responded to 40 standardized questions about optimal practices in psychotherapy. The results indicated considerable trans-theoretical convergence on the importance of novel exploratory activity, self-examination and self-development in psychotherapy. Behaviourists rated psychological change as significantly less difficult than did their colleagues of other persuasions unless they had been in psychotherapy themselves. In another study (Friedling *et al.* 1984), 85 psychodynamic and 110 behavioural psychologists reported on their use of operationally defined therapy activities. Over a half of these methods were used by both groups, 15 per cent were mutually rejected and only 29 per cent were employed exclusively by members of either orientation.

Furthermore, this convergence and informed pluralism have been accomplished without institutionalizing any one way as *the* way. The exclusive advancement of any one integrative strategy is premature in view of the early stage of development of the field, and is unrealistic in view of fundamental differences in the values, goals and philosophies of clinicians (Norcross 1991). Integration is still an open field in which different ways of thinking and acting are being proposed, explored and debated. This exploration has already been a healthy challenge to more established ways of thinking about psychotherapy.

Integrative perspectives have already opened up several new avenues for theory, research and practice in psychotherapy. One type of theoretical integration suggests new ways of thinking about therapy by integrating existing theories. Another type of theoretical integration, based on systemic interactions among affect, behaviour, cognition and social factors, has also begun to stimulate new thinking in the field. Both theoretical integration and common factors approaches have begun to suggest new research questions and strategies for therapy. Finally, technical eclecticism has been a stimulus for research in psychotherapy in its search for data on optimal matching strategies to improve therapy outcome. There have also been a number of integrative clinical proposals that suggested new therapy strategies.

In concluding, let us share a thought from Arthur Houts (from Norcross and Thomas 1988): We need to wait for whatever it is that will follow the post-modern era. We are in the post-modern era, but we do not yet know what comes next. There is an old Middle Eastern proverb that applies: 'He who plants dates does not live to eat dates.' We need to be careful to plant dates rather than pumpkins.

While psychotherapy integration has experienced, and will continue to experience, meaningful progress in our lifetimes, the greater legacy of the integrative movement will lie in the future. This legacy, for us, entails the promotion of open enquiry, informed pluralism, empirical research, intellectual relativism and enhanced clinical effectiveness. As with the clinical enterprise itself, the seeds we sow now may produce enticing flowers quickly, but may not bear the sustaining fruit for years to come. Our fervent hope is that we all work diligently enough and live long enough to partake of that fruit together.

Acknowledgements

Portions of this chapter were previously published in the *British Journal of Guidance and Counselling* (Norcross and Grencavage 1989) and in the *History of Psychotherapy: A Century of Change* (Arkowitz 1992). We gratefully acknowledge permission to reprint selected portions from those publications.

References

Adams, H.E. (1984) The pernicious effects of theoretical orientations in clinical psychology, *Clinical Psychologist* 37: 90–3.
Alexander, F. (1963) The dynamics of psychotherapy in light of learning theory, *American Journal of Psychiatry* 120: 440–8.
—— and French, T.M. (1946) *Psychoanalytic Therapy: Principles and Application*, New York: Ronald Press.
Alford, B.A. and Norcross, J.C. (1991) Cognitive therapy as integrative therapy, *Journal of Psychotherapy Integration* 1(3): 175–90.
Allen, D.M. (1988) *Unifying Individual and Family Therapy*, San Francisco: Jossey-Bass.
Allport, G.W. (1968) The fruits of eclecticism: bitter or sweet?, in G.W. Allport (ed.) *The Person in Psychology*, Boston: Beacon.
Andrews, J. (1991a) *The Active Self in Psychotherapy: An Integration of Therapeutic Styles*, Boston: Allyn & Bacon.
—— (1991b) Interpersonal challenge: the second integrative relationship factor, *Journal of Psychotherapy Integration* 1: 265–86.
Appelbaum, S.A. (1976) A psychoanalyst looks at gestalt therapy, in C. Hatcher and P. Himmelstein (eds) *The Handbook of Gestalt Therapy*, New York: Aronson, pp. 215–32.
—— (1982) Challenges to traditional psychotherapy from the 'new therapies', *American Psychologist* 37: 1002–8.
Arkowitz, H. (1984) Historical perspective on the integration of psychoanalytic therapy and behavior therapy, in H. Arkowitz and S.B. Messer (eds) *Psychoanalytic Therapy and Behavior Therapy: Is Integration Possible?*, New York: Plenum, pp. 1–30.
—— (1985) A behavioral-psychodynamic approach to depression, paper presented at the annual meeting of the Society for the Exploration of Psychotherapy Integration, May, Annapolis, Md.
—— (1989) The role of theory in psychotherapy integration, *Journal of Integrative and Eclectic Psychotherapy* 8: 8–16.
—— (1991a) Introductory statement: Psychotherapy integration comes of age, *Journal of Psychotherapy Integration* 1: 1–3.
—— (1991b) Psychotherapy integration: bringing psychotherapy back to psychology, invited address presented at the American Psychological Association August, San Francisco, Calif.
—— (1992) Integrative theories of therapy, in D.K. Freedheim (ed.) *History of Psychotherapy: A Century of Change*, Washington, DC: American Psychological Association.
—— and Hannah, M.T. (1989) Cognitive, behavioral, and psychodynamic therapies: converging or diverging pathways to change?, in A. Freeman, K. Simon, L. Beutler

and H. Arkowitz (eds) *Comprehensive Handbook of Cognitive Therapy*, New York: Plenum, pp. 144–67.

Arkowitz, H. and Messer, S.B. (eds) (1984) *Psychoanalytic Therapy and Behavior Therapy: Is Integration Possible?*, New York: Plenum.

Babcock, H.H. (1988) Integrative psychotherapy: collaborative aspects of behavioral and psychodynamic therapies, *Psychiatric Annals* 18: 271–2.

Bandura, A. (1969) *Principles of Behavior Modification*, New York: Holt, Rinehart & Winston.

—— (1977) *Social Learning Theory*, Englewood Cliff, NJ: Prentice-Hall.

Barlow, D. (1988) *Anxiety and its Disorders*, New York: Guilford.

Beck, A.T. (1991) Cognitive therapy as *the* integrative therapy, *Journal of Psychotherapy Integration* 1(3): 191–8.

—— and Weishaar, M. (1989) Cognitive therapy, in A. Freeman, K. Simon, L. Beutler and H. Arkowitz (eds) *Comprehensive Handbook of Cognitive Therapy*, New York: Plenum, pp. 21–36.

——, Rush, A.J., Shaw, B.F. and Emery, G.E. (1979) *Cognitive Therapy of Depression*, New York: Guilford.

Beckham, E.E. (1990) Psychotherapy of depression at the crossroads: directions for the 1990s, *Clinical Psychology Review* 10: 207–28.

Beitman, B.D. (1987) *The Structure of Individual Psychotherapy*, New York: Guilford.

—— (1989) Why I am an integrationist (not an eclectic), *British Journal of Guidance and Counselling* 17: 259–73.

——, Goldfried, M.R. and Norcross, J.C. (1989) The movement toward integrating the psychotherapies: an overview, *American Journal of Psychiatry* 146: 138–47.

Bergin, A.E. and Lambert, M.J. (1978) The evaluation of therapeutic outcomes, in S.L. Garfield and A.E. Bergin (eds), *Handbook of Psychotherapy and Behavior Change*, 2nd edn, New York: Wiley.

Beutler, L.E. (1979) Toward specific psychological therapies for specific conditions, *Journal of Consulting and Clinical Psychology* 47: 882–92.

—— (1983) *Eclectic Psychotherapy: A Systematic Approach*, New York: Pergamon.

—— (1986) Systematic eclectic psychotherapy, in J.C. Norcross (ed.) *Handbook of Eclectic Psychotherapy*, New York: Brunner/Mazel, pp. 94–131.

—— (1989a) Differential treatment selection: the role of diagnosis in psychotherapy, *Psychotherapy* 26: 271–81.

—— (1989b) The misplaced role of theory in psychotherapy integration, *Journal of Integrative and Eclectic Psychotherapy* 8: 17–22.

—— and Clarkin, J. (1990) *Selective Treatment Selection: Toward Targeted Therapeutic Interventions*, New York: Brunner/Mazel.

——, Mahoney, M.J., Norcross, J.C., Prochaska, J.O., Sollod, R.M. and Robertson, M. (1987) Training integrative/eclectic psychotherapists II, *Journal of Integrative and Eclectic Psychotherapy*, 6: 296–332.

——, Mohr, D.C., Grawe, K., Engle, D. and MacDonald, R. (1991) Looking for differential treatment effects: cross-cultural predictors of differential therapeutic efficacy, *Journal of Psychotherapy Integration* 1: 121–42.

Birk, L. (1970) Behavior therapy: integration with dynamic psychiatry, *Behavior Therapy* 1: 522–6.

—— (1988) Behavioral/psychoanalytic psychotherapy with overlapping social systems: a natural matrix for diagnosis and therapeutic change, *Psychiatric Annals* 18: 292–308.

—— and Brinkley-Birk, A. (1974) Psychoanalysis and behavior therapy, *American Journal of Psychiatry* 131: 499–510.

Blanck, G. and Blanck, R. (1976) *Ego Psychology* (Vol. 1), New York: Columbia University Press.

Brabeck, M.M. and Welfel, E.R. (1985) Counseling theory: understanding the trend toward eclecticism from a developmental perspective, *Journal of Counseling and Development* 63: 343-9.

Brady, J.P., Davison, G.C., DeWald, P.A., Egan, G., Fadiman, J., Frank, J.D., Gill, M., Hoffman, I., Kempler, W., Lazarus, A.A., Raimy, V., Rotter, J.B. and Strupp, H.H. (1980) Some views on effective principles of psychotherapy, *Cognitive Therapy and Research* 4: 269-306.

Brown, B.S. (1983) The impact of political and economic changes upon mental health, *American Journal of Orthopsychiatry*, 53: 583-92.

Brown, G.W. and Harris, T. (1978) *Social Origins of Depression: A Study of Psychiatric Disorder in Women*, New York: Free Press.

Budman, S.H. (ed.) (1981) *Forms of Brief Therapy*, New York: Guilford.

Cornsweet, C. (1983) Nonspecific factors and theoretical choice, *Psychotherapy: Theory, Research, and Practice* 20: 307-13.

Corsini, R.J. (ed.) (1981) *Handbook of Innovative Psychotherapies*, New York: John Wiley.

Davis, J.D. (1983) Slaying the psychoanalytic dragon: an integrationist's commentary on Yates, *British Journal of Clinical Psychology* 22: 133-44.

Dawes, R.M. (1971) A case study of graduate admissions: application of three principles of human decision making, *American Psychologist* 26: 180-8.

Dimond, R.E. and Havens, R.A. (1975) Restructuring psychotherapy: toward a prescriptive eclecticism, *Professional Psychology* 6: 193-200.

Dollard, J. and Miller, N.E. (1950) *Personality and Psychotherapy: An Analysis in Terms of Learning, Thinking, and Culture*, New York: McGraw-Hill.

Driscoll, R. (1987) Ordinary language as a common language for psychotherapy, *Journal of Integrative and Eclectic Psychotherapy* 6: 184-94.

Dryden, W. (1984) Issues in the eclectic practice of individual therapy, in W. Dryden (ed.) *Individual Therapy in Britain*, London: Harper & Row.

—— (1986) Eclectic psychotherapies: a critique of leading approaches, in J.C. Norcross (ed.) *Handbook of Eclectic Psychotherapy*, New York: Brunner/Mazel, pp. 353-75.

—— and Norcross, J.C. (1989) Eclecticism and integration in counselling and psychotherapy: introduction, *British Journal of Guidance and Counselling* 17: 225-6.

Elkin, I., Shea, M.T., Watkins, J.T., Imber, S.D., Sotsky, S.M., Collins, J.F., Glass, D.R., Pilkonis, P.A., Leber, W.R., Docherty, J.P., Fiester, S.J. and Parloff, M.B. (1989) National Institute of Mental Health Treatment of Depression Collaborative Research Program: general effectiveness of treatments, *Archives of General Psychiatry* 46: 971-82.

Eysenck, H.J. (1960) Learning theory and behavior therapy, in H.J. Eysenck (ed.) *Behavior Therapy and the Neuroses*, London: Pergamon, pp. 67-82.

—— (1970) A mish-mash of theories, *International Journal of Psychiatry* 9: 140-6.

Feather, B.W. and Rhoads, J.M. (1972a) Psychodynamic behavior therapy: I. Theory and rationale, *Archives of General Psychiatry* 26: 496-502.

—— (1972b) Psychodynamic behavior therapy: II. Clinical aspects, *Archives of General Psychiatry* 26: 503-11.

Feldman, L.B. and Pinsof, W.M. (1982) Problem maintenance in family systems: an integrative model, *Journal of Marriage and Family Therapy* 8: 295-308.

Fensterheim, H. (1983) Introduction to behavioral psychotherapy, in H. Fensterheim and H.I. Glazer (eds) *Behavioral Psychotherapy: Basic Principles and Case Studies in an Integrative Clinical Model*, New York: Brunner/Mazel.

Feyerabend, P. (1970) Consolations for the specialist, in I. Lakatos and A.E. Musgrave (eds) *Criticism and the Growth of Knowledge*, Cambridge: Cambridge University Press.

Fiedler, F.E. (1950a) The concept of the ideal therapeutic relationship, *Journal of Consulting Psychology* 14: 239-45.

—— (1950b) Comparisons of therapeutic relationships in psychoanalytic, nondirective, and Adlerian therapy, *Journal of Consulting Psychology* 14: 436-45.

Fischer, J. (1986) Eclectic casework, in J.C. Norcross (ed.) *Handbook of Eclectic Psychotherapy*, New York: Brunner/Mazel.

Fishman, D.B. and Neigher, W.D. (1982) American psychology in the eighties: Who will buy?, *American Psychologist* 37: 533–46.

Fitzpatrick, M.M. and Weber, C.C. (1989) Integrative approaches in psychotherapy: combining psychodynamic and behavioral treatments, *Journal of Integrative and Eclectic Psychotherapy* 8: 102–17.

Frances, A. (1988) Sigmund Freud: The first integrative therapist, invited address to the fourth annual convention of the Society for the Exploration of Psychotherapy Integration, May, Boston, Mass.

——, Clarkin, J. and Perry, S. (1984) *Differential Therapeutics in Psychiatry*, New York: Brunner/Mazel.

Frank, J.D. (1961) *Persuasion and Healing*, Baltimore: Johns Hopkins University Press.

—— (1973) *Persuasion and Healing*, 2nd edn, Baltimore: Johns Hopkins University Press.

—— (1974) Psychotherapy: the restoration of morale, *American Journal of Psychiatry* 131: 271–4.

—— (1979) The present status of outcome studies, *Journal of Consulting and Clinical Psychology* 47: 310–16.

—— (1982) Therapeutic components shared by all psychotherapies, in J.H. Harvey and M.M. Parks (eds) *The Master Lecture Series. Vol. 1. Psychotherapy Research and Behavior Change*, Washington, DC: American Psychological Association, pp. 73–122.

Franks, C.M. (1984) On conceptual and technical integrity in psychoanalysis and behavior therapy: two fundamentally incompatible systems, in H. Arkowitz and S.B. Messer (eds) *Psychoanalytic Therapy and Behavior Therapy: Is Integration Possible?*, New York: Plenum, pp. 223–48.

Freeman, A., Simon, K., Beutler, L. and Arkowitz, H. (eds) (1989) *Comprehensive Handbook of Cognitive Therapy*, New York: Plenum.

French, T.M. (1933) Interrelations between psychoanalysis and the experimental work of Pavlov, *American Journal of Psychiatry* 89: 1165–203.

Friedling, C., Goldfried, M.R. and Stricker, G. (1984) Convergence in psychodynamic and behavior therapy, paper presented at the annual convention of the Eastern Psychological Association, April, Baltimore, Md.

Garfield, S.L. (1973) Basic ingredients or common factors in psychotherapy?, *Journal of Consulting and Clinical Psychology* 41: 9–12.

—— (1980) *Psychotherapy: An Eclectic Approach*, New York: Wiley.

—— (1982) Eclecticism and integration in psychotherapy, *Behavior Therapy* 13: 610–23.

—— (1986) An eclectic psychotherapy, in J.C. Norcross (ed.) *Handbook of Eclectic Psychotherapy*, New York: Brunner/Mazel, pp. 132–62.

—— and Kurtz, R. (1974) A survey of clinical psychologists: characteristics, activities, and orientations, *Clinical Psychologist* 28: 7–10.

—— (1976) Clinical psychologists in the 70s, *American Psychologist* 31: 1–9.

—— (1977) A study of eclectic views, *Journal of Clinical and Consulting Psychology* 45: 78–83.

Gill, M.M. (1984) Psychoanalytic, psychodynamic, cognitive behavior, and behavior therapies compared, in H. Arkowitz and S.B. Messer (eds) *Psychoanalytic Therapy and Behavior Therapy: Is Integration Possible?*, New York: Plenum, pp. 179–88.

Goldfried, M.R. (1980) Toward the delineation of therapeutic change principles, *American Psychologist* 35: 991–9.

—— (1982a) *Converging Themes in Psychotherapy: Trends in Psychodynamic, Humanistic, and Behavioral Practice*, New York: Springer.

—— (1982b) On the history of therapeutic integration, *Behavior Therapy* 13: 572–93.

—— (1987) A common language for the psychotherapies: commentary, *Journal of Integrative and Eclectic Psychotherapy* 6: 200–4.

—— (1991) Research issues in psychotherapy integration, *Journal of Psychotherapy Integration* 1: 5–25.

—— and Newman, C. (1986) Psychotherapy integration: an historical perspective, in J.C. Norcross (ed.) *Handbook of Eclectic Psychotherapy*, New York: Brunner/Mazel, pp. 25–61.

—— (1992) A brief history of psychotherapy integration, in J.C. Norcross and M.R. Goldfried (eds) *Handbook of Psychotherapy Integration*, New York: Basic Books.

—— and Padawer, W. (1982) Current status and future directions in psychotherapy, in M.R. Goldfried (ed.) *Converging Themes in Psychotherapy: Trends in Psychodynamic, Humanistic, and Behavioral Practice*, New York: Springer.

—— and Robins, C.J. (1983) Self-schema, cognitive bias, and the processing of therapeutic experiences, in P.C. Kendall (ed.) *Advances in Cognitive-Behavioral Research and Therapy* (Vol. 2), New York: Academic Press.

—— and Safran, J.D. (1986) Future directions in psychotherapy integration, in J.C. Norcross (ed.) *Handbook of Eclectic Psychotherapy*, New York: Brunner/Mazel, pp. 463–83.

—— and Wachtel, P.L. (1987) Clinical and conceptual issues in psychotherapy integration: a dialogue, *Journal of Integrative and Eclectic Psychotherapy* 6: 131–44.

——, Greenberg, L.S. and Marmor, C. (1990) Individual psychotherapy: process and outcome, *Annual Review of Psychology* 41: 659–88.

Goldstein, A.P. (1962) *Therapist–patient Expectancies in Psychotherapy*, New York: MacMillan.

—— and Stein, N. (1976) *Prescriptive Psychotherapies*, New York: Pergamon.

——, Heller, K.H. and Sechrest, L.B. (1966) *Psychotherapy and the Psychology of Behavior Change*, New York: Wiley.

Grebstein, L.C. (1986) An eclectic family therapy, in J.C. Norcross (ed.) *Handbook of Eclectic Psychotherapy*, New York: Brunner/Mazel, pp. 282–319.

Greenberg, L.S. and Safran, J.D. (1987) *Emotion in Psychotherapy: Affect, Cognition, and the Process of Change*, New York: Guilford.

—— (1989) Emotion in psychotherapy, *American Psychologist* 44: 19–29.

Grencavage, L.M. and Norcross, J.C. (1990) Where are the commonalities among the therapeutic common factors?, *Professional Psychology: Research and Practice* 21: 372–8.

Guerney, L. and Guerney, B. (1987) Integrating child and family therapy, *Psychotherapy* 24: 609–14.

Gurman, A.S. (1981) Integrative marital therapy: toward the development of an interpersonal approach, in S. Budman (ed.) *Forms of Brief Therapy*, New York: Guilford, pp. 415–57.

Haaga, D.A. (1986) A review of the common principles approach to the integration of psychotherapies, *Cognitive Therapy and Research* 10: 527–38.

Halgin, R.P. (ed.) (1988) Special section: Issues in the supervision of integrative psychotherapy, *Journal of Integrative and Eclectic Psychotherapy* 7: 152–80.

Harper, R.A. (1959) *Psychoanalysis and Psychotherapy: 36 Systems*, Englewood Cliffs, NJ: Prentice-Hall.

Heilizer, F. (1977) A review of theory and research on Miller's response competition (conflict) models, *Journal of General Psychology* 97: 227–80.

Henle, M. (1986) Some problems of eclecticism, in *1879 and all that: Essays in the theory and history of psychology*, New York: Columbia University Press.

Higginbotham, H.N., West, S.G. and Forsyth, D.R. (1988) *Psychotherapy and Behavior Change: Social, Cultural, and Methodological Perspectives*, New York: Pergamon.

Hobbs, N. (1962) Sources of gain in counseling and psychotherapy, *American Psychologist* 17: 741–7.

Horowitz, M.J. (1988) *Introduction to Psychodynamics: A New Synthesis*, New York: Basic Books.

—— (1991) New theory for psychotherapy integration, *Journal of Psychotherapy Integration* 1: 85–92.

Howard, G.S., Nance, D.W. and Myers, P. (1987) *Adaptive Counseling and Therapy*, San Francisco: Jossey-Bass.

Izard, C., Kagan, J. and Zajonc, R. (eds) (1983) *Emotion, Cognition, and Behavior*, New York: Cambridge University Press.

James, J.R., Mulaick, S.A. and Brett, J.M. (1982) *Causal Analysis: Assumptions, Models, and Data*, Beverly Hills, Calif.: Sage.

Jayaratne, S. (1982) Characteristics and theoretical orientations of clinical social workers: a national survey, *Journal of Social Service Research* 20: 476–85.

Jensen, J.P., Bergin, A.E. and Greaves, D.W. (1990) The meaning of eclecticism: new survey and analysis of components, *Professional Psychology: Research and Practice* 21: 124–30.

Jones, E.E., Cumming, J.D. and Horowitz, M.J. (1988) Another look at the nonspecific hypothesis of therapeutic effectiveness, *Journal of Clinical and Consulting Psychology* 56: 48–55.

Karasu, T.B. (1977) Psychotherapies: an overview, *American Journal of Psychiatry* 134: 851–63.

—— (1986) The specificity versus nonspecificity dilemma: toward identifying therapeutic change agents, *American Journal of Psychiatry* 143: 687–95.

Kazdin, A.E. (1984) Integration of psychodynamic and behavioral psychotherapies: conceptual versus empirical syntheses, in H. Arkowitz and S.B. Messer (eds) *Psychoanalytic Therapy and Behavior Therapy: Is Integration Possible?*, New York: Plenum, pp. 139–70.

Kelly, E.L. (1961) Clinical psychology – 1960. Report of survey findings, *Newsletter, Division of Clinical Psychology* 14: 1–11.

Kendall, P.C. (1982) Integration: behavior therapy and other schools of thought, *Behavior Therapy* 13: 559–71.

Kiesler, D.J. (1966) Some myths of psychotherapy research and the search for a paradigm, *Psychological Bulletin* 65: 110–36.

Kilbourne, B.K. and Richardson, J.T. (1988) A social psychological analysis of healing, *Journal of Integrative and Eclectic Psychotherapy* 7: 20–34.

Klein, M., Dittman, A.T., Parloff, M.B. and Gill, M.M. (1969) Behavior therapy: observations and reflections, *Journal of Consulting and Clinical Psychology* 33: 259–66.

Korchin, S.J. and Sands, S.H. (1983) Principles common to all psychotherapies, in C.E. Walker (ed.) *The Handbook of Clinical Psychology* (Vol. 1), Homewood, Ill.: Dow Jones-Irvin.

Kubie, L.S. (1934) Relation of the conditioned reflex to psychoanalytic technique, *Archives of Neurology and Psychiatry* 32: 1137–42.

Kuhn, T.S. (1970) *The Structure of Scientific Revolutions*, 2nd edn, Chicago: University of Chicago Press.

Lambert, M.J. (1986) Implications of psychotherapy outcome research for eclectic psychotherapy, in J.C. Norcross (ed.) *Handbook of Eclectic Psychotherapy*, New York: Brunner/Mazel, pp. 436–62.

—— (1989) Contributors to treatment outcome, paper presented at the annual meeting of the Society for the Exploration of Psychotherapy Integration, May, Berkeley, Calif.

—— and DeJulio, S.S. (1978) The relative importance of client, therapist and technique variables as predictors of psychotherapy outcome: the place of 'nonspecific' factors, paper presented at the mid-winter meeting of the Division of Psychotherapy, March, American Psychological Association.

——, Shapiro, D.A. and Bergin, A.E. (1986) The effectiveness of psychotherapy, in S.L. Garfield and A.E. Bergin (eds) *Handbook of Psychotherapy and Behavior Change*, 3rd edn, New York: Wiley, pp. 157–211.

Landsman, J.T. (1974) Not an adversity but a welcome diversity, paper presented at the meeting of the American Psychological Association, New Orleans, La.

—— and Dawes, R.M. (1982) Smith and Glass conclusions stand up under scrutiny, *American Psychologist* 37: 504–16.

Langs, R. (1976) *The Bipersonal Field*, New York: Aronson.

Larson, D. (1980) Therapeutic schools, styles, and schoolism: a national survey, *Journal of Humanistic Psychology* 20: 3–20.

Lazarus, A.A. (1967) In support of technical eclecticism, *Psychological Reports* 21: 415–16.

—— (1971) *Behavior Therapy and Beyond*, New York: McGraw-Hill.

—— (1973) Multimodal behavior therapy: treating the BASIC ID, *Journal of Nervous and Mental Disease* 156: 404–11.

—— (1976) *Multimodal Behavior Therapy*, New York: Springer.

—— (1977) Has behavior therapy outlived its usefulness?, *American Psychologist* 32: 550–4.

—— (1981) *The Practice of Multimodal Therapy*, New York: McGraw-Hill.

—— (1984) The specificity factor in psychotherapy, *Psychotherapy in Private Practice* 2: 43–8.

—— (1985) *Casebook of Multimodal Therapy*, New York: Guilford.

—— (1986a) From the ashes, *International Journal of Eclectic Psychotherapy* 5: 241–2.

—— (1986b) Multimodal therapy, in J.C. Norcross (ed.) *Handbook of Eclectic Psychotherapy*, New York: Brunner/Mazel, pp. 65–93.

—— (1989a) *The Practice of Multimodal Therapy*, Baltimore: Johns Hopkins University Press.

—— (1986b) Why I am an eclectic (not an integrationist), *British Journal of Guidance and Counselling* 19: 248–58.

—— and Messer, S.B. (1988) Clinical choice points: behavioral versus psychoanalytic interventions, *Psychotherapy* 25: 59–70.

—— (1991) Does chaos prevail? An exchange on technical eclecticism and assimilative integration, *Journal of Psychotherapy Integration* 1: 143–58.

——, Beutler, L.E. and Norcross, J.C. (1992) The future of technical eclecticism, *Psychotherapy* 29(1).

Lebow, J.L. (1984) On the value of integrating approaches to family therapy, *Journal of Marital and Family Therapy* 10: 127–38.

Levis, D. (1970) Integration of behavior therapy with dynamic psychiatry: a marriage with a high probability of ending in divorce, *Behavior Therapy* 1: 531–7.

London, P. (1964) *The Modes and Morals of Psychotherapy*, New York: Holt, Rinehart & Winston.

—— (1983) Ecumenism in psychotherapy, *Contemporary Psychology* 28: 507–8.

—— (1986) *The Modes and Morals of Psychotherapy*, 2nd edn, New York: Hemisphere.

—— (1988) Metamorphosis in psychotherapy: slouching toward integration, *Journal of Integrative and Eclectic Psychotherapy* 7: 3–12.

—— and Palmer, M. (1988) The integrative trend in psychotherapy in historical context, *Psychiatric Annals* 18: 273–9.

Luborsky, L. (1984) *Principles of Psychoanalytic Psychotherapy: A Manual for Supportive-expressive Treatment*, New York: Basic Books.

—— and DeRubeis, R.J. (1984) The use of psychotherapy treatment manuals: a small revolution in psychotherapy research style, *Clinical Psychology Review* 4: 5–14.

——, Singer, B. and Luborsky, L. (1975) Comparative studies of psychotherapies: is it true that 'everybody has won and all must have prizes'?, *Archives of General Psychiatry* 32: 995–1008.

Lunde, D.T. (1974) Eclectic and integrated theory: Gordon Allport and others, in A. Burton (ed.) *Operational Theories of Personality*, New York: Brunner/Mazel, pp. 381–404.

Mahoney, M.J. (1974) *Cognition and Behavior Modification*, Cambridge, Mass.: Ballinger.

—— (1984) Psychoanalysis and behaviorism: the Yin and Yang of determinism, in H. Arkowitz and S.B. Messer (eds) *Psychoanalytic Therapy and Behavior Therapy: Is Integration Possible?*, New York: Plenum, pp. 303–26.

——, Norcross, J.C., Prochaska, J.O. and Missar, C.D. (1989) Psychological development and optimal psychotherapy: Converging perspectives among clinical psychologists, *Journal of Integrative and Eclectic Psychotherapy* 8: 251–63.

Mahrer, A.R. (1989) *The Integration of Psychotherapies*, New York: Human Sciences.

Malan, D.H. (1976) *The Frontier of Brief Psychotherapy*, New York: Plenum.

Marks, I.M. and Gelder, M.G. (1966) Common ground between behavior therapy and psychodynamic methods, *British Journal of Medical Psychology* 39: 11–23.

Marmor, J. and Woods, S.E. (eds) (1980) *The Interface between the Psychodynamic and Behavioral Therapies*, New York: Plenum.

Meichenbaum, D. (1977) *Cognitive Behavior Modification*, New York: Plenum.

Mendelsohn, E. and Silverman, L.H. (1984) The activation of unconscious fantasies in behavioral treatments, in H. Arkowitz and S.B. Messer (eds) *Psychoanalytic Therapy and Behavior Therapy: Is Integration Possible?*, New York: Plenum, pp. 255–94.

Messer, S.B. (1983) Integrating psychoanalytic and behavior therapy: limitations, possibilities, and trade-offs, *British Journal of Clinical Psychology* 22: 131–2.

—— (1986a) Behavioral and psychoanalytic perspectives at therapeutic choice points, *American Psychologist* 31: 1261–72.

—— (1986b) Eclecticism in psychotherapy: underlying assumptions, problems, and trade-offs, in J.C. Norcross (ed.) *Handbook of Eclectic Psychotherapy*, New York: Brunner/Mazel.

—— (1987) Can the Tower of Babel be completed? A critique of the common language proposal, *Journal of Integrative and Eclectic Psychotherapy* 6: 195–9.

—— (1989) Integrationism and eclecticism in counselling and psychotherapy: cautionary notes, *British Journal of Guidance and Counselling* 19: 275–85.

—— and Winokur, M. (1980) Some limits to the integration of psychoanalytic and behavior therapy, *American Psychologist* 35: 818–27.

—— (1984) Ways of knowing and visions of reality in psychoanalytic therapy and behavior therapy, in H. Arkowitz and S.B. Messer (eds) *Psychoanalytic Therapy and Behavior Therapy: Is Integration Possible?*, New York: Plenum, pp. 63–100.

Miller, M.H. (1985) We are good – they are bad, *Journal of Nervous and Mental Disease* 173: 279–81.

Mischel, W. (1973) Toward a cognitive social learning reconceptualization of personality, *Psychological Review* 80: 252–83.

Moultrup, D. (1986) Integration: a coming of age, *Contemporary Family Therapy* 8: 157–67.

Murray, E.J. (1983) Beyond behavioral and dynamic therapy, *British Journal of Clinical Psychology* 22: 127–8.

Murray, N.E. (1976) A dynamic synthesis of analytic and behavioral approaches to symptoms, *American Journal of Psychotherapy* 30: 561–9.

Norcross, J.C. (1981) All in the family? On therapeutic commonalities, *American Psychologist* 36: 1544–5.

—— (1985) For discriminating clinicians only, *Contemporary Psychology* 30: 757–8.

—— (ed.) (1986a) *Handbook of Eclectic Psychotherapy*, New York: Brunner/Mazel.

—— (1986b) Eclectic psychotherapy: an introduction and overview, in J.C. Norcross (ed.) *Handbook of Eclectic Psychotherapy*, New York: Brunner/Mazel.

—— (ed.) (1987) Special section: Toward a common language for psychotherapy, *Journal of Integrative and Eclectic Psychotherapy* 4: 165–205.

—— (1988) The exclusivity myth and the equifinality principle in psychotherapy, *Journal of Integrative and Eclectic Psychotherapy* 7: 415–21.

—— (1991) Prescriptive matching in psychotherapy: psychoanalysis for simple phobias? *Psychotherapy* 28: 439–43.

—— (1991) (Chair). *Tailoring the therapist's interpersonal stance to client needs: Four perspectives*, Symposium presented at the 99th annual convention of the American Psychological Association, August, San Francisco, Calif.

—— and Goldfried, M.R. (eds) (1992) *Handbook of Psychotherapy Integration*, New York: Basic Books.

—— and Grencavage, L.M. (1989) Eclecticism and integration in psychotherapy: major themes and obstacles, *British Journal of Guidance and Counselling* 19: 227–47.

—— and Napolitano, G. (1986) Defining our Journal and ourselves, *International Journal of Eclectic Psychotherapy* 5: 249–55.

—— and Prochaska, J.O. (1982) A national survey of clinical psychologists: affiliations and orientations, *Clinical Psychologist* 35: 1-2, 4-6.

—— (1988) A study of eclectic (and integrative) views revisited, *Professional Psychology: Research and Practice* 19: 170-4.

—— and Thomas, B.L. (1988) What's stopping us now?: obstacles to psychotherapy integration, *Journal of Integrative and Eclectic Psychotherapy* 7: 74-80.

——, Alford, B.A. and DeMichele, J.T. (1992) The future of psychotherapy: Delphi data and concluding observations, *Psychotherapy* 29(1): 150-58.

——, Dryden, W. and Brust, A.M. (1992) British clinical psychologists: I. A national survey of the BPS Clinical Division, *Clinical Psychology Forum* 40: 19-24.

——, Prochaska, J.O. and Gallagher, K.M. (1989) Clinical psychologists in the 1980s: I. Demographics, affiliations, and satisfactions, *Clinical Psychologist* 42: 138-47.

——, Beutler, L.E., Clarkin, J.F., DiClemente, C.C., Halgin, R.P., Frances, A., Prochaska, J.O., Robertson, M. and Suedfeld, P. (1986) Training integrative/eclectic psychotherapists, *International Journal of Eclectic Psychotherapy* 5: 71-94.

Omer, H. and London, P. (1988) Metamorphosis in psychotherapy: end of the systems era, *Psychotherapy* 25: 171-80.

Orlinsky, D.E. and Howard, K.I. (1986) Process and outcome in psychotherapy, in S.L. Garfield and A.E. Bergin (eds) *Handbook of Psychotherapy and Behavior Change* 3rd edn, New York: Wiley, pp. 311-81.

—— (1987) A generic model of psychotherapy, *Journal of Integrative and Eclectic Psychotherapy* 6: 6-27.

Papajohn, J.C. (1982) *Intensive Behavior Therapy: The Behavioral Treatment of Complex Emotional Disorders*, New York: Pergamon.

Parloff, M.B. (1976) Shopping for the right therapy, *Saturday Review* 21: 135-42.

—— (1979) Can psychotherapy research guide the policymaker?: a little knowledge may be a dangerous thing, *American Psychologist* 34: 296-306.

Patterson, C.H. (1989) Eclecticism in psychotherapy: is integration possible?, *Psychotherapy* 26: 157-61.

Paul, G.L. (1967) Strategy of outcome research in psychotherapy, *Journal of Consulting Psychology* 31: 109-18.

—— (1969) Behavior modification research: design and tactics, in C.M. Franks (ed.) *Behaviour Therapy: Appraisal and Status*, New York: McGraw-Hill, pp. 29-62.

—— (1987) Strategy of outcome research in psychotherapy, *Journal of Consulting Psychology* 31: 109-19.

Perry, W. (1970) *Forms of Intellectual and Ethical Development in the College Years: A Scheme*, New York: Holt, Rinehart and Winston.

Pinsof, W.M. (1983) Integrative problem-centered therapy: toward the synthesis of family and individual psychotherapies, *Journal of Marital and Family Therapy* 9: 19-35.

Powell, D.H. (1988) Spontaneous insights and the process of behavior therapy: cases in support of integrative psychotherapy, *Annals of Psychiatry* 18: 288-94.

Prochaska, J.O. (1984) *Systems of Psychotherapy: A transtheoretical analysis*, 2nd edn, Homewood, Ill. Dorsey.

—— (1991) Prescribing to the stage and level of phobic patients, *Psychotherapy* 28: 463-8.

—— and DiClemente, C.C. (1982) Transtheoretical therapy: toward a more integrative model of change, *Psychotherapy: Theory, Research, and Practice* 19: 276-88.

—— (1984) *The Transtheoretical Approach: Crossing the Traditional Boundaries of Therapy*, Homewood, Ill.: Dow Jones-Irvin.

—— (1986) The transtheoretical approach, in J.C. Norcross (ed.) *Handbook of Eclectic Psychotherapy*, New York: Brunner/Mazel.

—— and Norcross, J.C. (1983) Contemporary psychotherapists: a national survey of characteristics, practices, orientations, and attitudes, *Psychotherapy: Theory, Research and Practice* 20: 161-73.

Prochaska, J.O., Rossi, J.S. and Wilcox, N.S. (1991) Change processes and psychotherapy outcome in integrative case research, *Journal of Psychotherapy Integration* 1: 103–20.

Raimy, V. (1975) *Misunderstandings of the Self*, San Francisco: Jossey-Bass.

Rhoads, J.M. (1984) Relationships between psychodynamic and behavior therapies, in H. Arkowitz and S.B. Messer (eds) *Psychoanalytic Therapy and Behavior Therapy: Is Integration Possible?*, New York: Plenum, pp. 195–212.

—— (1988) Combinations and synthesis of psychotherapies, *Annals of Psychiatry* 18: 280–7.

—— and Feather, B.W. (1972) Transference and resistance observed in behavior therapy, *British Journal of Medical Psychology* 45: 99–103.

Robertson, M. (1979) Some observations from an eclectic therapist, *Psychotherapy: Theory, Research, and Practice* 16: 18–21.

—— (1986) Training eclectic psychotherapists, in J.C. Norcross (ed.) *Handbook of Eclectic Psychotherapy*, New York: Brunner/Mazel.

Rogers, C.R. (1951) *Client-Centered Therapy*, Boston: Houghton-Mifflin.

—— (1957) The necessary and sufficient conditions of therapeutic personality changes, *Journal of Consulting and Clinical Psychology* 21: 95–103.

Rosenzweig, S. (1936) Some implicit common factors in diverse methods in psychotherapy, *American Journal of Orthopsychiatry* 6: 412–15.

Rotter, J.B. (1954) *Social Learning and Clinical Psychology*, Englewood Cliffs, NJ: Prentice-Hall.

Ryle, A. (1987) Cognitive psychology as a common language for psychotherapy, *Journal of Integrative and Eclectic Psychotherapy* 6: 168–72.

Safran, J.D. and Segal, Z.V. (1990) *Interpersonal Process in Cognitive Therapy*, New York: Basic Books.

Schacht, T.E. (1984) The varieties of integrative experience, in H. Arkowitz and S.B. Messer (eds) *Psychoanalytic Therapy and Behavior Therapy: Is Integration Possible?*, New York: Plenum, pp. 107–32.

Schafer, R. (1983) *The Analytic Attitude*, New York: Basic Books.

Schofeld, W. (1964) *Psychotherapy: The Purchase of Friendship*, Englewood Cliffs, NJ: Prentice-Hall.

Schwartz, G.E. (1984) Psychobiology of health: a new synthesis, in B.L. Hammonds and C.J. Scheirer (eds) *Psychology and Health*, Washington, DC: American Psychological Association.

—— (1991) The data are always friendly: a systems approach to psychotherapy integration, *Journal of Psychotherapy Integration* 1: 55–69.

Sears, R.R. (1944) Experimental analysis of psychoanalytic phenomena, in J. McV. Hunt (ed.) *Personality and the Behavior Disorders*, New York: Ronald Press, pp. 297–323.

Segraves, R.T. (1982) *Marital Therapy: A Combined Psychodynamic–Behavioral Approach*, New York: Plenum.

Shengold, L.L. (1979) Child abuse and deprivation: soul murder, *Journal of the American Psychoanalytic Association* 27: 533–9.

Shoben, E.J. (1949) Psychotherapy as a problem in learning theory, *Psychological Bulletin* 46: 366–92.

Silverman, L.H. (1974) Some psychoanalytic considerations of non-psychoanalytic therapies: on approaches and related issues, *Psychotherapy: Theory, Research, and Practice* 11: 298–305.

Sloane, R.B., Staples, F.R., Cristol, A.H., Yorkston, N.J. and Whipple, K. (1975) *Psychotherapy vs. Behavior Therapy*, Cambridge, Mass.: Harvard University Press.

Smith, D.S. (1982) Trends in counseling and psychotherapy, *American Psychologist* 37: 802–9.

Smith, M.L., Glass, G.L. and Miller, T.I. (1980) *The Benefits of Psychotherapy*, Baltimore: Johns Hopkins University Press.

Stein, D.J. (1992) Schemas in the cognitive and clinical sciences: an integrative construct, *Journal of Psychotherapy Integration* 2.

Steuer, J.L., Mintz, J., Hammen, C.L., Hill, M.A., Jarvik, L.F., McCarley, T., Motoike, P. and Rosen, R. (1984) Cognitive-behavioral and psychodynamic group psychotherapy in treatment of geriatric depression, *Journal of Consulting and Clinical Psychology* 52: 180-9.

Stiles, W.G., Shapiro, D.A. and Elliot, R. (1986) Are all psychotherapies equivalent?, *American Psychologist* 41: 165-80.

Stricker, G. (1986) Some viable suggestions for integrating psychotherapies, paper presented at the second annual conference of the Society for the Exploration of Psychotherapy Integration, May, Toronto.

Strong, S.R. (1987) Interpersonal theory as a common language for psychotherapy, *Journal of Integrative and Eclectic Psychotherapy* 6: 173-83.

Strupp, H.H. (1973) On the basic ingredients of psychotherapy, *Journal of Consulting and Clinical Psychology* 41: 1-8.

—— (1982) The outcome problem in psychotherapy: contemporary perspectives, in J.H. Harvey and M.M. Parks (eds) *Psychotherapy Research and Behavior Change: 1981 Master Lecture Series*, Washington, DC: American Psychological Association.

—— and Binder, J.L. (1984) *Psychotherapy in a New Key: A Guide to Time-Limited Dynamic Psychotherapy*, New York: Basic Books.

Talley, P.F., Strupp, H.H. and Morey, L.C. (1990) Matchmaking in psychotherapy: patient–therapist dimensions and their impact on outcome, *Journal of Consulting and Clinical Psychology*, 58: 182-8.

Thoresen, C.E. (1973) Behavioral humanism, in C.E. Thoresen (ed.) *Behavior Modification in Education*, Chicago: University of Chicago Press, pp. 98-122.

Truax, C.B. and Mitchell, K.M. (1971) Research on certain therapist interpersonal skills in relation to process and outcome, in A.E. Bergin and S.L. Garfield (eds) *Handbook of Psychotherapy and Behavior Change*, 1st edn, New York: Wiley, pp. 299-344.

Wachtel, E.F. and Wachtel, P.L. (1986) *Family Dynamics in Individual Psychotherapy*, New York: Guilford.

Wachtel, P.L. (1975) Behavior therapy and the facilitation of psychoanalytic exploration, *Psychotherapy: Theory, Research, and Practice* 12: 68-72.

—— (1977) *Psychoanalysis and Behavior Therapy: Toward an Integration*, New York: Basic Books.

—— (1982a) What can dynamic therapies contribute to behavior therapy?, *Behavior Therapy* 13: 594-609.

—— (ed.) (1982b) *Resistance: Psychodynamic and Behavioral Approaches*, New York: Plenum.

—— (1983) Integration misunderstood, *British Journal of Clinical Psychology* 22: 129-30.

—— (1984) On theory, practice, and the nature of integration, in H. Arkowitz and S.B. Messer (eds) *Psychoanalytic Therapy and Behavior Therapy: Is Integration Possible?*, New York: Plenum, pp. 31-52.

—— (1987) *Action and Insight*, New York: Guilford.

—— (1991) From eclecticism to synthesis: toward a more seamless psychotherapeutic integration, *Journal of Psychotherapy Integration* 1: 43-54.

Wandersman, A., Poppen, P.J. and Ricks, D.F. (eds) (1976) *Humanism and Behaviorism: Dialogue and Growth*, Elmsford, NY: Pergamon.

Weitzman, B. (1967) Behavior therapy and psychotherapy, *Psychological Review* 74: 300-17.

Wills, T.A. (1982) *Basic Processes in Helping Relationships*, New York: Academic Press.

—— (1985) Supportive functions of interpersonal relationships, in S. Cohen and S.L. Syme (eds) *Social Support and Health*, New York: Academic Press, pp. 61-82.

Wolfe, B.E. (1989) Phobias, panic, and psychotherapy integration, *Journal of Integrative and Eclectic Psychotherapy* 8: 264-76.

—— (1992) Self-experiencing and the integrative treatment of the anxiety disorders, *Journal of Psychotherapy Integration* 2.

Wolfe, B.E. and Goldfried, M.R. (1988) Research on psychotherapy integration: recommendations and conclusions from an NIMH workshop, *Journal of Consulting and Clinical Psychology* 56: 448–51.

Wolpe, J. (1958) *Psychotherapy by Reciprocal Inhibition*, Stanford, Calif.: Stanford University Press.

—— and Rachman, S. (1960) Psychoanalytic 'evidence': a critique based on Freud's case of Little Hans, *Journal of Nervous and Mental Disorders* 131: 135–48.

Yates, A.J. (1983) Behavior therapy and psychodynamic therapy: basic conflicts or reconciliation or integration, *British Journal of Clinical Psychology* 22: 107–25.

2

Systemic Integrative Psychotherapy*

PETRŪSKA CLARKSON AND PHIL LAPWORTH

Introduction

Systemic Integrative Psychotherapy deserves to be contextualized against the general philosophical and scientific background of the late twentieth century. It is against such a backdrop that the psychoanalytic, behavioural and humanistic/ existential views of the nature of the person can be integrated by taking an inclusive perspective. This integrative psychotherapy approach, developed at *metanoia* Psychotherapy Training Institute, is facilitated by the recognition of *Physis*. Physis, first named by the ancient Greeks, is conceived of as a generalized creative force of evolution, both in human nature and in psychotherapeutic endeavour. It is in this sense that Systemic Integrative Psychotherapy has been developed at the Institute and remains in a constant process of creative evolution. In this chapter the influence of contemporary currents in psychotherapy and psychotherapy research of discovering commonality, communication and integrative principles is briefly considered. Another major integrative principle addressed is that of the research evidence that effective psychotherapy is more a factor of the relationship between the client and the therapist than the particular theory espoused. Among other systems principles, the notions of wholeness, homeostasis and evolution in particular lead to a primary focus on the *relationship* as the most important vehicle of therapeutic change from an integrative perspective. I see the emphasis on the centrality of relationship as a major practical application of systems theory in psychotherapy. A systems approach is thus offered at one level as a metatheoretical perspective on psychotherapy (individual or family). At another level the systemic interplay between homeostatic and evolutionary (developmental) mechanisms is also seen to apply to the psychological theory itself.

Five kinds of client–therapist relationship are identified which are hypothesized to be potentially present in any psychotherapy. This forms a primary

* Incorporating the Seven-Level Model by Petrūska Clarkson.

framework for psychotherapeutic integration which incorporates several major different theories of therapeutic change. Four domains of variation (client, psychotherapist, time and environment) are discussed separately, but they are conceived of as mutually interacting, dynamically evolving systems. The larger systems of time and environment are conceived of as the containing matrix for the interplay of all the other systems.

I describe a seven-level integrative perspective as a holistic view of the person. This model is also useful as a classificatory and integrative conceptual tool for separating out different layers of knowledge (epistemological areas or universes of discourse) in psychology and psychotherapy. It acts both as a categorization for different approaches as well as a tool for integration which depends not on the model itself but on the skilfulness of the integrator using it. This approach has also been found useful for psychotherapy integration at the concrete operations level or specific interventions level, providing a sorting tool for the multitude of interventions and strategies available to the integrating psychotherapist. I believe that psychotherapy integration is the task of each thinking and developing psychotherapist using singular or integrative theories, perspectives and tools gleaned from other workers, but essentially it concerns developing one's own individual integration with each unique therapeutic encounter. In this spirit my colleague, Phil Lapworth, has contributed a case-study, which although necessarily much abbreviated, reflects his own particular psychotherapeutic integration in practice.

The background of the times

The integration of psychotherapies is a growing movement throughout the world. For example, more psychologists now identify themselves as integrative than any other orientation in the USA, and in Britain and the rest of Europe interest is also growing apace. This *Zeitgeist* reflects an increasing openness to communication, cross-fertilization and divergent creativity. Simultaneously, it reflects decreasing allegiance to orthodoxy, unilateral perspectives and certainty regarding 'the truth' of any one particular approach to human behaviour. Some of the background factors which influence this concern are the increasing levels of complexity of information in the human sciences from biology to economics to chaos theory (Gleick 1988). There is a concomitant explosion in the very paradigms of thought such as are being discovered, articulated and indeed integrated in modern physics (Kuhn 1970; Capra 1982; Zohar 1990).

At a collective global level increasing openness to integration is reflected in some of the changes happening in different parts of the world. From Russia to Berlin to South Africa apparently irreconcilable polarities are beginning to break down and the struggles between mutually exclusive positions on right and wrong are being superseded by the hard work of finding common ground, negotiations, compromise and possible mutual enhancement – or war. Alongside such developments comes also the chaos of cultural transitions and paradigm shifts in philosophy, science and psychology. Currently there is widespread questioning about basic frames of reference in the philosophical, biological and physical sciences, as well as in the arts. The notion of one 'truth' or a single solution to complex problems is being challenged in all of the above fields. This appears to have led to a growing tolerance for multiple perspectives, often apparently paradoxical, for conceptualizing the same problem. People may be discovering many different but equally viable ways of dealing with issues relating to differing universes of discourse.

Intellectual relativism and open-minded curiosity appears to be a collective phenomenon of late twentieth-century psychological and historical developments. This climate has been described as post-modern. It is in this cultural idiom that the pluralistic tolerance of different perspectives in integrative psychotherapy can most fruitfully grow. Lyotard (1984) defines the post-modern as suspicion or incredulity of metanarratives – 'the grand narratives of the past' (traditional 'ultimate truths'). Post-modernism in art, architecture and literature embraces a heterogeneity which is opposed to consensus on the one hand and Fascism on the other. It favours, rather, the co-existence of many different 'language games' (Wittgenstein 1953). Its principle is the inventor's 'parology' – the invention of new knowledge. This is also the task of every individual integrative psychotherapist.

The problems facing the world on a macroscopic level, as well as psychotherapy on a microscopic level, have become too complex for many psychotherapists to continue to have unbridled faith in singular solutions or to insist on imposing such singular solutions on their trainees and colleagues. Economic pressure demands accountability from health services, insurance companies and psychotherapy providers. There is also accumulating research evidence that no one particular psychotherapy can be shown to be significantly more effective than another (Luborsky *et al.* 1975; Sloane *et al.* 1975; Bergin and Lambert 1978). The fact that the investment of time, money and availability can vary considerably across psychotherapeutic approaches causes serious economic, theoretical and ethical concern (Norcross 1986).

Theory

Common and integrative factors in psychotherapy

One of the primary reasons for the growth of interest and academic and clinical investment in Integrative Psychotherapy is the multiplication of so-called 'schools' of psychotherapy with estimates ranging between 250 (Corsini 1984) and 400. Yet since the Fiedler (1950) studies, no one approach to psychotherapy has been proved significantly better than another. (Fiedler found greater resemblances between senior practitioners of different schools than between trainees and such expert practitioners within the same school.) Rowan (1990) details the way different schools developed over time and also suggests that we are now in a period of integration rather than differentiation. Garfield (1980, 1982) is arguably the leading exponent of the view that certain therapeutic factors are common to most psychotherapeutic approaches. The factors he has identified as common across schools of psychotherapy are: the therapist–client relationship; interpretation, insight and understanding; catharsis; emotional expression and release; reinforcement in psychotherapy; desensitization; relaxation; information in psychotherapy; reassurance and support; modelling; confronting one's problems; clarifying and modifying client expectancies; and providing both a credible therapeutic framework for the client's problems and a credible rationale for the psychotherapy.

Marmor (1982) identified the following seven elements that produce change in analytic treatment:

(1) A basic matrix of a good patient–therapist relationship resting on both real and fantasied qualities that each brings to their work together . . . (2) Release of emotional tension . . . (3) Cognitive learning or the acquisition of insight . . . (4) Operant conditioning, by means of subtle and often nonverbal cues of approval or disapproval, as well as by corrective emotional experiences in the relationship with the analyst. (5) Suggestion and persuasion, usually implicit, occasionally explicit. (6) Unconscious identification with the analyst, both conceptually and behaviorally. (7) Repeated reality testing and 'working through' . . .

(p. 66)

The existentialist psychotherapist Yalom (1975) described 12 'curative' factors in effective group psychotherapy which overlap significantly with factors identified by Corsini and Rosenberg (1955). Different psychotherapies are thus seen by an increasing number of workers as deriving their potency from common factors.

Eysenck's (1952) challenge to prove the efficacy of psychotherapy has by no means been satisfactorily resolved, as has been shown in recent surveys of research literature in the field (Lambert 1986). Few of us claim to be over-optimistic about the likelihood that future research will ever give us a reliable and valid statistical proof of permanent psychological change on all possible parameters acceptable to all psychotherapists. This will be particularly true if qualitative research methods are not encouraged.

Research on psychotherapy outcome suggests that patients with a variety of problems are helped by many methods that may not have been put to the empirical test. The results of psychotherapy outcome research by no means suggest, however, that every participant gains from treatment to a clinically meaningful extent. The results are also compatible with the suggestion some clients may deteriorate during therapy.

(Lambert *et al.* 1977)

Thus the question is by no means resolved. Furthermore, substantial numbers of psychotherapists and many psychoanalysts hold the view that the measuring instruments so far available to psychological researchers do not fit the complexity and subtlety of the effects thought to be achieved in psychotherapy. The more cognitive-behavioural of therapies, as represented in Lambert (1986), take the problem extremely seriously and many of its advocates do diligent research. Humanistic-existential approaches have varied from participation in research statistically indicating high effectiveness (Bergin and Garfield 1978) to the rejection of previous scientific paradigms and the positing of post-Newtonian scientific paradigms (Merleau-Ponty 1962; Rogers 1986; Hawking 1988). Thus what is at question is not only the reliability, the validity, consistency and coherence of the psychotherapies themselves, but also the attempts to subject these to scientific scrutiny by methods about which practitioners are still extremely divided. Thus, despite the apparent fact that psychotherapeutic approaches which take wide-angle perspectives on human beings could be investigated by researchers, the question still remains whether indeed an effective post-Newtonian paradigm can or has been developed in psychology (Reason and Rowan 1981).

Whatever its fruits, psychotherapy generally has taken almost 90 years to reach its present stage of accountability. This applies equally to the three established streams or lineages of theoreticians/clinicians originating from Freud, Moreno and Pavlov respectively. In some sense each one of these ideological 'grand-fathers' can be seen as the primary three differentiated integrationists of their own time. However, the emergence of integrative psychotherapies as academic and clinical entities in their own right is comparatively recent, and already there are a large number of different forms of eclectic or integrative psychotherapy (Dryden 1984). The first official association for integrative psychotherapy, SEPI (the Society for the Exploration of Psychotherapy Integration), was formed as recently as 1983, with the British Society for Integrative Psychotherapy (BSIP), which is affiliated to International SEPI, being formed in 1987.

Psychotherapy integration therefore also needs to be placed in this historical context. In fairness it deserves to be given an equivalent number of decades as its historically older psychotherapeutic rivals, before the movement and its theories are judged as either unproven or unprovable. The value of theory is also by no means undisputed, even within ideological strongholds. From the Tavistock, Symington comments: 'The theories within psychoanalytic discourse have as much relation to psychoanalysis as a manual of sexual techniques have to being in love' (1986: 9). Utopian wishes for 'one finalised, true integrative psychotherapy' with consistency, coherence, scientific rigour, conceptual clarity, practical value and aesthetic appeal, will probably have to wait a while to be satisfied. At least it may have to be postponed until any one approach to psychotherapy does reach such idealized criteria. In the mean time, workers for integration within or between schools are developing communicative bridges and developing frameworks which may perhaps come closer to excellence than any one close-minded paradigm affiliation (Dryden and Norcross 1990). According to Smail (1978: 73):

> Because our experience of ourselves, other people, and of society . . . is infinitely more complicated . . . we cannot expect to quickly find a common language with which we can measure them. This demands a tolerance of different perspectives, a good will towards the experience of others, a patient groping after shared understandings, which will require a very different spirit from that in which psychological inquiry has largely been carried out in recent decades.

The integration of psychotherapies, however, is not new. An analysis of any particular psychotherapy will invariably unearth some borrowed form, theory, concept or technique from another psychotherapy or related discipline. Freud, for example, originally integrated Breuer's technique of discussing emotional problems of patients under hypnosis, to bring about catharsis within his developing psychoanalytic theory. Even within the humanistic psychotherapies, which independently evolved in the tradition of the psychodramatic work of Moreno, substantial integration (with or without acknowledgement) can be found. To take another example, the notion of 'self-realization' is anticipated in Aristotle (Lovejoy and Boas 1973: 450). Integration is thus a process, a development, an evolution itself:

> In spite of many deviations and retrogressions the record is one of cumulative observation, with gradual *evolution of concepts* and clarification of thinking over more than 4,000 years. Traces of the evolutionary process survive in current psychiatric terminology, and the evolution has been in part a reflection of advances in knowledge.
>
> (Brill 1967: 583, emphasis added)

Views of the person

The development of psychotherapies in the twentieth century can be conceptualized in terms of the three major streams of thought which originated around the beginning of this century: those emanating from Freud which lead to the *psychoanalytic tradition* and its developments; the *behaviourist tradition* which can be traced back to the work of Pavlov (1928) and the *existential/humanistic tradition* which can be seen to emanate from the spirit and practice of Moreno, the psychodramatist and pioneering group psychotherapist (Greenberg 1975). A necessarily abbreviated summary here suggests that the psychoanalytic tradition emphasizes the unconcious (Bowlby 1980, 1985; Greenberg and Safran 1987), drive theory (particularly *Thanatos* and *Eros*), transference and the repetition compulsion, ego psychology, object relations and more recently self-theory. The behaviourist tradition emphasizes the principles of learning reflexes and operant conditioning, models of reinforcement and scientific accountability, modelling, links between cognition and behaviour, and between emotion and cognition, as well as cognitive structures, schemas and scripts. The humanistic/existential tradition can be characterized by a focus on existence, choice, autonomy, responsibility, anxiety, death, despair, freedom, values, potential for change, self-actualization, social involvement and future orientation.

Maslow (1968) attached the term 'third force' to this latter grouping. It can also be associated with a third force or drive in human behaviour – *Physis*. This has been defined as a generalized creative 'force of Nature, which eternally strives to make things grow and to make growing things more perfect' (Berne 1969: 89). The pre-Socratics conceived of *Physis* as the healing factor in illness, the energetic motive for *evolution* and *creativity* in the individual and collective psyche (Guerriere 1980). *Physis* antedates *Eros* and *Thanatos*. It is conceived as more biological since it represents the evolutionary impulse inherent in every cell. It is also viewed as more spiritual since it implies that it is in the nature of the person and the planet to evolve creatively. Evolution is of course a *systemic* concept. This will be further discussed later in this chapter.

The three primary parent views of human beings (with the attendant value orientation and theories of each) are often seen as in contradiction or opposition to each other. The more the angle of the lens viewing human behaviour is nar-rowed, the more persuasive such differences can become. Alternatively, if one looks at them though a wide angle philosophical lens, these three philosophi-cal traditions could be seen as mutually complementary and enriching. A view of the person then emerges which arguably includes the person as a *learner* (behaviourism), the person as *reactor* (psychoanalysis) and the person as *creator* (humanistic/existential position). This is an integrative position based on inclu-sion, not exclusion. In practice this means that no one approach is believed to contain an exclusive claim to the 'truth', but that between these different views, a more complete and fully rounded appreciation of the human being can be construed.

Integration can then be conceived of as open and creative communication between these apparently conflicting and contradictory explanations of human beings (and how they think, feel, behave, grow and develop) and the coherently selective inclusion of useful and workable aspects of each (rather than the indis-criminate and total exclusion of one camp by another). Theories are understood as stories or metaphors used to make sense of ourselves, others and the world not representing facts or truth in and of themselves (see the theoretical level of the seven-level model to be discussed further on in this chapter).

Thus, though each of the above may have a story of human beings that differen-tiates one from the other, there are various themes or sub-plots that (like in all good stories) recur within each. There are naturally some common principles such as the recognition of human problems and life as process and develop-ment. Further, sometimes even the apparent oppositions can often be shown to be due to category confusion, not genuine contradiction (Ryle 1973). Perhaps psychotherapy integration, even where apparent conflicts exist, becomes increas-ingly possible as we take some of the understandings from modern physics into a post-Newtonian psychology. Creativity (which is most needed in the work of healing) often emerges when apparently contradictory positions can be tolerated (Rothenberg 1979). After all, even elementary particles 'seem to be waves on Mondays, Wednesdays and Fridays, and particles on Tuesdays, Thursdays and Saturdays' (Sir William Bragg quoted in Koestler 1972: 52). Psychotherapists can perhaps grow scientifically minded enough to tolerate or even welcome similar conditions in our field.

The figure/ground concept of gestalt (see Figure 2.1) can also be used to enable a mutually complementary perspective. This visual analogy makes it possible to see that two theories may be seen as incompatible in the sense of the assimilation or merging, of one into the other. While this may be the case from one point of view, it may appear quite different from another. It may also be necessary, more creative and useful to focus alternately from one to the other of two appa-rently mutually exclusive perspectives. Like in the gestalt figure/ground image where either two faces are seen, or alternately, a vase is seen, *both* may be needed if either is to be seen. In other words, their meaning is revealed in the relation-ship. What may be seen, for example, from the object relations perspective, as the depressive position incorporated into a person's later sense of guilt, may gain a useful counterbalancing view from a systems theory perspective of the need for a conscience within the social system. Neither need necessarily be exclusively

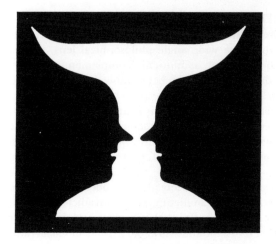

Figure 2.1   Gestalt psychology image of figure and ground

true. One or the other may shed some light on a patient's pain. Both views may be true from alternating perspectives. Some integration may be reached if seen as part of a mutually reinforcing system – the person experiencing guilt as a result of intrapsychic processes may be encouraged to continue in this role for the sake of the larger system.

It is anticipated that in the turbulent and troubled psychological waters of the end of this century communication may become more important than certainty, effectiveness more important than elegance for its own sake, and intellectual and moral questioning of basic assumptions more important than adherence to a single *via integrata* (one true way of integration). The suggestion here is that we become more systemic and metaphorically pull back the telescope that is solely directed at the behavioural planet (for example) and allow a wider-angled lens to include the other planets, the humanistic and the psychoanalytic in order to explore how they relate as a galaxy or *system* as a whole. This inclusivity neces-sitates a responsibility that is no longer to do with what is right or what is wrong, what is the truth and what is not the truth, but a responsibility to be able to explain why, when and how we select the theoretical constructs or the operational procedures that we do. Psychotherapy, like astronomy, is also a science, and as such it therefore needs to be teachable to others. Its practitioners need to be able to explain their thinking and their interventions in terms of what is important for a particular client at a particular moment, in particular circumstances, with a particular psychotherapist.

However, here is another application for the figure/ground gestalt. The vase of psychotherapy may be a science but the faces of psychotherapy constitute an art. The psychotherapist responds at an intuitive level to the client and inter-venes with perceptions and understandings that are seemingly mystical at times in their creativity and spontaneity, each forged anew in the existential moment of encounter between an 'I' and a 'You'. The changing figure/foreground perspective is thus also an image for the interplay between science and art, system and psyche, technology and intuition.

The possibility (philosophically as well as pragmatically) that there may be *three* drives, *Eros*, *Thanatos* and *Physis*, fuelling human lives and behaviourally interacting with the pervasive effect of conditioning, evolving and learning in relational systems, may seem a simple enough proposition. However, it may take another 100 years to work it out. Of course much precision may be lost in taking a wide angle view on the human condition. This macroscopic view needs to be complemented with attention to specific and smaller details. Naturally, what the microscope improves in terms of precision and minute observation it loses in large-scale perspective. Different instruments (telescopes or microscopes) are also, of course, suitable for different purposes. Obviously, for reasons of space, the discussion here has to be indicative rather than exhaustive, invoking the reader's existing knowledge, imaginative powers and collegial co-operation.

Systemic Integrative Psychotherapy

Systemic Integrative Psychotherapy is currently defined as a personal, conceptual and experiential integration of values, theories, strategies and specific interventions within a psychotherapeutic relationship which is based on a systems perspective. It begins specifically with systems theory which describes natural systems (e.g. von Bertalanffy 1969) in terms of relationships, as well as the systemic context of psychotherapy as a process of *evolution over time*. A systemic approach is considered applicable to group, family or organizational contexts, but naturally also to individuals.

The Shorter Oxford Dictionary defines a system as 'a whole composed of parts in orderly arrangement according to some scheme or plan. A set or assemblage of things connected, associated, or interdependent, so as to form a complex unity' (Onions 1973: 2227). On physical as well as psychological levels, living systems are made up of parts which themselves again constitute systems on a smaller scale (sub-systems). These are inevitably related to other systems in even larger organizations (supra-systems) which are hierarchically related. 'Thus the functional units on every level of the hierarchy are double-faced as it were; they act as whole when facing downwards, as parts when facing upwards' (Koestler 1989: 287).

Beutler (1986: 97) has also suggested that 'Systems theory is another general theory that might possibly serve as a vehicle for communication and as an umbrella under which all therapeutic approaches could be described'. It is a particularly useful approach to human behaviour and therapeutic change because: (a) as originally formulated by von Bertalanffy (1969) it does not necessarily imply adherence to any one particular philosophically based view of human beings; (b) it is an approach which focuses on wholes as wholes which are more than the sum of the component parts. This is different from the kind of holism which is sometimes the result of adding different levels of analysis as in many theories which are confined to psychology alone; (c) it particularly facilitates clarity and efficiency in making decisions as to which strategies, and particularly which interventions, are likely to have the largest effect in the shortest period of time on the whole person. Within the limited space available here I can but suggest that systems principles can act as practice guidelines for understanding, choosing, sequencing and implementing minimal interventions for maximum effect, also in individual or group psychotherapy. Much explanation, qualification and interpretation of context and process have to be assumed here for the sake of brevity and only some elements crucial to this discussion are highlighted. Despite great contributions particularly in family therapy and organizational work, the rich literature in systems theory is yet to be mined to its richest effect by current and future generations of clinicians in individual and group psychotherapy.

Systems theory is conceptualized by Cottone (1988) as metatheoretic to psychological theory. Depending on the level, it implies that even the way we view and interact with 'psychological evidence', ideological convictions or 'scientific knowledge' cannot be seen outside of the *relationship* with our social linguistic, philosophical or personally pathological contexts. The observer can no longer be considered separately from the observed. A systemic integration as a finally achieved integration would be nonsense since the systemic approach mandates an ongoing dialogic relationship with any model, *particularly* itself (Maturana 1980).

On a philosophical and theoretical plane, the systemic integrative approach considers that the integration of psychotherapies should therefore be a continually expanding and developing process whereby various theories, concepts and techniques are systematically employed within a clear framework to enhance the work between a particular psychotherapist and his/her client. Although it may be out of awareness, in a sense any psychotherapist (of singular, pluralistic or integrative persuasion) can be seen to be working within a systemic approach. Whether or not it is conceptualized as such, psychotherapy is the work of facilitating and intervening as complex living systems.

Although systems are self-regulating, and thus involve homeostatic mechanisms, workers in the field from Hoffman (1981) to Teilhard de Chardin (1970) have also emphasized systemic *development*. From Goldstein (1939) to Fivaz (1980) there has been evidence that healthy living systems tend to re-organize at increasing levels of complexity and actualization. Maruyama (1968) also studied systems and the evolution of systems in nature and society. Such evolution can be seen to be under the aegis of *Physis* in its guise as the evolutionary drive of Nature present in all living systems.

> The capacity of a system to evolve depends on an ability to move to more complex forms of differentiation and integration, greater variety in the system facilitating its ability to deal with challenges and opportunities posed by the environment.
>
>   (Morgan 1986: 47).

These principles may also be applicable to the evolution of psychology and psychotherapy as open systems which both seek to maintain homeostasis as well as facilitate their own evolution. (Such evolution may involve growth, decay or discontinuous second-order changes.) The originating developments of Freud, Pavlov and Moreno have evolved into the current rich diversity of approaches to psychotherapy. An emphasis on difference and disagreement even within 'schools' of thought has often provided the spur to creative developments and the dissolution of outdated conceptual structures (Samuels 1985). Conversely, an emphasis on difference may be restrictive; as Mahrer, an experiential psychotherapist wrote, 'It is always possible to emphasize *differences* in the larger theory of human beings, and these differences may be preserved and built up to prevent any real efforts at integration' (1989: 66–7).

This is not only true between different approaches to psychotherapy, but also within a particular approach. Rothstein, for example, after comparing the expositions of six psychoanalytic theories (the approaches of Freud, Klein–Bion, Sullivan, Self, Object-relations and Lacan) commented as follows:

> Analysts employ theories to create the illusion that they have an answer, or *the* answer, in the therapeutic encounter, an encounter that is intrinsically filled with uncertainty. Theories provide models, or puzzle solutions, terms and procedures, all of which, if properly employed enhance an analyst's self-esteem. In addition theories are associated with traditions and institutions which further enhance the analyst's self-esteem as he works within them and provides both illusions of security and tangible benefits such as referrals. This institutionalization of theory has contributed to an emphasis upon an exaggeration of differences and has interfered with more optimal communication between proponents of different points of view.
>
> (Rothstein 1985: 129–30)

(This state of affairs is, of course not unique to psychoanalysis, but may also apply to other psychotherapies.) Conversely, the psychoanalyst Sandler encouraged his colleagues at one of the Workshops for Mental Health Professionals which Rothstein recorded to 'try to listen to what other people are saying' (1985: 147). This has been echoed in Britain by Hinshelwood's comment on '. . . the hopeful atmosphere of integration in psychotherapy' (1989: 473). Pilgrim (1989) has also recommended that clinical psychologists in Britain embrace their own profession's rhetoric of successful eclecticism. He is, of course, *not* referring to what Dryden has called 'haphazard eclecticism' (1984: 351). Lazarus disparagingly caricatured such eclectics with the phrase 'I use whatever makes sense to me and whatever I feel comfortable with' (1981: 4–5).

Which particular theories, concepts, or techniques an experienced psychotherapist chooses to integrate can only be done on an individual and personal basis. Only then can there be a true integration for that person, in relationship with his or her own approach to psychotherapy. People and their problems should come before theories or techniques. The latter surely exist to serve the former. Any humane and effective approach to psychotherapy – from psychoanalysis to Gestalt – will hopefully honour this position. Systemic Integrative Psychotherapy is a process of considered integration rather than *ad hoc* or eclectic (in the worst sense) practice on the one hand or rigid prescriptionism on the other. It takes place within a systemic and holistic framework. It has to be forged anew from the knowledge and experience of each individual clinician. The exposition here is not an attempt to 'provide' a final true integration. It is an attempt to provide a framework which may be helpful to an experienced individual practitioner as he or she consciously and conscientiously *creates* (rather than reproduces) a

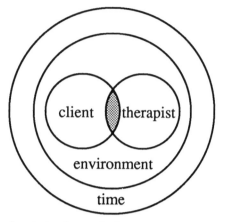

Figure 2.2   Domains of variation in psychotherapy

personally coherent system of applied integrative psychotherapy (whether it draws primarily from one theory base or twenty).

Four domains of variation

Any approach to psychotherapy has to account for at least four major domains of variation or difference. These are client variation, psychotherapist variation, variation over time and the variation of environment (Dryden 1986). Figure 2.2 schematically represents these domains of variation and their interaction (the overlap) by illustrating the relationship between client and therapist in the systemic context of time and space (environment). The fact that the client and psychotherapist areas are shown as both separate and overlapping is intended to facilitate conceptual and practical differentiation between the personal *internal world* of each individual and their *interpersonal* world and acknowledge the importance and mutual interaction of *both*. The intrapsychic or internal world, of course, comprises fantasy, internal objects, representational systems and so on while the interpersonal world consists for example of communication, verbal and non-verbal transactions between people. Stern's (1985) account of an integrative perspective in terms of child development which accounts for both the internal and the interpersonal worlds of the human infant is here generalized to be used for psychotherapy integration, practice, training and supervision.

It is also central to a *systems approach* to understand that

> Epistemologically, the things we see (people, objects etc.) exist only in relationship, and when analysed microscopically, they too, are best viewed as relationships. It is no secret in physics (Capra 1975, 1982) that the closer we analyse some 'thing' the less it appears as a thing and the more it appears as a dynamic process (things in relationships). Consequently, relationships become a primary source of our knowledge of the world. This can be taken to the ontological extreme by stating that things do not exist . . . that, in fact, things ultimately *are* relationships.
>
> (Cottone 1988: 360)

The client–therapist relationship system forms a natural unit throughout this discussion. It is within this matrix that the internal world of a person is externalized and becomes available for change. It is represented as the core of the psychotherapeutic system in Figure 2.2 (which is a cross-section of the summary diagram, Figure 2.4). Here, for the sake of discussion, sub-systems are differentiated. However, it is essential to keep in mind that all sub-systems are also all active, interacting, dynamic whole systems at other levels of analysis. Each element identified can also be studied as a complete system in itself.

Client variation

The individual *client as a system*, comprising the interacting relationships between many sub-systems, is sometimes a less familiar perspective in the psychotherapeutic literature than family systems theory. However, in the same way that one distinguishes, biologically, the cardio-vascular system from the digestive system, psychological systems of an individual person can also be differentiated and seen in mutual interrelationship. For example, belief systems, self-systems, value systems, autonomic response systems, cognitive construct systems (Kelly 1955) and so on are all systems which can be distinguished from each other and treated in interrelationship with each other.

Probably the most frequently used way of attempting to describe client difference in psychiatric and psychological circles is that of classical psychiatric diagnosis. Obviously this is an attempt to describe the idiosyncratic qualities of an individual taking into account larger patterns or frequently observed clusters of phenomena. Diagnosis attempts to describe what the person is presenting or what the symptoms, syndromes, problems and concerns are which the client is manifesting. There are many different systems of diagnosis ranging from constructive use of *DSM-III-R* (American Psychiatric Association 1987), Kernberg's classifications (1984), diagnosis in terms of Gestalt Interruptions to Contact (De Lisle 1988), or Beutler's dimensions of symptom complexity, coping style, reactance level and focal theme (1986). According to Dryden (1984) any psychotherapy, and particularly an integrative psychotherapy, must take account of client variation by one or more of these (or newly created) means. Systemic Integrative Psychotherapy does not prescribe which diagnostic approach (from phenomenological description according to Minkowski (1970) to the World Health Organization's classification of mental disorders (1978)) must be used. It does require that an individual practitioner be familiar with such systems and be able consistently to use one or more of them with some relevance to their practice – if only to communicate with other colleagues.

DSM-III-R diagnosis, for example, takes into account the psychiatric condition, the kind of personality, and the individual's physical and psychosocial world as well as their functional capacities. While this gives it a descriptive power exceeding unidimensional classification systems, it retains a channel of communication with psychiatry. Whether or not a psychotherapist uses a standard diagnostic procedure, it will be expected that they use or develop some way of describing individual differences, and appreciating commonalities, between patients. Sensitively used in the hands of psychotherapists skilled in the healing uses of relationship, clarity of diagnosis does not necessarily *have* to impede the integrity of existential psychotherapy, but can be seen to be complementary and even humane (Clarkson 1989c).

Assessment or diagnosis can also be seen as a way of describing how people present themselves in their existential world (Spiegelberg 1972). This, of course, is a combination of their heredity and their past and current environment and is represented as such on the summary diagram, Figure 2.4 (see p. 68). It is probably by now commonly accepted that 'nature' and 'nurture' interact as two major formative notions for regarding individual differences even though different workers ascribe greater or lesser importance to each. Modern child developmental theory (e.g. Stern 1985) emphasizes the interaction between nature and nurture, with the child as the agent of the interaction. Both nature and nurture refer to the origins of present constellations of a person's behaviour, feelings and attitudes, whereas diagnosis refers to what they present or manifest.

Variables from nature refers to people's predispositions (e.g. to cancer or alcoholism), temperamental preferences (e.g. intensity of stimulation or time of rising), intellectual ceiling (IQ range) and physical talents or limitations (athleticism or lack of height), their introversion/extroversion typologies (whether from Eysenckian or Jungian perspectives), archetypal propensities, their cortical excitation/inhibition balance (which according to Eysenck (1968) affects the speed of conditioning or learning), their vulnerability quotient (Anthony and Cohler 1987), their body type (Millon 1969) and gender influences from the biological determinism of Freud (1977) to feminist analyses (Mander and Rush 1974; Eichenbaum and Orbach 1983).

The influence of early environment, particularly the human care and interaction with the infant and child (from Bowlby 1953 to Mahler *et al.* 1975), forms a major portion of what constitutes psychological underpinnings for psychotherapy, particularly within the psychoanalytic and, to an important extent, humanistic/existential traditions. Here, nurture refers to the kind and extent of damage or adaptation due to the interaction between nature and nurture during developmental stages (whether conceived of in a Freudian or an Eriksonian (1977) paradigm) or developmental foci as in modern child development theories (from Stern 1985 to Pine 1985) which may later manifest in confusion, conflict or deficiency/effects of trauma.

The differentiation of detrimental effects of early childhood experience into the three foci of *confusion, conflict* and *deficit/trauma* was developed to aid clinicians in assessment and psychotherapy. It is more fully discussed elsewhere (Clarkson and Gilbert 1990b). This conceptualization has been found to have heuristic use – again for purposes of elucidation and improved understanding, not for finite exactitude. It posits three ways of thinking differentially about emphases in psychophysiological disturbance: (a) *confusion*, which here refers to affective and cognitive confusion – for example, Beck *et al.*'s approach to depression (1979), irrational beliefs (Ellis 1962), contaminations in Transactional Analysis (Berne 1975), transference phenomena, delusions or disassociative phenomena (Watkins 1976; Watkins and Watkins 1986); (b) *conflict* refers to the existence of internal conscious or unconscious conflict between different parts of the personality – however these may be conceived – from libidinal and anti-libidinal ego

(Fairbairn 1952) to sub-personality conflicts (Rowan 1990); (c) *developmental deficits* refers to psychological lacks or injuries caused by deficient, abusive or over-protective parenting, either chronically or traumatically (Balint 1968; Schiff *et al.* 1975), and consistent inadequate parenting (Sechehaye 1951; Kohut 1977) or *management of trauma* (Winnicott 1958; Miller 1985). There is of course no absolute dividing line between using any of these three demarcation aids as the primary focus for psychotherapy; they naturally merge and overlap. However, at any one time, maximum therapeutic leverage and improved creative anticipation may be derived from whichever one the psychotherapist is using as 'figure' or focus.

Psychotherapist variation
Psychotherapists are people too. They have their idiosyncratic styles, qualities and preferences and personality traits which are obviously influenced by *all* the factors discussed under client variation. In addition, their choice of training and learnt or developed skills and talents bear greatly upon their contribution to the psychotherapeutic encounter. Issues to do with transference and counter-transference dynamics, for example, projective identification (Hinshelwood 1989) and parallel process can be conceived of as belonging to the schematic overlap area between psychotherapist and client in Figure 2.2. The therapist, of course, also changes independently over time. Life issues such as pregnancy (Gottlieb 1989), ageing (Guy 1987) and stress (Kottler 1986) and/or increasing competency or disillusionment with the profession can be very powerful influences on the psychotherapy even though they may not directly have to do with an individual client.

There is a growing body of research, paying attention to the match between client and psychotherapist, which considers the influence of such factors as compatibility in terms of background, class, education and values (Garfield 1986). Furthermore, an impressive body of research shows that one of the most over-riding and influential factors in the outcome of psychotherapy is the relationship between psychotherapist and client (Frank 1979; Hynan 1981). In some discussions at the United Kingdom Standing Conference for Psychotherapy the following definition of psychotherapy has been used: ' . . . the systematic use of a *relationship* between therapist and patient – as opposed to pharmacological or social methods – to produce changes in cognition, feelings and behaviour' (Holmes and Lindley 1989: 3). (The integrative dimensions of affect, behaviour and cognition were identified by Beutler in 1971.) It is the responsibility of the psychotherapist to use the relationship with the client ethically and productively for maximun healing.

> We are born of relationship, nurtured in relationship, and educated in relationship. We represent every biological and social relationship of our forebears, as we interact and exist in a consensual domain called 'society'.
> (Cottone 1988: 363)

It is for this reason that the client (or patient) in systemic integrative psychotherapy is thought of as always in relationship whether this be conceived of in object relations terms or in subject relations terms (as in existential approaches).

In Figure 2.4 the centrality of relationship is diagrammatically carried through by showing the client in relationship to the therapist on every dimension.

An integrative psychotherapeutic framework of five possible modalities of client–therapist relationship has been identified by the author. It will be briefly summarized here since it forms the basis for the Integrative Psychotherapy Diploma training, as shown in the chapter on Integrative Training (see Chapter 11, this volume). This framework is one means of intellectually and experientially engaging with the systemic complexity of the relationship matrix. In order for 'help' to be of use a *working alliance* needs to be established in the first place. For example, patients actually have to take the medicine prescribed by their physicians. Research (e.g. Griffith 1990) shows that this cannot at all be taken for granted. Greenson in psychoanalysis (1967) and Berne (1975) in Transactional Analysis, among many others, have addressed the nature and use of this working alliance.

Second, there is the *transferential/countertransferential relationship* which is extremely well developed, articulated and effectively used within the theoretically rich psychoanalytic tradition and other approaches (Heiman 1950; Langs 1976; Racker 1982; Cashdan 1988; Clarkson 1992).

Third, the *developmentally needed/reparative relationship* can be differentiated as another kind of relationship which is potentially present and needed in psychotherapy. (This is a traditional intervention in psychotherapy from Ferenczi (1980) to Fromm-Reichmann (1974), Kohut (1977), and Schiff and Day (1970).) Here the psychotherapist intentionally provides the corrective/reparative replenishing parental relationship (or action) in cases where the original parenting was deficient, abusive or over-protective. According to many, including Balint (1968), it needs to be differentiated from untherapeutic gratification. Balint differentiates between malignant and benign regression in psychotherapy. Clearly, the therapeutically correct use of a developmentally needed reparative relationship (or interventions) should be carefully utilized in certain circumstances of benign regression.

Fourth, particularly within the humanistic/existential tradition, there is appreciation of the *person-to-person relationship* or *real relationship*. This kind of therapist–client relationship is similar to what Buber called the I–Thou relationship (1970). This has been retrieved and valued for its transformative potential in the psychotherapeutic arena *if* used skilfully and ethically (Rogers 1961; Laing 1965; Polster and Polster 1974). However, there has always been and there is again growing recognition within psychoanalytic practice that the real relationship between analyst and analysand – following Freud's own example – is a deeply significant, unavoidable and potentially profoundly healing force also within the psychoanalytic paradigm (Archambeau 1979; Malcolm 1981; Klauber 1986).

Finally, certainly within the Jungian tradition (Jung 1969a) and also within the humanistic/existential perspective (Rowan 1973), there is acknowledgement of the influence of the qualities which presently transcend the limits of our understanding ('There are more things in heaven and earth, Horatio, than are dreamt of in your philosophy' (*Hamlet* I. v. 166)). However defined, some implicit or explicit recognition of the possibility, if not the existence, of a *transpersonal relationship* between healer and healed as it unfolds within the psychotherapeutic *vas* (container) is gradually beginning to gain more acceptance (Clarkson 1990).

From a systemic integrative perspective these five forms of relationship in psychotherapy are all valid. Their intentional and informed use will of course depend on differences between individual patients and different phases in the psychotherapy over time. At any given moment in psychotherapy one of these relationships may predominate. For example, the development of the transference neurosis may appear to be antithetical to the furthering of the working alliance (Stone 1961; Greenson 1965, 1967) or reparative intentions. Often, it is unlikely that two or more

> . . . can be operative at the same moment. Which one is allowed to become figure, or focus, must depend on the nature of the psychotherapeutic task at a particular time with each unique patient. Other modes of therapeutic relationship may also be present but may be more in the background at a particular time.
>
> (Clarkson 1990: 150)

Variation over time

The psychotherapeutic relationship (whether it occurs in individual, family or group therapy) can only really be comprehensible in the context of time. This is a most important domain of variation in psychotherapy. People develop over time and their relationships develop over time. The qualities and idiosyncrasies of both partners in the psychotherapeutic journey evolve only in the context of time.

Within a systemic appreciation of the role of time in psychotherapy, it can be conceptualized as ranging back (downwards) to the *past*, through the *present* and on (upwards) to the *future*. This vast expanse of time in an individual's life is potentially the very stuff of psychotherapy. However, the time of one psychotherapy session is of course a mere moment on this scale. This moment of meeting is represented in the summary diagram of Figure 2.4 by the 50 minutes' time span at the far right-hand side, as an example.

The relationship in the existentially alive *present* may be the working alliance or the person to person relationship (or both). As the relationship 'goes back into the *past*' and possibly becomes more 'regressive' it can be seen in terms of transference/countertransference or in terms of the developmentally needed/ reparative (unfinished) relationship. As the relationship leaves the past and the present it may begin to dwell more on what is conceivable as represented by the *future*. It may then take on more of a transpersonal nature.

Many psychotherapies have developed models which incorporate these dimensions of relationship over time in terms of developmental psychotherapeutic stages. For example, the cycle of gestalt formation and destruction can be applied to the developing relationship between psychotherapist and client which is, from the beginning, directed towards termination (Clarkson 1989a). Similarly, general developmental stages have been identified by such workers as Lacoursiere (1980) and need to be taken into account in group psychotherapy. What is required by the integrative psychotherapist is the awareness of the influence of changes over time and a repertoire for effectively negotiating these to the benefit of clients.

These are also stages in the learning process which can be noticed in successful psychotherapy. They seem to proceed through the stages of awareness, accommodation and assimilation. The author and a colleague (Clarkson and Gilbert 1990a) developed this sequencing map from the learning phases described by Robinson (1974) as unconscious incompetence, conscious incompetence, conscious competence and unconscious competence. *Awareness* refers to the first phase which has to do with moving from unconscious incompetence to conscious incompetence – for example, a client may need to be made aware that negative thought patterns sustain depressive affect. *Accommodation* concerns the phase of moving from conscious incompetence to conscious competence – for example, instead of relying on the psychotherapist to interpret their dreams, the client learns how to use their dreamworld creatively as a key to self-understanding and personal growth. *Assimilation* here refers to the phase of psychotherapy whereby the client moves from conscious competence to unconscious competence – for example, when new feelings, attitudes and behaviours have become comfortably internalized. Thus, for example, the patient who used to be phobic of public speaking does so easily and well while in the assimilation phase, without recourse to will power, conscious use of 'technique' or undue self-consciousness. Similarly, the person who used to have a 'narcissistic personality disorder' develops enduring and mutually satisfying relationships with depth and spontaneity.

Environmental systems also change depending on the time-frame used. The current environment would include the setting and locality of the psychotherapy room as well as the client's current life experiences within the family/social system and the present economic and political, national and international, local and global environment. This is the time and ecological system within which the individual exercises his or her existential responsibility. 'All quantum systems (most especially human systems like ourselves) share this mechanism for creative self-discovery through a dialogue with their environment' (Zohar 1990: 176).

As the environment 'moves back in time' it encompasses the environmental influences of both nurture and nature. Nature is placed further back in time and includes both inherited variables (temperament, physical attributes, perhaps archetypal predispositions, and so on) as well as the presence of *Physis* (the life force which strives for healing, growth and actualization). Nurture is placed subsequent to nature to represent the early influences of our childhood experiences which lead to later *conflict*, *confusion* or *deficit*. It is within the matrix of nurture and nature that the individual finds the crucible for an autonomous life within his/her destiny. This is the context for consideration of what is known as object relations influences and psychological development.

The aspirational environment represents the unknown and uncharted environment of the *future* and involves that towards which the client (and the psychotherapist) may aspire, the goal towards which the psychotherapy may be directed or teleologically drawn, the self which the client may conceptualize or visualize. This kind of person–environment system is self-created or self-discovered and concerns whatever the person understands of themselves and their world in terms of the future.

Space does not permit more than an indicative mapping of many of the conceptual areas which are hypothesized to be central to the theory and practice of

Systemic Integrative Psychotherapy. What precisely an individual psychotherapist would choose to focus on is left to the individual's training, experience,
intellect, sensitivity and imagination. What is required, however, are viable and
comprehensible ways of organizing, managing and using our vast tracts of
psychological data at a multitude of levels of similar and different orders. The
interface between the patient and time is likewise not meant to be restrictive,
but to invite consideration of the ways in which patients change over time. Of
course the central overarching area is the space (environment) where all these
interact with each other.

Variation in environment
Since the client is always seen as belonging to and influencing, as well as being
influenced by, systemic relations, each of such dynamically alive systems can also
be encountered in the psychotherapeutic relationship over time.

> In the systemic viewpoints . . . the relationship as the therapeutic context
> [or psychosocial environment] is fully recognized. The larger social system
> (represented by the service delivery system) and the client's system(s) of
> influence (e.g. the client's family, peer group and/or cultural group) are
> linked through the counsellor–client relationship.
>
> (Cottone 1988: 367).

Many psychotherapists are familiar with systems approaches to families (Hoffman 1981), groups and organizations (Morgan 1986) where the therapy is accomplished through interventions in the larger system. Group therapy, couples work
or family therapy may well be the therapeutic setting of choice for a particular
individual. Equally the individual therapist may work through the means of the
systemic relationship between them.

Systemic variation must also take into account the surrounding social and
physical environment including environmental stresses. A comprehensive perspective may include consideration of global events such as ecological breakdown, international unrest and environmental factors such as the air we breathe
and the food we eat. The immediate environment in which the psychotherapy
takes place – i.e. the consulting room, the clinic, the hospital or centre; its location, decoration, ease of access, the internal and external constraints – also has
systemic implications. These can range from physiological disturbance (e.g.
noise) to socio-cultural effects (e.g. décor). Writers such as Rowan (1988), James
(1983) and Douglas (1976), among others, have paid attention to such factors.
Social class, race, disability, gender, sexual identity, religious belief, fashion,
culture and cultural 'drift', for example, the increase in unemployment, home-
lessness, an increasing number of people over the age of 50, also need to be taken
into consideration. Psychotherapy takes place within the larger context of the
Zeitgeist (the spirit of the times). In the psychotherapy situation, journeying back
to the client's childhood environment (e.g. the early nursing dyad or an extended
family system) and forward to an aspirational future environment (d'Ardenne
and Mahtani 1989) is considered to be potentially as influential as what is in the
current environment.

Practice

The parameters according to which a psychotherapist would develop, practise and sequence their behavioural strategies can clearly not be thoroughly
addressed within the scope of this chapter and are well represented in extant
psychotherapeutic literature. (*Strategies* are designed to eliminate, diminish, add,
maintain, enhance, change or replace problematic cognitive, affective or physiological behaviours.) For example, one strategic parameter may concern a psychotherapist's *style* which on the one hand may vary anywhere along the directive
to non-directive continuum and on the other hand encompasses such individual
qualities as warmth, wit, compassion and elegance. Another strategic parameter
concerns the *arena* for the psychotherapeutic activity – individual psychotherapy,
marital or family therapy, group psychotherapy, organizational consulting (e.g.
in a residential home for the elderly), or a strategic impact on a collective or community (e.g. a group of teenage West Indian friends). Strategies are of course
evolved from objectives, desires or *goals*. These may be articulated in terms of
growth, 'cure' or adjustment or, as in Clarkson's (1989b) *metanoia* paper, *evolutionary* change can be differentiated from *revolutionary change*. In any event it is vital
to discriminate between different kinds of changes as outcomes of psychotherapy
(Clarkson 1988) so that both client and psychotherapist are working together
towards the same objectives without getting involved in impossible or potentially
destructive collusions.

Systemic Integrative Psychotherapy mandates a holistic view of the person.
Such a view attempts to account for physiological, emotional, linguistic, socio-
cultural, rational, theoretical/metaphorical and transpersonal dimensions. These
are seven conceptualized levels of human experience and behaviour which
together are seen as constituting an integrative perspective on *the person as a whole*.

These seven levels may also be used as foci for psychotherapeutic theory,
strategy or interventions. This is one of many maps found useful for the conceptualizing and organizing of levels of attention in psychotherapy or human
experience. All psychotherapists, whatever their approach, probably develop
maps or organizing frameworks such as these as they develop and refine their
own individual models of thinking about and practising psychotherapy.

The seven-level model[1]

The five levels of psychotherapeutic relationship (discussed above) form the
integrative framework for psychotherapist activity and the psychotherapist's use
of self in the process of Systemic Integrative Psychotherapy (see Chapter 11,
this volume). The seven-level model offers both a *holistic view of the client as a person*
in most aspects of human functioning, *as well as a comprehensive, integrative view of
psychotherapy* with its multiplicity of emphases and applications to the person in
the wider context of their existence.

The seven-level model was developed as 'an attempt to construct a thinking
tool (or conceptual protractor) to provide a meaningful reference framework to
deal with knowledge and experience in the widest possible holistic fashion'
(Clarkson 1975). All seven levels are seen as co-existing. The healthy person will
not develop one level chronically at the expense of another, but will tend to realize

his/her potential on all of these levels. Psychopathology can be conceived of in terms of a person's confusion, conflict or deficit between or within structures and dynamics at these seven levels. Attention to any one concurrently implicates all others in the system.

This model is epistemological in the sense that it implies different analytical techniques which define boundaries for the processes of knowing (Bateson 1979). However, by ordering of knowledge (and ways of obtaining knowledge from the world in this way), different kinds of 'language games' (Wittgenstein 1953) played in these different universes of discourse can be differentiated and evaluated. As a result it can help to clarify kinds of interventions or to sort techniques, particularly therapists' behaviours and concretely specific operations in order that the psychotherapy achieves the *behavioural impact* which is of eminent practical importance. Analysis of antecedents and consequences, or the archaeology of infantile object relations, needs to be considered in terms of whether or not the person accomplishes the changes he or she desired – whether these concern insight into Oedipal conflicts (Freud 1977), resignation to the depressive position (Klein 1984), shouldering one's responsibility for being-in-the-world (Heidegger 1949) or the ability to ask for a refund on faulty goods (Dryden 1987).

The seven-level model is concerned with knowledge in two major ways. First, it can be used to differentiate how we obtain knowledge about the world using different levels of conceptualization, different universes of discourse and different criteria for establishing validity, sense or 'truth' (epistemology in a philosophical sense). It is epistemological for the psychotherapist in the sense that people can sort their experiences into these different categories. Psychotherapeutic areas of knowledge, theories and procedures can also be discriminated by this means, and it can therefore be useful to guide the choice of concretely specific operations.

The seven-level model is a map rather than the territory; a map that can assist the psychotherapist practising in complex territory created in the face-to-face encounter of psychotherapist and client and the life experiences brought by each into the psychotherapeutic arena. It is important to emphasize that it is a sorting device or a kind of protractor, to be used as a guide and measure of practice rather than a directive to dictate the psychotherapeutic journey. Since it is less well known than some of the other component parts of Systemic Integrative Psychotherapy, it requires a more, if vastly summarized, explanation. (For reasons of space, this discussion will exclude its epistemological and ontological implications for psychotherapy as a system.) It is presented here as a holistic view of the person as well as a major map usable as an integrative conceptual and practice-guiding tool for psychotherapists from many different orientations or to help a single psychotherapist order, prioritize and/or include a wide range of interventions which may complement or extend his/her usual range.

At no point is it to be conceived that one level is necessarily higher or better than another. It is thought that the healthy human being will be functioning well on *all these levels* simultaneously, with the biological at least as significant as any other. It is postulated that these 'universes' of discourse are frequently confused in the theory and in the practice of psychotherapy leading to category errors, apparently irreconcilable differences and spurious contradictions.

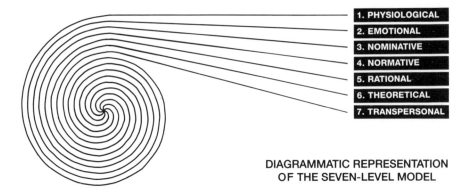

1. PHYSIOLOGICAL
2. EMOTIONAL
3. NOMINATIVE
4. NORMATIVE
5. RATIONAL
6. THEORETICAL
7. TRANSPERSONAL

DIAGRAMMATIC REPRESENTATION
OF THE SEVEN-LEVEL MODEL

Figure 2.3   Diagrammatic representation of the seven-level model

The seven-level model can also be useful to assist in the incorporation of the great variety of specific operating procedures from different psychotherapies which are built on very different universes of epistemological discourse. It is suggested that these can be effectively used together provided the practitioner is willing and able to discriminate between different perspectives (e.g. how to 'prove' a particular hypothesis within that theory) and to think for themselves, at least within the four domains of variation outlined above. For example, integration may include other theoretical and strategic approaches such as Gestalt body work, object relations, a developmental perspective, self-theory and a phenomenological approach to diagnosis (Jaspers 1963).

The seven levels (Figure 2.3) are currently identified as: (1) Physiological, (2) Emotional, (3) Nominative, (4) Normative, (5) Rational, (6) Theoretical and (7) Transpersonal. I set out below a brief, and by no means exhaustive, synopsis of possible aspects of experience and the psychotherapeutic approaches which may be emphasized at each level.

Level 1, the *Physiological*, concerns the person as an 'amoeba' or 'body' with biological, physical, visceral and sensational experience, temperament, body type and predispositions. It concerns body processes, psychophysiology, sleep, food, physical symptoms of disease, the physical manifestation of anxiety and general sensory awareness. Bioenergetic and body-oriented approaches – the work of Lowen (1969), Reich (1972), Keleman (1985), and perhaps Wolpe (1961) – can be seen to be primarily focused on this level. Methods of working primarily with the body, such as classical conditioning, desensitization, breathing and relaxation techniques, can also primarily be located at this level. Sometimes psychotherapy at this level may be complemented with the use of medication, surgical intervention (e.g. plastic surgery), acupuncture, homoeopathy and osteopathy. Relaxation techniques (such as those of Jacobson 1964) and breathing and body-posture procedures and techniques (such as those of Bioenergetics) would also have a place here, as would massage (e.g. in the treatment of clients who are 'stroke deprived') – which may be done by complementary health practitioners as an adjunct to psychotherapy – Gestalt techniques for enhancing sensory awareness, and methods which emphasize the importance of breathing in psychological health and freedom from anxiety.

Level 2, the *Emotional*, concerns the person as 'mammal'. It its essentially a preverbal area of experience and activity and concerns affect and emotion in psychology. The theoretical and experiential foci here are bonding, attachment, nursing and deprivation (Bowlby 1953; Winnicott 1960 and Rutter 1972). Theories and approaches to experiencing and expressing affect in psychotherapy often primarily operate at this level. The methodologies and techniques of Gestalt, Primal Therapy, Rebirthing, and Pre-natal work are relevant here, as is the work of Greenberg and Safran (1987).

At this level are included the experiencing and expression of affect over and above physiological presence; the person's fear, anger, sadness, joy, rage and despair. 'Resonance' phenomena and hypnotic induction procedures would probably be emphasized at this level of experience. This could include affective work towards the cathartic release of emotion (whether situationally current or archaic), the expression of emotion within the therapeutic relationship with the psychotherapist or group members and the expression of repressed emotion in the context of 'childhood scenes' (Miller 1985). Specific therapeutic operations, such as Focused Expressive Psychotherapy used by Daldrup *et al.* (1988), Gestalt (e.g. polarity work), Primal Therapy (dealing with pre-verbal experience), Psychodrama, Bioenergetics, Rechilding (Clarkson and Fish 1988) and Redecision work of Transactional Analysis (Goulding and Goulding 1979) could be located at this level (depending on how they are used). The use of visualization techniques to influence psychophysiological conditions could be seen to operate primarily at this level (Rossi and Cheek 1988).

Level 3, the *Nominative*, concerns the person as 'primate'. Under this heading are included the awareness and labelling of experiences and the validation of experience through naming. Since at least the earliest biblical times people have known that the 'giving of names' develops 'dominion', ownership and the feeling of mastery over the existential world and the transformation of human experience. The naming of feelings and sensations, the naming of ego states (Watkins 1976; Watkins and Watkins, 1986) and the naming of personified introjects, are relevant to this level. Those interventions described by Watzlawick *et al.* (1967, 1974), including the concept of second-order change in which reframing, making overt the covert, utilizing resistance and paradoxical interventions play a part, belong under this heading. The work of Enright (1980) on the renaming of symptoms in Gestalt, Haley's (1963) and Erickson's (1967) paradoxical and strategic interventions are also approaches which centralize the nominative level of enquiry. All these approaches emphasize the transformative potential of 'what things are called'.

The naming and labelling of experience according to psychotherapeutic orientation would also come under this heading. For example, it would include the 'top-dog/underdog' of Gestalt Therapy, the 'placator/blamer/computer/distractor' of Satir's Family Therapy (1967), the 'archetypes' of Jungian analysis (Jung 1968, 1969a), the sub-personalities of Psychosynthesis (Assagioli 1971) and other approaches (Rowan 1990), and the 'Parent/Adult/Child' of Transactional Analysis all provide labels in order to assist understanding. Other approaches used here include Neurolinguistic Programming, the awareness phase of the Gestalt cycle, Phenomenology (e.g. Merleau-Ponty 1962), Rogers's (1986) reflective process, empathic attunement (Rowe and MacIsaac 1989) and reframing (Bandler and Grinder 1982). The naming and labelling of experience under the headings of diagnostic categories (whether the kind of assessment refers to reactance levels, feeling or thinking function (Jung 1944), borderline personality organization, or failure at the *rapprochement* stage (Mahler *et al.* 1975)) could also be seen as basically belonging here.

Level 4, the *Normative*, concerns the person as social animal. It refers to norms, values, collective belief systems, societal expectations. Strategies and interventions from this level would tend to deal with facts, knowledge of attributes and practices regarding people as 'cultural beings' – the tribe, the group, the community. This level corresponds to the psychoanalytic notion of the super-ego or equally, the borrowed egos of Federn (1977) or Parent egos of Berne (1975). Statistical and cultural norms are affected by individual differences and the concept of 'consensual reality'. Glasser's Reality Therapy (1965), the Cathexis approach (Schiff *et al.* 1975) and Peck (1978) all deal in important ways with norms and values. The Values Clarification movement (Simon *et al.* 1972) also provides major contributions to psychological thinking and intervention at the normative level. This level attends to the relation between the individual and the group, and how culture is built and ecology maintained. It also underpins cross-cultural considerations in psychotherapy, for example the role of cultural pressures in addictions and compulsions (Orbach 1978).

Both statistical and cultural norms are included at this level. It refers to the measurements by which we assess some of the 'oughts' of our belief-systems, how to do things, what things mean in our culture, what is the 'usual' and what the 'unusual'. This is not to suggest that psychotherapy plays a normative role in the sense of encouraging conformity or providing further oughts, rather it looks at norms in terms of their appropriateness, usefulness and application in specific circumstances. While the acceptance of some norms may be useful in certain circumstances, psychotherapies differ in how much they emphasize aims such as autonomy, integration, growth, awareness and self-actualization. These can challenge and transcend many cultural and societal 'norms'. (The 'stiff upper lip' norm of the white British male, for example, or the 'apartheid' norm of white South Africa – both are contradictions of health, integration, well-being and growth and as such will be refuted in an approach to psychotherapy in which everyone is held equally to have worth, value, freedom of expression and dignity.) Child Development material could be used here as a model of normal developmental needs in the light of which cultural and familial norms can be examined. TA procedures such as Self-Reparenting (James 1974) and Spot-Reparenting (Osnes 1974) can be used to work with identified deficits. Clearly the social environment acts as a reinforcing system in terms of stimulus–response interactions both for the group's need for cohesion and the individual's need to belong to the group.

Level 5, the *Rational*, concerns 'Homo sapiens' – the person as thinker. This layer of knowledge and activity includes thinking, making sense of things, examination of cause and effect, frames of reference, working with facts and information, and reading skills. 'Reality testing', developing rationality, experimentation (e.g. Kelly's (1955) Inquiring Man model), form the ways by which knowledge is gained or experience differentiated on this level. Approaches particularly relevant here are: RET – Rational-Emotive Therapy (Ellis 1962) – which provides three stages to assist in disputing irrational beliefs – namely, defining, distinguishing and debating (Dryden 1987); aspects of Cognitive Therapy (Beck *et al.* 1979, 1985); 'insight' in most psychotherapies and decontamination work in Transactional Analysis (Berne 1975).

In Transactional Analysis this level is dealt with by decontamination of the Adult ego state (Berne 1975), differentiating between Parent prejudices and beliefs, Child magical thinking and delusions and the clear factual thinking of the Adult, in order for psychotherapy of each distinct ego state to be possible. Here TA develops basic psychoanalytic theory where the ego is seen as the reality-testing function according to Federn (1977) and Weiss (1950) and similar to the objective ego of Fairbairn (1952).

Level 6, the *Theoretical*, throws into relief the person as 'storyteller' – as a meaning maker, making sense of human experience through symbolism, story and metaphor. This is based on the notion of theoretical plurality and relativity: theories can be seen as 'narratives' – stories that people tell themselves – interesting, exciting, depressing, controlling, useful and relative but no one forever true. 'Theories' are in a different logical category from that of facts. Both in psychological theory and individual experience, it is important to separate these where possible. It is, for example, quite likely that the psychological theories or explanations we have developed to support the empirical evidence science has accumulated at Level 5 may be 'mistaken' and in time replaced by other (better?) theories (Kuhn 1970). The history of science can certainly tell many such tales. The theories, explanations, metaphors and stories that humans have created in order to explain why things are as they are and why people behave as they do are included at this level. The many and varied psychotherapies each provide their own narratives or stories to explain people's behaviour and to create ways of changing it. Moreover, the Oxford philosopher Farrell (1979) pointed out that each story in psychotherapy tends to manufacture material that will fit it.

Psychoanalysis has several stories (Freud, Winnicott, Klein, Lacan, Kohut), Behavioural Therapy has others and Humanistic Psychotherapy has yet several more. Within these are further stories or metaphors which may be very different or very similar, overlap or interface, but all of which attempt to make some sense of our human experience. Thus at this level it may be useful for the client to use stories from one or more of the humanistic psychotherapies in order to gain clarity or a frame of reference that makes sense of a particular problem or aspect of therapy. It is also possible to integrate part-stories from the other schools of psychotherapy – for example, 'modelling' theory from Behavioural Therapy may usefully explain how parental messages may be given or reinforced at a non-verbal level. Or Self-theory from the psychoanalytic and Jungian traditions may enrich our understanding of the development of the Self and assist in identifying Confusion (e.g. where parts of the Self are denied, repressed, disowned or split off), Conflict (e.g. the Real Self and False Self) and Deficit (e.g. the interpersonally developed Self lacking adequate object relationships for healthy development). What is required, though, is that the ideological convictions of 'true beliefs' at Level 4 (in the absence of consensually accepted factual evidence at Level 5) be differentiated from the possible theoretical explanations which have become attached to them. Theories are to be judged by criteria other than facts or normative beliefs.

Level 7, the *Transpersonal*, refers to the epistemological area concerned with people as 'spiritual beings'. Beyond rationality, facts and even theories are the prescient regions of dreams, altered states of ecstatic consciousness, the spiritual, the metaphysical, the mystical, the existentially paradoxical, the unpredictable and the inexplicable. Religion both experientially and theoretically impacts psychological perspectives. It is represented in several approaches to psychotherapy and human development, for example the influence of eastern philosophies (Fromm 1960), and the creation-centred spirituality of Fox (1983). Also included at this level are those experiences which may be described as the surreal, the transcendent and the synchronous.

At this level belongs Jung's (1968) work on archetypes and the collective unconscious, much of his approach to dreams and symbols (Jung 1977), as well as transpersonal psychotherapies such as Psychosynthesis, Gestalt and sectors of TA which include a spiritual dimension within their parameters. Perhaps even included are tools for human healing and evolution derived from the 'I Ching' (Wilhelm 1988), the Tarot, Transcendental Meditation, Yoga, Taoism and T'ai Chi. Vaughan (1985: 20–1) writes,

> The spiritual quest is, above all, a search for truth . . . Truth can become a strong force for healing once the commitment is made. In psychotherapy, telling the truth about experience is an essential part of the process, but its relevance to spiritual well-being is rarely recognized.

In the paper 'A multiplicity of psychotherapeutic relationships' (Clarkson 1990), this spiritual healing-force within the therapeutic relationship itself is recognized in several approaches to psychotherapy. Archambeau (1979), for example, implies that the mutual unconsciousness of partners transforms their relationship beyond that of the I–Thou relationship to something greater than the sum of its parts, something that happens in the 'between' of the relationship (the 'third self' of James and Savary 1977).

The physical, body-process considerations of Level 1 may *seem* unrelated, but what links these and all the other levels is that they are precisely the levels at which we experience ourselves and our environment and the relationship between the two. Such a holistic approach to the client is essential to our integrative psychotherapy training. All aspects of our human experience can find inclusion under these seven levels (if not, we need to find other means). This conceptual structure has provided a useful framework for assessing, selecting, focusing and enhancing the work of several generations of psychotherapists by the integration of relevant theories and procedures from various models of psychotherapy. One of the strategies for psychotherapy integration recommended by Mahrer (1989) – that of *concretely specific working therapeutic operations* – can be facilitated by using a model such as the one presented here. In other words, integration is comparatively eased when it has to do with what psychotherapists do with clients at the basic nuts-and-bolts level, what they say to the clients or instruct them to do in order to attain some change, reinforcement or response. This may include (using some of Mahrer's examples) clarifying the role of the patient, providing information on therapeutic arrangements, telling the patient how to focus attention, inviting the patient to express him- or herself with more feeling, drawing the patient's attention to the therapist–patient relationship, and so on. Millions of interventions or techniques on each of the seven levels (which are based on different epistemologies) can be divided into different types, as in Heron's (1990) six category intervention analysis and Rowan's (1973) model.

Depending upon the required outcome, these interventions will have differing styles, foci and intentions, and will be paced, timed and weighted in intensity differently at different points in the psychotherapy. Using this strategy for psychotherapy integration, it generally follows that, for example, the integration of some aspects of Cognitive-Behaviour Therapy with psychoanalysis (Fonagy 1989) becomes more workable because of the inclusion that is possible at the concretely specific operating procedures level of integration.

> This rich pool of operating procedures is part of the public marketplace. Any therapist, regardless of approach, can obtain operating procedures from this public pool. No therapeutic approach has exclusive rights of ownership over any of these operating procedures.
>
> (Mahrer 1989: 81)

It is likely that most psychotherapists in the course of training, supervision, personal psychotherapy, through attendance at conferences and psychotherapy workshops and seeing other psychotherapists at work, have accumulated a valuable resource of specific operating procedures that can be integrated into psychotherapeutic work. In this sense, whether acknowledged or not, every learning, developing, questing psychotherapist is probably an integrator.

Case-study

This case example clearly does not represent the totality of the client's psychotherapy as only certain highlights can be indicated within the available space. The seven-level model may be a more unfamiliar conceptualization than the other major parameters; so this case-study takes a vertical view of the psychotherapy in its terms rather than the more usual chronological progression. Of course each psychotherapy, however we attempt to describe it, in fact diverts, converges, winds and unwinds through chronological and existential time, environmental systems and relationship dimensions in unique and unrepeatable configurations.

Introduction to the client

Susan, a school counsellor, entered psychotherapy three years ago, aged 29. During the first meetings with her male psychotherapist, she was very nervous

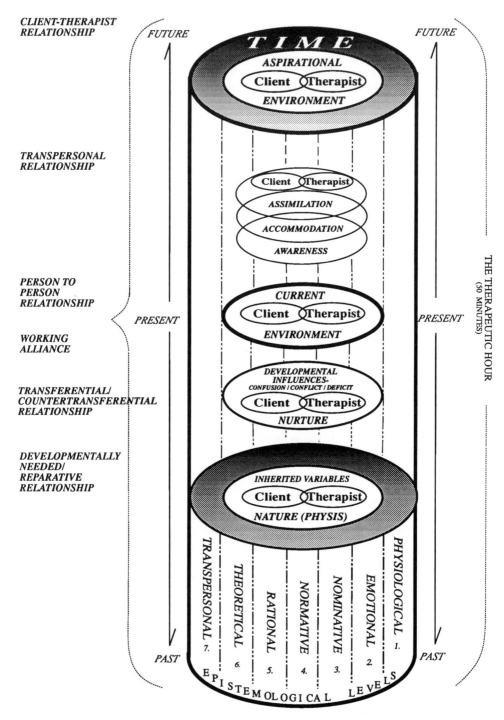

Figure 2.4 Summary Diagram (by Phil Lapworth)

and avoided any eye contact. She was often sad, depressed and had very low self-esteem. She felt inadequate in friendships and potential sexual relationships due to finding it difficult to get close to people. She spoke of loathing herself as a person and particularly disliking her body which she described as fat.

The psychotherapist's response to Susan was one of warmth and an intuitive feeling that they could work together well. They agreed upon weekly individual psychotherapy in order to provide a regular arena in which to explore and change, through the one-to-one relationship, her self-image and self-loathing – crucial aspects reinforcing her feeling depressed. They also discussed the possibility of her entering a psychotherapy group when the time was appropriate in order to allow exploration of her interpersonal relationships, including her rivalry with women who reminded her of her sister and her feeling of inadequacy in relation to others. A psychotherapy group would also provide her with opportunity and a safe space to experiment and practise new behaviours with both male and female peers.

Susan came from a working-class family in the North of England. Her mother was a forceful woman who was constantly critical of Susan. Her father was an odd-job man, often absent from home, in trouble with the law and having 'secret' affairs with women. Her younger sister was born with a congenital hearing loss. Because of this, the sister was the centre of attention and affection, particularly favoured by dad. Susan spent much of her time as a child living with her maternal grandparents whom she felt cared for her more than her parents.

In thinking about Susan in classical diagnostic terms (*DSM-III-R*), she showed no symptoms to justify any psychiatric diagnosis on Axis I. The way in which she had learnt to relate interpersonally indicated Avoidant personality traits (on Axis II) accompanied by chronic stomach tension (which could be indicated on Axis III). Axis IV refers to psychosocial stressors (her current systemic context and environment). These were rated as moderate because of discord in her current relationship with her boyfriend. She was also rated as moderate on Axis V in terms of a global assessment of her functioning, as she was currently functioning at a low moderate level due to her flattened affect and poor social relationships, but this was not particularly different from her level of functioning in preceding years.

Summary of psychotherapy

Susan entered psychotherapy aware of feeling depressed, not liking herself or her body. She did not know why she was feeling as she was nor how to change. She was confused in her thinking and feeling about herself, believing that there was something 'wrong' with her. The psychotherapist's initial warm acceptance towards Susan helped in establishing a therapeutic working alliance in which Susan's wants and needs were identified and clarified. Further, this enabled the development of the other four dimensions of psychotherapeutic relationship which at various later stages become catalytic media for change.

Over the course of her time in psychotherapy Susan became aware of how her childhood experiences influenced her self-esteem. Lack of empathic attunement and mirroring as an infant had left her with a fear of closeness and precarious sense of self and self-support. As she became conscious of how neglected her 'inner child' had become, she gradually understood how she perpetuated similar experiences in the present – for example, in her rivalrous feelings towards her favourite sister. Early in childhood she had also introjected her mother's constant and destructive criticism of herself. In cognitive-behavioural terms, this criticism became the incessant refrain of her self-talk, or she constantly experienced a persecuting bad object. After some time she also allowed into her awareness the previously repressed experience of being sexually abused by her grandfather. She associated this with her fear of closeness, her lack of trust and her feeling of 'wrongness'. Though painful, this knowledge helped Susan unravel some of the confusion she had had about herself and enabled her to relive and work through those repressed unconscious childhood feelings and fantasies that had been interfering with her healthy adult functioning.

Accommodation and assimilation of this knowledge of her experience involved exploring and resolving the resultant inner conflicts – for example, between such polarities as feeling/non-feeling, love/hate, closeness/distance, creative/destructive and libidinal/anti-libidinal forces. Thus her inner conflicts also illuminated where her deficiencies lay and where focus needed to be given in terms of nurturing, self-care, recognition of skills, successes and achievements. The psychotherapist enabled her to develop a more nurturing and benign internal Parent to take care of the needs of her inner child. She was used to forming relationships with friends and colleagues where she looked after the lame ducks. This was the way in which she maintained the deprivation from her early family in her current environment.

The transference, however, did not remain positive throughout the psychotherapy. The group experience restimulated Susan's childhood experiences with her father and her sister. She felt rivalrous with other women in the group and rejected by the psychotherapist. This was worked through by open confrontation, exploration, discussion and current reality testing. She grew in taking responsibility for herself from asking for her needs to be met in the group to experimenting and to being more demanding with her friends.

Towards the termination of her therapy, Susan re-entered a negative transference with her therapist, again feeling unloved and unwanted. In fact she repeated most of her former psychotherapy issues at an even more intensive and acted-out level of transference before finally resolving the hurt resultant of her rejecting father, her critical mother and preferred sister. This later negative transferential period was one to which the psychotherapist could respond by containing her negative feelings while continuing to accept her and allowing *Physis* and her Psyche to do battle.

Subsequent to this 'regression' (a common phenomenon towards the end of therapy) Susan has increased her self-esteem enormously by visualizing and aspiring towards a conceivable Self unfettered by destructive introjects. She is more spontaneous, appropriately trusting and clear in what she feels and what she thinks. She has increased her circle of friends and allows herself to be as emotionally and physically close as she chooses. She thoroughly and appropriately mourned the termination of her relationship with the psychotherapist. She has begun training for a new career and has ended her psychotherapy in a spirit of resolution of the past, satisfaction with the present and optimism for the future.

Some of the psychotherapy with Susan will now be highlighted and explored in terms of the seven levels of experience as used in practice.

Level 1 – physiological

Using Rowe's (1988) definition Susan would be described as an 'introvert', her 'preference' being for the progressive development of her individuality in terms of clarity, achievement and authenticity. She is a fast learner and very much an 'ideas' person who emphasizes the importance of control and keeping things in order. Bearing in mind the desirability of creating a better balance between introversion and extroversion, Susan's preference for thoughts and ideas was a 'way in' to further work concerning her more extrovert desires, in particular wanting to make more satisfying contact with others.

It was important in working with Susan and her concern about her body that the possibility of any medical explanation (e.g. thyroid problems) be eliminated by medical consultation, before moving on to approaches at other levels (e.g. cultural norms in Level 4). Interventions of a dietary nature were decided against, having made sure that over-eating and unhealthy eating were not a part of the problem. Thus it was decided not to intervene at this level but to explore the issue at other levels.

In her second year of psychotherapy, the working alliance between client and psychotherapist was well-established. A positive transferential relationship developed until Susan accessed the memory of sexual abuse by her grandfather of which she had been unconscious until this time. The positive transferential relationship here appears to have intensified Susan's underlying conflict between wanting to be close and being scared to be close. Her stomach tension had increased and did not respond to any anxiety-reducing interventions at this level until the trauma of her sexual abuse had been brought into consciousness. In other words, her stomach pain appeared to be a somatization of the trauma.

Her breathing became very shallow for several weeks. Relaxation techniques were used as a coping strategy to deal with this physiological response while working at other levels (namely, Emotional, Nominative and Normative). Bioenergetic breathing techniques and body postures were used to release repressed emotions and muscular 'holding' subsequent to the trauma.

It was noted that Susan's breathing pattern in general was to breathe out more than she breathed in. This was experienced by her as a reflection of her belief in a world that could not support her and where sustenance was in short supply. She inhabited an existential world in which she felt required to 'give out' in order to survive. Of course, this had been true when she was a child in her family. Correction of her breathing pattern by direct instruction from the psychotherapist was an intrinsic part of the updating of her experience of the world. Deficit during childhood, originating with her birth when she was induced two weeks prematurely due to septicaemia, delivered by forceps and needed oxygen (delivered by mask) in her first few hours of life, required reparative experiences – containment, acceptance and permission to live. The psychotherapist would pay close attention to her breathing and, at times when it was clear that Susan's intake of breath was shallow, would facilitate her to breathe in more and regulate her out-breath to provide a more balanced and self-supportive pattern.

In connection with this 'world view' and in the service of liking herself and getting close to others, Susan was encouraged to experiment with varying degrees of physical closeness to others in the psychotherapy group. She gradually began to experience these bodily sensations and contacts, such as touching hands, as both pleasurable and safe. In other words, over time, beginning with Awareness of the need for contact, she has allowed herself to Accommodate her need for closeness and contact and is moving through to the Assimilation of such needs by getting close to others in a more spontaneous way. This has helped to bring about a shift in her view of her body as well as a shift in her view of the world: a significant step for someone whose only experience of physical closeness was with her grandfather who later abused her.

Level 2 – emotional

At times when it would have been more appropriate and useful to feel angry or scared, Susan resorted to crying as a defensive means to cutting-off from others. It was not a loud 'relief' crying but a withdrawn, almost sulky sadness. At such times, the psychotherapist suggested that Susan explore any possible anger she may be feeling, for example: 'Supposing there were something you might be angry about, what would it be?' When encouraged to express it she moved out of her sad, withdrawn state into an energetic mode in which she was more able to deal actively with her problems in the past and in the present. The expression of anger can be seen as moving into her authentic feeling (True Self) and out of her inauthentic adaptation (False Self) (Winnicott 1958) – the means by which she had maintained past frames of reference in the here and now. In Gestalt terms, the expression of her anger in response to figures from the past can be seen as 'closing' the gestalts that have remained incomplete, or which resulted in fixated, repetitive, physio-affective and behavioural patterns.

The focus of therapy for several months was one of allowing Susan to get in touch with her memories and feelings connected with being sexually abused. She contacted the 'frozen child' (Winnicott 1958) within herself. Miller's (1983) understanding of the importance for the abused person of re-experiencing the trauma (bringing the past into the present) now with the reparative support of a witness and ally became very significant for Susan. Feeling safe and supported by the psychotherapist in the relationship they had built up over time, and trusting of the other group members, she eventually chose to re-experience the scene of abuse within the psychotherapy group (a source of several allies and witnesses) with the psychotherapist at her side. During this therapeutic work, Susan re-experienced her original terror (connected with the stomach tension referred to at the Physiological level). She moved through this to express other feelings repressed at the time of the original trauma. This included anger which she abreacted with loud shouts and self-protective pushing and hitting of the soft furniture, sadness, disgust and despair expressed in loud sobs and physical shaking, until at the end of the work she expressed a joyous relief, expressed by laughter, in the present. In this way she contacted her True Self – not an object used by others but an autonomous person with a full emotional response, unlike the passive False Self adaptation within which she felt almost deserving of abuse. Thus, within a safe and supportive current environment and trusting relationships, Susan was able 'to go back in time' to her childhood environment to heal the trauma of abuse. A period of mourning followed (as she worked through the loss of this special relationship with her grandfather, however painful it had been) until she could psychologically assimilate it over time.

Level 3 – nominative

Naming is one way of working through Confusion in order to resolve Conflicts. It was fundamental to Susan's recovery that she name the perpetrator of her abuse in childhood. She had to do this in order to 'let go' of his 'possession' of her in the present and thus allow herself to be close to others. This can be seen in terms of Awareness, Accommodation and Assimilation of the trauma which clearly did not happen all at once but was developed in the therapeutic environment and the psychotherapeutic relationship at several levels.

By naming her grandfather, she was able to take her own power by re-experiencing the event and resolving it within her psyche. For Susan, it was also important that she name her experience as 'abuse'. This was difficult to accept – 'How could someone who loves me abuse me?' But accepting that she was abused helped put responsibility back with her grandfather where previously she had felt 'bad' or 'wrong' or 'guilty'.

The chronic stomach tension noted on Axis III *DSM-III-R* was also primarily dealt with in a nominative way. In fact, it was by naming the physical sensation in her stomach as 'fear' that Susan was eventually able to access the experience of her sexual abuse. In Gestalt terms, Susan moved through the Sensation stage (stomach tension) of the Gestalt Cycle to Awareness (naming of fear) which led to the Mobilization of her energy to protect herself appropriately or seek protection (the reparative relationship with her therapist) in order to take Action (re-experiencing) and seek the origin through Contact (redecision) and eventual Satisfaction (resolution) in order to Withdraw from a now satisfactorily closed gestalt.

Level 4 – normative

Susan used her body shape as a 'reason' for not being close to others. This belief may have served a protective role at some stage but in reality it was more Susan's withdrawal and distancing behaviour that prevented closeness. The psychotherapist suggested looking at cultural norms within our society (Wolf 1990). Together they observed that slimness is a requirement of the media while 'real' people come in a multiplicity of shapes and sizes. This helped Susan to take steps towards 'enjoying owning and being in my body so that I enjoy the experiences of massage, swimming, sex, clothes and other body-linked experiences' which she did by attending body-work sessions, joining in physical activities within the group and photographing herself.

Susan's avoidance of eye-contact was confronted in a normative way by the psychotherapist. He explained that it is an evolved cultural norm to make some eye contact while speaking. So, after some time in therapy when Susan failed to make eye contact, he would bring this to her attention and encourage her to experiment with looking at him. Such interventions as 'This is how I know you are talking to me' or 'This is how I know you are in contact with me as I speak to you' have encouraged this normative aspect of communication. The Awareness, Accommodation and Assimilation process is naturally played out around single interventions, such as an interpretation in a single session, as well as over the longer period of an entire psychotherapy.

The normative level was particularly important within the developmentally needed/reparative relationship with the psychotherapist. Where deficit and trauma had been the originating problems, Susan received various permissions and corrective messages from various ages and stages of development. This was achieved through empathic attunement, modelling, repetition and reassurance and through other familiar reparenting procedures. For example, towards the end of the second year of psychotherapy, having well-established an open and trusting relationship, Susan spent about 15 minutes of each session sitting close by the psychotherapist's side while the rest of the group continued their work. During this time the psychotherapist affirmed her right to be there and told her that her inner child's needs were OK with him in order to normalize her need of closeness and attention which had been made 'abnormal' by her father's selective and preferential relationship with her sister.

Clearly, later in her psychotherapy and with termination in sight, the person-to-person relationship between psychotherapist and client increasingly became the norm while the reparative relationship became the exception.

Level 5 – rational
For Susan, work at this level primarily took place within the working alliance with her psychotherapist – the relationship within her current psychosocial environment. It has included the following rationalizations using techniques including interrogation explanation, information, illustration, persuasion, confirmation, even exhortation in dealing with areas of Confusion. This process has involved the confrontation of discounting behaviours and redefinitions from TA along with the three-stage cognitive change techniques of RET to assist in disputing Susan's irrational beliefs, namely (1) distinguishing between rational and irrational beliefs, (2) debating with Socratic questioning and (3) defining to help her make increasingly accurate definitions. The following statements summarize the reality gains Susan made at this level:

• That she did not inherit congenital deafness was fortunate but in no way was it her fault that her sister contracted the disease.
• That she did not deserve to be ignored by her father. He did not ignore her because she was 'bad'. All children need care and attention from their parents to grow healthily.
• That her grandfather's sexual abuse of her was wrong. She was not the guilty one. She did nothing to be ashamed of. She was the victim of the situation, not the perpetrator.
• That her mother was unkind and critical of her because of her own inadequacies, not Susan's.

- That it is safe to trust some people and to be close to them.
- That some men get close to women for reasons other than sex.
- That parents and grandparents are responsible for their children while they are young. Children are not responsible for their parents or grandparents.

Level 6 – theoretical (metaphorical)

In the course of her psychotherapy and through her own wide reading, Susan became increasingly 'psychologically minded'. She became familiar with TA's Script theory, RET's theory of the perpetuation of psychological disturbance by negative beliefs in response to negative events, Gestalt's 'fixed gestalts' at points around the 'cycle' and some object relations theory. Suffice it to say that in the course of her psychotherapy Susan accepted at the very least the basic theoretical principle that events in the past have influenced the way she feels, thinks and behaves today (the 'nurture' theory). In the following extract Susan is thinking through her experiences on this theoretical level and interpreting her current behaviour in the light of her past experience:

> What do I need to be forgiven for that I'm often so ashamed and humiliated by criticism? I remember the constant criticism of my mother. I especially remember this excruciating feeling of embarrassment when, having not even entered the High School entrance exam, my mother lied to a friend of hers that the grammar school uniform I was wearing was, in fact, the High School uniform. Of course, the friend knew better and challenged her on it. I wanted to disappear. That's what I've been doing up to now – trying to make myself invisible and unnoticeable and disappear in the face of perceived criticism from others which is really the mother in my head. In my therapy, I'm standing up to her, I'm telling her how embarrassed I was, how cruel she was, how hurt I felt and how I hated her for her constant criticism. I'm standing up to her for the first time and I'm not afraid of her. I feel strong and powerful. I do not disappear in the face of criticism. I stay in the present. I am healing my childhood.

In a similar way, the past was brought into the present through the transferential relationship. It is impossible in a few lines to do justice to this vital aspect of the psychotherapy. Suffice it to say that the transference was used in the reworking of her relationship with both her father and mother. At times the psychotherapist was seen and responded to as the idealized and wished-for-father, at others he was seen and responded to negatively as the original withholding and rejecting father (or the cruel and critical mother). At other times, Susan felt identified with what she perceived as the 'needy child' of the psychotherapist.

The psychotherapist's countertransference ranged from experiencing feelings towards Susan of protective caring (and using this in a 'good-enough' rather than 'perfect' reparative way) to dismay when Susan oft-repeated a negative transference which attempted to devalue and destroy the good work she was doing in her psychotherapy. The latter took a lot of working through: the psychotherapist needing to tread a narrow path between interpreting, confronting or simply accepting the negative transference while remaining unrejecting and uncritical of Susan. He responded to her projection of a needy child on to him by understanding her desire to look after him as disguised information as to how she wanted to be looked after herself.

Bringing unconscious or subconscious material to consciousness by the interpretation of dreams was also useful in understanding Susan's past. Prior to therapy, Susan rarely remembered her dreams. Her psychotherapist asked her to speak to her subconscious and ask it to help her retain her dreams in consciousness – since then she has dreamed many dreams and kept a rich and fascinating dream diary. For example, she dreamt of looking over a wall at people having fun until she is soaked by a wave of black water. She dreamt she had been given a new party dress on which she spilt something and stained it. Her friends said it didn't show but she tried to get rid of it, failed, and missed the party.

Susan saw both these dreams as symbolizing her difficulty with intimacy. She understood the wall and the stain as barriers that she used to employ against closeness. The wave of black water she associated with her fear of being close and of being overwhelmed by emotions if she allowed herself to feel them. She felt the stain as her belief that there was something wrong with her. When others accepted her, they were 'fools' not to see it. Susan says,

> I was 'stained' by my childhood experiences but instead of blaming myself and trying to scrub them out, I'm finding that time and caring have faded the stains. My self-compassion is transforming the stain into part of the new pattern I am creating.

Level 7 – transpersonal

The transpersonal relationship between Susan and her psychotherapist, so hard to describe, is based upon a genuine, mutual, high regard and acceptance (developed over shared time) that transcends the other definable relationships that have occurred in the course of the psychotherapy.

This relationship was 'felt' implicitly as existing in the 'between' of the relationship – the relationship between the unconscious of the psychotherapist and the unconscious of the client – those moments of being-together in a dimension which is impossible to articulate exactly (Clarkson 1990). It was, along with a shared belief in change, in a true self and in transformation, a powerful healing force within the psychotherapy.

The inexplicable and the synchronous have also played their part in Susan's psychotherapy. On her birthday, following a psychotherapy session where she had talked of her fear of 'standing on my own two feet', she twisted her ankle. She had twisted her ankle once before on her fifth birthday and at that time had suffered emotional as well as physical hurt by being ignored. Though regretting her injury, Susan took heart in the very different environment (with caring friends) in which she now exists and two nights later was given further symbolic encouragement from her subconscious when she dreamt she was being presented an award at the school at which she works. Two other staff were awarded toys. She was awarded, to her delight and much applause, a pair of running shoes.

Finally, an even more inexplicable and synchronous event happened towards the end of her psychotherapy, when Susan was disturbed at repeating some transferential attitudes towards her psychotherapist. At the point at which she was complaining that she didn't know what to do, a picture she had drawn of a magician which was on the consulting room wall revolved quite slowly until the magician came to rest upside down. It can be seen as an example of synchronicity (the acausal connecting principle identified by Jung (1969b)). Though quite accepting of the message, Susan appropriately (considering the wish-fulfilling magical nature of the former transference) remained unimpressed by the form of this 'instruction' from the cosmos.

Conclusion

In the course of this chapter, including an illustrative case example, an attempt has been made to describe and clarify the complexities of developing a systemic integrative approach to psychotherapy. Variations and dimensions within the psychotherapeutic field have been outlined as necessary considerations for this task. Hopefully, what the reader is left with is a useful framework for further exploration so that, together, we may better serve the people we aspire to serve and improve communication with each other as practising psychotherapists.

Note

1 My model is published here at the insistence of colleagues and students who have found it valuable for integrating philosophical/theoretical *and* strategic/practical issues, both in psychotherapy itself and also for individual patients. It could be compared with Lazarus's BASIC ID (1981) on the one hand, and with Wilber's (1980) on the other, although it was developed and taught at Pretoria University in 1975 before I had heard of either.

References

American Psychiatric Association (1987) *Diagnostic and Statistical Manual of Mental Disorders*, 3rd edn revised, Washington, DC: American Psychiatric Association.

Anthony, E.J. and Cohler, B.J. (eds) (1987) *The Invulnerable Child*, New York: Guilford Press.

Archambeau, E. (1979) *Beyond Countertransference: The Psychotherapist's Experience of Healing in the Therapeutic Relationship*, San Diego: California School of Professional Psychology Doctoral Dissertation.

d'Ardenne, P. and Mahtani, A. (1989) *Transcultural Counselling in Action*, London: Sage.

Assagioli, R. (1971) *Psychosynthesis: A Manual of Principles and Techniques*, New York: Viking.

Balint, M. (1968) *The Basic Fault: Therapeutic Aspects of Regression*, London: Tavistock.

Bandler, R. and Grinder, J. (1982) *Reframing: Neuro-Linguistic Programming and the Transformation of Meaning*, Moab, Ut.: Real People Press.

Bateson, G. (1979) *Mind and Nature: A Necessary Unity*, London: Wildwood House.

Beck, A.T., Emery, G. and Greenberg, R.L. (1985) *Anxiety Disorders and Phobias: A Cognitive Perspective*, New York: Basic Books.
——, Rush, A.J., Shaw, B.F. and Emery, G. (1979) *Cognitive Therapy of Depression*, New York: Guilford Press.
Bergin, A.E. and Garfield, S.L. (eds) (1978) *Handbook of Psychotherapy and Behavior Change*, 2nd edn, New York: Wiley.
—— and Lambert, M.J. (1978) The evaluation of therapeutic outcomes, in A.E. Bergin and S.L. Garfield (eds) *Handbook of Psychotherapy and Behavior Change*, 2nd edn, New York: Wiley.
Berne, E. (1969) *A Layman's Guide to Psychiatry and Psychoanalysis*, London: André Deutsch.
—— (1975) *Transactional Analysis in Psychotherapy*, London: Souvenir Press (first published 1961).
Bertalanffy, L. von (1969) The theory of open systems in physics and biology, in F.E. Emery (ed.) *Systems Thinking*, Harmondsworth: Penguin, pp. 70–85.
Beutler, L.E. (1971) Attitude similarity in marital therapy, *Journal of Consulting and Clinical Psychology* 37: 298–301.
—— (1986) Systemic eclectic psychotherapy, in J.C. Norcross (ed.) *Handbook of Eclectic Psychotherapy*, New York: Brunner/Mazel, pp. 94–131.
Bowlby, J. (1953) Some pathological processes set in motion by early mother–child separation, *Journal of Mental Science* 99: 265.
—— (1980) *Attachment and Loss: Vol. 3: Loss*, London: Hogarth Press.
—— (1985) The role of childhood experience in cognitive disturbance, in M.J. Mahoney and A. Freeman (eds) *Cognition and Psychotherapy*, New York: Plenum Press, pp. 181–200.
Brill, H. (1967) Nosology, in A.M. Freedman and H.I. Kaplan (eds) *Comprehensive Textbook of Psychiatry*, Baltimore: Williams and Wilkins, pp. 581–9.
Buber, M. (1970) *I and Thou* (W. Kaufmann, trans.), Edinburgh: T. & T. Clark (first published 1923).
Capra, F. (1975) *The Tao of Physics*, London: Wildwood House.
—— (1982) *The Turning Point: Science, Society and the Rising Culture*, London: Wildwood House.
Cashdan, S. (1988) *Object Relations Theory: Using the Relationship*, New York: W.W. Norton.
Clarkson, P. (1975) Seven-level model, Invitational Paper delivered at University of Pretoria, November.
—— (1988) Script cure? – a diagnostic pentagon of types of therapeutic change, *Transactional Analysis Journal* 18(3): 211–19.
—— (1989a) *Gestalt Counselling in Action*, London: Sage.
—— (1989b) Metanoia: a process of transformation, *Transactional Analysis Journal* 19(4): 224–34.
—— (1989c) Metaperspectives on diagnosis, *Transactional Analysis Journal* 19(1): 45–50.
—— (1990) A multiplicity of psychotherapeutic relationships, *British Journal of Psychotherapy* 7(2): 148–63.
—— (1992) Transference and countertransference in TA, in P. Clarkson *Transactional Analysis Psychotherapy: An Integrative Approach*, London: Routledge.
—— and Fish, S. (1988) Rechilding: creating a new past in the present as a support for the future, *Transactional Analysis Journal* 18(1): 51–9 (first published in Spanish translation 1986).
Clarkson, P. and Gilbert, M. (1990a) The training of counsellor trainers and supervisors, in W. Dryden and B. Thorne (eds) *Training and Supervision for Counselling in Action*, London: Sage.
—— (1990b) Transactional analysis, in W. Dryden (ed.) *Individual Therapy: A Handbook*, Milton Keynes: Open University Press, pp. 199–225.
Corsini, R. (ed.) (1984) *Current Psychotherapies*, Itasca, Ill.: F.E. Peacock.
—— and Rosenberg, B. (1955) Mechanisms of group psychotherapy: processes and dynamics, *Journal of Abnormal and Social Psychology* 51: 406–11.

Cottone, R.R. (1988) Epistemological and ontological issues in counselling: implications of social systems theory, *Counselling Psychology Quarterly* 1(4): 357–65.

Daldrup, R.J., Beutler, L.E., Engle, D. and Greenberg, L.S. (1988) *Focused Expressive Psychotherapy: Freeing the Overcontrolled Patient*, London: Cassell.

De Lisle, G. (1988) *Balises II: A Gestalt Perspective of Personality Disorders*, Montreal: Le Centre d'Intervention Gestaltiste, Le Reflet.

Douglas, T. (1976) *Group Work Practice*, London: Tavistock.

Dryden, W. (1984) Issues in the eclectic practice of individual therapy, in W. Dryden (ed.) *Individual Therapy in Britain*, London: Harper & Row, pp. 341–63.

—— (1986) Eclectic psychotherapies: a critique of leading approaches, in J.C. Norcross (ed.) *Handbook of Eclectic Psychotherapy*, New York: Brunner/Mazel, pp. 353–75.

—— (1987) *Counselling Individuals: The Rational-Emotive Approach*, London: Taylor & Francis.

—— and Norcross, J.C. (eds) (1990) *Eclecticism and Integration in Counselling and Psychotherapy*, Loughton: Gale Centre.

Eichenbaum, L. and Orbach, S. (1983) *Outside In . . . Inside Out – Women's Psychology: A Feminist Psychoanalytic Approach*, Harmondsworth: Penguin.

Ellis, A. (1962) *Reason and Emotion in Psychotherapy*, New York: Lyle Stuart.

Enright, J. (1980) *Enlightening Gestalt: Waking Up from the Nightmare*, Mill Valley, Calif.: Pro-Telos.

Erickson, M.H. (1967) *Advanced Techniques of Hypnosis and Therapy*, New York: Grune & Stratton.

Erikson, E. (1977) *Childhood and Society*, London, Triad Granada (first published 1951).

Eysenck, H.J. (1952) The effects of psychotherapy: an evaluation, *Journal of Consulting Psychology* 16: 319–24.

—— (ed.) (1968) *Handbook of Abnormal Psychology*, London: Pitman Medical Publishing.

Fairbairn, W.R.D. (1952) *Psycho-analytic Studies of the Personality*, London: Tavistock.

Farrell, B.A. (1979) Work in small groups: some philosophical considerations, in B. Babington Smith and B.A. Farrell (eds) *Training in Small Groups: A Study of Five Methods*, Oxford: Pergamon Press, pp. 103–15.

Federn, P. (1977) *Ego Psychology and the Psychoses*, London: Maresfield Reprints (first published 1953).

Ferenczi, S. (1980) *Further Contributions to the Theory and Technique of Psycho-Analysis*, London: Maresfield Reprints (first published 1926).

Fiedler, F.E. (1950) A comparison of therapeutic relationships in psychoanalytic, non-directive and Adlerian therapy, *Journal of Consulting Psychology* 14: 436–45.

Fivaz, R. (1980) Une Evolution Vers l'Impasse?, *Polyrama*, Ecole Polytechnique Fédérale de Lausanne, 45, 9–11.

Fonagy, P. (1989) On the integration of cognitive-behaviour theory with psychoanalysis, *British Journal of Psychotherapy* 5(4): 557–63.

Fox, M. (1983) *Original Blessing: A Primer in Creation Spirituality*, Santa Fe, NM: Bear & Co.

Frank, J.D. (1979) The present status of outcome studies, *Journal of Consulting and Clinical Psychology* 47: 310–16.

Freud, S. (1977) Introductory lectures on psycholanalysis, in A. Richards (ed.) and J. Strachey (trans.) *The Pelican Freud Library Vol. 1*, Harmondsworth: Penguin (original work published 1915–17).

Freud, S. (1977) Three essays on sexuality, in A. Richards (ed.) and J. Strachey (trans.) *The Pelican Freud Library, Vol. 7*, Harmondsworth: Penguin, pp. 33–170 (original work published 1905).

Fromm, E. (1960) *Psychoanalysis and Zen Buddhism*, London: Allen & Unwin.

Fromm-Reichmann, F. (1974) *Principles of Intensive Psychotherapy*, Chicago: University of Chicago Press (first published 1950).

Garfield, S.L. (1980) *Psychotherapy: An Eclectic Approach*, New York: Wiley.

—— (1982) Eclecticism and integration in psychotherapy, *Behavior Therapy* 13: 610–23.

Garfield, S.L. (1986) An eclectic psychotherapy, in J.C. Norcross (ed.) *Handbook of Eclectic Psychotherapy*, New York: Brunner/Mazel, pp. 132–62.

Glasser, W. (1965) *Reality Therapy*, New York: Harper & Row.

Gleick, J. (1988) *Chaos: Making a New Science*, London: Heinemann.

Goldstein, K. (1939) *The Organism*, Book 6, New York: America Books.

Gottlieb, S. (1989) The pregnant psychotherapist: a potent transference stimulus, *British Journal of Psychotherapy* 5(3): 287–99.

Goulding, M.M. and Goulding, R.L. (1979) *Changing Lives Through Redecision Therapy*, New York: Brunner/Mazel.

Greenberg, I.A. (ed.) (1975) *Psychodrama: Theory and Therapy*, London: Souvenir Press (first published 1974).

Greenberg, L.S. and Safran, J.D. (1987) *Emotion in Psychotherapy: The Process of Therapeutic Change*, New York: Guilford Press.

Greenson, R.R. (1965) The working alliance and the transference neuroses, *Psychoanalytic Quarterly* 34: 155–81.

—— (1967) *The Technique and Practice of Psychoanalysis*, Vol. 1, New York: International Universities Press.

Griffith, S. (1990) A review of the factors associated with patient compliance and the taking of prescribed medicines, *British Journal of General Practice* 40: 114–16.

Guerriere, D. (1980) Physis, Sophia, Psyche, in J. Sallis and K. Maly (eds) *Heraclitean Fragments: A Companion Volume to the Heidegger/Fink Seminar on Heraclitus*, Alabama: University of Alabama Press, pp. 87–134.

Guy, J.D. (1987) *The Personal Life of the Psychotherapist*, New York: Wiley.

Haley, J. (1963) *Strategies of Psychotherapy*, New York: Grune & Stratton.

Hawking, S. (1988) *A Brief History of Time*, London: Bantam Press.

Heidegger, M. (1949) *Existence and Being*, Chicago: Henry Regnery (first published 1929).

Heiman, P. (1950) On countertransference, *International Journal of Psychoanalysis* 31: 81–4.

Heron, J. (1990) *Helping the Client: A Creative Practical Guide*, London: Sage.

Hinshelwood, R.D. (1989) *A Dictionary of Kleinian Thought*, London: Free Association Books.

Hoffman, L. (1981) *Foundations of Family Therapy: A Conceptual Framework for Systems Change*, New York: Basic Books.

Holmes, J. and Lindley, R. (1989) *The Values of Psychotherapy*, Oxford: Oxford University Press.

Hynan, M.T. (1981) On the advantages of assuming that the techniques of psychotherapy are ineffective, *Psychotherapy: Theory, Research and Practice* 18: 11–13.

Jacobson, E. (1964) *Anxiety and Tension Control: A Psychobiologic Approach*, Philadelphia: Lippincott.

James, J. (1983) Cultural consciousness: the challenge to TA, *Transactional Analysis Journal* 13(4): 207–16.

James, M. (1974) Self-reparenting: theory and process, *Transactional Analysis Journal* 4(3): 32–9.

—— and Savary, L. (1977) *The New Self: Self Therapy with Transactional Analysis*, Reading, Mass.: Addison-Wesley.

Jaspers, K. (1963) *General Psychopathology* (J. Hoenig and M.W. Hamilton, trans.), Chicago: University of Chicago Press (first published 1913).

Jung, C.G. (1944) *Psychological Types* (H.G. Baynes, trans.), London: Trench Trubner.

—— (1968) Archetypes of the collective unconscious, in H. Read, M. Fordham and G. Adler (eds) R.F.C. Hull (trans.) *The Collected Works, Vol. 9 Part 1*, 2nd edn, London: Routledge & Kegan Paul (original work published 1934).

—— (1969a) Psychology and religion, in H. Read, M. Fordham and G. Adler (eds) R.F.C. Hull (trans.) *The Collected Works, Vol. 11*, 2nd edn, London: Routledge & Kegan Paul (original work published 1938).

—— (1969b) Synchronicity: an acausal connecting principle, in H. Read, M. Fordham and G. Adler (eds) R.F.C. Hull (trans.) *The Collected Works, Vol. 8*, 2nd edn, London: Routledge & Kegan Paul (original work published 1952).

—— (1977) Symbols and the interpretation of dreams, in H. Read, M. Fordham and G. Adler (eds) R.F.C. Hull (trans.) *The Collected Works, Vol. 18*, London: Routledge & Kegan Paul (original work published 1961).

Keleman, S. (1985) *Emotional Anatomy: The Structure of Experience*, Berkeley, Calif.: Center Press.

Kelly, G.A. (1955) *The Psychology of Personal Constructs*, Vols 1 & 2, New York: W.W. Norton.

Kernberg, O.F. (1984) *Severe Personality Disorders: Psychotherapeutic Strategies*, New Haven, Conn.: Yale University Press.

Klauber, J. (1986) Elements of the psychoanalytic relationship and their therapeutic implications, in G. Kohon (ed.) *The British School of Psychoanalysis: The Independent Tradition*, London: Free Association Books, pp. 200–13.

Klein, M. (1984) *Envy, Gratitude and Other Works*, London: Hogarth Press and Institute for Psychoanalysis (first published 1957).

Koestler, A. (1972) *The Roots of Coincidence*, London: Hutchinson.

—— (1989) *The Act of Creation*, London: Arkana (first published 1964).

Kohut, H. (1977) *The Restoration of the Self*, New York: International Universities Press.

Kottler, J.A. (1986) *On Being a Therapist*, San Francisco: Jossey-Bass.

Kuhn, T.S. (1970) *The Structure of Scientific Revolutions*, 2nd edn, Chicago: University of Chicago Press.

Lacoursiere, R. (1980) *Life Cycle of Groups*, New York: Human Sciences Press.

Laing, R.D. (1965) *The Divided Self*, Harmondsworth: Penguin.

Lambert, M.J. (1986) Implications of psychotherapy outcome research for eclectic psychotherapy, in J.C. Norcross (ed.) *Handbook of Eclectic Psychotherapy*, New York: Brunner/Mazel, pp. 436–62.

——, Bergin, A.E. and Collins, J.L. (1977) Therapist-induced deterioration in psychotherapy, in A.S. Gurman and A.M. Razin (eds) *Effective Psychotherapy: A Handbook of Research*, New York: Pergamon Press, pp. 452–81.

Langs, R. (1976) *The Bipersonal Field*, New York: Jason Aronson.

Lazarus, A.A. (1981) *The Practice of Multimodal Therapy*, New York: McGraw-Hill.

Lovejoy, A. and Boas, G. (1973) *Primitivism and Related Areas in Antiquity*, New York: Ferrar, Strauss & Giraux.

Lowen, A. (1969) *The Betrayal of the Body*, New York: Collier-Macmillan.

Luborsky, L., Singer, B. and Luborsky, L. (1975) Comparative studies of psychotherapies: is it true that 'Everybody has won and all must have prizes'?, *Archives of General Psychiatry* 32: 995–1008.

Lyotard, J.F. (1984) *The Postmodern Condition: A Report on Knowledge* (G. Bennington and B. Massumi, trans.), Manchester: Manchester University Press.

Mahler, M.S., Pine, F. and Bergman, A. (1975) *The Psychological Birth of the Human Infant*, London: Hutchinson.

Mahrer, A.R. (1989) *The Integration of Psychotherapies: A Guide for Practicing Therapists*, Ottawa: Human Sciences Press.

Malcolm, J. (1981) *Psychoanalysis: The Impossible Profession*, New York: Knopf.

Mander, A.V. and Rush, A.K. (1974) *Feminism as Therapy*, New York: Random House.

Marmor, J. (1982) Change in psychoanalytic treatment, in S. Slipp (ed.) *Curative Factors in Dynamic Psychotherapy*, New York: McGraw-Hill.

Maruyama, M. (1968) The second cybernetics: deviation-amplifying mutual causal processes, in W. Buckley (ed.) *Modern Systems Research for the Behavioral Scientist*, Chicago: Aldine, pp. 304–13.

Maslow, A. (1968) *Toward a Psychology of Being*, 2nd edn, New York: Van Nostrand.

Maturana, H.R. (1980) Biology of cognition, in H.R. Maturana and F.J. Varela

Autopoiesis and Cognition: The Realization of the Living, Boston, Mass.: D. Reidel (first published 1970), pp. 1–58.

Merleau-Ponty, M. (1962) *The Phenomenology of Perception* (Colin Smith, trans.), London: Routledge & Kegan Paul.

Miller, A. (1983) *The Drama of the Gifted Child and the Search for the True Self*, London: Faber & Faber.

—— (1985) *Thou Shalt Not Be Aware: Society's Betrayal of the Child* (H. & H. Hannum, trans.), London: Pluto Books (first published 1981).

Millon, T. (1969) *Modern Psychopathology: A Biosocial Approach to Maladaptive Learning and Functioning*, Philadelphia, Pa: W.B. Saunders.

Minkowski, E. (1970) *Lived Time* (N. Metzel, trans.), Evanston, Ill: Northwestern University Press (original work published 1933).

Morgan, G. (1986) *Images of Organization*, Beverly Hills, Calif.: Sage.

Norcross, J.C. (1986) Eclectic psychotherapy: an introduction and overview, in J.C. Norcross (ed.) *Handbook of Eclectic Psychotherapy*, New York: Brunner/Mazel, pp. 3–24.

Onions, C.T. (ed.) (1973) *The Shorter Oxford English Dictionary*, 3rd edn, Oxford: Oxford University Press.

Orbach, S. (1978) *Fat Is a Feminist Issue*, London: Arrow.

Osnes, R.E. (1974) Spot-reparenting, *Transactional Analysis Journal* 4(3): 40–6.

Pavlov, I.P. (1928) *Lectures on Conditioned Reflexes* (W.H. Ganff, trans.), New York: International Publishers.

Peck, S. (1978) *The Road Less Travelled: A New Psychology of Love, Traditional Values and Spiritual Growth*, New York: Simon & Schuster.

Pilgrim, D. (1989) The rise and rise of clinical psychology, *Changes* 7: 44–6.

Pine, F. (1985) *Developmental Theory and Clinical Process*, New Haven, Conn.: Yale University Press.

Polster, E. and Polster, M. (1974) *Gestalt Therapy Integrated*, New York: Vintage (first published 1973).

Racker, H. (1982) *Transference and Countertransference*, London: Maresfield Reprints (first published 1968).

Reason, P. and Rowan, J. (eds) (1981) *Human Inquiry: A Sourcebook of New Paradigm Research*, Chichester: Wiley.

Reich, W. (1972) *Character Analysis*, 3rd edn, New York: Simon & Schuster.

Robinson, W.L. (1974) Conscious competency – the mark of a competent instructor, *Personnel Journal* 53: 538–9.

Rogers, C.R. (1961) *On Becoming a Person: A Therapist's View of Psychotherapy*, London: Constable.

—— (1986) *Client-Centred Therapy*, London: Constable.

Rossi, E.L. and Cheek, D.B. (1988) *Mind-Body Therapy: Ideodynamic Healing in Hypnosis*, New York: W.W. Norton.

Rothenberg, A. (1979) *The Emerging Goddess*, Chicago: University of Chicago Press.

Rothstein, A. (ed.) (1985) *Models of the Mind: Their Relationships to Clinical Work*, Madison, Conn.: International Universities Press.

Rowan, J. (1973) *The Reality Game*, London: Routledge.

—— (1988) Counselling and the psychology of furniture, *Counselling: The Journal of the British Association for Counselling* May, 64: 21–4.

—— (1990) *Subpersonalities: The People Inside Us*, London: Routledge.

Rowe, C.E. and MacIsaac, D.S. (1989) *Empathic Attunement: The 'Technique' of Psychoanalytic Self Psychology*, Northvale, NJ: Jason Aronson.

Rowe, D. (1988) *The Successful Self*, London: Fontana.

Rutter, M. (1972) *Maternal Deprivation Reassessed*, Harmondsworth: Penguin.

Ryle, G. (1973) *Dilemmas: The Tarner Lectures 1953*, Cambridge: Cambridge University Press.

Samuels, A. (1985) *Jung and the Post-Jungians*, London: Routledge & Kegan Paul.

Satir, V. (1967) *Conjoint Family Therapy*, Palo Alto, Calif.: Science and Behavior Books.
Schiff, J. and Day, B. (1970) *All My Children*, New York: Pyramid Publications.
Schiff, J.L., with Schiff, A.W., Mellor, K., Schiff, E., Schiff, S., Richman, D., Fishman, J., Wolz, L., Fishman, C. and Momb, D. (1975) *Cathexis Reader: Transactional Analysis Treatment of Psychosis*, New York: Harper & Row.
Sechehaye, M. (1951) *Reality Lost and Regained: Autobiography of a Schizophrenic Girl, with Analytic Interpretation by M. Sechehaye* (F. Urbin-Ralson, trans.), New York: Grune & Stratton.
Shakespeare, W. (1951) *Hamlet*, in *The Complete Works*, P. Alexander (ed.), London: Collins.
Simon, S.B., Howe, L.W. and Kirschenbaum, H. (1972) *Values Clarification: A Handbook of Practical Strategies for Teachers and Students*, New York: Dodd, Mead & Co.
Sloane, R.B., Staples, F.R., Cristol, A.H., Yorkston, N.J. and Whipple, K. (1975) *Short-term Analytically Oriented Psychotherapy versus Behavior Therapy*, Cambridge, Mass.: Harvard University Press.
Smail, D.J. (1978) *Psychotherapy: A Personal Approach*, London: J.M. Dent.
Spiegelberg, H. (1972) *Phenomenology in Psychology and Psychiatry*, Evanston, Ill: Northwestern University Press.
Stern, D.N. (1985) *The Interpersonal World of the Infant*, New York: Basic Books.
Stone, L. (1961) *The Psychoanalytic Situation*, New York: International Universities Press.
Symington, N. (1986) *The Analytic Experience: Lectures from the Tavistock*, London: Free Association Books.
Teilhard de Chardin, P. (1970) *The Phenomenon of Man*, London: Fontana (original work published 1955).
Vaughan, F. (1985) *The Inward Arc*, Boston: Mass.: New Science Library.
Watkins, J.G. (1976) Ego states and the problem of responsibility: a psychological analysis of the Patty Hearst case, *Journal of Psychiatry and Law* Winter: 471–89.
—— and Watkins, H.H. (1986) Hypnosis, multiple personality, and ego states as altered states of consciousness, in B.B. Wolman and M. Ullman (eds) *Handbook of States of Consciousness*, New York: Van Nostrand Reinhold, pp. 133–58.
Watzlawick, P., Helmick Beavin, J. and Jackson, D.D. (1967) *Pragmatics of Human Communication: A Study of Interactional Patterns, Pathologies, and Paradoxes*, New York: W.W. Norton.
Watzlawick, P., Weakland, J.H. and Fisch, R. (1974) *Change: Principles of Problem Formation and Problem Resolution*, New York: Norton.
Weiss, E. (1950) *Principles of Psychodynamics*, New York: Grune & Stratton.
Wilber, K. (1980) *The Atman Project: A Transpersonal View of Human Development*, Wheaton: The Theosophical Publishing House.
Wilhelm, R. (trans.) (1988) *The I Ching*, London: Routledge & Kegan Paul (original work published 1951).
Winnicott, D.W. (1958) *Collected Papers: Through Paediatrics to Psychoanalysis*, London: Tavistock.
—— (1960) *The Maturational Processes and the Facilitating Environment*, London: Hogarth Press.
Wittgenstein, L. (1953) *Philosophical Investigations*, Oxford: Blackwell & Mott.
Wolf, N. (1990) *The Beauty Myth*, London: Chatto & Windus.
Wolpe, J. (1961) The systematic desensitization treatment of neuroses, *Journal of Nervous and Mental Disease* 132: 189–203.
World Health Organization (1978) *Mental Disorders: Glossary and Guide to Their Classification*, Geneva: WHO.
Yalom, I. (1975) *The Theory and Practice of Group Psychotherapy*, 2nd edn, New York: Basic Books.
Zohar, D. (1990) *The Quantum Self*, London: Bloomsbury.

3

Cognitive-Analytic Therapy (CAT)

ANTHONY RYLE AND PAULINE COWMEADOW

Psychotherapists are concerned with people whose lives are going badly. Going badly in this sense may mean suffering from psychologically induced physical symptoms, from distressing mood changes, from impaired capacities or from uncontrollable, harmful behaviours. Such features occur usually in relation to unsatisfactory close personal relationships and to negative or highly conditional attitudes towards the self. A theory of psychotherapy must aim to encompass a wide field, therefore, considering the relationship between thinking, feeling, action and bodily function on the one hand, and the development of the self and of the individual's relation to others and to society on the other. Such a theory, moreover, needs to give an account both of how difficulties arise and of how therapy may resolve them.

No theory can hope to cover all this ground, and one explanation for the apparent disparities between the rival schools of psychotherapy is the fact that different theories attend to different aspects of the problem, often, however, being less than modest in their claims to cover the whole field. Part-theories may in fact generate quite efficient therapies, for distressed people are helped by more or less any socially accredited professional through non-specific effects on morale. Moreover, even neurotic humans are skilled learners, able to make use of a wide number of kinds of therapy to gain better control over their lives.

In view of the above it seems best to start this chapter by describing the scope and underlying assumptions of the theory on which CAT is based.

Theory

The Procedural Sequence Model (PSM)

The underlying theory (called the Procedural Sequence Model) is concerned with intentional, aim-directed activity. Human activity takes place in a social and historical context and each individual's personality and intellectual functioning are shaped in accordance with his or her particular experience, mediated through the tools, language and ideas of the general culture and of his or her particular family. According to both psychoanalytic theory, especially object relations theory, and the developmental psychology of Vygotsky (Wertsch 1985), this learning takes place crucially through the process of internalization, whereby what is first experienced and enacted in an interpersonal relationship (initially of a child with its parents and other adults) generates (or becomes transformed into) intrapsychic functions. Through this process each of us acquires a second 'voice' in an internal conversation; human personality thus becomes essentially dialogic. In this way we gain access to the range of conceptual tools offered by our culture and acquire our capacity for abstract thought; from the same experiences are derived our systems of self-observation, self-care and self-control but also our proneness to inner conflict. Internalization is the key to human personality development and growth; problems arising during it can lead to those distorted, limited or conflicted personalities which are the concerns of psychotherapy.

Psychotherapy as a learning process is to some degree analogous to early adult–child learning in that the therapist uses his or her relationship with the client as an arena within which new attitudes and new skills may be acquired. In contrast to the teaching of intellectual skills, however, the therapist will often need to recognize and modify the ways in which a client cannot enter into or distorts this learning relationship, that is to say the therapist must deal with the issues described in psychoanalysis as transference.

The PSM is so called because the unit of description is the procedural sequence or procedure. A procedure, as is the case with a committee's procedures, describes the way in which a regular sequence of mental and behavioural acts are unfolded in pursuit of a given aim. This sequence involves mental processes, action and environmental events and consequences. Procedures are interrelated hierarchically; a given procedure, for example to attend a lecture, will represent one sub-procedure of a higher order one, for example to become qualified in a particular subject, and may well be enacted in turn through lower order sub-procedures, such as catching the bus to the lecture. The distinction made by Vygotsky's followers between the three levels of motivated *activities* occurring in a social context, *actions* directed towards specific goals and *operations* representing the use of specific means within a given context, offers a useful sub-division of this hierarchy. The procedures of concern to psychotherapists are those to do with the maintenance of the self and of social existence – that is to say they are role procedures, and are hence complex ones with acquired beliefs and values playing an important role and with both cognitive and affective processes being involved.

The basic procedural sequence may be described in the following seven stages:

1 The formation of an aim in relation to an environment or environmental event.
2 The evaluation of the personal meaning of the aim in this context. This involves both unconscious 'affective processing' indicating the personal meanings involved and also cognitive processes concerned with memory and with checking the aim's congruence with other aims and values.

3 The prediction (a) of one's capacity to achieve the aim and (b) of the likely consequences of achieving it.
4 Possible means (sub-procedures) are considered.
5 Enactment.
6 The effectiveness of the act is judged and the consequences are considered.
7 The aim is either pursued further, modified or abandoned and the means are either confirmed or revised.

It will be apparent that stage 1 involves perception of the environment, stages 2 to 4 and 7 are mental, stage 5 is action in the world and produces responses and consequences which are considered in stage 6. Such circular sequences are repeated, normally without reflection, and are normally open to modification. According to this theory neurosis is best understood as the persistent use of, and failure to revise, damaging or ineffective procedures.

Three main ways in which people fail to modify ineffective procedures have been identified, namely traps, dilemmas and snags. *Traps* are circular; a negative belief or assumption generates action which provokes consequences which serve to confirm this initial assumption. *Dilemmas* occur at stage 4; they represent restrictions due to the narrowing of choices of acts or roles to polarized alternatives; in most cases one pole is repeated for fear of the consequences of enacting the opposite one. In the case of *snags*, appropriate aims are abandoned due to the prediction of negative consequences (stage 3); such consequences may be the reactions of others (truly or falsely predicted) or internal and not always fully recognized, for example guilt or the fear of envy. For example, the child of quarrelling and abusive parents who finally get a divorce might feel irrationally guilty and become self-sabotaging (a snag). In relationships, the choices might seem to be between either being abusive *or* a submissive martyr (a dilemma). One aspect of the latter might be the attempt to gain affection by submission, leading to the acceptance of neglect or abuse and an increased sense of worthlessness (a trap). The particular problem procedure used by an individual patient will be listed in the reformulation as Target Problem Procedures (see below).

The relation of the Procedural Sequence Model to other theories

This model can incorporate the essentials of cognitive-behavioural therapy approaches. Cognitive therapists, for example, identify and challenge distorted meanings and inferences and the ensuing emotions (stage 2); they challenge negative self-evaluations ('learned helplessness') and distorted predictions of consequences (stage 3); they help in the choice of appropriate plans (stage 4) and they aid accurate evaluation of the consequences of action (stage 6); they may in addition use behavioural techniques by guiding graded exposure to new situations or practice in new skills, by modelling appropriate action (stage 4) or by manipulating outcomes (stage 6).

The PSM aims, however, to incorporate in addition some of the ideas of psychoanalysis. For instance, the basic model, as described above, can incorporate the main 'ego defences', understood as particular examples of cognitive 'editing' as follows:

A *Denial*: Aspects of reality likely to produce too much anxiety do not reach consciousness (stage 1).

B *Repression*: Aspects of memory and desire are not acknowledged (stage 2).

C *Dissociation*: The incompatibility of different plans or values is not acknowledged (stage 2 and stage 6).

D *Reaction Formation*: This represents the exaggerated adherence to one pole of a dilemma (stage 4).

E *Symptom Formation*: This represents an alternative to the enactment of a subprocedure which was disallowed (stage 4), the 'primary gain' being the avoidance of what is internally forbidden. Alternatively or additionally a symptom can be seen as the replacement of an abandoned procedure by one producing some alternative reward (secondary gain).

A full understanding of these neurotic mechanisms, however, requires a more elaborate model of personality structure. In the PSM, as described above, the processes of evaluation and choice involve reference to a system of self-organization which is developmentally derived from the infant's earliest interactions with adult caretakers and which reflect the infant's particular experiences. To understand this process, key ideas, derived from object relations theory but also influenced by the developmental psychology of Piaget and Vygotsky, are required.

The development of personality

The infant at birth is utterly dependent upon the providing care of the mother but at once becomes an active participant in the relationship through inborn attachment behaviours. Over the first months of life the process of differentiating her own body from external objects and from the mother takes place and early 'role procedures' are elaborated whereby the hungry baby conveys her needs, the uncomfortable baby conveys her pain and the frustrated baby conveys her anger and so on. These communicative procedures are rudimentary but they already reflect the special nature of role procedures, namely that the enactment of a role contains affective elements and aims to elicit, or must match, the reciprocal role of the other. The early reciprocal role procedures are 'bit parts', governing discrete interactions with aspects of the mother; only later do they become integrated to form a more or less complex whole person reciprocal role procedure. In going through this developmental process the child both elaborates her own procedures and internalizes the reciprocating parental role procedures. In due course these other-derived roles are enacted, for example in the child's feeding the mother, or looking after a doll, and they are also manifest in her care and control of herself. These internalized self-to-self procedures are the basis of the internal relationship which develops between a parentally derived, caring and controlling 'I' and the spontaneous child-derived 'me' and are the basis of the individual's capacity for self-consciousness and for conflict.

Adverse parenting, whether restrictive, inconsistent, rejecting or abusive, will damage the process of integrating the originally segmental role procedures. Such damage may leave the individual with extreme and disconnected ways

of viewing the self and the world (described in psychoanalytic theory as splitting). Parallel to this, polarized patterns of relating to others are manifest in 'projective identification' in which self-to-self roles are paralleled in self–other roles,
the others being elected to play one or other pole of the complementary roles.
The common pattern in personality disorders is of a split between a safe, undif-
ferentiated, idealized mode of relating (reflecting the earlier stages of the infant's
total dependence on the mother) and the contrasted conflicted state within which
roles are seen to be starkly polarized between being either abusive or abused.
Such individuals may be self-abusing and may engage in relationships with the
self playing either the abusing or abused role, the other playing the reciprocal
one.

In contrast to the views of most psychoanalytic writers, splitting and non-
integration of the personality are seen to represent failures to complete integration rather than being primarily defensive. Some of the results of this pattern
of development can be expressed in terms of dilemmas for these can be seen
to represent two kinds of polarization. In one the distinction is between originally parent- and originally child-derived roles, for example: as if *either* power-
fully care-giving *or* submissively depending. In the other pattern, polarization is
between non-integrated, segmental reciprocal role procedures (within each of
which there may also be parent–child-type dilemmas operating). An example
here would be of the so-called narcissistic personality disorder in which the
characteristic personality dilemma would be between *either* seeking admiration
from admired others *or* relating as if the choice were *either* to be contemptible *or*
contemptuous.

In the clinical understanding of patients with personality disorders of the
borderline type it is often necessary to represent failures of integration more
elaborately. This may involve considering and describing a large range of contrasting 'sub-personalities' or states of mind. Each such sub-personality or state
will be characterized by its particular pattern of reciprocal role procedures and
self–self procedures, by a typical emotional tone and by the operation of particular
defences (see Horowitz 1979). Each such state will differ in these respects from
other states. The bewildering or bizarre experiences of borderline personality
patients become comprehensible with the help of such descriptions. Understanding is best achieved by working with the patient to plot a sequential diagrammatic
reformulation (SDR) in which state characteristics and the sequences between
states and the triggers for state transitions are identified. An example is given
in the final section of this chapter.

To recapitulate, the theoretical model on which CAT is based has the following
features:

1   It is concerned with aim-directed activity, in a social context, mostly to do with
    the maintenance of the self and of relationships.
2   Such activity is described in terms of the procedural sequence of mental,
    behavioural and environmental events.
3   Anticipation and feedback and evaluation in terms of personal significance are
    integral to the maintenance of the procedural sequence.
4   The human personality is structured on the basis of internalized parent–child

interactions; these form the basis both for self–self procedures and for reciprocal role procedures.
5 Neurosis is the persistent, unrevised use of damaging or ineffective procedures
   (referred to in what follows as problem procedures).
6 Personality disorder reflects the incomplete integration of initially discrete role
   procedures.

It will be seen that the theory uses a form of description drawn from cognitive
psychology (Miller *et al.* 1960; Neisser 1967) and influenced by artificial intelligence. The understanding of the structure of human personality is derived from
developmental psychology on the one hand and from object relations theory on
the other. In this way it aims to integrate the main theories underlying present-
day psychotherapy with the broader field of developmental and cognitive psychology and to offer an understanding of neurotic and personality disorders and of
therapeutic intervention.

Practice

The theory and practice of CAT developed hand in hand. The initial impetus
came from the recognition that there was no research evidence to indicate the
unique value of any one approach to therapy; hence it was a logical step to try
combining methods including those that had previously been seen to be incompatible. My own interest (AR) in psychotherapy outcome research had involved
the use of the Repertory Grid (derived from Kelly (1955) and his Personal Construct Theory) and this had given me the experience of using two kinds of language with my patients, one primarily psychoanalytic and the other the plainer
cognitive language derived from the Grid. Moreover, there was a need to be clear
about the aims of therapy if one were to show how far they had been achieved,
and this led to an increasingly direct involvement of patients in defining their
problems. This task was partly guided by the Grid and the kind of description
emerging from it. This experience led to an increased understanding of how
helpful such descriptions were to the process of therapy itself.

The practice of CAT, as it has evolved, shows traces of this history, notably
in the use made within it of techniques drawn from many different sources
(although centrally from cognitive therapy and psychoanalysis) and the emphasis
placed upon the joint working out by patient and therapist of the best description
possible of the processes which therapy aims to change. This reformulation,
whereby the patient's story is recast in a way conveying an understanding of
how the life had been and describing the patient's current contribution to his
or her own difficulties is central to CAT; achieving it is one aspect of the very
active patient participation in the process. In the early sessions of the therapy
this reformulation is worked out together and the final written-down version
serves as the 'scaffolding' of the treatment process, within which many different
therapeutic tools may be made use of. The therapist's role is to be skilful at the
task of reformulation, to be good at identifying and dealing with problems in the
patient–therapist relationship which block or distort the therapeutic work, and

to be able to use the reformulation to overcome these difficulties and to guide, regulate and maintain the thrust of therapy.

CAT has been applied largely in under-resourced NHS conditions where time-limited work is essential if the needs of populations are to be met. Most patients are offered 16 sessions but some may be helped by 8 or 12; others may have intermittent therapy with 8–12 sessions alternating with intervals of two to three months. The active time-limited nature of the therapy does not induce regression, and CAT proves to be safe and often effective across the whole range of neurotic and personality disorders; the worst outcome is that further therapy is indicated and in such cases the 'trial of therapy' experienced in the CAT intervention is a good guide to what is indicated thereafter. CAT methods are also applicable to couple and groupwork but these extensions of it will not be discussed in this chapter.

Reformulation

The essence of CAT is reformulation which represents the description of the patient's difficulties in the form of most use to the therapeutic task. 'Most use' implies that these descriptions focus upon the procedures which need to be changed and on how the patient is actively responsible for maintaining them. These descriptions need to be accurate and fully comprehended by the patient; to this end patients must play an active part in the process of reformulation and the final form must be checked in detail with them before it is recorded in writing.

Reformulation is normally completed at the fourth session. The main sources on which it is based are the clinical history and the patient's behaviour in relation to the therapist in the early sessions. These sources, however, may be supplemented by a number of other devices, notably (a) patients are instructed to self-monitor variations in mood, behaviour or psychological symptoms, along the lines developed by cognitive therapists, noting the provoking situations and their accompanying thoughts or mental images; (b) patients are given the Psychotherapy File to read (see Appendix at the end of this chapter). In reading this they identify which descriptions seem to apply to them and these are further discussed with the therapist: (c) other pencil and paper procedures may be used (see Ryle 1990). At this point you might like to read the File (see Appendix) which will serve to introduce you to the approach as it does the patient.

At the fourth session the therapist will usually present a draft reformulation to the patient for discussion and elaboration. The first part of this is in the form of a letter or may be written in the first person as if in the patient's voice; the aim is to recount in a straightforward way the past difficulties experienced by the patient and to note the means used to cope. These means in turn will be related to the ways in which the patient currently continues to use procedures which are no longer essential or effective. This reformulation will be initially discussed verbally and the written text will be considered together and modified if the patient does not agree with aspects of it or finds it unclear. A final copy is then typed and therapist and patient each retain this. The emotional impact of this letter is often profound; as patients feel that their experience has been understood and validated they often become silent or may cry and this moment often cements the therapeutic alliance. The second part of the reformulation condenses from the written account a list of current target problems (TPs) and target problem procedures (TPPs). The latter are of crucial importance for they describe in the present tense how the patient is actively maintaining his or her difficulties, identifying the dilemmas, traps and snags in ways which explain how it is that revision has not been possible so far. The solutions or 'exits' from these problem procedures will be explored over the next few sessions. The Psychotherapy File (see Appendix) offers a list of commonly encountered TPPs.

In many cases, and in all cases of patients with personality disorders suffering from major shifts in mental state, this written list will be supplemented or replaced by a Sequential Diagrammatic Reformulation (SDR). Such diagrams (developed from those used by Horowitz 1979) will be constructed jointly on the basis of the observed states and state sequences exhibited by the patient. In constructing the diagrams it is often helpful first to describe the key features of the 'core state'. This concept, which is based on object relations theory, will name the patient's dominant harmful self-to-self procedures; these represent unresolved childhood issues. The description of a core state, for example, might read 'critical and conditional to deprived, striving and angry'. Patients have variable access to the feelings identified in this core and any which are hypothesized but are not directly experienced, or which are hard to acknowledge, should be written in brackets. From this core state will emanate a number of 'procedural loops' representing life strategies designed to pursue ordinary life enterprises or to remedy or avoid the painful feelings associated with the unfinished business of the core state.

In patients with a personality disorder there is frequently a dominant 'coping' mode such as compliance (the 'false self') or perfectionism; these are ways of going about life which make the world manageable but which conceal but do not heal the underlying problem. Other loops may represent the search for intimacy or relationships and these are often best described in terms of the dilemmas listed in the Psychotherapy File. Others again may represent symptomatic alternatives to avoided behavioural procedures.

Reformulation carried out in this way has a number of effects. In the first place patients' active involvement strengthens their sense of ability and efficacy and recruits them to an active co-operative role in therapy. In the second place the various activities involved, which extend from unstructured talking to specific homework tasks, reveal in most cases the ways in which the patient's particular difficulties are provoked by and manifest in the therapeutic situation. Reformulation may be based in part upon the evidence of such 'transference' issues and in any case will anticipate, in its delineation of problematic interpersonal procedures, what difficulties are likely to arise in the course of treatment. For the therapist, therefore, reformulation offers an accessible tool for recognizing transference and countertransference issues. Third and crucially, the task of reformulation calls for considerable thought and sensitivity on the part of the therapist. The fact that the results of the process are written down is daunting but the fact that what is written down is discussed and modified with the patient means that, once completed, the reformulation provides a firm shared basis upon which the rest of the therapeutic work can be built.

Active treatment

While reformulation itself usually initiates therapeutic change therapy changes gear once it has been completed. The main task for the remaining sessions, usually numbering between 8 and 12, is for the patient to learn to recognize and begin to modify these problematic procedures. Reformulation represents the forging of a new conceptual tool from which can grow a new way of understanding and integrating the self, but the patient will take time to learn to apply this new tool. Some of this learning takes place in the patient's daily life and to this end patients are asked to keep diaries in which they record the occasions on which they find themselves repeating one of their 'target procedures'. These diaries are discussed in the session when, in addition, the therapist will be alerted to detect manifestations of problem procedures both in the patient's account of his or her life and, crucially, as they are enacted in the therapy itself. When sequential diagrams are used patients will consider their lives in relation to the diagram at least once daily, tracing which procedures or loops they have been through. At the end of each session it is helpful for patients to rate how far they have been controlled by their TPPs or ineffective loops and, as alternative modes ('exits') are defined, it will be helpful also to rate their use of these. This rating serves to bring together the work of each session and to relate it to the target issues of the therapy. The repeated demonstration of these procedures usually leads quite rapidly to a much greater capacity to recognize consciously what has hitherto been performed automatically and hence initiates the possibility of change.

In essence this approach represents the use of a learning paradigm based on the kind of learning typical of the child's learning from parents and teachers, in which what is enacted within the relationship and the tools, words or concepts supplied (by the parent or teacher or therapist) provide the basis for revising harmful procedures and for integrating hitherto poorly connected aspects of the self. The essential tools are description and demonstration; interpretations of the developmental origins of present experiences or of the presumed unconscious impulses concealed behind defences are largely avoided. The reason for this is that the interpreter, in claiming to know something the patient does not or cannot know, can seem threatening to the already anxious patient, especially for the patient whose sense of self is already fragile or fragmented. Any kind of interpretation in such cases can feel critical and undermining. The need for cautious timing of interpretation is fully recognized by psychoanalysts but jointly elaborated descriptions seem to be containing rather than destabilizing. This does not mean, however, that CAT leaves undisturbed the defences of repression, denial and so on; as the patient's sense of safety and control is enhanced through the therapeutic relationship and reformulation, forgotten memories and avoided feelings become accessible.

Through the active phase of therapy and up to termination the main content of sessions will be determined by the patient, as in dynamic therapy, but the main comments of the therapist will be concerned with demonstrating how problem procedures are manifest and in clarifying how they can be modified. A part of each session, however, will be spent in elaborating appropriate 'homework' tasks and in going over work done by the patient on such tasks between the sessions. Some patients will pursue their work conscientiously and effectively using the therapist in an uncomplicated way, like a good teacher. Others, however, in their failures and forgettings, in their over-compliance or passive resistance or in their swings between idealization and dismissal, manifest, in their involvement with the therapist, versions of the difficulties for which they have consulted. Such manifestations are taken as further grist to the therapeutic mill, that is to say as examples of TPPs needing to be challenged and modified. Other patients may acquire with apparent conviction new understandings of what they are doing and may even begin to act differently without experiencing any central emotional change. For these patients the need may be to work more directly with feelings, learning both what the patient seems to be avoiding and perhaps more importantly being able to name directly, with reference to the therapy issues and within the framework of the therapeutic relationship, what the therapist is feeling also. The fact that the therapist can acknowledge and contain, for example, his or her disappointment, affection, desire, irritation or frustration at the absence of feeling, within the understood framework of a therapeutic contract, may make it far safer for the patient to do likewise. In other cases where past painful issues have been incompletely dealt with, as for example in incompletely resolved grief reactions, more direct methods for freeing feeling, such as Gestalt techniques, may be useful. Other patients may find the use of writing or painting a way to contact feelings. At various stages specific cognitive or behavioural methods may be used in relation to particular procedures. In summary, within the agreed framework of the reformulation, therapists are able to employ a wide range of specific methods.

Termination

Most patients are emotionally damaged and needy when they come to therapy and one of the advantages of time-limited work is that such patients are freed from the hope of actually getting enough and they are hence often able to take on board something of value. No therapy ever makes up for what was missing or damaged in childhood; the main therapeutic gift is to offer something real linked with a manageable degree of disappointment. In CAT this 'something real' is not only a metaphorical make-weight for what was missing, it is also a pilot guide and tool-kit. This is not to say that the therapist may not acquire considerable emotional importance but it is an importance based upon a working together rather than a giving to and receiving; the therapist has respected and equipped the healthy part of the patient and, together with the patient, begun the task of clearing road blocks and diminishing self-damage.

In so far as the therapist is internalized as a more caring and coping figure than the patient's own internal parents may be, she will be internalized as the bearer of understanding and the initiator of active change, not as the all-powerful carer of the passive needy child in the patient; if the passive needy part of the patient has been contained by patient and therapist together then this subsequent capacity to care may well endure. Finally, the therapist, like the parent who allows children to leave home, will allow the leaving of therapy to be felt but will balance the pain of loss with reminders of what has been learnt and can be taken away. To make these features clear it is usual for the therapist and patient to exchange 'good-bye letters' at the end of therapy. These are usually read out at the penultimate session so they can be modified before being written in a final version. Such letters serve to continue the work of therapy and to aid in the internalization of the therapist through the period between termination and follow-up, which is usually arranged about three months after therapy ends, but which may be sooner for more deprived or disturbed individuals. At this meeting further follow-up or treatment will be arranged for about one in four patients.

Outcomes in psychotherapy reflect patient selection (less ill patients do better) and the measures used (symptom scores change more readily than indices of personality or social functioning). CAT has been applied to a very wide and often severely disturbed range of patients and seems a safe first intervention; there is no evidence of dangerous negative effects in terms of breakdown or suicide. A comparitive study (Brockman *et al.* 1987) showed that CAT effected more cognitive change than did a similar psychodynamic therapy; other outcome studies are underway.

Kate: a case history

Kate was a 32-year-old Canadian physiotherapist who had been suffering from episodes of depression for four years since the suicide of her brother Paul. These episodes usually lasted several weeks and were characterized by feelings of worthlessness, despair and suicidal feelings, and would sometimes alternate with periods when she felt 'high' and very confident, active, sociable and energetic. Six months before therapy she had been diagnosed as having a serious but curable malignant illness. She was referred by the doctor treating her because of her depression which had become more severe during this period. She began a 16-session CAT while still receiving medical treatment.

Assessment phase of therapy: sessions 1–4

At her first session of CAT, Kate described how she had been depressed for the past six weeks. This episode was severe and associated with extreme inertia, almost complete social withdrawal and marked suicidal feelings. She had thought of ending her life by overdosing but was held back by remembering the grief caused by her brother's suicide.

This bout of depression had been preceded by a few weeks of feeling 'high', beginning while she was on holiday with friends. During this time she had ended a long-standing relationship with a boy-friend, feeling she was too dependent on him and had begun a new relationship with another man.

Apart from these 'high' episodes, which were usually short-lived, Kate described herself as generally lacking in self-confidence, feeling socially inadequate, incompetent at work and, most painfully of all, as feeling 'unworthy of being a person'. These feelings of unworthiness were experienced most acutely during her depressions, but reflected a lifelong lack of self-esteem and contributed to her general inability to make decisions about her life or to make plans for the future.

During this session she appeared sad but cut off from her feelings. She expressed concern about the increasing severity of both her depressive and 'high' moods and at the seemingly arbitrary shifts between these two states. She was given the Psychotherapy File (see Appendix) and asked to monitor her moods in a 'mood diary', noting especially any triggers associated with changes of mood.

In the second session of the therapy, Kate reported that through self-monitoring she had observed that her depressions were sometimes related to feeling socially inadequate and to feeling rejected by her boy-friend. Some significant memories of childhood were discussed in this session, notably the lack of a satisfactory relationship with her father since the age of three due to her parents' separation. From that time Kate's contact with her father had been infrequent, being confined to letter writing for some years; and in spite of more contact in recent years, she thought of him as more like a penpal or distant friend than a father. Nor did her stepfather, who was critical and disapproving, provide her with the father figure she missed. In respect of her work history she reported many changes between jobs, professional trainings and college courses, none of which ever seemed to be quite what she wanted.

During this session Kate looked very depressed and cut off, and appeared to have difficulty thinking and talking. When asked if she had reservations about starting psychotherapy she replied that she found it easier not to think about things and preferred to 'blank everything off'.

To the third session Kate brought a list of 'positive' and 'negative' self-attributes and also a written description of her relationships with men; in the course of doing this she had begun to recognize some of her habitual procedures, and to link cognitions and feelings with behaviour. She described feeling that she had 'no self-worth of her own' and that she did not know who she was. She thought that these feelings made her seek 'validation' through close relationships with men, with whom, however, she tended to feel inferior and submissive. She felt that she 'catered for the needs of others' at the expense of her own needs and realized that she never let anyone do anything for her and never asked for anything from others. She summarized, 'I feel unworthy of an existence without a man's approval . . . I haven't got an autonomous identity'. When considering her list of positive self-attributes, Kate dismissed most of them as consisting of qualities assumed in order to elicit approval from others, rather than representing 'true' aspects of herself. When the therapist commented on her difficulty in accepting that any of these qualities might come from her rather than from others, she wept, repeating 'I don't know who I am'.

A few days after her third session Kate experienced a suicidal crisis and arrived unexpectedly in the psychotherapy clinic, greatly distressed, saying that she felt desperate, that she could no longer bear the 'pain' and that she felt unable to go on unless she talked to someone. In the absence of her own therapist she was seen by another therapist to whom she expressed her guilt and grief about her brother's suicide. She blamed herself for not preventing his death by failing to recognize the depth of his depression and despair, which she felt she could understand now because she was experiencing these feelings herself. She had bought Paracetamol tablets earlier that day, intending to kill herself with these if she failed to gain relief from these painful feelings. By the end of her session she felt less suicidal and was able to cope until the next planned meeting with her own therapist.

During the fourth session Kate recognized that this severe episode of depression had been triggered off by her feelings of rejection after she and her boy-friend had decided to end their relationship. Her subsequent despair seemed, she said, to encompass everything: feelings about her parents' separation, her brother's death, and her fears about getting in touch with painful feelings during therapy. She also discussed her tendency to idealize her relationships with men, which often resulted in disillusionment, disappointment and feelings of rejection when the relationships inevitably fell short of her expectations.

Reformulation: session 5

After the fourth session the therapist prepared a reformulation, drawing together the various strands gathered in the assessment phase of therapy. It was written in the first person, as if in her own words; many of the phrases are indeed hers. It began by describing her 'central pain' which she had recently experienced intensely during her suicidal crisis. The origins of these painful feelings were located in early experience, and the procedures that she had evolved to cope with these feelings were described. These problem procedures offered protection against being overwhelmed by painful feelings, but, while unrevised, also served to maintain the feelings in their original painful state. The Reformulation read as follows:

> Most of my life I have felt as though I am unworthy of being a person and that I don't know who I am. These feelings of worthlessness and lack of a sense of self are rooted in my early childhood. Due to my parents' separation I failed to receive the safe, supportive care that I needed in order to develop a sense of belief in my own ability to confront with confidence the uncertainties of life.
>
> My father left home when I was three and I have had little contact with him since, except as a penpal. Although I see him more frequently now, he is more of a distant friend than a father. Nor was my stepfather the father figure that I wanted, because he was very critical and disapproving.
>
> I felt unsafe as a child because of the inconsistent and rejecting behaviour of important adults and this has led to feelings of unworthiness, as if I don't deserve care, and also to a general lack of certainty about myself. Because I feel as though I don't know who I am, I lack a sense of direction and have difficulty in following through new enterprises and making plans for the

future. This sense of lacking a consistent, coherent self has been increased by unpredictable shifts in my moods which can leave me feeling frightened and out of control of my feelings. As a child I felt abandoned by my father, and as an adult I continue to feel and act as if people are going to abandon me. These feelings have increased since the tragic death of my brother Paul and the end of my relationship with John the following year. When I was diagnosed as having cancer last year I again feared that I would be abandoned by family and friends and that no one would be around to help me through the shock or to support me through the long unpleasant treatment. My response to these fears was to blank off from my feelings so that now, on looking back, it seems as though it didn't really happen to me.

My lack of sense of self, which began in childhood and which is associated with feelings of unworthiness and fear of being abandoned, has persisted into adult life, where I have dealt with it in three main ways:

1 Blanking off. I try to avoid painful feelings by blanking them off, which creates a temporary relief but makes me feel cut off and as if I am not really here. This contributes to my sense of not knowing who I am. When the feelings I am trying to avoid are very painful, I sometimes feel as though the only way to successfully block them off is by taking my own life.

2 I have sought a sense of identity by looking after others whether as a physiotherapist, or as a friend or girl-friend. My kindness, sympathy and patience find expression through caring for others, but I feel that this is only part of the picture. I find it hard to assert myself and my needs in relationships and feel resentful because I am fitting in with others' ideas about who I am, as if the 'real me' is left out of the picture.

3 As if to compensate for the lack of a consistent caring father figure in childhood, I have tended to make heavy emotional investments in relationships with men, as though seeking perfect care in the security of a permanent relationship. I also look for a sense of myself through men, as if my existence can only be validated through affection and acknowledgement from others. My sense of self is so bound up with approval that if an important relationship ends, or if I feel rejected in any way, I fear that I may fall apart and lose myself. Although I realize that putting so much value on another's recognition is likely to put undue pressure on relationships, my need to find a secure source of affection and approval seems to become greater with every loss, as if only a permanent loving relationship could begin to make up for past losses and give me enough confidence to claim an identity and a life of my own.

Psychotherapy offers me the chance to develop a sense of self that belongs to me rather than representing reflections from others. This will involve bringing together contradictory feelings and qualities that express different bits of me into a more coherent and consistent whole. Putting the picture together in this way may involve getting in touch with painful areas that I would rather avoid and blank off. Another difficult aspect of psychotherapy may be the fact that it is time-limited, which may rekindle fears about my being abandoned. Closely linked to this may be anxieties that any sense of self I achieve may disappear after the end of therapy. A crucial aim of therapy will be to discover a sense of self that I will be able to own, develop and incorporate after therapy ends. This will be achieved through the process of mutual discussion, sharing of ideas, and working things out together during the course of therapy.

The target problems and procedures identified in the reformulation were recorded with their respective aims or alternative procedures on a rating sheet. These read as follows:

Target problems:

1 Feeling depressed, worthless and suicidal.
   Aim: To feel positive about myself.
2 Blanking off when faced with difficult feelings.
   Aim: To be able to find and express feelings to put me back in touch with who I am.

Target problem procedures:

1 I feel bad about myself so I look after others, with the result that my own needs are not met so I feel resentful or depressed and bad about myself.
   Aim: To be able to ask for things for myself.
2 In relationships with others it is as if the choice is either: involved, vulnerable and likely to get hurt or: cut off, in control but lonely.
   Aim: To be able to feel safe and myself when involved with others.
3 In my sense of myself it is as if I either: feel depressed, hopeless and worthless or unrealistically high, as if capable of anything.
   Aim: A more continuous sense of self despite mood changes.

Ratings on these TPs and TPPs were completed by Kate during each subsequent session. The wording of the aims was worked out jointly with her therapist. She was also given a Sequential Diagrammatic Reformulation (SDR) (Fig. 3.1) which provided a more graphic demonstration of the self-perpetuating nature of the procedures described in the prose reformulation. The box on the left side of Kate's diagram contains a summary of her core state, derived from early experience. From this box emerge three main loops which correspond to the main coping or problem procedures described in the reformulation. Each of these loops converge on the right to generate suicidal thoughts and feelings, which both evoke powerful reverberations of, and reinforce the core state feelings, from which the problem procedures originally derived.

Active treatment: sessions 6–16

At the fifth session the final version of the reformulation was read out; after discussion it was agreed without further change. This marked the transition from the assessment phase to the active treatment phase of therapy. The aim from now on was to increase Kate's understanding of her problem procedures and their

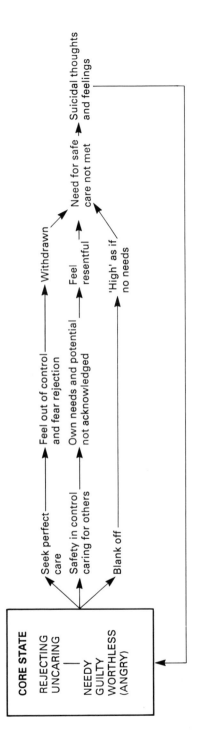

Figure 3.1 Sequential diagram

contribution to what she felt to be her central problem, her lack of a sense of self, and also to help her to recognize the operation of these procedures in different settings, including the transference, and to encourage her to try out alternative procedures, described as aims on the rating sheet.

By focusing on the dilemmas involving relationships and placation, Kate was able to modify her placatory, approval-seeking behaviour and assert her own needs and feelings more easily. For the first time in her life she began to ask for help and support from her friends and family. This process was facilitated by understanding how her feelings of unworthiness maintained these procedures. She reduced her unrealistic expectations of her relationships with men so that she was more open to receiving the care and affection they were prepared to offer. The relationship with her therapist provided her with an experience of a relationship in which she was neither the controlling care-giver nor the idealizing seeker of perfect care, but which contained mutuality, in the sense of shared discussion and working things out together. In this way was demonstrated a new model for close relationships, in which Kate could both acknowledge painful limitations and make use of the care available.

An important part of Kate's therapy was the treatment of her unresolved grief reaction to her brother's death. This was achieved through focusing on her procedure of blanking off. After reformulation she began to realize that she blanked off not just from painful events and feelings but in many other situations as well and she related this to her frequent lapses of memory. This made her feel as if whole areas of herself, her past and her experience were inaccessible; 'it's all behind a closed door'. Through self-monitoring, she became aware of entering a blanked-off state, and could sometimes bring it to an end. Towards the end of therapy she could recognize when she was blanked off within a session. In her eighth session, after a difficult Christmas week during which Kate had again felt depressed, suicidal and blank, she burst into tears saying that she wanted to say 'goodbye' to her brother Paul. She described the events surrounding his death and her guilt at not having been sufficiently aware of his feelings. The therapist suggested that Kate write a 'goodbye letter' to Paul, and she brought this to the next session. In the letter she described not only her grief and sense of loss at his death but also her determination that she should live her life despite his death. The writing of this letter marked a turning point in the therapy, in that from then on Kate appeared less blanked off and more in touch with her feelings. She also experienced glimpses of 'being herself' when she was aware of being less restrained by feelings of worthlessness and fears of others' disapproval or rejection so that she felt more able to do what she wanted and to 'feel good' about it.

The ensuing improvement from this time, in both symptoms and problem procedures, was reflected in a marked upturn in her ratings of her TPs and TPPs between sessions 10 and 12. During this period she was also able to discuss her feelings about her recent illness, which she had experienced on one level as a punishment for what she saw as her failure to be available for her brother when he needed help. Kate was unsure of what to do with her goodbye letter to Paul, and it was suggested that she should use it in some kind of ritualized farewell which might represent a symbolic 'letting go' of her grief for him. Towards the end of therapy she decided to take the letter to Paul's grave where she read it out 'to him', and then tore it up before scattering it in the river near the grave-yard. Kate found this hard to do because it seemed very final, but she felt it was an important step towards accepting the reality of her loss.

Ending therapy

Kate's past experiences of poorly managed loss contributed to the anxiety about ending therapy which emerged in the twelfth session. In subsequent sessions there was a recurrence of blanking off in various forms, for example forgetting to come for a session, losing her reformulation and rating sheets, and a return to her vague and cut-off manner, reminiscent of the assessment phase of therapy. In addition she experienced a return of feelings of worthlessness, feeling that she did not deserve any more therapy. Also at this time she experienced a short-lived 'high' mood, during which she disclaimed her need for therapy and ended a supportive long-standing male friendship which she had resumed during therapy. In her final session, however, she was able to express appropriate feelings of sadness, realistic anxieties about the future, and gratitude for the changes made during therapy. Her TP and TPP ratings indicated improvement of between 60 and 90 per cent. In the final session the therapist and patient exchanged and discussed their respective goodbye letters. These read as follows:

Therapist's goodbye letter

During the last four months we have looked at how you grew up with a sense of lacking the safe, warm, supportive care you needed. Your father was absent much of the time, or distant, and your mother was not always as emotionally available as you needed her to be. This has left you feeling a lack of sense of self, and as if unworthy of being a person, and also perhaps, unworthy of having a life of your own. We have related this central issue to your feeling directionless and out of control, especially in relation to feelings and 'mood swings'. These swings have been intensified by loss of or separation from 'valued' people, and also by your recent illness, which you felt might have been related in some way to Paul's death, as if you deserved punishment for not having looked after him well enough.

We have looked at three main ways in which you have coped with painful feelings to do with your sense of unworthiness and loss of valued others:

1 Blanking off
2 Looking after others and seeking their approval
3 Looking for perfect care in 'permanent' relationships.

We have discussed how these three ways of coping have both distanced you from painful feelings and diminished rather than enhanced your sense of self. We have looked at ways of doing things differently.

1 Using your diary, you have identified triggers for mood swings which, in the past, were frightening (because poorly understood). Your depressive moods are often the result of feared or anticipated rejection from

others. Sometimes you misconstrue others' reactions as rejection when in fact they aren't. Your 'high' moods may be related to idealizing hopes of relationships (perfect care) or may represent a denial of your needs – as if feeling so good that you don't need anyone.

2 Using your diary and self-observation you have recognized the extent and effects of blanking off, in terms of lapses of memory and not being fully in touch with your feelings and thus yourself.

3 You have found the courage to face up to painful feelings, particularly those to do with Paul's death. You have been able to mourn his loss more fully than before and have been able to say 'goodbye' to him. This has allowed you to feel both closer to him and also that, despite his death, you are entitled to a life for yourself.

As a result of being less blanked off, less placatory, and more realistic in your expectations of others, you have experienced two important changes during therapy:

1 You have begun to feel a stronger sense of self, so that you are more confident about who you are and what you want.

2 You feel more able to express yourself with others and feel accepted for what you are.

The experience of therapy has shown you a way of achieving 'safe closeness' with me, based on sharing of feelings, ideas and observations, discussion and working things out together. Ending our regular sessions may feel as if this is another rejection or abandonment. This may make you fearful of losing the gains you have made, especially the sense of a more coherent and definite self you have got in touch with.

I feel confident that you will be able to take away and hold on to and develop further the changes you have made during therapy, and that as a result, you will be able to live life more fully in the future.

Kate's goodbye letter

Coming into therapy was like shedding a skin and exposing raw emotions and painful memories. Something I was very frightened of. I saw therapy as my LAST chance and only hope, as at the time I started I was experiencing very morbid suicidal thoughts as the only means of ending my constant depressions, particularly that current one which was the worst ever. Therefore my expectations of you and therapy were huge. With your help I realized that certain problems have been crippling my capacity for happiness for years. My extreme low sense of self-esteem and reasons for it seem to me to be the main issue we worked on. In recognizing 'why' through therapy, I have begun to allow myself choices in behaviour . . . I am now more in touch with painful feelings and am experimenting with how to deal with them safely (for me).

Through therapy I have got in touch with an autonomous identity independent of any sense of self I may have when I am involved with a man.

This admittedly is not a very strong feeling, but I recognize it is there and that I am beginning to get in touch with ME. The risk of slipping back into other routines is great, but I know now what my needs are and can ask for them to be met from friends and family, not just in intimate relationships with men. Being rejected and fear of disapproval has been another major issue. My comment on this is 'I have stopped running away'. I'm beginning to face situations more assertively and in a more adult fashion and feel less fearful in general of other people's reactions. I now try to rationalize and intellectualize their and my behaviour, instead of feeling rejected, paranoid, worthless and anxious, resulting in black depressions.

Saying goodbye is always difficult and sad, though sometimes a relief. I've felt relieved a few times recently when saying goodbye. I'm (a) relieved and (b) fearful of saying goodbye to you: (a) because of the nature of therapy and disclosure of painful and sometimes uncomfortable thoughts; (b) because not having your support and guidance makes me feel slightly vulnerable.

Thank you for working with me and for helping me to turn round and face me and my problems; having been given the opportunity to do so makes me feel humbly grateful, as I had little faith four months ago in myself or anyone. That is now restored and I am looking forward to a new beginning that will come from this ending.

Follow-up

When Kate was seen for follow-up by her therapist ten weeks after the end of therapy, she reported that she had been feeling very well, not depressed, and that her mood had been stable, somewhere in between 'neutral' and 'high'. She had been aware of the risk of going 'too high', in response to feeling liked or appreciated by friends, but had resisted this and avoided idealizing other people or forming unrealistic expectations of them. She described how for the first time in her life she felt free of being dominated by the need for a relationship with a man, and no longer felt a 'sense of void' without such a relationship. She appreciated the fact that she had more time to enjoy with her friends, with whom she now felt she was being more selective, seeing those whom she wanted to see rather than those she felt she ought to be seeing. She felt that she had been generally more in touch with her feelings and not blanked off and had noticed an improvement in her memory, so that she could remember music she had heard and books she had read.

It seemed, therefore, that the changes described by Kate, which had begun during therapy, had continued subsequently. This was reflected in further improvements in her ratings on the Target Problems and Target Problem Procedures at follow-up, confirming the therapist's impression that Kate had indeed gained a fuller and more effective sense of herself.

Appendix: The Psychotherapy File

An aid to understanding ourselves better

We have all had just one life and what has happened to us, and the sense we made of this, colours the way we see ourselves and others. How we see things is for us, how things are, and how we go about our lives seems 'obvious and right'. Sometimes, however, our familiar ways of understanding and acting can be the source of our problems. In order to solve our difficulties we may need to learn to recognize how what we do makes things worse. We can then work out new ways of thinking and acting.

These pages are intended to suggest ways of thinking about what you do; recognizing your particular patterns is the first step in learning to gain more control and happiness in your life.

Keeping a diary of your moods and behaviour

Symptoms, bad moods, unwanted thoughts or behaviours that come and go can be better understood and controlled if you learn to notice when they happen and what starts them off.

If you have a particular symptom or problem of this sort, start keeping a diary. The diary should be focused on a particular mood, symptom or behaviour, and should be kept every day if possible. Try to record this sequence:

1 How you were feeling about yourself and others and the world before the problem came on.
2 Any external event, or any thought or image in your mind that was going on when the trouble started, or what seemed to start it off.
3 Once the trouble started, what were the thoughts, images or feelings you experienced?

By noticing and writing down in this way what you do and think at these times, you will learn to recognize and eventually have more control over how you act and think at the time. It is often the case that bad feelings like resentment, depression or physical symptoms are the result of ways of thinking and acting that are unhelpful. Diary keeping in this way gives you the chance to learn better ways of dealing with things.

It is helpful to keep a daily record for 1–2 weeks, then to discuss what you have recorded with your therapist or counsellor.

Patterns that do not work, but are hard to break

There are certain ways of thinking and acting that do not achieve what we want, but which are hard to change. Read through the list that follows and mark how far you think they apply to you.

Applies strongly + + Applies + Does not apply ○

Traps

Traps are things we cannot escape from. Certain kinds of thinking and acting result in a 'vicious circle' when, however hard we try, things seem to get worse instead of better. Trying to deal with feeling bad about ourselves, we think and act in ways that tend to confirm our badness.

Aggression and assertion   People often get trapped in these ways because they mix up aggression and assertion. The fear of hurting others can make us keep our feelings inside, or put our own needs aside. This tends to allow other people to ignore or abuse us in various ways, which then leads to our feeling, or being, childishly angry. When we see ourselves behaving like this, it confirms our belief that we shouldn't be aggressive. Mostly, being assertive – asking for our rights – is perfectly acceptable. People who do not respect our rights as human beings must either be stood up to or avoided.

Examples of traps

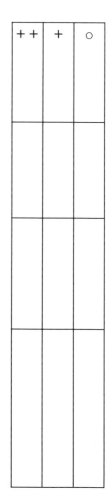

1 **AVOIDANCE**: We feel *ineffective and anxious* about certain situations, such as crowded streets, open spaces, social gatherings. We try to go back into these situations, but feel even more anxiety. Avoiding them makes us feel better, so we stop trying. However, by constantly avoiding situations our lives are limited and we come to feel increasingly *ineffective and anxious*.

2 **DEPRESSED THINKING**: Feeling *depressed*, we are sure we will manage a task or social situation badly. Being depressed, we are probably not as effective as we can be, and the depression leads us to exaggerate how badly we handled things. This makes us feel more *depressed* about ourselves.

3 **SOCIAL ISOLATION**: Feeling *under-confident* about ourselves and anxious not to upset others, we worry that others will find us boring or stupid, so we don't look at people or respond to friendliness. People then see us as unfriendly, so we become more isolated from which we are convinced we are boring and stupid – and become more *under-confident*.

4 **TRYING TO PLEASE**: Feeling *uncertain about ourselves* and anxious not to upset others, we try to please people by doing what they seem to want. As a result (1) we end up being taken advantage of by others, which makes us angry, depressed or guilty, from which our uncertainty about ourselves is confirmed; or (2) sometimes we feel out of control because of the need to please, and start hiding away, putting things off, letting people down, which makes other people angry with us and increases our uncertainty.

Dilemmas (false choices and narrow options)

We often act as we do, even when we are not completely happy with it, because the only other ways we can imagine seem as bad or even worse. These false choices can be described as dilemmas, or either/or options. We often don't realize that we see things like this, but we act *as if* these were the only possible choices.

Do you act as if any of the following false choices rule your life? Recognizing them is the first step to changing them.

Choices about yourself: I act as if:

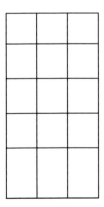

	+ +	+	○
1 Either I keep feelings bottled up or I risk being rejected, hurting others, or making a mess.			
2 Either I feel I spoil myself and am greedy or I deny myself things and punish myself and feel miserable.			
3 If I try to be perfect, I feel depressed and angry; if I don't try to be perfect, I feel guilty, angry and dissatisfied.			
4 If I must, then I won't (other people's wishes, or even my own, feel too demanding, so I constantly put things off, avoid them etc.).			
5 If other people aren't expecting me to do things, look after them etc., then I feel anxious, lonely and out of control.			
6 If I get what I want, I feel childish and guilty; if I don't get what I want, I feel angry and depressed.			
7 Either I keep things (feelings, plans) in perfect order, or I fear a terrible mess.			

Choices about how we relate to others

Do you behave with others as if:

1 If I care about somebody, then I have to give in to them.

2 If I care about somebody, then they have to give in to me.

3 If I depend on someone, then they have to do what I want.

4 If I depend on someone, then I have to give in to them.

5 Either I'm involved with someone and likely to get hurt, or I don't get involved and stay in charge, but remain lonely.

	++	+	o

6 As a woman, I have to do what others want.

7 As a man, I can't have any feelings.

8 Either I stick up for myself and nobody likes me, or I give in and get put on by others and feel cross and hurt.

9 Either I'm a brute or a martyr (secretly blaming the other).

10 Either I look down on other people, or I feel they look down on me.

Snags

Snags are what is happening when we say 'I want to have a better life, or I want to change my behaviour but . . .'. Sometimes this comes from how we or our families thought about us when we were young; such as 'she was always the good child', or 'in our family we never . . .'. Sometimes the snags come from the important people in our lives not wanting us to change, or not able to cope with what our changing means to them. Often the resistance is more indirect, as when a parent, husband or wife becomes ill or depressed when we begin to get better.

In other cases, we seem to 'arrange' to avoid pleasure or success, or if they come, we have to pay in some way, by depression, or by spoiling things. Often this is because, as children, we came to feel guilty if things went well for us, or felt that we were envied for good luck or success. Sometimes we have come to feel responsible, unreasonably, for things that went wrong in the family, although we may not be aware that this is so. It is helpful to learn to recognize how this sort of pattern is stopping you getting on with your life, for only then can you learn to accept your right to a better life and begin to claim it.

You may get quite depressed when you begin to realize how often you stop your life being happier and more fulfilled. It is important to remember that it's not being stupid or bad, but rather that:

(a) we do these things because this is the way we learned to manage best when we were younger;
(b) we don't have to keep on doing them now we are learning to recognize them;
(c) by changing our behaviour, we can learn to control not only our own behaviour, but we also change the way other people behave to us;
(d) although it may seem that others resist the changes we want for ourselves (for example, our parents, or our partners), we often under-estimate them; if we are firm about our right to change, those who care for us will usually accept the change.

Do you recognize that you feel limited in your life:

	++	+	o

(a) for fear of the response of others

(b) by something inside yourself.

Difficult and unstable states of mind

Indicate which, if any, of the following apply to you:

	+ +	+	o
1 How I feel about myself and others can be unstable; I can switch from one state of mind to a completely different one.			
2 Some states may be accompanied by intense, extreme and uncontrollable emotions.			
3 Others by emotional blankness, feeling unreal, or feeling muddled.			
4 Some states are accompanied by feeling intensely guilty or angry with myself, wanting to hurt myself,			
5 or by feeling that others can't be trusted, are going to let me down, or hurt me,			
6 or by being unreasonably angry or hurtful to others.			
7 Sometimes the only way to cope with some confusing feelings is to blank them off and feel emotionally distant from others.			

References

Brockman, B., Poynton, A., Ryle, A. and Watson, J.P. (1987) Effectiveness of time-limited therapy carried out by trainees: comparison of two methods, *British Journal of Psychiatry* 151: 602–10.

Horowitz, M.J. (1979) *States of Mind: Analysis of Change in Psychotherapy*, New York: Plenum Press.

Kelly, G.A. (1955) *The Psychology of Personal Constructs*, New York: Norton.

Miller, G.A., Galanter, E. and Pribram, F.H. (1960) *Plans and the Structure of Behavior*, New York: Holt.

Neisser, U. (1967) *Cognitive Psychology*, New York: Appleton.

Ryle, A. (1990) *Cognitive-analytic Therapy: Active Participation in Change: A New Integration in Brief Psychotherapy*, Chichester and New York: John Wiley.

Wertsch, J.V. (1985) *Vygotsky and the Social Formation of Mind*, Cambridge, Mass. and London: Harvard University Press.

4

Multimodal therapy

ROY ESKAPA

Theory

Origins

Arnold A. Lazarus was the first to introduce the terms 'behaviour therapy' and 'behaviour therapist' into the scientific and professional literature (Lazarus 1958). Nevertheless, due to the overwhelming limitations of behaviour therapy and mounting evidence of unacceptably high relapse rates for orthodox or 'narrow band' behaviour therapy, Lazarus extended and refined the field, developing a more innovative and flexible broad-spectrum or what is now termed 'cognitive-behavioural' therapy. The position was detailed with the publication of Lazarus's (1971) exceedingly well-received book *Behavior Therapy and Beyond.*

Broad-spectrum behaviour therapy was a vast improvement on the traditionally oriented 'narrow-band' behaviour therapy. However, in the style of the scientist that he is, Lazarus reconsidered his position because the data showed that 'broad-spectrum' behaviour therapy (or cognitive-behaviour therapy) was still far too incomplete – behaviour therapy was unimodal and cognitive-behaviour therapy was essentially bimodal. These considerations then gave rise to *multimodal* therapy which is a systematic and innovative approach to therapy where clients are assessed and treated across seven modalities: *B*ehaviour; *A*ffect; *S*ensation; *I*magery; *I*nterpersonal; and *D*rugs/Biology. (BASIC ID is a convenient acronym for these modalities.) Over the course of the last 20 years, multimodal therapy was pioneered and refined by Lazarus in the United States. Lazarus (1989a) writes that there is a strong overlap between William James's (1890) view of functionalism and multimodal eclecticism, and that 'direct precursors (of multimodal therapy) date back to the 1950s, when (he) was a student at the University of the Witwatersrand in Johannesburg, South Africa where, although the psychotherapeutic climate was predominantly Freudian and Rogerian' (Lazarus 1989a: 510), he was nevertheless exposed to the works of Salter (1949, 1953), and observed Wolpe's early behavioural methods.

While still in South Africa, Lazarus's clinical observations led him to conclude that *performance-based* methods were invariably more effective than cognitive
or verbal interventions when used exclusively. While the psychotherapy establishment viewed behaviour as the expression of deep, intangible and complicated intrapsychic processes, neobehaviourists emphasized the observability and
measurability of behaviour as paramount. It became patently apparent that
clients could develop deep insight into their problems *without* terminating self-
destructive behaviour.

> Yet, after *behaving* [my italics] differently, it was evident that people were
> inclined to feel and think differently . . . The observation and quantifica-
> tion of significant actions became firmly established as a crucial starting
> point for effective clinical intervention. Coupled with the search for relevant
> antecedents as well as maintaining variables, the focus on maladaptive
> behaviours and their remediation resulted in positive outcomes.
>
> (Lazarus 1989a: 511)

However, it was precisely as a result of high relapse rates in clients who were
treated with behavioural methods *alone* that techniques *beyond* behaviour therapy
were invoked. For instance, even in the early days of behaviour therapy, when
Lazarus (1956) began treatment of a serious alcoholic, he employed a *broad-based
educational approach* involving conventional medicine, techniques from behaviour
modification (aversion therapy, anxiety relief conditioning, assertiveness training, desensitization, imagery, behaviour rehearsal), hypnosis and family therapy.
Once again, the roots of this eclectic attitude are found in Lazarus's early
writings. As far back as 1956 he stated that

> the emphasis in psychological rehabilitation must be on a *synthesis* which
> would embrace a diverse range of effective therapeutic techniques, as well
> as innumerable adjunctive measures, to form part of a wide and all-
> embracing re-educative programme.
>
> (Lazarus 1956: 707–10)

Training and status of multimodal therapy

British and European students are, as a rule, generally not as aware of multimodal therapy as their counterparts in the United States. To familiarize British
and European readers with the status of multimodal therapy in the United States,
it should be emphasized that multimodal therapy has been rated by American
clinical practitioners as among the most influential forms of therapy (Smith
1982). Furthermore, large-scale surveys of clinicians revealed that Arnold
Lazarus (together with Freud, Rogers, Ellis and Wolpe) is considered among the
top five most influential therapists in America, and his text *Multimodal Behavior
Therapy* (Lazarus 1976) was, after Garfield and Bergin's (1978) *Handbook of
Behavioral Psychotherapy and Change*, the most influential textbook of psychotherapy
at the beginning of the 1980s (Smith 1982: 808).

Arnold Lazarus holds the chair of Distinguished Professor at the Graduate School of Applied and Professional Psychology, Rutgers University, New Jersey. He has received numerous awards for his service to both academic and applied psychology, has contributed over 150 journal articles and is the author of several texts in the field. Training in multimodal therapy has been conducted at Rutgers since 1972 and former students teach at various universities around the United States. In Holland, Kwee and his associates have carried out considerable research into multimodal methods and have applied them clinically (e.g. Kwee and Roborgh 1987; Kwee 1990).

Despite all of this, Lazarus himself remains opposed to all attempts at commercializing his approach. He has deliberately avoided becoming a charismatic guru – in my opinion, something he could easily have done over the course of the years.

Technical and systematic eclecticism

Multimodal Therapy is a *systematic* and *practical* approach to tackling psychological problems. It emphasizes a personalistic and individualistic outlook. Consequently, it consciously avoids making patients or clients conform to treatment. In fact, imposing a delimited treatment on a client would be considered not only anti-humanistic and counterproductive, but essentially unethical. Instead, treatment is tailored to individual needs, demanding 'a diligent scrutiny for individual exceptions to general rules and principles' where the 'search is for appropriate interventions for each person' (Lazarus 1989a: 503). This is crucial to the philosophical outlook of multimodal therapy and should be underscored at the outset.

Lazarus describes multimodal therapy as a systematic or technically eclectic approach. This position directly contrasts with theoretical eclecticism (see Thorne 1973; and Norcross 1986) which refers to the unsystematic, haphazard use of many epistemologically incompatible notions. Instead, technically eclectic therapists use procedures of varied origin – without feeling obliged to accept the theories that spawned these particular procedures. For instance, a multimodal therapist might, as part of a wide armamentarium of techniques, prescribe a form of meditation from Eastern yogic tradition to enhance relaxation in a patient suffering from 'stress'. However, he or she might not necessarily subscribe to the philosophy behind the meditation technique. In the same vein, a multimodal therapist might employ techniques such as 'free association' or 'paradoxical intention' without accepting classical psychodynamic or group systems explanations as to the relationship between theory and outcome. The reason for this stance is that multimodal therapists endorse the scientific and the parsimonious as opposed to the non-scientific and the confusingly complex. Above all, multimodal therapists advocate being as practical as possible. They recognize both the complexities and the practicalities inherent in working with human problems. Although 'humanistic' in outlook, multimodal therapists are aware that *compassion* is not sufficient *in itself* as a complete and effective agent of change.

At the same time it is important to note that technical eclecticism is systematic. Norcross (1986) describes technical eclecticism as resulting from years of solid clinical and theoretical work. Unlike unsystematic eclecticism[1] it does not imply an atheoretical orientation. Numerous practitioners and students of psychotherapy have observed, often with trepidation, how bewildering, complex and disorganized the field of psychotherapy can be. Norcross also described the astonishing, even alarming, growth in the number of psychotherapeutic approaches available: in 1959 there were about 36 defined systems of psychotherapy; by 1976 there were over 130 organized approaches to therapy, each one claiming to be more original than the next. This almost arithmetic proliferation of psychotherapy continued, so that by 1980 Herinck's (1980) *The Psychotherapy Handbook* outlined 250 forms of psychotherapy.

In view of the foregoing, it should be stressed at the outset of this chapter that multimodal therapy is philosophically opposed to the irresponsible and glib 'theoretically eclectic' position (see Thorne 1973) 'I use whatever technique feels best at the time'. This would be considered confusing and unprofessional at best. By contrast, multimodal therapists are *systematically eclectic* –'they base their endeavors on data from the threefold impact of patient qualities, clinical skills, and specific techniques' (Lazarus 1990: 36). By the same token, the philosophical position of multimodal therapy is at odds with the newer theories of integration.

Multimodal perspectives on integration

According to Lazarus (1989a) the psychotherapy integration movement of the 1980s arose out of the frustration with the virtual uncontrolled proliferation of various psychotherapeutic schools. The existence of several hundred identifiable 'schools' of psychotherapy resulted in much confusion and ideological splitting within the field. The ideological battlefield became such that the Freudian and post-Freudian era was characterized by extremists who created their own inner circles or cults and advocated their methods as the only way. Further, many originators of 'new therapies' were said to have become Messianic, doctrinaire and dogmatic leaders who spawned adoring devotees and took poorly to outside criticism (Lazarus 1991).

The Society for the Exploration of Psychotherapy Integration (SEPI) was founded in North America in 1983, essentially to help cope with the increasingly toxic divisions in the psychotherapy and counselling arena. The idea behind SEPI was to help reduce the ideological strife and to emphasize convergence, similarity or *integration* among therapies. Alas, from a multimodal perspective, this cannot be condoned.

One of the main reasons why integration does not fit in with the multimodal perspective is that it endeavours to marry diverse therapy techniques and personality theories from fundamentally incompatible persuasions. For instance, from a multimodal perspective, it does not make sense to combine family systems theory with Gestalt theory, nor does it make sense to amalgamate psychodynamic theory with learning theory. While there may be several similarities or commonalities between various systems of therapy, there may also be *far greater differences*. Arnold Lazarus is fond of illustrating the problem to his students by saying,

Imagine two identical glasses in front of you. One is filled with water, the other vodka. From a distance, you cannot tell the difference. Obviously there are similarities between them. But there are also *fundamental* differences.

Indeed, both substances might be fluids, transparent, and wet to the touch. But they have different specific gravities, molecular structures and densities. One is flammable and the other puts out fire. One is a powerful drug and the other purifying, and so on. Thus, while there might be similarities between say, Kohut's analytic learning theory and Bandura's social learning theory, there are unique and insurmountable incompatibilities. The differences are so vast, in fact, that it is like trying to use a computer program designed for an IBM machine on a Macintosh computer – impossible because the operating systems (languages) are fundamentally different. Freud does not blend with Adler who does not mix with Jung, who is fundamentally at odds with Perls, whose theory and language is not compatible with Skinner's, and so on.

A multimodal therapist using the 'empty chair' technique does so in an entirely different vein from Gestalt therapists (Yontef and Simkin 1989). From a multimodal perspective, the 'empty chair' technique is seen as a variant of role-playing and behaviour rehearsal, while from a Gestalt therapy perspective, the 'empty chair' technique is a way of 'working through' existential angst, of becoming 'authentic' and cutting through 'conventional thought that obscures or avoids acknowledging how the world is' (Yontef and Simkin 1989: 324). Thus, it is clear that as we begin to scratch the surface there are more differences than similarities between the two approaches.

The problem with attempts at integration is that we need fewer theories and more facts. Despite purist objections that all observations are 'theory laden' (Steven Herman, personal communication, 1990), multimodalists are concerned more with *observations* than with theories. For instance, patients are often observed to relate to others in the present in much the same way as they did towards significant others in the past. Psychoanalytic theory accounts for this observation in terms of 'transference' – a desire to rekindle repressed, unconscious infantile fantasies from the past. Behavioural theory, on the other hand, would tend to account for such phenomena in terms of 'response and stimulus generalization'. The point is that there is no common language between the different theoretical systems, and therefore, from a multimodal therapy perspective, attempts at integration prevent meaningful communication, are futile and are best avoided.

Practice

Since 'the effects of psychotherapy . . . is always the study of the effectiveness of techniques' (London 1964), multimodal therapy endorses a 'technical eclecticism' which has been described as the use of different techniques within a preferred theory (Norcross 1986). Multimodal therapists use a range of methods from many sources recognizing that 'methods and techniques may be effective for reasons other than those their originators propound' (Lazarus 1981: 40). While non-conscious processes and defensive reactions are seen to play an important role in human functioning, they are not confused with reified psychodynamic ideas of 'the unconscious', which imply 'topographical boundaries, separate divisions, putative complexes, and intrapsychic functions . . . tied into an elaborate mosaic of untenable state, stage, and trait theories of personality development' (Lazarus 1981: 37).

Multimodalists, for example, would view 'defensive reactions' more directly and simply, without resorting to complicated neo-Freudian and psychodynamic theories. These invariably account for events in complex terms of intrapsychic hydraulics where *the* 'super-ego' suppresses *the* 'id' as a result of a 'phallic introject', 'displacement', 'repression', 'denial' or 'Oedipus' and 'Electra' complexes. Rather, from a multimodal perspective, individuals are acknowledged to misattribute feelings to others (projection), engage in cognitive dissonance, fool themselves, mislabel affective processes, and so on. For instance, when a client arrives late for a therapy session multimodal therapists do not assume that the tardiness is a 'defence' related to 'projection' or transference. *All possibilities are entertained by the therapist.* Thus, it may be concluded that the patient is late for one of a number of reasons: he or she may, for instance, be avoiding a confrontation *or* difficult period of therapy, *or* the train actually may have been delayed – or it may have been a combination of both. By analogy, multimodal therapy would endorse Common Law where the individual is presumed innocent until proven otherwise – as opposed to more orthodox, traditional psychotherapeutic creeds in which Napoleonic Code is assumed – where guilt is presumed and innocence has to be proven.

Multimodal therapy aims 'to reduce psychological suffering and to promote personal growth as rapidly and as durably as possible' (Lazarus 1981: 13). Since human problems and their solutions are viewed as 'multileveled and multi layered', individuals are assessed across seven 'discrete but interactive modalities'. *Essentially, human beings are viewed as organisms who move, feel, sense, image, think/believe, and relate to one another* (Lazarus 1981). In addition, people share the common denominator of being biochemical/neurophysiological beings. Unique to multimodal therapy is the pervasive outlook that personality, for want of any cogent theory, is best described in terms of seven 'discrete yet interactive' modalities:

- Behaviour
- Affect
- Sensation
- Imagery
- Cognition
- Interpersonal Relationships
- Drugs/Biology (BASIC ID).

Change in any one modality is likely to affect functioning in other modalities. Individual personality is seen as the combined result of genetic diathesis, environmental learning and socio-educational histories. Environmental learning includes concepts from classical and operant conditioning (such as 'association', 'stimulus generalization', 'discrimination', 'higher-order conditioning', 'extinction', 'stimulus control', 'self-reinforcement' and 'schedules of reinforcement') as well as principles drawn from social learning theory (such as 'modelling', 'identification', 'imitation', 'observation' and 'vicarious learning').

In addition to acknowledging the importance of the interplay between genetic endowment (nature) and social learning (nurture), the multimodal theoretical position makes use of the concept of *thresholds* (Lazarus 1989a). People are acknowledged to have different 'constitutions' or thresholds that influence personality. Different autonomic thresholds exist for pain, stress tolerance, and tolerance of stimuli in the form of light, sound, and touch. Someone who cannot tolerate or is very easily disturbed by loud noise will have a different predisposition or 'personality' from the person for whom loud noise presents little irritation.

While 'trait theory' is not highly regarded from a multimodal perspective, Lazarus says that people tend to prefer some of the BASIC ID modalities to others. People are said to be 'sensory reactors' or 'cognitive reactors' or 'imagery reactors'. In other words, if someone values the cognitive modality, they are more likely to respond to the world in an 'intellectual' or cognitive manner. Imagery reactors are likely to be right-hemispheric dominant, whereas cognitive reactors are liable to be left-hemispheric dominant. One way of getting at an individual's BASIC ID is to construct a 'Structural Profile' (Table 4.1) (Ferrise 1978) of the person in question. These are different from the 'Modality Profiles' that describe problems and their treatments across the BASIC ID (see Lazarus 1981: 68–72).

Structural profiles are used both diagnostically and therapeutically. For instance, in couples therapy it is often useful to have partners complete structural profiles of how they see themselves as well as how they *think* their partners

Table 4.1 Structural profile

The following are rated on a 6-point Likert scale which can be graphically plotted out in the form of a bar graph.

1 *Behaviour*: How active are you? How much of a doer are you? Do you like to keep busy?

2 *Affect*: How emotional are you? How deeply do you feel things? Are you inclined to impassioned or soul-stirring inner reactions?

3 *Sensation*: How much do you focus on the pleasures and pains derived from your senses? How tuned in are you to your bodily sensations – to sex, food, music, art?

4 *Imagery*: Do you have a vivid imagination? Do you engage in fantasy and daydreaming? Do you think in pictures?

5 *Cognition*: How much of a thinker are you? Do you like to analyse things, make plans, reason things through?

6 *Interpersonal*: How much of a social being are you? How important are other people to you? Do you gravitate to people? Do you desire intimacy with others?

7 *Drugs/Biology*: Are you healthy and health conscious? Do you take good care of your body and physical health? Do you avoid overeating, ingestion of unnecessary drugs, excessive amounts of alcohol and exposure to other substances that may be harmful?

see them. Enquiry into the meanings and significance of each rating often yields important insights for both partners.

The bulk of the accumulated data points to the undeniable impact of 'learning theories' on human behaviours, thoughts and feelings. Many phobias are 'classically conditioned' responses. For instance, a client said that he had been listening to a Beethoven sonata after surgery when he had been feeling nauseous. He subsequently felt sick every time he heard that sonata (Lazarus 1989a). Similar regard is accorded the role of operant conditioning, which refers to the fact that behaviour is often a function of its consequences. For instance, if a parent rewards a child by giving him or her a present contingent on coming 'first in class' the child will not be *intrinsically* motivated to do well. In fact, he is liable to start doing poorly when presents (rewards) for doing well are stopped. We may say that the child has been given the wrong message about motivation, but really what has happened is that he has been operantly conditioned to 'fail'. In addition to classical and operant conditioning, multimodalists have a high regard for social learning theory (Bandura 1977, 1986) from which observations clearly demonstrate that people learn by *observing models (modelling and vicarious processes)*. In other words, imitation, observation and identification with others in the environment are relevant to the development of personality. Thus, the implications for multimodal therapy are that techniques from 'behaviour therapy' play an important role in therapy. Multimodalists are therefore trained to apply techniques like relaxation, desensitization, flooding, behaviour rehearsal, imagery, hypnosis and so on.

Multimodal therapists are also acutely aware of the significance of cognitive factors in mediating the individual's perception of the environment, and the therapy draws on the work of cognitive theorists like Ellis (1962), Mahoney (1974) and Beck (1976). These perspectives imply that individuals often respond, not to the real environment, but to their private perceptions and evaluation of the environment. Cognitive factors addressed include

> the idiosyncratic use of language, semantics, problem-solving competencies, encoding and selective attention, expectancies, and goals and performance standards, as well as specific impact of beliefs, values, and attitudes on overt behavior.
>
> (Lazarus 1981: 3b)

Beck (1976), Ellis (1962, 1987), Lazarus and Fay (1977), Meichenbaum (1977) and a host of others have stressed that faulty cognitions or unrealistic, irrational thinking invariably impair functioning, precipitating among other things anxiety and depression. A significant, but by no means sole objective in multimodal therapy, therefore, is to attempt to disabuse the client of his or her misperceptions about the world. Misperceptions about the world include the following: categorical imperatives, perfectionism, overgeneralization, dichotomous thinking, catastrophizing, excessive approval-seeking and insisting on fairness. In line with the multimodal emphasis on *therapy-as-education*, this is accomplished first by educating the individual to recognize cognitive errors, and then by helping to replace self-defeating cognitions with more salubrious, self-actualizing attitudes and beliefs.

The similarities between multimodal therapy, cognitive behaviour therapy and rational-emotive therapy can be summarized in the following way: (1) Difficulties are assumed to arise from faulty and deficient social learning processes; (2) The therapist–client relationship is conceptualized in terms of the 'trainer–trainee' model rather than that of a (superior) doctor ministering to an (inferior) patient; (3) Therapeutic change is not viewed as automatic. It is considered as being accomplished through an active process of homework and performance-based assignments; and (4) Nosological or pathological psychiatric labels (e.g. DSM IIIR) are eschewed in favour of behavioural and operational descriptions.

While multimodal therapy acknowledges a special debt to the cognitive therapies, it departs from the purist and delimited nature of these therapies (e.g. Ellis's rational-emotive therapy or Beck's cognitive therapy). Instead of putting all patients through the same mill, it fully endorses Paul's (1967: 109) cogent enquiry, '*What* treatment, by *whom*, is most effective for *this* individual, with *that* particular problem, and under *which* set of circumstances?' Clients with seemingly similar classical diagnoses might receive entirely different psychotherapeutic interventions. Thus, while one alcoholic might be referred to Alcoholics Anonymous (AA) as part of his or her treatment, another might be warned away from such a group precisely because the AA group (and its attendant religio-social belief systems) for *that* individual at *that* time is personally and clinically contraindicated. The same might be said for numerous other interventions. The maxim 'One person's meat is another person's poison' is a concept that pervades clinical interventions throughout multimodal therapy. Other examples might include prescribing meditation and relaxation procedures for one patient, but not for another. While generally salubrious, relaxation procedures in some clients, albeit few, have produced serious, unwanted side-effects (Lazarus and Mayne 1989). Contrary to the *trimodal* or *biomodal* positions of some cognitive therapy practitioners, like Ellis or Beck, once a thorough *multimodal* assessment has been conducted for a particular 'depressed' patient, it may be concluded that he or she should *not* be exposed to a cognitive therapy to undo faulty thinking. Depending on the circumstance, it may prove wiser to employ family therapy (interpersonal modality), coupled with medication (biological modality) and relaxation procedures (sensory modality) as a first line of attack. The cognitive therapy may be employed at a later stage, if at all.

Multimodal therapy places strong emphasis on a thorough understanding of the person and his or her social environment. While assessment is a continuous process over the course of therapy, it is initiated through initial interviews and administration of the Multimodal Life History Questionnaire (LHQ). This instrument acts as a 'blueprint for therapy', enabling the clinician not only to gather an extensive social history of the client, but also to gather information across each modality. (The LHQ is reprinted in the appendix of *The Practice of Multimodal Therapy* (Lazarus 1989c).)

Since therapist–patient rapport is considered the 'soil' in which techniques will flourish, the multimodal approach encourages flexibility and versatility of the therapist. This is central to multimodal therapy, and cannot be understated. Thus, a multimodal therapist would tend to relate in a formal manner with a client who is offended by excessive warmth and empathy. Conversely, the situation may call for a person-centred stance where affective processes need clarification (after the work of Carl Rogers), while active modelling and social skills training may be required in cases of response deficits. In short, 'the therapist is called upon to treat the same client with tenderness and sympathy on some occasions, and with a tough-minded pragmatism on others' (Lazarus 1981: 62).

The *goodness of fit* between client and therapist (client expectancies, therapist–client matching and compatibility) is paramount. When fundamental incompatibility arises between therapist and client, or when a therapist is presented with problems outside an area of expertise, clients are judiciously referred to qualified professionals with whom it is felt they may be more compatible. However, when other treatment impasses occur, *second-order BASIC ID* assessments and/or *tracking* and *bridging* procedures (procedures distinctive to multimodal therapy) are conducted.

Second-order assessments are conducted when a problem requires magnification. Thus, antecedent and maintaining factors can be highlighted and effectively dealt with by re-evaluating a problem across each modality of the BASIC ID. For instance, a second-order modality profile revealed that the client described in the case below had fears of driving which were rooted, not only in irrational fears that other drivers would jeer at him on the road, but also in his close identification with his father who was also afraid of driving. (A second-order BASIC ID assessment is described in full below.)

Multimodal therapy is also distinguished from other therapies via its emphasis on 'tracking'. Tracking refers to an examination of the 'firing order' of the BASIC ID modalities. For instance, some clients experience distress by first thinking (cognition) of disaster. They subsequently dwell on negative images (imagery) which leads them to experience physiological stress (sensation) resulting in avoidance behaviour (behaviour). These clients appear to fit a C–I–S–B pattern (Cognition–Imagery–Sensation–Behaviour). Other clients may experience similar distress but generate it via entirely different 'firing orders'. Tracking is described in the case presented below.

In Multimodal Therapy, *bridging* is a 'procedure in which the therapist deliberately tunes into the client's preferred modality before branching off into other dimensions that seem likely to be more productive' (Lazarus 1989a: 505). Thus, in the case of an 'intellectualizer' who uses excessive rationalization or cognition to defend against confronting painful emotions, it is best to join the client in his or her preferred cognitive modality prior to dealing with cognitive content. The following exemplifies *bridging* in action:

> *Client*: I think that my daughter became schizophrenic when my mother died. The doctors are probably wrong in their diagnosis.
> *Therapist*: How did that make you feel?
> *Client*: I realize it may be both genetic and because of us. But we have only had one opinion, I mean there could be many explanations couldn't there?
> *Therapist*: [*Joining rather than opposing the client's cognitive inclinations*] I agree,

schizophrenia is often attributed to both biological and environmental factors. What else happened around the time of your mother's death?

Client: Well, there were the funeral arrangements and people and documents to attend to.

Therapist: When you think about all of this, do you have any physical sensations?

Client: What?

Therapist: When you think about all of the events that occurred around the time of your mother's death, and your daughter being diagnosed with schizophrenia, are you aware of any particular sensations in your body?

Client: [*Pausing for a full 30 seconds*] Well, come to think of it, I feel a bit nauseous.

Therapist: Can you focus your attention on the sensation of nausea for a moment? Try to concentrate on the sensations or feelings.

Client: It feels like my stomach is all tied up . . .

Therapist: Do you feel sensations in other areas?

Client: My head is aching slightly, I am afraid I am going to cry. [*Tearfully*] I broke down and fell apart for three whole days when my mother died, my world fell apart, I should never have done so. She [*the daughter*] became ill then, and started to see people with red faces and hear voices and tell us she hated us and that Granny was still alive.

While the therapist wanted to focus on affective areas at the outset, he first decided to go along with the client's 'intellectualizing' or cognitive preferences. By staying with the client in his or her preferred modality, the therapist was able to access some very painful and confusing emotions. 'Failure to tune into the clients presenting modality often leads to feelings of alienation – the client feels misunderstood or may conclude that the therapist does not speak his or her language' (Lazarus 1989a: 506). It is worth emphasizing that it is not unusual for clients to say they 'feel understood' or that they 'feel as though I have known you for a long time' after the deliberate use of *bridging*.

Multimodal theory and practice described above is now illustrated in the case of Roman, described below.

Case example

In terms of multimodal therapy, there is no such thing as a 'typical case'. Each client is special and presents a unique situation for treatment. The therapy has been employed by a wide range of practitioners in varying circumstances. For instance, multimodal therapy has been used with sexual offenders, substance abusers, family and marital therapy, the psychoses, a wide array of affective disorders, so-called neuroses, with children, and in hospital situations, to name but a few.

Nevertheless, for the purposes of this chapter, I have attempted to present, as closely as possible, a 'run-of-the-mill' case in the hope that it will illustrate how to proceed multimodally. Due to chapter constraints it is only possible to present a single case history. Since it is impossible to do justice to the multi-modal approach through the presentation of only one case, the interested reader is referred to *Multimodal Behavior Therapy* (Lazarus 1976), *The Practice of Multimodal Therapy* (Lazarus 1989c) and *A Casebook of Multimodal Therapy* (Lazarus 1985) for further case presentations.

Presenting situation

As a rule, multimodal therapists are trained to observe the basic mental status of the patient. Thus, when Roman came to see me, I conducted a rather basic mental status examination. Roman was a 26-year-old Caucasian man of average height and above-average weight. He was well dressed and groomed, co-operative, and appeared alert to time, place, and person. His speech was expressive and earnest, and although somewhat accented, was clearly intelligible. His affect appeared to be in the normal range and was appropriate to the content of discussion. If anything, he seemed to project an overly strong desire to please, giving the impression of a possible 'smiling depressive'. (He scored 12 on the Beck Depression Inventory, which reflects a mild mood disturbance.) Cognitively, his thought processes appeared to be logical and directed, and his memory was good. Delusional or hallucinatory activity was not evident, and he reported no suicidal ideation. However, he was anxious, and his thought content focused on his lack of self-confidence, procrastination, and generalized fear of the world. He was con-cerned about his chances of improving his life. His judgement seemed reasonably sound and his intelligence was estimated to be in the above-average to superior range.

Furthermore, in keeping with the multimodal *principle of parity* (Lazarus 1981), by the second session it was decided that we would relate with each other on a first-name basis. This outlook is predicated on the belief that human beings are all essentially equal to one another. Just as there are 'no superior human beings – not royalty, heads of state, religious leaders, heads of large corporations, famous actors, athletes, doctors, lawyers, or teachers' (Lazarus and Fay 1977: 88) so therapists are not superior to their clients or patients. I should point out that some of my patients refer to me as Dr Eskapa and, in the best interest of the therapy, I return the formality.

Roman was referred to me by his general practitioner. He had sought therapy after reading one or two self-help books and, during the first interview, he gave the impression of being somewhat aware of his problems but said that he did not know what to do about them. Despite his unhappiness and obvious anxiety, he seemed very eager to please. He complained of 'insecurity', a 'lack of con-fidence', 'excessive worrying', 'too much smoking and drinking', 'procrastina-tion', and 'terrible untidiness'. He also said that he was 'scared to death of the world', was 'too sensitive', and like his father, was 'too afraid to drive a car'. His problem began when he was in primary school and he blamed both his parents and teachers in the Polish educational system, which he described as 'sadistic' and 'bigoted'. In high school his problems worsened when a girl refused his overtures after her parents implied that he did not come from an acceptable family. On the Multimodal Life History Questionnaire (LHQ) Roman rated his problems as 'very severe'.

Multimodal assessment

The continuous process of assessment is initiated through initial interviews and administration of the Multimodal Life History Questionnaire. This is designed to enable client and clinician to agree on the most appropriate courses of action, which, if necessary, are modified during treatment.

The Modality Profile set out in Table 4.2 was constructed using information obtained from Roman's Multimodal Life History Questionnaire and over the first two interviews. (It should be stressed that all these interventions are not implemented at once. Rather, they serve as a 'blue-print' or guide for both therapist and client. Depending on circumstances, clients are often informed about available strategies.)

Roman's *strengths* included his presentation as a likeable, intelligent and eloquent young man who was serious about improving his life. He was punctual, courteous and optimistic about the outcome of therapy. In addition, he was trusting enough from the outset to establish a good working rapport, giving the impression that he was willing to work at change. He also described himself as a good cook and said that he basically liked people.

Roman's primary presenting problems centred around pervasive and persistent anxieties. Essentially, he was constantly worried, insecure and 'scared to death of the world'. From the perspective of DSM IIIR, his symptoms appeared to fit the pattern for a diagnosis of Generalized Anxiety Disorder in that he experienced motor tension (muscular tension, inability to relax), autonomic hyperactivity (excessive sweating, numbness) apprehensive expectation (worry, fear, rumination, gloomy outlook) and excessive vigilance (constantly 'on edge', hyper-attentiveness to the environment – particularly in social situations). While Roman exhibited some depressive features in the form of hopelessness and feelings of worthlessness, his symptoms did not appear to rise to the level of an actual affective disorder. Subsequent examination by a GP helped confirm a psychological versus physiological basis for Roman's anxiety (i.e. hyperthyroidism and other endocrinological problems were ruled out, as was cardiopathy).

Although multimodal therapists do not revere nosological diagnostic labels, it was noteworthy in Roman's case that his symptoms overlapped to some extent with those for Social Phobia (DSM IIIR:300.23) and Avoidant Personality (DSM IIIR:301.82).

Roman was very reclusive and it was a major ordeal for him to use public transportation over which he experienced anticipatory anxiety. Nevertheless, he appreciated that his fear that other passengers might somehow harm him was largely irrational. Further, Roman's 'fear of the world' and of failure in general kept him isolated – away from dating, driving and seeking employment.

The assessment also pointed to an enduring history of low self-esteem, an overly strong motivation to please and a hypersensitivity to social rejection, public humiliation and shame. For example, the ridicule Roman experienced both at school and at home was reflected by his unusually low self-esteem as

Table 4.2 Modality profile

Modality	Problem	Intervention
Behaviour	Phobic avoidance: reclusive, withdrawn, avoids 'standing up for myself', dating, driving and finding a job.	RET, assertiveness training, contingency contracting (risk-taking exercises) role-playing, attend driving school, organize a job search campaign.
	Procrastination and excessive untidiness at home.	Cognitive disputation of perfectionistic beliefs, organizational skills development, and contingency contracting (e.g. start arranging paperwork, and tidy room for ten minutes per day).
Affect	Anxiety: worry, rumination, apprehension, excessive fear of failure, rejection and criticism.	Bibliotherapy, cognitive restructuring, social skills training, cognitive restructuring (replace self-defeating with positive self-statements), assertiveness training, time projection.
	Isolation, loneliness, and pervasive insecurity.	Assertiveness training (risk-taking in approaching others). Actively seek work. Cognitive restructuring to overcome fear of rejection. Role-playing, join social groups.
	Fear of authority, being hurt and ridiculed.	Social skills training (e.g. role-playing, how to use paradox) feeling-identification (owning anger/rational disputation), bibliotherapy.
Sensation	Muscular tension, numbness fatigue, excessive sweating.	Differential relaxation (relaxation tapes), deep abdominal breathing exercises.
Imagery	Pictures self failing driving test, and being beaten.	Coping imagery exercises: picturing self passing test and imagine self travelling safely.
	Pictures self being ridiculed.	Step-up technique: (imagining the worst and then picturing survival), thought/image stopping, time projection.
Cognition	Many self-negating beliefs: (e.g. 'I will always be a loser, I will fail, never have a girl-friend, I am worthless' etc.).	Cognitive restructuring: read, write and recite positive self-statements daily. Bibliotherapy.
	Perfectionistic thinking: (e.g. 'I should never make mistakes'. 'If you don't try you can't fail').	Challenge absolutistic thinking (musts, oughts and shoulds). Bibliotherapy.

Table 4.2 *continued*

Modality	Problem	Intervention
	Generalized attitude that it is always important to please the whole world (e.g. 'It's terrible if I upset anyone').	Disputation of faulty cognitions and assignments to express needs and disagreements with others. Bibliotherapy.
Interpersonal relationships	Excessive approval-seeking.	Cognitive restructuring.
	Overly sensitive to perceived insults, criticism and put-downs by his small circle of friends (consisting almost exclusively of Turkish students in the US).	Teach, via role-playing and discussion, the use of paradox and humour to stand up to others. Risk-taking assignments.
	Social isolation. Over-dependent on and fearful of father.	Consider sharing an apartment, putting together a resumé and applying for jobs even if not 'perfect'. Join a youth group, and/or find social recreation.
Drugs/biology	Over-weight, eats junk food, smokes, drinks too much coffee and alcohol.	Consult physician. Self-control procedures: self-monitoring, imagery exercises, cognitive restructuring, stimulus control. AA if indicated.

an adult. He would not drive because he was afraid that if he made an error, other drivers would jeer at him. He would not apply for a job in case he was rejected, or worse still, in case the job was not acceptable in the eyes of significant others.

Treatment objectives

Since the Modality Profile revealed numerous areas requiring intervention, it was necessary to prioritize goals and to begin with tasks that have a greater chance of proving successful initially, thereby enhancing the therapist's credibility and the therapeutic alliance (Lazarus 1986). Soon after initial rapport was established, Roman agreed that the following areas were salient if he seriously wanted to improve the quality of his life:

1 start taking more care of basic health (e.g. losing weight, exercising, stop smoking and reduce caloric intake in general)
2 take specific steps to reduce anxiety (e.g. worry, rumination, fear of failure, rejection and criticism)
3 raise the overall level of Roman's self-efficacy (e.g. job searching, dating, level of organization, driving, assertiveness, reduce dysfunctional beliefs, and so on).

Treatment

The first few sessions involved carefully *listening* to Roman discuss his problems, building rapport and inspiring hope. Roman said that he would like to 'get to know' me as a 'friend' to whom he could 'tell everything'. His relief at being able to express his frustrations, anxieties and fears without being judged was evident. It appeared that we were well matched, and I felt that there was a good chance of helping him.

Sensing that Roman harboured notions that I would 'magically cure' him, I emphasized that we would have to work together as 'a team' if we wanted to get results. Roman's initial over-enthusiasm prompted him to request as many sessions per week as possible. In my opinion, this was both clinically unwarranted and far too costly (even though he was being seen at a reduced fee). We settled on two sessions per week at the outset. He approved of my suggestion that it would probably be most beneficial if we approached therapy as an educational experience. The idea was to communicate that responsibility for successful treatment lay with both of us. I emphasized that homework assignments, ranging from practising new skills to risk-taking and exercise, were designed to 'coach' him along. Roman diligently tape-recorded each session to listen to outside the office. He also kept a detailed journal of thoughts and feelings to share with me during therapy sessions.

Our initial treatment agreement included discussing techniques and various homework assignments that could be implemented with minimal anxiety. The object was to begin with assignments that would most likely result in success. For instance, Roman was in the process of applying for status as a permanent resident in Britain. This was a source of immense anxiety for him. His lawyers were unresponsive and uncooperative over the telephone, he was afraid of authority figures, and allowed himself to be intimidated by bureaucracy. Further, Roman's disorganization at home made it extremely difficult for him merely to find his immigration papers. The problem was dealt with in a typical multimodal fashion. Roman agreed to listen to standard relaxation tapes (sensation), to *begin* tidying his room for only ten minutes per day (behaviour). We also practised letter-writing and role-played telephone conversations with immigration lawyers (interpersonal). Coping imagery exercise assignments were also useful in having Roman visualize himself dealing effectively with both his immigration lawyers and the Polish consulate who had been uncooperative in extending his military service deadline (imagery). In addition, we used stress-inoculation (cognition) to help him become more positive. Roman agreed to use coping self-statements, which were stuck on his refrigerator, and to use the 'stop technique' whenever he found himself becoming overwhelmed or putting himself down. He would emphatically tell himself to 'STOP!' and then gently but firmly think thoughts like, 'One step at a time'; 'I'm not perfect'; 'I can succeed'; 'I'm just beginning to take charge of my life'; 'Well done'. These simple procedures coupled with his reading of *I Can If I Want To* (Lazarus and Fay 1977) produced immediate improvements. Roman was less anxious when calling his solicitor and viewed me as a sort of 'permission giver'. By the twelfth session, his level of hope was rising, reinforced by being assertive with his solicitor, tidying up his apartment, and starting to jog and diet.

While Roman's fear of public transportation was not overwhelming enough to prevent him from taking the bus to and from therapy and around his own locality, he was still reluctant to take the train into London. Roman was required to travel to London from the country to see solicitors and the Polish consul about permanent residence in the United Kingdom – a daunting proposition in his view. An analysis of the firing order regarding his fear of public transportation followed a Cognition–Imagery–Sensation–Affect–Behaviour (C–I–S–A–B) pattern. Roman would first *think* 'I'll be attacked by thugs'. He would then picture himself being beaten up and robbed. These cognitions and images resulted in muscular tension and sweating, which in turn resulted in fear and despair. Finally, Roman would avoid going to London by train.

An understanding of the sequence of events seemed to help Roman travel into the city with greater ease: he learned actively to dispute his catastrophic thoughts, calmly visualize the journey into London, and finally make several trips without incident. He was also able subsequently to visit friends living in Paris. Nevertheless, Roman's deeply ingrained lack of self-worth continued to hamper his life. During therapy, we explored how his childhood and adolescent experiences continued to influence him. Roman discovered that he was fulfilling his father's 'script' for failure: 'I can just hear him telling me how I am like my uncle who doesn't work, never got married, and is supported by the family even though he's over sixty.' Roman had come to believe these injunctions, and slowly began to realize that unless he *did* something, he really might fulfil his father's expectations.

Since performance-based interventions are often more effective than cognitive interventions alone (Wilson 1980), an obvious tactic was for Roman to obtain his driving licence. Apart from directly confronting his father's powerful prophesies of failure, it was also important that Roman begin to occupy his time constructively. Yet he was reluctant to have driving lessons. A second-order BASIC ID assessment revealed the following:

Behaviour:	I would have no excuse not to look for a job.
Affect:	I would feel anxious about having an accident.
Sensation:	I would freeze up on the road, be unable to react.
Imagery:	I can see myself being honked at on the road.
Cognition:	If I fail the test it will be terrible.
Interpersonal:	I would have to go out on dates.

Once Roman realized that having a driving licence did not mean that he would *have* to date, get a job, get tense on the road, and if he failed the test or if other drivers honked at him the world would not end, he agreed at least to try driving lessons. It turned out that he was fortunate enough to find a sympathetic teacher and his self-confidence was visibly improved when he passed the driving test three months later.

Nonetheless, Roman still avoided applying for a job. His thinking was absolutistic and distorted. He unrealistically believed that in order to win approval in the eyes of others he would have at least to be the manager of a five-star hotel. I introduced him to *Thoughts and Feelings* (McKay *et al.* 1981) and we began to work on improving awareness about distorted thinking, and the importance of taking risks. Roman recognized that he was an expert 'catastrophizer' and that his perfectionism was preventing him from trying to get a job. He saw that his expectations were unrealistic and that he was sabotaging his chances for employment. I pointed out the advantages of being employed, even if the job was not exactly perfect. He would have the opportunity of meeting new people, and that doing nothing all day was a 'soul-destroying' activity, which fuelled his lack of self-acceptance. At worst he would supplement his income and begin the process of financial emancipation from his father – whose frequent international calls from Poland reinforced feelings of guilt and worthlessness ('We sacrifice for you'; 'Why haven't you got a job?; 'Why haven't you got your work papers?'; 'Why aren't you married?').

Roman finally typed out his curriculum vitae, contacted friends and acquaintances to let them know he was serious about finding a job, and begin a campaign of looking for jobs advertised in newspapers. Roman's problems with his father were also 'worked through' using a technique called 'bridging' (described above). During therapy sessions, Roman and I would spontaneously act out conflicts with his father and others. I would re-enact some of these scenes with him, modelling more appropriate responses. For instance, we role-played conversations he might have with his father once he obtained the job. This 'anti-future shock' strategy proved useful when, as predicted, his father belittled the job Roman had secured working for a civil engineering business as a technician. Using imagery exercises both in the office and at home, Roman vividly pictured his childhood home, and was able to visualize the atmosphere between his parents and himself. At times these images were powerful enough to bring tears to his eyes. Roman was able to reconstruct a picture of his father as an 'infant in an adult's body': he was identifying his anger and declared that mature adults did not throw tantrums or deliberately take pleasure in inducing guilt in and physically hurting their children. We began the process of cognitively reframing his father as a 'frightened little boy' whose frustration was directed at Roman, and that all of this had originated in his father's own harsh childhood. Thus, instead of reacting in his usual over-sensitive manner, Roman learned how to humour his father and respond in a more mature fashion. He stated that he was 'forgiving my father for his own ignorance'.

Roman's over-sensitivity to perceived criticism impinged on his work and his social life. We began to explore how he had developed a pattern of allowing others to walk over him. Identifying feelings of anger and frustration was relatively new to him, and he began to acknowledge assertiveness as an important tool. I suggested that Roman obtain a copy of Fensterheim and Baer's (1975) *Don't Say Yes when You Want to Say No*. Through risk-taking assignments and role-playing, he learned to stand up for himself at work by saying 'no' to other employees who wanted him to do their work. We also role-played using humour and paradox to deal with perceived slights. Roman's Polish friends would call him and say, 'You have a job. Well why are you still taking money from your parents?' To this Roman learned to respond with, 'You're right. I'm just a worthless good for nothing who can't support myself'. The result was that everyone laughed and tension diffused. Roman was able to generalize these skills to other difficult interpersonal situations. He also started to play cards with his co-workers and began to joke around and socialize with them outside the plant. Six months into therapy Roman had improved throughout his BASIC ID, and continued to use the weekly sessions as a safe place to vent his frustrations and anxieties.

Roman decided to move out of his bed-sit to share a larger flat with a room-mate. He had also lost a great deal of weight (over 15 kg), stopped smoking completely, and was looking and feeling much better. He also met a young woman through a friend at work and began the first serious dating in his life. The two 'hit it off' superbly. Roman was no longer a virgin, and was reading Alex Comfort's (1973) *The Joy of Sex*. Roman's level of 'self-efficacy' soared. He said, 'If I can make it in London I can make it anywhere'. I was delighted at this good fortune, yet aware of the 'dangers' involving a possible 'flight into health' and of the ramifications of a potential rejection. I attempted to induce 'survival cognitions' (e.g. 'She is not my emotional oxygen', 'I might be disappointed and hurt if I am rejected, but I will survive without her', and so on) if Roman were to be rejected. Ironically these apprehensions proved unfounded. It was Roman who was considering seeing other women, and feeling a little guilty about it as well.

Roman's guilt was partly based on dichotomous thinking: either he should get married or get out of the relationship. In addition, his girl-friend was not Catholic – what would his family say? During therapy Roman came to see the futility of making the 'either/or' distorted thinking mistake, and realized that he could remain in the relationship without getting married. However, his conflict over the religious differences continued, and he looked to me for answers. By this stage of the therapy, I had been encouraging Roman to be less dependent on me and responded by saying that I was not in the position to provide 'the answer'. Nevertheless, questions were posed and some basic problem-solving ensued. Roman had almost completely missed the developmental stage of dating during adolescence. Shouldn't he keep things in perspective, be less rigid, and less intense about the whole thing? Growing up involved making mistakes and learning from errors. Even if she were Catholic, was he really prepared for marriage? What were the issues for and against inter-marriage? Did he really need family approval? After all, whose life was it anyway? Needless to say, the conflict was not totally resolved, but at least Roman was developing several cognitive strategies, and other tools that might enable him to deal with similar problems after therapy.

Two years after therapy, Roman appeared to have maintained the gains he had made during therapy. He had become the assistant manager of a large hotel, was able to drive his car to and from the city, and was contemplating marriage. While Roman and I had developed an excellent rapport, I feel certain that with a modicum of rapport, any multimodal therapist would have been as effective with Roman. Despite a recent controversial attempt by Paul Whitby in *The Psychologist* (1990) to show that therapists should be careful about attributing positive results to their own ministrations, in my opinion, there is no doubt that the technical and systematically eclectic nature of multimodal therapy – which *emphasized improvements across the BASIC ID* – proved highly conducive for Roman's overall well-being.

Note

1 In the end, this type of unsystematic eclecticism will do the same disservice to systematic and technical eclecticism as Hans Eysenck did profoundly, if ironically, to set
   back the reputation and application of behaviour therapy in the profession at large. The
   interested reader should refer to Arnold Lazarus's excellent chapter on the subject
   entitled 'On sterile paradigms and the realities of clinical practice: critical comments
   on Eysenck's contribution to behaviour therapy' (Modgil and Modgil 1985).

Acknowledgements

Sincere thanks to Ashley Conway, Windy Dryden, Steve Herman, Arnold Lazarus,
Mike Owen, Brian Roet and Paul Whitby for their valuable comments and help.

References

American Psychiatric Association (1987) *Diagnostic and Statistical Manual of Mental Disorders*,
   3rd ed – revised, Washington, DC.
Bandura, A. (1977) *Social Learning Theory*, Englewood Cliffs, NJ: Prentice-Hall.
—— (1986) *Social Foundations of Thought and Action*, Englewood Cliffs, NJ: Prentice-Hall.
Beck, A.T. (1976) *Cognitive Therapy and the Emotional Disorders*, New York: International
   Universities Press.
Comfort, A. (1973) *The Joy of Sex*, London: Quartet Books.
Corsini, R.J. and Wedding, D. (eds) (1989) *Current Psychotherapies*, Itasca, Ill.: F.E.
   Peacock, Inc.
Ellis, A. (1962) *Reason and Emotion in Psychotherapy*, New York: Lyle Stuart.
—— (1987) The impossibility of achieving consistently good mental health, *American
   Psychologist* 4: 364–75.
Fensterheim, H. and Baer, J.S. (1975) *Don't Say Yes when You Want to Say No*, New York:
   McKay.
Ferrise, F. (1978) Personal Communication to Arnold Lazarus, in A.A. Lazarus (1981)
   The Practice of Multimodal Therapy, New York: McGraw-Hill, p. 68.
—— (1980) Personal Communication to A.A. Lazarus.
Garfield, S.L. and Bergin, A.E. (eds) (1978) *Handbook of Psychotherapy and Behavioral Change*,
   New York: Wiley.
Herinck, R. (1980) *The Psychotherapy Handbook*, New York: New American Library.
Herman, S. (1990) Personal Communication, Stanford, California.
James, W. (1890) *Principles of Psychology*, New York, Macmillan.
Kwee, M.G.T. (1987) *Multimodale Therapie*, Lissa: Swets & Zeitlinger.
—— (1990) Cognitive and behavioural approaches to meditation, in M.G.T. Kwee (ed.)
   Psychotherapy, Meditation, and Health, London: East–West Publications.
—— and Roborgh, M. (1987) *Multimodale therapie: Pratiijk, theorie, en onderzoek*, Lisse, The
   Netherlands: Zwets and Zeitlinger.
Lazarus, A.A. (1956) A psychological approach to alcoholism, *South African Medical Journal*
   32: 707–10.
—— (1958) New methods in psychotherapy: a case study, *South African Medical Journal*
   32: 660–4.
—— (1971) *Behavior Therapy and Beyond*, New York: McGraw-Hill.
—— (1976) *Multimodal Behavior Therapy*, New York: Springer.
—— (1981) *The Practice of Multimodal Therapy*, New York: McGraw-Hill.

—— (1985) *A Casebook of Multimodal Therapy*, New York: Guilford.

—— (1986) Multimodal therapy, in J.C. Norcross (ed.) *Handbook of Eclectic Psychotherapy*, New York: Brunner/Mazel.

—— (1989a) Multimodal therapy, in R. Corsini and D. Wedding (eds) *Current Psychotherapies*, Itasca, Ill.: F.E. Peacock.

—— (1989b) Why I am an eclectic (not an integrationist), *British Journal of Guidance and Counselling* 17(3): 248–58.

—— (1989c) *The Practice of Multimodal Therapy: Systematic, Comprehensive, and Effective Psychotherapy*, Baltimore: Johns Hopkins University Press.

—— (1990) Why I am an eclectic (not an integrationist), in W. Dryden and J.C. Norcross (eds) *Eclecticism and Integration in Counselling and Psychotherapy*, London: Gale Centre Publications.

—— (1991) Does chaos prevail? An exchange on technical eclecticism and assimilative integration, *Journal of Psychotherapy Integration* 1(2): 143–58.

—— and Fay, A. (1977) *I Can If I Want To*, New York: Warner Books.

—— and Fay, A. (1982) Resistance or rationalization? A cognitive-behavioral perspective, in P.L. Wathcel (ed.) *Resistance: Psychodynamic and Behavioral Approaches*, New York: Plenum.

—— and Mayne, T.J. (1989) Relaxation: some limitations, side effects, and proposed solutions, *Psychotherapy* 27: 261–6.

London, P. (1964) *The Modes and Morals of Psychotherapy*, New York: Holt, Rinehart & Winston.

McKay, M., Davis, M. and Fanning, P. (1981) *Thoughts and Feelings: The Art of Cognitive Stress Intervention*, Oakland, Calif.: New Harbinger Publications.

Mahoney, M.J. (1974) *Cognition and Behavior Modification*, Cambridge, Mass.: Ballinger.

Meichenbaum, D. (1977) *Cognitive-Behavior Modification*, New York: Plenum.

Modgil, S. and Modgil, C. (1985) *Hans Eysenck: Consensus and Controversy*, Philadelphia and London: The Falmer Press.

Norcross, J.C. (ed.) (1986) *Handbook of Eclectic Psychotherapy*, New York: Brunner/Mazel.

Paul, G.L. (1967) Strategy of outcome research in psychotherapy, *Journal of Consulting Psychology* 31: 109–18.

Salter, A. (1949) *Conditioned Reflex Therapy*, New York: Farrar, Strauss.

—— (1953) *The Case against Psychoanalysis*, New York: Medical Publications.

Smith, D. (1982) Trends in counseling and psychotherapy, *American Psychologist* 82(7): 807–9.

Thorne, F.C. (1973) Eclectic psychotherapy, in R. Corsini (ed.) *Current Psychotherapies*, Itasca, Ill.: F.E. Peacock.

Whitby, P. (1990) Assumed usefulness, *The Psychologist* 3(7): 308–10.

Wilson, G.T. (1980) Toward specifying the 'nonspecific' factors in behavior therapy: a social learning analysis, in M.J. Mahoney (ed.) *Psychotherapy Process*, New York: Plenum.

—— and O'Leary, K.D. (1980) *Principles of Behavior Therapy*, Englewood Cliffs, NJ: Prentice-Hall.

Yontef, G.M. and Simkin, J.S. (1989) Gestalt therapy, in R.J. Corsini and D. Wedding (eds) *Current Psychotherapies*, Itasca, Ill.: F.E. Peacock.

5

Counselling skills:
an integrative framework

SUE CULLEY

Introduction

This chapter presents a model of counselling that is essentially skills-based. While theory provides counsellors with ideas and concepts, skills form the *substance* or *reality* of counselling. It is skills which enable each counsellor to put his or her particular theoretical perspective into operation. Skills are what each counsellor needs to make counselling happen. The model is therefore concerned with the *process* of counselling. It is derived from the work of Truax and Carkhuff (1967) and Egan (1977, 1990) and offers a guide both to understanding what is happening between counsellors and clients – that is, how they are working together – and to facilitating the progress of the counselling work.

The model has its theoretical foundation in both the person-centred (Mearns and Thorne 1988) and cognitive-behavioural approaches (Trower *et al.* 1988). It attempts a systematic and coherent integration of the central theoretical aspects of both these approaches. I will briefly review each of these approaches in turn.

Person-centred

Person-centred counselling (Rogers 1951, 1961, 1970) has its roots in the existential-humanistic tradition. At its core it is a *relationship* model. By that I mean that it is the quality of the relationship which the counsellor creates with clients that is in itself healing or therapeutic. The view of what it means to be a human being espoused by person-centred counsellors is that each of us has the fundamental capacity to grow and to change. It is a positive view which holds that people, at their core, are good and, if given the right conditions, will strive both to take charge of their lives and ultimately to self-actualize. The conditions under which people will experience the freedom to grow are those which are free of judgement, which hold people as valuable because they are human and which validate the individual's experiences of self and the world. Rogers identified these core attitudes or conditions, essential to creating a therapeutic relationship, as *unconditional positive regard, empathic understanding* and *congruence*.

Unconditional positive regard or *acceptance* means that the counsellor's view of clients as worthy is not tarnished by an evaluation of their behaviour, thoughts or feelings. This does not mean that counsellors do not make assessments or must condone destructive behaviour; rather, it means separating individuals from their actions. *Empathic understanding* means demonstrating to clients that their experiencing has been heard and understood. *Congruence* means being real and without façade. A congruent counsellor is one who communicates herself accurately, is open and whose outward behaviour matches her inner experiences. In the model I am describing, I have used Tyler's (1969) terminology for the core conditions – namely, *acceptance, understanding* and *sincerity*.

The focus of person-centred counselling is not on the use of techniques to problem-solve, but on helping clients to tap their inner resources, to get in touch with their inner valuing process and so better face their concerns. Creating these *necessary* conditions has more to do with the counsellor as a person than it does with techniques and strategies. The way to change is via the individual's *felt sense* or organismic valuing process. Freed from their sense of worth being conditional, that is that they have value *only* if they feel, think or behave in certain ways, clients will begin to learn about themselves, to find meaning and significance in their experiences and harness their capacity for change. Enabling clients in this way demands that the counsellor create a threat-free, respectful and containing relationship, where clients can begin to divest themselves of their defences, their negative self-evaluation and the selves they believe they *ought* to be, and start to explore and to know themselves at their most *real*.

Cognitive-behavioural

A cognitive-behavioural approach integrates thought and behaviour. This is a re-educative approach and counsellors are involved in helping clients create the conditions in which new learning can take place. Cognitive-behavioural counsellors are primarily interested in the clients' ideas or cognitions about themselves and their worlds and how from the many possible interpretations of their experiences they choose the ones that they do. They are also concerned with how these interpretations or *frames of reference* influence clients' behaviour. Like the person-centred approach it is not concerned with childhood experiences, although these may usefully be explored to help clients see themselves in context. While the cognitive-behavioural approach sees the counsellor–client relationship as important, the relationship is not seen as therapeutic in itself. The way to change is through clients' thought processes. The basic assumption about people is that they are born with the capacity for rational thinking, and through their life experiences, learn to engage in self-defeating thoughts or to make evaluations based on faulty thinking (Dryden 1990).

The aim of the cognitive-behavioural approach is to help clients become aware of how they judge themselves and others and to substitute more realistic thinking.

Central to this approach is the challenging of clients' irrational beliefs by disputing both the beliefs and the inferences drawn from these beliefs. The role of practice and action in changing irrational and self-defeating beliefs is also stressed. Constructive behavioural change will follow from the client's ability to think in less maladaptive ways. Cognitive-behavioural counsellors also use specifically behavioural techniques (Meichenbaum 1977). They emphasize the importance of behaviour and the identification of behavioural objectives. They may work with clients to discover precisely what behaviours clients wish to change and to set specific goals for change. The techniques used involve, among others, stress management, assertiveness training or developing a self-management programme.

The beginning stage of the skills-based model is concerned with relationship-building and communicating core values. It has its roots in the person-centred approach. This is seen as crucial to the entire helping process, because without it clients will neither feel secure enough to share what concerns them nor take the risk of owning their problems. The middle stage has to do with using the basic trust of the relationship to challenge clients to explore their feelings and thoughts more deeply and to discover new and more liberating ways of viewing their concerns. It is in this stage that the integration of the person-centred and the cognitive-behavioural approaches becomes most apparent. Clearly, clients are helped to re-assess their concerns when their thinking about these concerns is directly challenged (Nelson-Jones 1989). They will also gain new perspectives by being helped to find deeper significance in their feelings, to stay in close contact with their counsellor and to use the relationship to explore their feelings, thoughts and behaviour. Finally, the ending stage uses concepts from behavioural counselling, such as setting clear and specific goals, developing a reward system, monitoring action in the light of preferred change and helping clients to transfer their learning.

The model identifies the communication skills and strategies necessary at each stage of the counselling process (Culley 1990). For example, if counsellors wish to communicate their acceptance of clients, they will need to know what behaviours are likely to be effective in doing that. I have used the term *integrative* to signify that these skills have been organized according to some conceptual plan. The plan will enable you to identify where you are now in the counselling process, to comprehend what has been happening, and to discern what needs to happen next in order to enable clients to achieve their goals. The model represents, I believe, an intelligible template for your counselling work; it is a description neither of the counselling encounter nor of the behaviour of the participants.

Box 5.1 gives an outline of the model in full and, as you will see, I have used stages as the organizing framework. This is common to many approaches to counselling and therapy (Egan 1986; Ivey *et al.* 1987; Nelson-Jones 1988) and is a way of introducing order into what is in operation an intricate, fluid and sometimes elusive activity. The notion of stages can also help counsellors to identify the points at which the focus of their work with clients needs to change. For these reasons, I have conceptualized the counselling process as having three stages, and have labelled them simply Beginning, Middle and Ending.

Box 5.1　An integrative counselling skills model

THE BEGINNING STAGE

Aims
to establish a working relationship
to clarify and define problems
to make an assessment
to negotiate a contract

Strategies
exploration
prioritizing and focusing
communicating core values

Foundation skills
attending
observing clients
listening
reflective skills
probing skills
being concrete

THE MIDDLE STAGE

Aims
to reassess problems
to maintain the working relationship
to work to the contract

Strategies
to challenge by:
confrontation
giving feedback
giving information
giving directives
self-disclosure
immediacy

Skills
listening, reflective and probing skills

THE ENDING STAGE

Aims
to decide on change
to implement change
to transfer learning
to end the counselling relationship

Strategies
goal-setting
action planning
evaluating action and sustaining change
closure

Skills
skill sequences for listening and challenging

I have identified key aims for each stage plus the strategies and skills essential for achieving these aims. Counselling is a purposeful activity (Ivey 1983). While at the beginning it is important for counsellors to suspend judgement both about what changes clients will make and how they will resolve their concerns, it is crucial that they have clear aims for the counselling process. These aims are the intended outcomes for each stage and are guidelines by which to assess the progress of the work.

By the term 'strategy', I mean procedure. For example, exploration is a key strategy, particularly during the Beginning Stage. It is through exploration that clients begin to gain the sort of clarity, understanding and insights that are the fundamental precursors to change.

The skills are basic component parts of any counselling session; the competencies in communication which enable each of us to put our particular approach into operation. Thus, each strategy will involve the use of different combinations of skills. This model both identifies and organizes the core skills necessary for helping clients to engage productively in the counselling work.

Counselling is, of course, much more than the development and use of communication skills and strategies (Bond 1989). It is a unique, difficult and fundamentally human activity, which offers clients the protected space and opportunity to discover ways of living more resourcefully. However, unless counsellors are adept at the skill level, they are unlikely either to counsel sensitively or purposefully.

Who is the model for?

I think this model will provide a useful process map for both beginning and experienced counsellors, as well as those who counsel as part of their wider work role. It is inappropriate to discuss the differences between counselling and psychotherapy in this chapter. However, as a crude 'rule of thumb', I define therapy as working towards constructive personality change with clients, while counselling has a more focused brief, that of enabling clients to manage and resolve particular problems and concerns.

I consider this model to be a counselling model and therefore most suitable for use with clients who present for shorter-term, focused work. I do not think it is suitable for work with clients who have psychiatric diagnoses or who would benefit from regression work. The model is also limited to verbal and some aspects of non-verbal communication. It would be inappropriate for clients who would benefit from more active therapies, such as bodywork or psychodrama. Finally, while I believe that some clients do present with more intractable problems than others, the skill is not in the model, it is in the user.

Basic assumptions about people

Before turning to look at the model in detail, I want to summarize the basic assumptions about people which are inherent in its structure.

1 *People deserve acceptance*: This means counsellors distinguishing between clients themselves and their behaviour, valuing them as individuals while not necessarily valuing or condoning their behaviour.

2 *People create their own meaning*: Clients will have their own interpretation of their worlds based on their beliefs and reinforcing experiences. What may seem unhelpful or self-sabotaging to counsellors may have a sense of *rightness* for clients. They will interpret their experiences to fit their views of themselves and their worlds.

3 *People are experts on themselves*: Clients know best how they feel and what they believe and think. However, clients are often out of touch with themselves. They may not be used to thinking about what they want or they may have had a lifetime of denying their feelings. Enabling clients to know what they want as opposed to what they think they *ought* to do is an important aim of the helping process.

4 *People want to realize their potential*: Clients have the capacity to become more proactive and to take greater charge of their lives. Helping clients to take a realistic census of their resources, to own their strengths and to tap their under-utilized potential is essential if they are to respond more creatively to the challenges which face them.

5 *People are capable of change*: Clients do have the ability to learn to think, to feel and to behave differently. They may come to counselling believing that they are stuck with the lives that they have. Challenging clients' beliefs and helping them to make creative changes is a fundamental value in this model.

6 *People will work harder for their own goals*: Clients are likely to work harder and commit themselves to outcomes which they value, rather than outcomes which have been imposed. Goal-setting must be a collaborative process, in which clients are helped to marshal their energy towards the changes they value.

I now want to describe the model in detail. I will be integrating the case material both to describe the model in practice and to illustrate the counselling process.

The beginning stage

Aims

The fundamentally important aim of this stage is establishing a 'working relationship' with clients. This is a relationship characterized by trust, support and emotional closeness, in which clients begin to feel secure enough to reveal their concerns (Rogers 1961; Brammer 1988). Clients are often anxious, particularly if they have never been clients before (Storr 1980). Understanding and acceptance from the counsellor will be crucial to encouraging their participation in the work.

The other aims are:

1 *Clarifying and defining concerns*: This means that the issues brought by clients are understood as clearly as possible by both clients and counsellors (Gilmore 1973). However, this is not such an apparently straightforward process; clients

Box 5.2   The Beginning Stage

AIMS
to establish a working relationship
to clarify and define problems
to make an assessment
to negotiate a contract

STRATEGIES
exploration
prioritizing and focusing
communicating core values

FOUNDATION SKILLS
attending
observing clients
listening
reflective skills
probing skills
being concrete

themselves may be unclear about what bothers them or they may have several concerns and not know where to start. Not untypically, some may 'present' counsellors with a problem to test whether or not it is safe for them to reveal what deeply concerns them.

2 *Making assessments*: The process of making assessments is an important aspect of both the beginning and subsequent stages of counselling. Assessment involves using theoretical frameworks to develop hypotheses about clients and their concerns, and make tentative plans for the counselling work. It is not within the scope of this chapter to discuss assessment frameworks. However, the other approaches described in this book provide a range of valuable theoretical perspectives.

3 *Contracting*: As a way of helping, counselling stresses the importance of enabling individuals to discover or recover their potential to take greater charge of their lives. Making a contract is a behavioural way of demonstrating this value. The contract is a clear, negotiated agreement which has three aspects. The first is the contract for counselling, meaning that clients agree that counselling is what they want and know that is what they are receiving. The second covers aspects such as, length, times and number of sessions, confidentiality and payment. Third, both counsellors and clients need to agree what changes clients want to make. Working to a contract is a powerful way both of focusing the work and of making it a shared enterprise.

Strategies

I have identified three strategies; they are Exploration, Prioritizing and focusing and Communicating core values.

Exploration

This involves enabling clients to examine their behaviour, articulate their thoughts and express their feelings in order to gain greater understanding both of themselves and their concerns. It is also crucial to developing mutual understanding. Exploration, of course, continues throughout counselling and is not limited to the beginning stage. However, during initial contact, counsellors typically focus on what clients are expressing explicitly. In subsequent stages, in order to enable clients to reassess their concerns, counsellors encourage a shift in focus to what is implicit or 'below the surface'. It is the move from what clients are openly stating to the hidden messages which gives exploration a deeper and more intense quality.

Prioritizing and focusing

This means deciding with clients both in what order they will tackle their concerns and what the foci will be. Clients often have multiple and complicated problems. They may feel overwhelmed and unable to separate what is most important from what can be suspended for a while.

Communicating core values

This means demonstrating both acceptance and understanding of clients (Tyler 1969). Acceptance means valuing clients because they are human, respecting their uniqueness and their ability for self-determination. At its core, it is a robust affirmation of clients' potential to change and to grow. Mollifying clients or colluding with unhelpful behaviours and self-defeating beliefs does not constitute acceptance as it is defined here.

Understanding or empathic understanding means the ability to understand clients' perspectives on their concerns, to see clients' worlds as they see them. It does not mean counsellors acknowledging to themselves how they would react in their client's place, and using those insights to inform their practice. Demonstrating a willingness to work with clients to understand them, both validates their experience and builds trust.

These core values are essential to the helping process (see Rogers (1951) and Gilmore (1973) for a further discussion) and are as much to do with the counsellor as a person as they are with skills. However, communicating these values has both a behavioural and a skill component. The skills outlined in the next section will enable counsellors to do that.

Let us now turn to the communication skills essential for implementing the preceding strategies. I have called them *foundation skills*, meaning that they are the indispensable basis of the counselling process.

Skills

Let us look first at attending and listening. Although I will discuss them separately, these skills are interdependent. Counsellors will not be attending fully to clients if they do not listen to them, and conversely attending fully puts counsellors in a good position to listen to clients.

Attending
You will need to demonstrate by your non-verbal behaviour that clients have your undivided attention and that you are 'with them'. Good attention is conveyed by sustaining eye contact, sitting with an 'open' posture, putting your chairs at an appropriate distance, making sure they are of equal height and comfort and being aware of what your facial expression is communicating (Jacobs 1985; Egan 1986, 1990). Your attending or non-verbal behaviour will carry powerful messages. The effect of what you say will be diminished if your attending behaviour is poor.

Listening
Clearly, listening is essential to counselling, as well as being one of the finest acknowledgements you can give clients. Listening is a complex skill, involving attending, hearing and understanding the information which clients convey both verbally and non-verbally. Counselling effectively involves *active listening*. This means listening with the purpose of understanding the client's core message, sorting information, making assessments and responding in an enabling way. The following framework will help you to focus both your listening and attending with a view to assessing both content and process.

Framework for listening and attending
- *Experiences*: Clients often want to tell of their experiences – that is, what has happened to them or is currently happening in their lives. When clients talk about their experiences, they will be focusing on what others do and say to them or fail to do or say.
- *Behaviour*: Clients may report how they behaved in and describe how they have acted in certain situations. Counsellors will also be interested and want to observe the behaviour of the client in relation to them in the counselling room.
- *Feelings*: This refers not only to what feelings clients describe but also to the feelings they express in the counselling session.
- *Thoughts*: What sense clients make of their own and others' behaviour, and what beliefs they have about themselves, other people and events in their lives is obviously important to the change process.

The counsellor's aim will be to enable clients to talk specifically about their own behaviour, thoughts and feelings, because that is what they have most control over. The behaviour of others towards them is not so amenable to change. However, clients may need recognition of their sadness at the behaviour of others before they can begin to explore how they have responded. Using this framework will enable counsellors to assess what clients are exploring and what they are failing to explore.

I want briefly to mention some hindrances or *filters* to listening. First, none of us listens in a completely objective way. The impact of our culture, gender and life experiences will inevitably influence the way we receive and process information. Our cultural norms and values are the most difficult to transcend and may become particularly salient when working with clients whose cultural backgrounds are different to ours (see Ivey *et al.* 1987; d'Ardenne and Mahtani 1989).

Second, the theoretical perspectives we espouse will provide another source of bias.

Other typical hindrances will arise from issues in our own lives which distract or preoccupy us, thinking about what to say next, seeking confirmation for our hypotheses and ignoring contradictory information and finally becoming defensive when clients attempt to correct us.

However, while listening is important, it is not usually enough; clients need a response from you. The following section deals with the skills of responding verbally to clients. I have classified them into two skill groups, namely *reflecting* and *probing* skills. You will need to develop proficiency in both.

Reflective skills

Reflective skills are those which enable you to focus primarily on the client's perspective or frame of reference. Nelson-Jones (1988) refers to understanding *the internal frame of reference* – meaning how clients view themselves and their concerns. The common element in this skill group is identifying clients' core message and offering it back to them in your own words. When you do this, you will be imposing minimal direction on the exploration and giving clients space to say what is important to them. Accurate use of reflective skills is an excellent way of communicating your acceptance and understanding. Your purpose in using these skills will be to follow clients, to facilitate exploration and to build trust.

The reflective skills are:

1 *Restating* what you believe to be a significant word or phrase which the client has used, for example:

> *Client*: I felt real *despair*.
> *Counsellor*: [*restating*] Despair.
> *Client*: Yes, I can't remember feeling so low or that life was so hopeless before. It was like I couldn't imagine ever feeling happy or content again.

The counsellor has focused on an emotionally loaded word and by simply restating has let the client know she has heard. The choice of direction of the ensuing conversation is with the client.

2 *Paraphrasing* involves expressing in your own words clients' core messages. You may focus on the content or the feelings which clients are expressing – for example:

> *Client*: [*with an angry tone*] I suppose I felt irritated when he asked me to lend him the money. It's not as though I'm broke or anything. I can afford it. I don't know what it was but I can remember not wanting to seem miserly.
> *Counsellor*: You felt annoyed when he asked you and didn't want him to think you're mean.

3 *Summarizing* is a way of offering clients a précis of the information they have given you. A summary is essentially a longer paraphrase and should not be given as a list of facts but as an organized overview of important themes or

clusters of concerns. These are called *attending summaries* (Ivey *et al.* 1987) because you will be summing up what clients have said, without adding another perspective.

Appropriate use of reflective skills means being both tentative and direct in your manner. You should not add to or make any interpretations about what clients have been saying.

Probing skills

Probing skills express the counsellor's perspective or *external frame of reference* (Nelson-Jones 1988). When you probe, you will usually be following your agenda and focusing on aspects which you believe are important. At times, you will want to influence the direction of the exploration and probing will enable you to do this. Probes are interventions which increase counsellor control and their overuse may invite clients into passivity. For these reasons, they should be used sparingly, particularly in the early stages of counselling.

The probing skills are:

1 *Questioning*: The most useful forms of questions are called *open* questions. They begin with 'what', 'how', 'when' or 'where'. Your intention in asking them will be to invite a full, descriptive response from clients. For example, if you were exploring a relationship difficulty with a client, you might ask: 'How do your quarrels usually start?'; 'What happens when you quarrel?'; or 'When do you usually quarrel?'

Let us turn briefly to forms of questions which are unhelpful because they do not encourage open dialogue. First, '*closed questions*' are those which encourage a 'yes/no' answer, for example: 'Do you love your wife?', 'Have you talked to your son?' Overuse of 'closed' questions is inhibiting for clients and may set up a pattern of question and answer which is hard to break. Conversely, if you want to check some information, a closed question can be an efficient way of doing so. For example: 'Do you write poetry?' rather than 'How do you express your poetic tendencies?'

Second '*leading questions*' are those that communicate to clients that they are expected to give a particular answer. As the label suggests, these questions both lead clients and impose the counsellor's values. They do not stimulate clients to explore what is important for them. An example of a leading question is: 'I don't think money is *that* important, do you?'

Third, '*either/or questions*' are generally restrictive and leading because they offer options which the counsellor has chosen. For example: 'Have you told your daughter how you feel or are you keeping your feelings to yourself?'

Fourth, '*multiple questions*' involve asking two or more questions at once. This is both inefficient and confusing. Invariably, you will not know which question the client has answered. For example: 'What did she say when you told her you were angry, did she accept what you felt or did she contradict you, I mean, do you think you've cleared the air between you now?'

Finally, '*why questions*' generally invite a search for reasons and may promote rumination rather than exploration. One of the aims of counselling is increased self-understanding for clients, but this is rarely achieved by asking 'why'. These types of questions do not encourage description and may appear interrogative. For example: 'Why don't you like her?' might be more profitably explored by asking 'What is it about her that you don't like?'

For a more detailed discussion about the use of questions see Benjamin (1974).

2 *Making statements* is another way of probing. Statements are softer probes and tend to be less intrusive than questions. For example, instead of asking a client 'What did you say when she asked you to leave?' you might say 'I'm not sure how you replied when she asked you to leave'. They are especially useful for focusing clients on their own behaviour, thoughts and feelings. For example: 'I have a clear picture of your partner's reservations, what I'm less clear about is what you think.'

Being concrete

I want to introduce the skill of *being concrete*. If clients are to make changes in their lives, they will first need specific information about what they are doing now, and in what ways that is unhelpful or destructive both for them and others. One of the ways you can invite a more specific description from clients is to ask for or offer a concrete example. For example: 'If you were being more open, what would you be doing that you're not doing now?' [*counsellor asks a hypothetical question to invite a concrete description*] or 'Would sharing your feelings with your partner be an example of you being more open?' [*counsellor offers a concrete example*]

This is a particularly useful skill in forming contracts where you will be helping clients to focus on the outcomes they want from counselling.

Skill sequence for exploration

Effective counsellors use a good mix of both reflective and probing skills. As you will see from the case-study, skills may be used in sequence. A useful sequence for exploration is to paraphrase before asking a question or making a statement. This has the effect of showing acceptance and understanding of what clients have said before moving on.

Case-study – Jane

Let us turn now to Jane, the client in the case-study. Jane has referred herself for counselling because of 'relationship difficulties'. The counsellor gained the following biographical information both from the initial telephone contact and during the first session.

Jane is 28 years old and has been working as an administrator for a large public company. Three years ago she decided to embark on a part-time degree course. She enjoys her course enormously, both for the academic and social opportunities it offers. She lives alone and has a partner of two years' standing called Alan. She describes him as 'caring, easy-going but not very confident of his abilities'. The counsellor notices that she is very concerned to describe Alan in positive terms, almost as if she is defending him. Jane begins by saying angrily that she feels 'put on'. The counsellor uses a mix of skills to help Jane explore her thoughts, feelings, experiences and behaviour.

Counsellor: You feel angry because others take you for granted. [*paraphrase which focuses on feelings and content*]

Jane: [*in a tense tone*] Yes, I am. I'm always being expected to help others out, look after them, take care of them. I've been feeling really irritated lately and have wanted to yell 'Go away and do it yourself – you're an adult now, the same as me and if I've learned to cope so can you!'

The counsellor has a choice here, to focus on Jane's feelings or to ask for specific information – for example, who usually makes demands on her. She decides to stay with Jane's feelings.

Counsellor: It sounds as though you feel frustrated and from the way you said 'always', I imagine you've been supporting others for a long time. [*paraphrase plus a statement to probe*]

Jane: Uhm, [*with a hollow laugh*] a hell of a long time! Although things have been getting worse recently. Alan expects me to make most of the decisions. This may sound awful but sometimes he's like a clinging child. He keeps telling me he's not as bright as me and my friends don't like him. None of which is true. It's not just him though, if it was I wouldn't feel so used.

Counsellor: You're feeling so used. [*counsellor reflects Jane's last statements to prompt further exploration*]

Jane tells the counsellor about three of her close women friends from college.

Jane: I'm really irritated about the way they lean and 'dump' on me. I realize I get so little back from them. I'm beginning to want to avoid them!

Counsellor: What would be an example of the demands they make on you and your response to them? [*open question to gain concrete information*]

Jane: Well! one of them has just bought a computer and because I'm used to word processing and have some programming she thinks I have nothing else to do but teach her. She phoned me four times yesterday and moaned about how she couldn't get the hang of it. She's got a manual but she says she can't understand it. So, I end up spending time on the phone or driving to her place to help her out. I've got my own work to do.

Counsellor: So you feel resentful and think she's using you. Whenever she calls you help her out, even though you don't want to. [*paraphrase to separate feelings, thoughts and behaviour*]

Jane recognizes what she does and how she feels in response to others' demands. She continues by describing aspects of her childhood and adolescence. She is the eldest of three children. Her parents owned a pub and for almost as long as she can remember, Jane has been taking responsibility for her siblings. As a child, when she expressed any resentment about this, she was usually called mean or ungrateful. She says, she feels almost compelled to help others and wants to explore that idea. The counsellor and Jane contract for six sessions. They agree to focus on Jane's behaviour in relationships with the aim of both understanding her urge to 'rescue' and discovering how she will develop more equal relationships.

The counsellor's assessment is that Jane has a strong belief or 'should', learned in childhood and reinforced by negative labelling ('you're mean and ungrateful'), that her needs are not important and that others' needs come first. She also hypothesizes that, out of awareness, Jane both attracts and is attracted to people who are less resilient than she is. Jane can then, despite feeling anger and resentment, continue to be the ever-available 'prop'. The counsellor believes that changing the pattern of her relationships will require Jane to see her own needs as important and to recognize her part in creating this uncomfortable yet familiar pattern. The counsellor's hypotheses will be important in helping Jane to reassess her behaviour. This is the work of the Middle Stage, to which we will now turn.

The middle stage

The focus of the counselling work changes in the Middle Stage. Your aim is to help clients to gain the sort of new understanding crucial for making changes. This is the process of reassessment. For example, without reassessment, Jane is likely to stay trapped, believing that she has no other options but to bail others out and may feel increasingly resentful and guilty.

Let us now turn to the aims, strategies and skills of the Middle Stage.

Box 5.3 The Middle Stage

AIMS
to reassess problems
to maintain the working relationship
to work to the contract

STRATEGIES
to challenge by:

confrontation
giving feedback
giving information
giving directives
self-disclosure
immediacy

SKILLS
listening, reflective and probing skills

Aims

The Middle Stage has three aims.

Reassessment

This involves helping clients to understand themselves and their concerns from a different and more liberating perspective. A metaphor I use for describing reassessment is that of taking a familiar route by car and instead of driving, being the passenger. Freed from the responsibility of driving, you are likely to discover aspects of the scenery that you had not noticed before. Now that you have noticed them, you will not overlook them in future, even when driving. So it is with clients, becoming aware of what they have hitherto been unaware of, overlooking or avoiding, transforms their perspectives on their concerns. Clients will take varying lengths of time before they are prepared to modify or relinquish their 'old' views and adopt a different perspective.

Maintenance of the working relationship

Reassessment is often painful for clients and it is important that you are experienced by them as acting in their best interests. A secure relationship, based on the core values of acceptance and understanding, will be significant in enabling them to examine their beliefs, feelings and behaviour at a deeper level. The relationship you have developed will be your 'interpersonal power base' for influencing clients to explore and develop new perspectives (Strong 1968).

Working to the contract

The contract agrees the boundaries of the work and the outcomes clients want to achieve. You will need to keep the contract in mind because your interventions should be geared to helping clients move in the direction you have both agreed they will move in.

Strategies – Challenging

'Challenging' is the generic term I use for the following group of strategies which encourage clients to the kind of deeper exploration essential to reviewing their perspectives on their concerns. Each strategy has a particular focus. I will describe each of them and discuss how the counsellor challenges Jane, the client in the case-study.

Confrontation

You will use confrontation when you want to enable clients to face and to explore the distortions or discrepancies which they employ to inhibit change. Discrepancies may be between: what clients say they want and what they are doing to get it; clients' views of themselves and how others view them; clients' verbal and non-verbal behaviour.

For example, Jane tells the counsellor that she is determined to stop taking decisions for her partner, Alan. Her voice has a flat tone and she sits in a hunched position. The counsellor thinks she sounds anxious rather than determined. She confronts her:

> *Counsellor*: Jane, I can understand that you want change. As I listened to the way you were describing what you would do, my hunch was you sounded anxious and burdened rather than determined. Does that make any sense to you?

Jane considers what the counsellor has said. She reveals that her lack of determination is based on an underlying fear that he will not be able to cope if she changes. The counselling moves to a deeper level. As Jane explores her fears she begins to realize that it is her beliefs about herself and others which are inhibiting her. She believes that ohers *must have* her help, that they are incapable of managing their problems on their own.

Giving feedback
This involves letting clients know how you experience them in their interaction with you. Giving feedback to clients means offering them another different and more *objective* view of themselves. Hearing how another person experiences them is a challenge to clients' current self-understanding. The outcome is that clients will begin to explore and to modify the ways in which they see themselves.

For example, Jane described herself as 'selfish' and 'self-centred'. Her counsellor experiences her as having little regard or concern for her own needs. Hearing the counsellor's view encourages Jane to examine which of her needs she fulfils by being at others' 'beck and call'.

Giving information
This is similar to giving feedback and involves providing clients with specific information about an aspect of their problems. Information challenges clients because, used appropriately, it invariably prompts them to take a different perspective on themselves and their concerns. For example, if a client believes that he will have little trouble entering a popular training course, some figures on the number of applicants may encourage him to reassess what he needs to do to obtain a place. Information should not be used as a subtle means of discouraging clients or telling them what they should do. Rather, it is a way of helping clients to understand themselves and their situations in a different way, in order that they may set clear goals and take the necessary action to achieve their goals.

Giving directives
As the label suggests, 'giving directives' is the strategy whereby the counsellor assumes greater control of the process. This is a powerful strategy most appropriately used when the relationship between counsellor and client has developed into a robust and secure one. Used prematurely, clients may feel dominated. Some directives you may want to give are, for example, 'Stay with what you're feeling now', or 'Put some words to that feeling'. Giving directives is a way of focusing clients' attention on significant behaviour or feelings. It is the focusing of attention which challenges clients to explore more deeply and

to discover new meanings in what they have hitherto been avoiding or been unaware of.

Jane rarely shows her anger, she covers it with sarcasm or a joke. Focusing on her anger helps her to discover new insights into her behaviour.

Counsellor: You sound angry Jane.

Jane: I am, [*with a wry smile*] but what good does being angry with you do for me?

Counsellor: Stay with your anger. [*gives a directive*]

Jane: [*after a few moments*] I feel worn out and . . . I feel sad. I've always taken care of others and . . . well, I feel embarrassed telling you this, I feel frightened at the thought of being dumped, rejected if I don't do what they want. Thinking back to what I said about Alan, I think I've always had boy-friends who were less competent than me. I've always been the organized, capable one. I don't want friendships to be like this, but somehow they are. I didn't realize being left was such an issue for me.

Counsellor self-disclosure
This strategy involves counsellors sharing something of their own experiences with clients. Self-disclosure challenges clients because it invites them to explore their own material in the light of another's and from there to begin to form different perspectives. Although self-disclosure may be good modelling for clients in how to articulate thoughts, to label and to express feelings, it should be used sparingly and only when counsellors believe it would be enabling for clients. Using the strategy to relieve your own feelings or give yourself a boost is burdening clients and not helping. Any disclosure should also be experiences with which you think clients will be able to identify. For example, describing your thoughts and feelings about the time when you failed to obtain a management position to a client whose job is redundant is likely to antagonize rather than encourage. The following is an example of counsellor self-disclosure which enables Jane to begin to see her concerns from a new angle. Jane is saying how miserable she feels after successfully saying no to a request from a friend.

Jane: I feel awful, really guilty and such a heel. I know that I hate being put on and yet when I do stand up for myself, I feel bad too. Yet this friend was fine about me saying 'no'. She said, she was glad I'd been honest and felt that she could always ask me because she'd get a straight answer.

Counsellor: I grew up with the clear message that refusing requests was mean and uncaring. I learned to judge myself harshly and punish myself. It sounds to me like that is what you're doing now.

Jane: Yes, I've been telling myself what a lousy friend I am, that I'm greedy and unsupportive. Those are exactly the messages I grew up with and they're not true. Hearing you say that, I realize how strong those rules still are for me and I don't like that one bit. They have got to go.

The counsellor's disclosure helps Jane to articulate her beliefs about herself and to understand her own process. She now knows that she has learned to punish herself for breaking the 'family rules', just as her parents punished her when she was little. Once Jane is aware of what she believes, then her beliefs are available for updating.

Immediacy

What is going on 'here and now' in the counselling relationship is the focus of immediacy. You may use this strategy to explore either what is happening 'now' with a client or the relationship patterns you think are emerging. Using immediacy challenges clients because it not only presents them with the counsellor's view of the relationship, but also provides a chance to explore the relationship and to identify self-defeating patterns and themes. Clients, like Jane in the case-study, often have relationship difficulties; and the patterns and themes which become apparent in counselling may reflect their difficulties with relationships outside the counselling room. Immediacy faces both you and clients with the dynamics of your relationship, and used appropriately will bring you into closer contact. It is not an opportunity to tell clients what they have been doing that is unhelpful; rather, it is an invitation to explore the relationship as a way of helping clients to reassess themselves and their behaviour.

The following is an example of 'relationship immediacy'. The counsellor realizes that Jane is often rebellious and complaining in sessions. She avoids focusing on change.

> *Counsellor*: Jane, I'd like to say what I think is going on between us. I've noticed that you often complain about how others treat you. I've realized when I've asked you to consider how you might act differently, you sound angry as if I've dismissed what you've been saying. Perhaps I'm moving to action too quickly for you but it's almost as if you're telling me how important it is for you to be heard. Does that make any sense to you?
>
> *Jane*: [*angrily*] So I'm not allowed to complain here. It's easy for you sitting there, criticizing me and telling me what to do. You don't have to take the risk, do you?
>
> *Counsellor*: You sound angry with me now and it sounds as though you heard what I said as criticism of you. [*counsellor uses immediacy again*]
>
> *Jane*: [*looking sad*] Yes, I was angry and I don't want you to criticize me or to think I'm not trying. It's like no one has recognized how much it costs me to keep on minding about others. I feel anxious when you talk about changing. I know what to do but it's so risky doing it.
>
> *Counsellor*: So, you feel sad when you think I'm criticizing you and scared at the thought of changing.
>
> *Jane*: Yes, I don't want you or anyone to think badly of me and dump me, I suppose. I know that you won't but I still feel scared.
>
> *Counsellor*: I'm not going to reject you and I want you to be able to do more than complain effectively as a result of counselling.
>
> *Jane*: [*laughing*] So do I and you know, I've just had a thought. It was always

alright to moan about being hard done by in our family, as long as no one tried to change anything.

Jane continues to explore her fear of rejection. The counsellor offers her the hypothesis that she seeks friends and lovers who will allow her to do what she has learned to do – act as a prop. She realizes that this is both a fear and a pattern she has carried with her since childhood. With her counsellor, she updates her view of herself and her relationships. She begins to see that as an adult, she does not have to assume responsibility for friends as if they were her younger siblings. She ends by telling her counsellor that she wants to look at how she can change. In owning that she has responsibility for her choice of friends and in telling the counsellor that she 'wants to say no', Jane shows that she is ready to explore what she might do differently. The next stage of counselling focuses on precisely what changes Jane will make and the action which she will take to achieve the outcomes she wants.

Skills of challenging

The reflective and probing skills are again used in sequences. Sensitive challenging involves recognizing the client's perspective by paraphrasing the core content; adding your understanding of what they have been communicating in a brief summary; returning the focus to the client and inviting exploration of what you have offered. You may do this by making statements, for example: 'I imagine you have some thoughts about what I've just said', or asking an open question: 'How does that sound to you?'

Any new perspective you offer clients should be close to the message the client has been conveying. Challenging is not indulging in extravagant speculations. I like to understand the process as 'discovering the obvious'. By that I mean giving clients a view which makes enough sense to them that they wonder how they could have overlooked it.

The purpose of challenging is to enable clients to make a reassessment of their concerns. Reassessment can be both empowering and painful for clients as they face their problems squarely and prepare to take the risk of changing. The ending stage focuses on helping clients to harness their energy and desire for change by working with them to identify specific and realizable goals.

The ending stage

The Ending Stage typically has to do with planning for and taking effective action. Ending the counselling relationship is also an important aim for this stage. There are four aims.

Aims

Deciding on change

If clients are to make changes, then they will need to know what changes are possible and what particular outcomes they want. You will also want to explore

Box 5.4   The Ending Stage

AIMS

to decide on change
to implement change
to transfer learning
to end the counselling relationship

STRATEGIES

goal-setting
action planning
evaluating action and sustaining change
closure

SKILLS

skill sequences for listening and challenging

with them what impact any changes will have on issues that concern them (Munro *et al.* 1989). For example, Jane may tell her counsellor that a change she wants to make is to cease her friendship with those who lean on her. This will not help her to learn to be equal in friendships, to learn to negotiate for what she wants or to be clear about the limits to the support she is prepared to give.

Implementing change
Changing involves taking some action; it means doing some things and stopping doing others. Clients may need help in both choosing what action to take and acting. For example, Jane talking about refusing requests from friends is not the same as her doing it. She may need some coaching/teaching in assertiveness techniques. Jane and her counsellor may engage in role-play or guided fantasy. Some clients will need the support of the counsellor while they take action. It is sometimes the case that clients stumble while they are trying out new behaviours.

Transferring learning
What clients learn in counselling about themselves and the different options open to them will need to be transferred to their life outside the counselling room. For example, Jane and her counsellor contracted that Jane would ask her counsellor for what she wanted. Jane became used to asking for feedback, expressing preferences and taking more control in sessions. However, Jane needs to transfer this learning and apply it in her other relationships.

Ending the counselling relationship
The counselling relationship will have been a very important relationship for most clients. For many it is the first time they have experienced so much genuine interest from another, been challenged constructively and supported while they struggle with their difficulties. Ending must be concerned with the loss of this relationship as well as the fulfilment of a contract.

Let us now turn to the Strategies.

Strategies

Goal-setting

As a result of the reassessment of the Middle Stage, clients will be change-oriented. However, they will still need to decide precisely what outcomes they want. Goal-setting provides a valuable framework for both identifying and assessing change.

Goals are defined by Egan (1986) as 'valued outcomes' and should meet the following criteria:

1 *Wanted by the client*: You will be helping clients to decide what they want to do, rather than what they think they should do or what others want them to do. This is not to imply that clients should be encouraged to act only out of self-interest; rather, that they identify goals which are in tune with their values. Counsellors are influential people in clients' lives and it is important that you distinguish between challenging clients to explore and discover what they want and leading clients to fulfil either your or others' expectations. Clients are likely to work harder for goals that are in keeping with their values and wanted by them. Clues that clients are not doing what they want are statements such as, 'My partner thinks we should. . . .' . You will also need to be alert to incongruence between verbal and non-verbal behaviour.

2 *Specific*: Goals which are clear and specific enable clients to focus their energy and resources and plan appropriate action. For example, Jane began by saying that she wanted more equal relationships. This is fine as a starting-point, but it is a vague statement and needs tailoring into a specific goal.

3 *Realistic*: By this I mean within clients' emotional, physical and financial resources. This involves helping clients to take a census of their resources and challenging them when you think they are overlooking important strengths or obstacles. Discovering what is realistic with clients may be done by using the following simple *sentence completion* exercise. You might say to clients. 'Imagine you are resolving this problem, and this time you are doing something different. What are you doing?' The answers which clients give will form the basis for exploration about what might be realistic options.

   Another way in which clients' goals may be unrealistic is in their attempts to set goals for others. Clients have most control over their own behaviour and while they may influence others to change, this is not the focus of goal-setting. The client's behaviour is the target.

4 *Observable and assessable*: How will Jane know that her relationships are more equal? What will she be doing that she is not doing now and how will she assess her progress towards this goal? Identifying some criteria for assessment helps clients both to decide if at any point in the process they need to modify their goals and to know when they have achieved their goals.

Clients are more likely to succeed in making changes if they choose from a number of options. There is usually more than one way of managing or resolving a problem and 'brainstorming' is a useful technique for generating alternatives. Brainstorming can be a pleasurable activity, which encourages clients to use their creativity and imagination. It involves suspending critical judgement and generating as many options as possible for solving a problem. All solutions, however unusual, are recorded. Options are then evaluated for their desirability and efficacy.

Let us now return to the client, Jane. She has a clear idea about the patterns in her relationships and has decided she is no longer prepared to rescue her friends and partner. Her aim is more equal and reciprocal relationships. You will see that the counsellor uses the strategies of exploration and challenging in helping Jane to shape goals.

> *Counsellor*: Jane, what would a more equal relationship be like?
>
> *Jane*: Well, I'd be supported by my friends, Alan wouldn't keep leaning on me financially and emotionally.
>
> *Counsellor*: You've told me what others would be doing. If you imagine yourself behaving differently, what changes would you have made?
>
> *Jane*: I'd be feeling that I had a right to refuse, without feeling guilty. I'd feel better about myself. I'd say 'no' more often, particularly when I get a twinge in my stomach, which is a sure sign that I don't want to do something.

Jane thinks that if she learned to say 'no', she would have greater self-esteem and greater control over her life. She describes how she gets into a downward spiral of acquiescing to others, feeling used and believing she is valueless. Her counsellor asks her what the costs might be if she pursued this goal.

> *Jane*: What costs? Well, the one I've always dreaded I suppose, that friends will reject me. That won't happen though.
>
> *Counsellor*: Jane, my understanding is that you sustain many of your relationships by ignoring your own needs. You told me at our first meeting that you noticed Alan becoming more clinging, the more confident you became. I don't want to be negative, but it seems to me that some friends may not want to stay around when the balance of power shifts and you become more assertive. What do you think?
>
> *Jane*: Yes, I guess you're right and I'm sad about that, but I don't want to be like this. I want to be respected for *me*, not just for what I will do.

Any goals and any action which clients plan should be assessed for costs and benefits. No change is without its costs to clients and sometimes to their families and social circle. The question you will be addressing with clients is, 'Is the cost too exorbitant?' You will also need to keep in mind that some clients will be satisfied with smaller changes than you think they are capable of making. An excellent technique for assessing options and action plans is called *force-field analysis* (Lewin 1969). Each one of us can conceptualize our lives as having a 'space' or 'field'. Our spaces contain our physical surroundings, relationship ties, personal characteristics such as interests, values, strengths and achievements. Whenever we decide to make changes, there will be certain aspects or 'forces' in our lives which will assist us and others that will hinder us. The list of 'pros' and 'cons' which you help clients to generate will be a census of the important aspects of their lives. Reviewing the list will enable them to assess the feasibility of any goal or action plan.

Action planning
Just as there is usually more than one way of managing a problem, so there are different ways that clients can achieve their goals. Jane decided she would start with learning to say 'no' to friends when they asked for more help than she wants to give. That is her goal. She lists what action she could take, as follows:

- take a course in assertiveness skills
- role-play saying 'no' in counselling
- tackle the issue before it occurs again
- learn positive messages to replace the negative ones of 'you're mean and thoughtless, if you don't do what others want'
- widen her circle of friends
- read some books about developing interpersonal skills.

Jane decided she wanted to rehearse using role-play in counselling. She put the assertiveness training 'on hold' until she had finished her studies. The notion of tackling the issue with friends appealed to her but she felt anxious about what she thought was 'jumping too far ahead'. In the role-play, her counsellor encouraged her to be aware of her bodily responses when faced with a request she did not want to meet and to give herself time before answering. Jane discovered how quickly and almost automatically she leapt to be helpful. The counsellor again asked her to put some words to her feelings; she says:

Jane: This is risky, you should help. Something bad will happen if you don't. You're a bad person. Others are more important than you.

The counsellor and Jane worked out a believable, positive sentence which Jane could substitute for the abusive ones she had been running through her head.

Evaluating
Any action that clients take needs to be evaluated. The important question for clients is, 'Is this action helping me to obtain the outcomes I want?' Jane reported a mixture of success and stumbling. She discovered both how difficult it was for her to change a life-long pattern and how empowered she felt when she stated what she would like in a direct, assertive way. The counsellor asked her to describe her experiences in a concrete way and together they discussed the options for tackling the pitfalls Jane had identified. This is new behaviour for Jane and she is still experimenting to find a style which suits her. Jane decided she would end counselling, knowing that she still had some distance to travel but that she had done enough for the moment.

Ending
From the beginning of counselling the end is in sight. You will have been working towards the time when clients leave, having made the changes they sought. Endings will usually occur when clients have fulfilled their contracts. Clients may have experiences of endings which are painful, and ending with you may be evocative of those times. Alerting them to the possibility of sadness may help them to express what feelings they do have. You will also be concerned to encourage clients to express any feelings that are 'left over' from previous

sessions. Your aim will be to enable clients to end well with you. By this I mean that they are changing in the ways that are valuable for them, they have cleared any 'unfinished business' with you and recognized and expressed any feelings of loss (Ward 1984). Jane decided to end with her counsellor. In reviewing the work, she confirmed her strategy for coping with unwanted demands. She had experienced a relationship with her counsellor where her wants were recognized and respected. Her self-esteem and self-assurance had increased as a result of being accepted and valued by the counsellor. She was still undecided about her relationship with her partner but was not ready to make a decision about her future with him.

During the ending session Jane and her counsellor explored a plan for how she might sustain the changes she had made. They discussed how Jane could identify situations where she might feel vulnerable. For example, she thought that a man on her course was going to ask her to do a joint project with him. She enjoyed his company but did not want to work with him. She also decided she would keep a diary and record both the praise she received and her achievements. This would be a tangible record to turn to when she failed to sustain change.

Finally, they addressed the end of the relationship. The counsellor asked Jane if she had any unexpressed resentments or left-over feelings about their work.

Jane: Well, I had, but even you asking me has somehow defused them. I was really angry when you said I chose friends who would let me rescue them. I wish I'd said so at the time. I told someone at work and they said that I did have choice over who I picked to spend time with. I know now that taking responsibility for myself is what I hadn't been doing.

Counsellor: I wish you had said so too and that I had picked up on your feelings. I'm interested in whether telling me now has cleared the issue for you and also what you'll take away from that session?

Jane: Yes, I'm clear with you and I think what I learned I was in some way repeating my patterns. Not saying how I was feeling and hanging on to resentment.

The session ends with the counsellor giving Jane some positive feedback about how she has experienced working with her over the past six sessions.

Conclusion

This model is, I believe, a metamodel of counselling. It is a 'content-free', process model which can be integrated with other theoretical approaches. Whatever theory you espouse, you will need the strategies and the skills with which to implement that theory. Just as counsellors need theories which attempt to explain how individuals have developed as they have and provide models of healthy development, so they need frameworks to understand process. This model conceptualizes process and enables you to translate theory into practice. Using this model and being aware of your intentions as well as developing your skills by practising so

that you communicate what you actually intend to communicate seems to me a
responsible way to approach counselling.

References

Benjamin, A. (1974) *The Helping Interview*, 2nd edn, Boston: Houghton Mifflin.
Bond, T. (1989) Towards defining the role of counselling skills, *Counselling: The Journal
    of the British Association for Counselling* 69: 3–9.
Brammer, L.M. (1988) *The Helping Relationship: Processes and Skills*, 4th edn, Englewood
    Cliffs, NJ: Prentice-Hall.
Culley, S. (1990) *Integrative Counselling Skills in Action*, London: Sage.
d'Ardenne, P. and Mahtani, A. (1989) *Transcultural Counselling in Action*, London: Sage.
Dryden, W. (1990) *Rational-Emotive Counselling in Action*, London: Sage.
Egan, G. (1977) *You and Me*, Monterey, Calif.: Brooks-Cole.
—— (1986) *The Skilled Helper: A Systematic Approach to Effective Helping*, 3rd edn, Monterey,
    Calif.: Brooks/Cole.
—— (1990) *The Skilled Helper: A Systematic Approach to Effective Helping*, 4th edn, Monterey,
    Calif.: Brooks/Cole.
Gilmore, S.K. (1973) *The Counselor-in-Training*, Englewood Cliffs, NJ: Prentice-Hall.
Ivey, A.E. (1983) *Intentional Interviewing and Counseling*, Monterey, Calif.: Brooks/Cole.
——, Ivey, M.B. and Simek-Downing, L. (1987) *Counseling and Psychotherapy: Integrating
    Skills, Theory and Practice*, 2nd edn, Englewood Cliffs, NJ: Prentice-Hall.
Jacobs, M. (1985) *Swift to Hear*, London: SPCK.
Lewin, K. (1969) Quasi-stationary social equilibria and the problem of permanent change,
    in W.G. Bennis, K.D. Benne and R. Chin (eds) *The Planning of Change*, New York: Holt,
    Rinehart & Winston.
Mearns, D. and Thorne, B. (1988) *Person-Centred Counselling in Action*, London: Sage.
Meichenbaum, D. (1977) *Cognitive-Behavior Modification*, New York: Plenum.
Munro, A., Manthei, B. and Small, J. (1989) *Counselling: The Skills of Problem Solving*,
    London: Routledge.
Nelson-Jones, R. (1988) *Practical Counselling and Helping Skills*, 2nd edn, London: Cassell.
—— (1989) *Effective Thinking Skills: Preventing and Managing Personal Problems*, London:
    Cassell.
Rogers, C. (1951) *Client Centred Therapy: Its Current Practice, Implications and Theory*, Boston:
    Houghton Mifflin.
—— (1961) *On Becoming a Person*, London: Constable.
—— (1970) *On Encounter Groups*, New York: Harper & Row.
Storr, A. (1980) *The Art of Psychotherapy*, New York: Methuen.
Strong, S. (1968) Counseling: an interpersonal influence process, *Journal of Counseling
    Psychology* 15: 215–24.
Trower, P., Casey, A. and Dryden, W. (1988) *Cognitive-Behavioural Counselling in Action*,
    London: Sage.
Truax, C.B. and Carkhuff, R.R. (1967) *Toward Effective Counseling and Psychotherapy*,
    Chicago: Aldine.
Tyler, L.E. (1969) *The Work of the Counselor*, 3rd edn, New York: Appleton Century Crofts.
Ward, D.E. (1984) Termination of individual counseling: concepts and strategies, *Journal
    of Counselling and Development* 63: 21–5; in W. Dryden (ed.), *Key Issues in Counselling in
    Action*, London: Sage, 1989.

6

Behavioural–systems couple therapy: selecting interventions according to problems presented

JANE RIDLEY AND MICHAEL CROWE

Introduction

The behavioural–systems approach (Crowe and Ridley 1990) takes its origins from two forms of couple and family therapy: (a) behavioural marital therapy and (b) family therapy based on systems theory. It is however more than a simple combination of these two types of therapy, and integrates them, together with some specific techniques developed in our own clinic setting, to produce a form of therapy well-suited to dealing with relationship problems in a short-term, focused way. In order to assist the therapist to assess the couple and to choose the most useful approach for each couple we have also developed the alternative levels of intervention (ALI) hierarchy. This is a method of choosing the best approach to a particular couple, based on the way they present their problem and the degree of 'rigidity' in the relationship, and will be described later in the chapter with accompanying vignettes of couples being treated within each level on the hierarchy. We also show how during therapy couples may be treated using different approaches, moving up the hierarchy where they are fixed or rigid in their interaction, or are heavily symptomatic, and down the hierarchy as they develop greater flexibility. In addition we describe how sexual difficulties can be dealt with in the context of relationship therapy.

Origins of the approach

Behavioural marital therapy has been practised for over two decades (Stuart 1969; Liberman 1970). It is well researched and there are many controlled outcome studies confirming its effectiveness. It has always been recognized, however, that it is most effective with those couples whose problems are acknowledged as relationship problems and who are not excessively distressed as individuals. This led us to seek for other approaches which would be useful for those couples who were complaining of individual symptoms in addition to their relationship difficulties; and it appeared that the systems approaches developed for the treatment of families with a symptomatic member would be a good supplement for the well-established but limited behavioural marital therapy.

The particular techniques we use are derived from the structural therapy of Minuchin (1974) and Sluzki (1978) and the strategic approach of Haley (1976). In addition we make some use of the systemic interventions of Selvini Palazzoli *et al.* (1978). Our approach is, however, constantly evolving, and we have developed some specific interventions for various problems, such as timetables for morbid jealousy and sexual refusal and the encouragement of arguments over trivial issues for couples in which one partner seems to be depressed or unassertive. We also find that in most cases it is more helpful for the therapist to work from a 'de-centred' position rather than to talk directly with either or both partners.

In addition to these specific techniques within sessions and in homework tasks we describe the general goals of therapy and strategies to maintain both the momentum within the session and the motivation of the couple towards change.

The setting

The Maudsley couple therapy clinic is an out-patient clinic of the Maudsley Hospital. Couples referred to the clinic therefore reflect the variety of problems which are presented at a postgraduate psychiatric teaching hospital. These can range from simple relationship difficulties to quite severe psychiatric symptoms or behavioural difficulties experienced by one partner. At the clinic, over successive years of team discussion and practical experience, the behavioural-systems approach has been developed and is under constant review and modification.

Behavioural marital therapy, as mentioned above, has been demonstrated to have lasting benefit for couples who have relationship problems with or without milder psychiatric difficulties (Crowe 1978). In cases with more severe symptoms, however, it is often necessary to seek for interventions of other types to facilitate change. The systems approach provides a theoretical framework for approaching these more problematic couples.

While using the systems approach we are very aware that there is little research to substantiate claims made for its effectiveness and that we are therefore relying to a much greater extent upon clinical experience and therapeutic ingenuity.

While we are fairly confident that many such symptomatic couples can be helped by systemic interventions both to improve their interaction and lose their symptoms, there are some problems, notably the psychoses and organic brain diseases, which cannot be expected to respond to couple therapy alone, despite the over-optimistic ideas of earlier workers (see McFarlane 1983). In these cases couple therapy has to be seen as a supplementary approach, helping the partners to adjust to the illness and to reduce the added burden produced by the relationship difficulties.

General goals and strategy of therapy

Goals of therapy

The behavioural–systems approach is a short-term therapy which focuses on improving the present relationship of the couple. The primary goals are to help the couple learn to negotiate and communicate more effectively and to develop more flexible ways of relating to each other by increasing their repertoire of interactions.

We would also in many cases expect as a result some improvement in the symptoms or the behaviour which caused the distress. On the other hand, as mentioned above, we might decide with the couple that their expectations are too high and that they may be best helped by learning to live with, and cope more effectively with, symptoms or behaviour. Where change does not occur we prefer not to blame the couple for such a failure; rather we assume that we have not yet developed a suitable therapeutic strategy to help them with their problem.

Our overall goals can be summarized as:

1 Improved marital adjustment (communication, negotiation and satisfaction)
2 Increased flexibility of interaction in the relationship
3 Reduction of any symptoms or individual problems
4 Decrease in the labelling of one partner as the 'problem'
5 If the relationship or the individual problems cannot be improved, reduce expectations and 'live with it'
6 Any improvement should be able to last without further therapeutic help.

General strategy for therapy

Most of the referrals to the clinic are from general practitioners, although a small proportion come from social workers, probation officers, community nurses and other professionals.

The first contact which the clinic has with each couple is through an appointment letter and a questionnaire which asks the couple to give details of their personal history and to describe the problem for which they are seeking help. Each partner is asked to give his or her own account of the problems and the history of the relationship. The way in which this is given can convey much about their relationship. Language or literacy skills can also be picked up from this first postal contact.

Most therapy is carried out using a one-way screen room with a supervision group behind the screen who can both observe and communicate with the therapist. The couple are told of these arrangements in the appointment letter. When therapy is videotaped the couple's written permission is always sought.

The therapist will usually see the couple for 30–40 minutes and then take a break in the session to discuss with the observation team the process of therapy and what message, timetable or task may be given to the couple at the end of the session. During this break the couple may continue with some work the therapist has suggested they carry out or go for a cup of tea. The camera and microphone are always switched off during the session break.

Therapists new to this way of working worry that couples may find the one-way screen intrusive; our general impression is, however, that couples are reassured to find their difficulties being taken seriously by the team. If couples are worried about being observed they may be introduced to the team behind the screen. Occasionally we may choose to see a couple without the screen if particularly sensitive areas are being discussed, such as the more intimate aspects of a sexual relationship. However, we usually find that it is helpful for both therapist and couple to use the one-way screen for most problems.

A central concern in therapy is to engage the couple in working together on their relationship and we try to ensure that this begins to happen within the first session. We would also hope in most cases to send the couple away after the first session with some small piece of homework which builds on the work begun in the clinic.

There are several ways in which the therapist can facilitate this early engagement of the couple in working together on their difficulties. The therapist first establishes a reasonable rapport with both partners by helping each of them to state what they are hoping for in coming for therapy.

Even at this early stage of therapy the therapist keeps in mind and acts upon several principles: to keep the focus of therapy on their interaction, to keep up the momentum of the session, to encourage positive suggestions rather than criticism, to help the couple avoid excessive rationalization and explanation and to concentrate on the present and future rather than the past.

Focus on the interaction is often best facilitated by the therapist working from a de-centred position. This means asking the couple to turn their chairs to face each other and to talk together. From a de-centred position the therapist stays out of the couple's interaction, only intervening to help them continue their dialogue. It is helpful to avoid non-verbal contact with the couple, who will usually attempt to bring the therapist back into the action. Many therapists accustomed to working with individuals find this difficult, and continue to intervene to interpret each partner to the other, rather than encouraging direct contact between the partners.

The therapist keeps up the momentum of interaction by ensuring that one partner is not allowed to talk too long, and that they stick to the topic. Too much emphasis on history and explanations is discouraged. One important result of focusing on the present is that, if some small change can be produced in the session, the couple's morale may be improved and they may become more hopeful and more co-operative. Often at this stage the therapist may be carrying most of the hope that things can change, and should be gentle but persistent and not easily deflected by protests from the couple that they have tried it all before.

Where symptoms are presented as one partner's problem there is often an initial difficulty in engaging the non-symptomatic partner in therapy. S/he may express great reluctance about even being present and may have introduced him/herself by saying 'I am only here because of him/her'. In these circumstances the therapist tries to focus on their interaction, and if this cannot be done directly other indirect approaches may be needed.

For example, where the couple present their difficulties as being the intense jealousy of one partner, the non-jealous partner can be involved in therapy by being asked to say how s/he is affected by the jealousy. We find that this is more helpful in terms of their interaction if the jealous partner is encouraged to elicit this information from the non-symptomatic partner. An alternative intervention might be to ask the non-symptomatic partner to speak about times when s/he might have had similar pangs of jealousy or envy. Again this can be achieved from the de-centred position in a way which encourages direct interaction between the partners.

By these means the therapist constantly encourages one partner to help the other to speak about aspects of their relationship which have not previously been discussed. Using systems language the therapist may ally with one partner (often the symptomatic partner) in order to unbalance the system and raise that partner to a position of competence which s/he did not previously have.

In this way we hope to reframe the problem as interactional and shared between the couple. By encouraging the non-symptomatic partner to become involved s/he may modify some aspects of their relationship which in turn may lead to a diminution of the symptom. For example, if the non-jealous partner is able to speak about occasional bouts of jealousy or insecurity and can perhaps reduce their own rather flirtatious attitude to others and pay more attention to their relationship, this may help the other partner to bring his/her jealousy under control and feel more secure within the relationship.

Where couples are very stuck and the session is very slow-moving, the momentum can be enhanced by the use of circular questions. This method of questioning is derived from the Milan School (Selvini Palazzoli *et al.* 1980) who consistently and regularly use circular questioning with families. We use a modified form of circular questioning to facilitate a change of tempo in the session and to try to draw out from the couple any differences in their behaviour or perception. Examples of questions which might be used are: 'Which one of you finds it more difficult to cope with your son's untidiness?' or 'If you were to separate who do you think would be the most lonely/independent/able to cope?' Questions of this comparative nature can also be used to facilitate the interaction by, for example, asking the man to answer the question and then to check with the woman if she agrees.

As part of the ongoing process of therapy we usually formulate a message, which is designed in the session break, and is given to the couple at the end of the session. Such a message may be a very simple statement of concern for their present situation, or may include more details about their difficulties. We would usually wish to give positive feedback to the couple at the beginning of the message and even the most dysfunctional couple can be reminded that by choosing to seek therapy and by actually keeping the appointment together they are showing concern for their relationship.

The message will often include a task or timetable for the couple to undertake before their next appointment. The task or timetable is likely to be most useful if it arises directly out of work done in the session even if some of the details are worked out by the therapist in the session break.

Any message given should be simple and understandable and in the language and metaphor of the couple. Where the message to be given is paradoxical, extra care is taken to ensure that the wording and tone are empathic with the couple's difficulties.

The alternative levels of intervention (ALI) hierarchy

Within the therapy session we have to decide at any one stage what kind of intervention to use. The behavioural–systems approach gives us a wide reper- toire of such interventions, from direct negotiation between the partners to the use of paradoxical messages at the end of the session. The ALI hierarchy (Figure 6.1) is a simple method of assessing and making choices about how to inter- vene with each couple according to the problem presented. We use the word 'hierarchy' as the most practical way of describing our approach, although we recognize that hierarchy carries with it some unfortunate connotations of status or purity which we do not wish to imply. The hierarchy is used to describe an ascending series of alternative interventions depending upon the flexibility or rigidity of the couple and the degree of symptomatology in one partner. As the therapist ascends the hierarchy and changes the interventions so he or she must rely less upon the couple's stated goals and more upon therapeutic hypotheses and ingenuity.

The characteristics of the couple: the vertical axis

In Figure 6.1 the vertical axis represents the couple characteristics, and as one moves up the hierarchy there is an increase in three main areas:

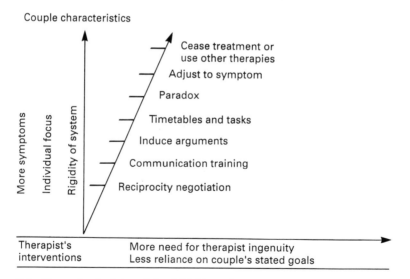

Figure 6.1 General principles of the ALI hierarchy

1 the symptoms
2 the individual focus
3 the rigidity of the system.

A couple near the top of the hierarchy is likely to present (if indeed they both come for therapy) by saying that they both agree that only one partner has a problem: for example, wife – 'I've brought him along because he is depressed; other than that we have a good relationship'; or, husband – 'I've only come to be with her; she needs help because she's gone off sex and thinks she may be frigid. There is nothing wrong with our relationship.' In such cases the partner will usually agree.

At the bottom of the hierarchy the couple is likely to present by saying, 'We have difficulty with our relationship'.

Therapeutic choices: horizontal axis

The horizontal axis represents the ways in which the therapist may choose to intervene according to the intensity of the symptom, the individual focus and the rigidity of the couple's interaction. As one ascends the hierarchy and uses structural or strategic interventions the therapist relies more upon hypotheses which reflect upon the circularity of the couple's interaction and the rules which appear to act 'as if' they govern the way the couple relate to each other (Jackson 1965).

Rigidity

The rigidity of the system is a somewhat complex concept. In general, it describes couples in which change is difficult to achieve. Occasionally a couple may seem very flexible and capable of negotiating; but when encouraged to do so, the old patterns of interaction may readily reassert themselves and negotiation is seen to be impossible.

Where the couple is very rigid it may be necessary to use a paradoxical intervention, suggesting that they have many good reasons for preferring to stay as they are and, for the moment, should not attempt to change.

Although we use the paradox, we prefer initially to see whether a couple can be helped to change by using interventions from lower down the hierarchy. This might be to use negotiation in the session to find what they want of each other which they are not getting. This might be followed up by a small timetabled activity at home based on their expressed areas of discontent. A useful beginning point for a timetabled activity is the end of the working day when a couple meet together; each may be encouraged to alter their behaviour in specific small ways such as exchanging hugs and sitting together with a cup of tea for ten minutes, taking five minutes each to tell the other about their day.

Where systemic interventions from the top of the hierarchy have been used in the early stages of therapy and the couple become more flexible, the therapist can then choose interventions from lower down the hierarchy. In this way the hierarchy can be used throughout therapy, changing interventions as the couple change.

Therapist characteristics: flexibility and the ability to live with contradictions

In order to use the behavioural–systems approach the therapist develops a flexibility which allows the possibility of thinking and acting from within different conceptual frameworks. This means being able at times to work from a de-centred and neutral position, observing and intervening to help the couple to negotiate or changing the manner in which they communicate; for example, to ask them to use 'I' rather than 'we' when talking about feelings and opinions. At other times the therapist may be thinking and working systemically. Examples might be to ally heavily with one partner to encourage him/her to speak about hidden resentments; to formulate and present a message which may reframe a symptom such as depression as shared between the couple; or to design tasks in couples with symptoms such as jealousy, continuous complaints, depression or sexual deviation by suggesting that they can be given expression by allocating specific times for these behaviours.

Within the behavioural approach each partner is assumed to be responsible for his or her own actions, and is therefore able to choose to change the way s/he negotiates or communicates. When thinking systemically, however, the therapist no longer focuses on observed behaviour, and does not assume that the individual is responsible for his/her own behaviour. Rather, the individual is conceptualized as being caught up in a complex web of interacting parts being both the responder to and the initiator of interactions.

The therapist who moves back and forward between the two approaches must be able to live with these theoretical contradictions. It is a bit like changing gear to go up a hill, or using different lenses for different subjects. The benefits for the therapist are a wider repertoire of interventions, a flexibility which allows for greater creativity and ingenuity, and a lack of dogma and rigidity about the value of one theoretical approach over another.

Thinking systemically: therapeutic ingenuity

When thinking and working systemically the therapist is concerned with the circularity of the interactions over time, and processes rather than detail are paramount. Here the therapist works with greater ingenuity, hypothesizing the possible utility of the present behaviour pattern to the couple and to the system.

Many alternative ways of viewing the couple's interaction are now of value and much use can be made of concepts derived from psychoanalysis as well as developmental theory. Knowledge of the impact of life events upon couples, family myths, intergenerational alliances or significant events which have occurred and are linked in some time sequence – all may be relevant to the couple's present inability to break out of the circular pattern of interaction which is causing discomfort.

Hypothesizing

Some of the hypotheses which seem to fit many couples who attend the clinic are as follows (for further discussion see Crowe and Ridley 1990):

- The problem may be functioning as a distance regulator, in which the couple may be avoiding sexual intimacy, physical or non-verbal closeness, emotional empathy or operational closeness.
- Symptoms may be hypothesized to be a protection against other more painful problems, or ways of maintaining the permanence of the family unit.
- Affairs may be thought of as ways of avoiding boredom, bringing excitement, or a sense of being needed into a relationship.
- Sexual refusal might be seen as part of a power struggle in which one partner dominates the non-sexual interaction and the other partner dominates in their sexual relationship.

These are some of the kinds of hypotheses therapists may be constructing while developing their interventions higher up the hierarchy.

Take, for example, a couple where the presenting problem is female reluctance to have intercourse and where the partners say they have a good relationship because they 'never argue'. Therapists may wish to consider alternative hypotheses such as the lack of arguments in their daily life being a way of protecting the couple from the pain of disagreement and discord; while their sexual difficulties might be hypothesized as being the more acceptable way of expressing resentment. One might also hypothesize a fear of greater intimacy which is expressed in both their daily life and their sexual life; in such a situation their current relationship may appear to operate as a 'distance regulator' (Byng-Hall 1985), the feared consequence of greater intimacy being the expression of differences which might precipitate rejection. These ideas are not shared with the couple like interpretations, but instead are used as the basic thinking behind systemic interventions.

Using such an hypothesis an appropriate intervention might be to encourage arguments over trivial issues. In order to facilitate this the therapist might ally with one partner and encourage greater assertiveness, thus enabling some disagreement or resentment to emerge. In this way the couple may gain a 'contained' experience in the session that it is safe to disagree. To link this to the above hypothesis, having experienced an argument over a trivial issue the couple may have gained a sense that it is safe to come a little closer; or that to disagree does not end in rejection.

Within this approach hypotheses are thought of as tools for the use of the therapist rather than truths which can be tested. The therapist therefore thinks flexibly about alternative hypotheses without according to them any ultimate validity, and changes the focus of interventions as the partners change their interaction.

A light touch and a sense of humour

Regardless of the level on the hierarchy at which the therapist is working, a light touch and a sense of humour are useful. Inexperienced therapists sometimes feel they are being rude or intrusive when they interrupt a couple's negative interaction and ask them, for example, to make specific requests for positive change rather than continuing with their generalized complaints. The therapist who can smilingly tell them they are skilled at complaining and that they are being asked to practise being simpler and more positive may make it easier for the couple to engage in a more playful or experimental interaction.

Couples may occasionally feel they are being treated as children, or are reminded of being back at school, and the therapist who is aware of this and can cheerfully suggest that they may view her as a bit of a 'schoolteacher' may well win them over.

We like the idea of play and experimentation. The therapist who conveys a quiet confidence and a sense of humour can often lighten even the darkest relationship.

How couples present themselves, as a guide to the choice of therapeutic approach

As already suggested, couples tend to present in two ways: first, those who recognize that they have a relationship difficulty, and second, those who present either as an individual or as a couple, but with a common agreement that only one partner has a problem or a symptom.

Couples who present with relationship difficulties

Couples who fall into this category often find themselves having continuous arguments, or power struggles about almost anything, without any ability to compromise or make decisions. They may be weary of their relationship believing that they are doing their best to sort out the difficulties and feeling quite pessimistic that, although they may still have a lot invested in the relationship, their joint efforts are not rewarded by an improvement. Their experience is often that the harder they try, the more difficult their relationship becomes.

Other couples may acknowledge that they have difficulties but find it hard to identify them. With such couples, smouldering resentments tend to surface in the way they communicate with each other through much mutual criticism, 'mind-reading' of the other partner, or reasonable interactions which end with a 'sting in the tail', such as 'thanks for getting my magazine for me, but I do wish you would stop leaving the newspapers all over the bedroom floor, I can hardly move for them'.

Sexual difficulties may present as relationship difficulties or as one partner's problem. When they are presented as a relationship difficulty it is often in terms of one partner's motivation, i.e. 'I've gone off sex'. This may often be accompanied by statements that there is little else wrong with the relationship. The therapist, however, can often detect hidden resentments in their communication, in the way they have shared out their joint responsibilities, or in attitudes to family members or other relationships.

Since these couples describe their difficulties as being within the relationship, we recommend that therapists begin by using reciprocity negotiation or communication training to see if the partners can negotiate for changes in their relationship. However, such couples may be very stuck or rigid in their interaction, and it may become necessary to move up the hierarchy in order to help the couple.

Couples who present with symptoms lodged in one partner

Most therapist will recognize the pattern where one partner says 'I've only come to accompany my partner, because she's depressed'. Jealousy, sexual reluctance or behavioural difficulties such as gambling, alcohol or drug abuse, or one partner's affair, may also be presented as one partner's problem.

From our perspective we would usually want to see if the couple can be helped to make some adjustments within their relationship which would enable the symptom to be modified; or to develop some ability to see the problem as shared, and hence to work together to seek some more acceptable solutions. However, interventions from the upper levels of the hierarchy such as structural or strategic techniques are often necessary with these couples.

Where there are medical or psychiatric symptoms such as multiple sclerosis, diabetes or chronic schizophrenia, the couple may be helped to understand the illness and to make adjustments to it.

Occasionally we find the need to refer couples on to other approaches where, for example, an individual prefers to seek personal therapy; and of course couples occasionally decide that they do not want to continue in therapy.

The ingredients of the behavioural–systems approach

As already indicated behavioural–systems couple therapy draws from several different therapeutic approaches, notably those of reciprocity negotiation and communication training from within the behavioural approach, and structural and strategic therapy from within systems therapy. A brief picture of each approach is now described.

Reciprocity negotiation

Reciprocity negotiation is the beginning point of the hierarchy. Thibault and Kelly (1959) developed their 'social exchange theories' which became the basis upon which successive therapists designed reciprocity negotiation skills (Stuart 1969; Liberman 1970; Azrin *et al.* 1973; Birchler *et al.* 1975; Gottman *et al.* 1977; Crowe 1982; Mackay 1985).

In social exchange theory, satisfactorily functioning marriages are thought to depend upon each partner receiving positive reactions from the other, accompanied by a willingness to respond by exchanging mutually rewarding behaviour in a 'give to get' interaction. Reciprocity negotiation is therefore designed to capitalize upon this by helping a couple to learn how to negotiate changes in behaviour which are mutually rewarding.

Although simple to describe, the method requires of the therapist some complex skills, including an ability to empathize with a couple about the extent of their difficulties while assisting them to focus down on discrete pieces of behaviour which they are encouraged to attempt to change in a reciprocal manner. It also requires a keen sense of observation of verbal and non-verbal behaviour, and an ability to focus on the present interaction of the couple rather than upon the individual dynamics or the personal or social history of the couple. The therapist has to learn to intervene early in the session and persist with the task, often working hard to encourage the couple that small changes are possible, or at least worth experimenting with as a first step towards an improved relationship.

The basic process is quite simple, and stated in terms of the steps which are required, these are:

1 complaints become wishes
2 wishes become tasks
3 tasks are reciprocal
4 the tasks are monitored.

The concepts are modified so that:

1 past becomes present
2 negative becomes positive
3 general becomes specific
4 destructive becomes constructive.

Example: Amy and Bob

This example demonstrates the use of reciprocity negotiation in the early stages of therapy to focus on achievable goals while simultaneously attending to their sexual relationship. Amy (26 years) and Bob (27 years of age) were Australian graduates who had come to London to 'get away from overintrusive parents'. They were not married but lived together in a communal dwelling house with little money. Amy had stopped enjoying sex. Bob felt he wanted to help.

Although this couple presented with a request to help them with Amy's difficulty in enjoying sexual intercourse, they were also uncertain whether their relationship would last. Amy had a five-year history of depression and had been in hospital when they met. Bob found her very sensitive, and she felt he took her seriously. Their main source of income was now Social Security, supplemented by the occasional cheque from her father.

Since their sexual relationship was the presenting problem, they were asked to agree, for the moment, to a ban on sexual intercourse; they were given a handout on relaxation techniques and they agreed to help each other to practise these twice a week (see the section on Sexual relationship problems, pp. 175–7).

When asked to discuss a common problem they agree that managing money was really difficult as Amy became anxious and pestered Bob for solutions: Bob would ignore the problem, and leave bills unopened or hidden.

The therapist de-centred herself and concentrated on helping the couple to talk to each other and to stick to the topic. The aim was to help each partner make a simple request of each other as a first step towards solving their financial problem bearing in mind steps 1–4 above. In this way the task was honed down from 'how to manage our finances' to the following requests:

> Amy asked that they sit together one evening and go through all the unopened bills, including those which Bob kept hidden in a box, and sort them out so that they could clearly see what needed to be paid. The repeat bills would be thrown away.

> Bob asked that Amy refrain from constantly nagging him about this task for the rest of the week on the understanding that they would work together on sorting out the 'mess', on one specific evening.

With the therapist's help they agreed that this would happen on Thursdays between 7.30 p.m. and 9.00 p.m. They were to ensure that they were not interrupted by any one else during this time and that if they had not managed the task by 9.00 p.m. they would set it aside until the same time the following week.

This detailed work is often experienced by the therapist as tedious but it is necessary so that the tasks can be more easily achieved. At the next appointment the couple had indeed done the task and they were beginning to feel more hopeful about their relationship.

Communication training

Communication training is based upon the assumption that couples wish to have an easy and open communication with each other. Many marital and family therapists have been involved with the development of knowledge and skills of how couples communicate and what seems to occur within the communication pattern of distressed couples. There is not space here to chronicle that development. There are, however, common elements which are summed up by Olson *et al.* (1983):

> Positive communication skills include the following: sending clear and congruent messages, empathy, supportive statements and effective problem-solving skills. Conversely, negative communication skills include the following: sending incongruent and disqualifying messages, lack of empathy, non supportive (negative) statements, poor problem solving skills, and paradoxical double bind messages

An important aspect of communication is the non-verbal interaction, and research tends to suggest that distressed couples are less likely to look into each other's eyes, and judge their spouse's behaviour more negatively than do non-distressed couples. This is particularly true of eye contact, facial expression and gesture (Schaap and Jansen-Nawas 1987).

Bateson (1971) identified the double bind as a communication pattern which he thought was peculiar to families where one member had been diagnosed as schizophrenic. Further investigation has demonstrated that patterns of interaction such as the double bind are common to many families. Many of us use patterns of communication, such as the double bind, which are inadequate, but in the majority of families these communications appear to do no harm. However, in dysfunctional couples the therapist has to be particularly alert to recognize when a particular communication style is causing relationship difficulties.

Each couple tends to develop its own distinctive style. Some couples constantly quarrel as though this were a protection from facing difficulties. Other couples develop ways of avoiding issues: each time the 'problem area' is approached a partner may change the topic. Going over old ground seems to be a safe way of detouring around difficulties too sensitive to be discussed. Other couples may bring in family members or affairs as a way of avoiding talking together about their relationship. Yet others talk amicably about some subjects but have ways of avoiding others by getting angry, leaving the room, crying or turning on the television.

In order to establish how each couple communicate it is helpful for the therapist to de-centre him/herself and ask the couple to talk together about an aspect of their relationship which causes them difficulty. In this way the therapist observes their interaction and where necessary intervenes to help the couple to change their communication style.

One partner speaks for the other
A common pattern is when one partner speaks for the other: for example, if the therapist is enquiring how Caroline relates to David's daughter from his previous marriage, David replies, 'Caroline can't stand Mandy, my eldest daughter. She gets quite upset when Mandy comes to stay because the two of them don't get on', and Caroline allows him to speak for her by saying nothing.

'We' statements rather than 'I' statements
Other couples have a variation of the above, namely, that one partner speaks for both of them, often making very sweeping statements which the other does not challenge. For example, the therapist is trying to find out from Fred what he enjoys doing with Edith; and Edith replies for them both saying,

> We always like to spend the weekend with either Fred's parents or mine, and then on Thursdays we both love to go with my sister and her husband to the local pub, and sometimes we will also go out with them on Saturdays.

For his part, Fred may neither interrupt nor challenge this statement.

Mind-reading
Mind-reading can be said to occur when one partner speaks for the other without checking whether what is said is accurate or not. It often occurs in the following form:

> *George*: You feel that I spend too much time at work, and you feel that I don't pay attention to you because my mind is occupied with other things.

The partner may have adopted the same style and respond with,

> You think that I constantly want you to be at home so that I can get you to do the odd jobs that need to be done, and so that I can take time off to go out on my own.

This pattern, like the others, may be quite pervasive.

The sting in the tail
An example of a sting in the tail has already been given (see p. 164). Such 'stings' usually follow a positive statement and this may be why they are often missed by therapists.

The therapist's interventions
The first task of the therapist is to be able to recognize the communication style of the couple which is usually quite evident within the first few minutes of the session. When intervening to alter the couple's communication style there are some guidelines which can be followed. In general we would:

1 Encourage the partners to take each other seriously
2 Encourage each partner to speak for him/herself
3 Suggest that they constantly check with the partner whether they are each being understood correctly
4 Change complaints into positive requests for change
5 Increase positive interaction
6 Discourage negative interactions such as 'sting in the tail' or detouring around subjects
7 Encourage a mutual exchange of emotional messages
8 Encourage mutual responsibility for their communication style
9 Encourage a widening of the couple's repertoire of interactions
10 Encourage a sense of play, experimentation and lightness about 'doing it differently'.

Structural techniques

Structural techniques are useful for couples where one partner is moderately depressed or is passive or dependent within the relationship. They can also help where one partner is reluctant to have sexual intercourse and this is accompanied by unstated resentments. They are also quite useful for couples who, despite clear reasons for resentments, never argue and maintain total politeness together.

Equally structural techniques may be used to bring momentum into a stuck situation or to change the non-verbal interaction of a couple whose interaction in the session is 'frozen'.

Structural techniques, like strategic interventions described in the next section, are derived from systems thinking. This means that the interventions are based upon hypotheses which the therapist or team have developed rather than upon the couple's stated goals.

It is therefore necessary to think about the circularity of the couple's inter-actions and the consistency with which the patterns of behaviour appear to repeat themselves. Thought may be given to possible 'rules' which may appear to be guiding the couple's relationship, such as 'good couples never argue', or 'one partner must always be seen to win'. Overt or covert alliances within the family system can be explored, and questions of enmeshment or over-involvement, as well as the way boundaries are maintained or ignored by the couple in their rela-tionship with each other and the extended family members, can be thought through. In developing hypotheses for each couple the therapist can also consider what positive function these behaviour patterns may have for the couple and for the family (see sections on Therapeutic choices, Thinking systematically and Hypothesizing, pp. 161, 162 and 163 respectively).

Structural interventions are designed to give the couple an experience of a different way of interacting within the session. Within the behavioural–systems approach we usually follow up the work done in the session by setting home-work tasks which are timetabled, with details agreed in the session between the couple.

The therapist draws upon a wide range of both verbal and non-verbal alter-natives, and it is here that sculpts, role-play and reverse role-play and exercises, which ask the couple to experiment with a different interaction, are used.

One such exercise explores in a light-hearted way their different tolerance of space, or physical closeness. Each partner in turn stands still while the other walks towards him/her. The still partner is asked to indicate when the other is about to come too close, by saying, 'stop now'. Couples are often surprised by the choices made by their partners. However, even if the couple do not learn some-thing new about each other, the exercise can help free them to talk about issues such as their need for closeness, or possible fears of being engulfed.

If the couple have been experimenting in the session with different non-verbal behaviour, they may be asked to continue this experimentation at home between sessions. For example, if one partner has been trying to soften a strident voice tone and the other partner to speak louder in-session, this can be included in any message or timetable given at the end of the session.

A structural intervention which we have developed is that of encouraging arguments over trivial issues in the session. We find this useful for couples where one partner is unassertive or depressed. It is also useful for couples where the man is reluctant to have sexual intercourse and the relationship is between a rather dominant and articulate woman and a somewhat submissive and hesitant man.

Since these couples may fear the whole process of arguing, it is important that the couple choose a topic which they agree is trivial but has not yet been resolved. Where one partner is less assertive it is important that this partner is involved in the choice of the issue and feels comfortable that it is sufficiently trivial. A favourite example which we quote (Crowe and Ridley 1990) is that in which the man was reluctant to have sexual intercourse with his wife. She was a very capable and organized person of whom her husband said there were no com-plaints or trivial issues to discuss. However, the therapist pursued the possibility that there might be one trivial issue about which he felt his wife was somewhat over-fastidious. After some encouragement he introduced the question of the 'toilet seat'. It would seem that after urinating he occasionally left the toilet seat up, about which his wife complained.

This issue was chosen for discussion. The therapist allied with the husband and encouraged him to see if he could at least state to his wife his disagreement with her. It took time and some gentle but patient support of the husband but it was achieved. After this they had further discussions in later sessions about more emotive issues, including whether they should separate, which they decided against. Their sexual relationship began to improve after the husband successfully disagreed with his wife about the 'toilet seat'.

Not all successful arguments over trivial issues are followed by such a significant change in their relationship. However, where couples are rather stuck and rigid in their interaction and the therapist hypothesizes the presence of unstated resentments, low self-esteem or difficulties with assertiveness, then encouragement of arguments in the session may help the couple to feel safer while exploring their differences and becoming more flexible.

We usually like to follow up any in-session therapy with a message, which may include a task which has been timetabled. Timetables for arguing are rather complicated and it may be best to suggest other tasks until the couple have had more experience in the safety of the session.

Where couples are asked to find time to discuss some of their disagreements at home, details should be decided in the session, so that the time, place and ending are clearly agreed with the therapist's help. It may also be helpful to choose who will start and how the time can be shared equally between them. We suggest that when couples find discussions of trivial issues difficult, timetables of 20 minutes, two or three times a week are likely to be as much as can be managed.

For some couples it may be preferable to suggest that they do some other task, such as spending some time doing something apart as well as finding time to do an enjoyable activity together. This too can be seen as structural changes in their relationship.

Within systems thinking focusing on small issues does two things: it intensifies the interaction, and it changes the length of time spent on the topic. This changes the structure of the repetitive sequences. By following the in-session discussions with a homework task the restructuring of their relationship is continued in the intervening weeks before the next session.

Strategic interventions

Within behavioural–systems therapy, strategic techniques sit near the top of the hierarchy and as such constitute an intervention best used for couples where the interaction is quite rigid and where one partner is heavily symptomatic.

An essential ingredient of strategic couple therapy is that of relabelling the symptom, or some of its characteristics, as shared between the couple. For example, where one partner gambles and the other worries incessantly about how they can manage financially, it may be possible to ask the gambling partner what s/he worries about and find out from the non-gambling partner in what way s/he gambles. The worrying and the gambling can then be described as joint concerns shared between the partners.

Tasks and timetables are now used to bring out-of-control symptoms within the control of the couple or to normalize the symptoms. They may be used to share the symptom between the partners and to challenge the assumptions being made by the couple about the source of their difficulties.

For example, where one partner is presented as being the cause of their difficulties because s/he drinks too much when left alone while the other partner is engrossed in many projects, the task may be to suggest that they do something enjoyable together and then have a glass of wine as part of the occasion.

The paradox is one of the main strategic interventions and was developed in its most extreme form by Mara Selvini Palazzoli and her Milan team (Selvini Palazzoli *et al*. 1978). For us the paradox is an intervention which we use when all else fails; or when we feel that a couple's interaction is extremely rigid.

Crowe has described three aspects which need to be considered when using a paradox (Crowe 1985):

1 The symptomatic behaviour
2 The reciprocal behaviour, i.e. the behaviour in the partner which can be said to be maintaining the symptom
3 The feared consequences of removing the symptom and the reciprocal behaviour.

In formulating a paradoxical message the following elements should be included:

1 Positive connotation of the symptom and the reciprocal behaviour
2 Reasons why these are useful behaviours for the couple
3 A statement about the feared consequences
4 Prescribing the symptom.

Because the paradox is an uncertain therapy in that the outcome cannot be predicted, we sometimes prefer to use a paradox as part of a split team message. In such a message the couple will be told that the team (or the therapist) cannot decide what is happening for the couple. For example,

> Half of the team think you are ready to perform a simple task at home (a task would be described) but half of the team think that for the moment you are not ready to change and to complete the task, and for the stated reasons should not attempt to change for the moment.

While including the paradox within the hierarchy of alternative levels of intervention we feel that therapists should be cautious when using the paradox. It should never be used just because the therapist is feeling frustrated at a couple's lack of movement. Instead the therapist can use these feelings of frustration to think about the symptom, the reciprocal behaviour and the feared consequences of any change, and develop a more empathic attitude towards the couple's dilemma. When delivering a paradox the therapist should always feel a certain empathy with the couple's inability to change. When this occurs the paradox no longer feels so paradoxical (Dell 1981).

Adjust to the symptom

There are many couples whose relationship is affected by an illness or accident. For some couples it is sufficient that they come to understand the illness or the effect of the accident upon the partner. Other couples may need help in continuing with a relationship and making adequate adjustments to whatever symptoms are present.

The work done by Leff and Vaughn (1985) and Falloon *et al.* (1984) with families where one member has been diagnosed as schizophrenic can be modified for use with couples. A problem-solving approach is used. The couple is asked to focus on small practical problems and work together to make choices about how these can be tackled. Delabelling, sharing the problems and encouraging greater assertiveness in the less able partner can all be used to help the couple strengthen their relationship and cope more effectively with symptoms.

Other examples might be where one partner has multiple sclerosis, or where severe arthritis or heart trouble is affecting the couple's relationship. The sexual relationship of such couples may well be severely affected by these changes and help can be given to modify their expectations and where necessary to find alternative ways of showing affection and giving physical and sexual pleasure (see section on Sexual relationship problems, pp. 175–7).

Cease treatment or use other therapies

Not all couples can yet be helped and it may therefore be necessary to end therapy. Some couples will make choices for themselves that they prefer other treatments or that they wish to seek individual treatment or simply drop out of treatment. There is no sense in which we feel that couple therapy has the monopoly of efficacy.

Moving up and down the hierarchy

The alternative levels of intervention (ALI) have been described briefly to show how one might work at each level. However, it is also possible to move up and down the hierarchy as the partners themselves change. As a couple learns for example, through arguing over trivial issues, that it is safe to disagree, it may become possible to move down the hierarchy and work with them in a session on their communication style before moving down again in order to help them negotiate for changes they both would like to occur.

Equally a couple may have made some changes in the early sessions but appear to have got stuck later in therapy when it may be wise to use a paradoxical message to help them make a further shift. For example, a couple may have negotiated changes in their own relationship but have been unable to accept that their 27-year-old daughter should be allowed to leave home. For such a couple a paradoxical message might include a statement such as,

> for the moment, you should continue to treat your daughter as though she were a young teenager and not trust her to be able to live independently because you may fear that you cannot cope as a couple without her.

In these ways the hierarchy and the alternative interventions can be used to match the couple's relationship and the different factors which seem to be affecting it at a particular time.

Special situations

Some particular interactions where jealousy, depression or female sexual refusal are involved have been quite difficult to treat in the past. We have developed a series of interventions which offer some scope for working with these more intractable difficulties. This section deals very briefly with some of the interventions we have been using with these couples.

Where jealousy is affecting a relationship the jealousy can be viewed in systemic terms and given a positive reframing such that it can be described as bringing excitement and reassurance into a relationship in which both partners may feel insecure.

Structural interventions such as role-play and role reversal may be used in-session, and the non-jealous partner may be asked to speak about his/her occasions of jealousy or uncertainty about the relationship.

The jealousy can be brought under some control and normalized by setting daily timetables for discussing it, at which time the partner is to take the jealousy seriously. They are asked not to speak of the jealousy at other times and to help each other to bring jealous feelings to the regular discussion time. As with most timetables the length, time and place should be decided with the therapist in-session.

The paradox can be used to good effect so long as it is carefully and empathically framed to reflect the detail of each individual couple's interaction.

Where depression in one partner is affecting the relationship, interventions which seek to put the depressed spouse into a caring (and therefore more competent) position may be used. This spouse may also need to be given support to be more assertive and make requests for change from the non-depressed spouse, while the non-depressed spouse may be helped over time to speak about anxieties or difficult feelings which have so far been kept hidden. In these ways the symptom is set within the context of the relationship and the depressed spouse is, as much as possible, taken out of the patient role.

This is not achieved without patient and supportive help to both partners. As the relationship changes, the non-depressed spouse may also need encouragement and praise for being able to adjust to a less passive and more assertive partner and for being prepared to share his/her more vulnerable self.

Where the woman is finding sexual intercourse less and less satisfying although having previously enjoyed sex, and the partner is pressurizing for sex, the following interventions can be considered.

At the same time as working on relationship issues the couple is asked to agree to have intercourse on a timetabled basis once or twice a week only. This is presented to the woman as a way in which she will not be pressurized by her partner during the rest of the week, and to the man as a way in which he is assured of sexual intercourse at least once a week.

It is important that the man agrees to stop pressurizing the woman and that she feels free to be affectionate towards him without assuming that he will demand sex.

The woman seems to accept this approach more easily than the man, even though one might have hypothesized the opposite reaction. She is also told that she should not expect to enjoy sexual intercourse on the timetabled occasions and can be encouraged to 'pretend' if she feels that is necessary.

It is equally important to finalize in the session the details as to which night will be chosen for intercourse; and possibly to go through some of the details such as whether they would like wine with a meal beforehand, music, the door locked, a warm room and no interruptions from children or pets and so on.

The timetable for sexual intercourse seems to act as a holding measure which enables the conflicts which have been occurring in their sexual life to be set aside for the moment. At the same time it seems to allow resentments which have been simmering to surface and to be opened up for discussion and adjustment. Frequently the female partner is somewhat passive and unassertive and the therapist may need to ally quite strongly with her to help her to speak about some of these resentments. As the experience of using the timetable is reviewed by the therapist some of the pressurizing behaviour of the man and the difficulties the woman has in asking for what she wants can be attended to.

Other specific problem areas in which couple therapy may be useful are: where there has been physical or sexual abuse of a child, where one or other partner has a past or present affair, where bereavement or other life events such as retirement or the 'empty nest' are affecting the relationship, or where divorce or separation are being discussed. More details of therapy with these problems are given in Crowe and Ridley (1990).

Sexual relationship problems

The sexual relationship is a central part of most intimate relationships, whether the couple are married, cohabiting or simply relating. Sexual function is not a subject that the couple therapist can safely ignore, because it interacts all the time with non-sexual aspects, and sexual dysfunctions and difficulties can undermine what is otherwise a perfectly satisfactory relationship. Similarly we would advise any therapist dealing with sexual dysfunctions to pay full attention also to the non-sexual aspects, because these can contribute strongly to sexual problems. It is usual to recognize three components in sexual function – desire, arousal and orgasm – each of which has physical, cognitive and emotional aspects. Thus, a man may be very attracted to his partner and be physically aroused when he is approaching her, but may lose his erection when intercourse is attempted because he is afraid of her criticism. Again, a woman may be able to become sexually aroused in intercourse, but unable to allow herself to experience orgasm, perhaps because her upbringing has led her to think that she does not deserve to experience pleasure.

Sexual therapy has to take account of both the physical factors in dysfunctions, the individual psychological aspects and the interaction with the rest of the relationship. This brief account cannot begin to address the full complexity of sexual therapy; but we feel that it is vital that anyone practising as a couple therapist should at least understand some of the factors leading to sexual problems and what can be done to help. Useful detailed information can be found in Bancroft (1989), while more practical guidelines are provided in Crowe and Ridley (1990) and in Hawton (1985).

The factors leading to sexual problems

These can be present in one or in both partners, and any combination of factors can coexist in the causation of a problem. Physical factors causing loss of desire can include, in men, low testosterone levels, and in women, the menstrual cycle, childbearing and the menopause. In both sexes the use of sedatives and tranquillizers can lead to loss of interest, and the drugs of addiction, including alcohol, have the same effect. The ageing process is somewhat unpredictable in its effect, but in both sexes there is a tendency for sex to be less frequent as age increases. Depression, anxiety, sleep loss, overwork, stress and loss of self-respect can all reduce desire. Previous bad experiences, including rape and childhood sexual abuse, can all reduce desire. Finally, relationship factors contributing to this problem can include, as might be expected, criticism, resentment, hostility and violence, but also too much politeness, caring and protection and an inability to 'close the bedroom door'. Simple lack of communication, especially on sexual matters, may also be an important factor. One further point to beware of is that the label of 'lack of desire' may be applied to a woman whose sexual appetite, although within normal limits, is much lower than that of her partner: it is then a matter of persuading the couple that the problem lies in the relationship and seeking for a compromise.

The factors leading to disorders of arousal (by which we mean erection in the male and relaxation and lubrication in the female) are many, and can include most of the factors listed above which inhibit desire. Loss of erection can be the result of many physical causes affecting the nerve and blood supply of the penis, including diabetes and multiple sclerosis, by a number of medications including beta-blockers, diuretics and anti-depressants, and by the effects of alcohol. Lack of arousal in the woman can also result from similar causes, but these are not so well documented as in the male. In addition, vaginal infections and pelvic disease can cause painful intercourse. It is, however, important to remember that many cases of poor arousal in both men and women are mainly psychogenic, and even in the most clearly physical cases there is the almost inevitable complication of performance anxiety: the sexual approach leads to anxiety, which in itself causes a further exacerbation of the problem.

Disorders of orgasm (premature and delayed ejaculation and female anorgasmia) are in most cases either psychogenic or of unknown cause. Occasionally delayed orgasm may be caused by anti-depressant drugs, and spinal and neurological diseases can also lead to these problems. In most cases, however, we have to consider psychological factors, including relationship aspects and performance anxiety.

Treatment principles

This does not pretend to be an exhaustive account of the treatment of sexual problems, but in the context of couple therapy it seems appropriate to mention at least the basic approaches and techniques used in treatment.

Following a full assessment including both physical, individual and relationship factors, the partners are encouraged to talk together about the problem, and if there are difficulties the therapist will try to help them to be more open and explicit. It is sometimes necessary to teach the couple some of the basic facts of sex, and if there are doubts about possible physical illness a medical opinion may need to be sought.

The next step will depend on the type of problem. If there are problems of desire, it may well be appropriate to focus immediately on the relationship, and if necessary on past experiences of both partners, without specific sexual tasks (see section on Strategic interventions, p. 171). In those cases with dysfunctions we would usually spend more time assessing the problem, including physical investigations if necessary. In most such cases we then set a homework task based on Masters and Johnson's (1970) 'sensate focus' – a form of prolonged foreplay avoiding the genital areas with a ban on intercourse. The couple are also given physical relaxation exercises.

In cases of impotence and of lack of arousal, as long as there are no major physical causes or complications, the reduction of anxiety and improved communication produced by the therapy sessions and the homework exercises are often enough to reverse the problem. In other conditions specific exercises are given, including the stop–start technique for premature ejaculation, the 'superstimulation' approach for delayed ejaculation, the use of vibrators for anorgasmia and the use of graded relaxation and dilatation for vaginismus (Hawton 1985).

Results are in the main quite good in the treatment of sexual problems, although it is important to remember that these are best thought of as improvements rather than cures. One difficult area for sexual therapy is probably those cases of impotence where there are either clear organic problems or where factors such as the ageing process or relationship difficulties are affecting the situation. There are now some physical treatments available, including the use of yohimbine capsules and the use of papaverine by self-injection into the penis, and these two approaches have brought, albeit artificially, some improvement to these previously intractable problems.

Conclusions

Behavioural–systems couple therapy is a form of brief therapy for relationship problems which is not simply eclectic but in fact integrates the two types of therapy from which it was formed. The ALI hierarchy is the mechanism for this integration, and in moving up and down the hierarchy the therapist matches the intervention to the type of problem s/he is dealing with. The behavioural interventions are simpler and more stereotyped while the systemic ones are more complicated and depend more on the formation of hypotheses and less on the goals as stated by the two partners.

In this approach the elements of negotiation and communication training are quite similar to those of behavioural marital therapy, with the addition in our work of the de-centred position for the therapist. The use of circular questioning and paradox is less rigid than that of the Milan group which developed them; we tend to use them only when we are in a 'stuck' situation with a couple, and to move out of that way of working as soon as possible. In the use of trivial arguments we are to some extent following the structural approach of Minuchin, and in general our approach is perhaps nearer to that of Minuchin than to other models; but again this is simply one in a whole series of techniques which we have found to be useful in making changes in couple interaction.

The use of timetables and tasks is one of our more original developments, and especially in regard to jealousy and in sexual refusal we feel that we have a very valuable method at our disposal.

In other ways we feel that new ground is being broken by this therapeutic approach. The linking of sexual and relationship therapy in the same clinical setting is, we think, a very sound one, and is helpful to both forms of therapy. In the past sex therapy has seemed to be in some ways an extension of individual therapy, with only limited attention being paid to the relationship in which the sexual problem is occurring. The integrative aspects of what we do have yet to be evaluated, but have the potential for considerable growth.

The behavioural systems approach is highly compatible with other forms of treatment besides sexual therapy. Most forms of behavioural therapy or individual counselling as well as psychiatric treatment can be carried out concurrently with this form of couple therapy. Only intensive dynamic psychotherapy, with its rather different emphasis on exploring internal conflicts and unconscious meaning, seems to cause some motivational problems in individuals who are in couple therapy, and it may be preferable to delay the couple therapy until the individual therapy is completed. The question should be asked as to how effective behavioural–systems couple therapy is. This cannot be answered directly, since there has not been a specific trial of the combined approach. However, there have been numerous studies comparing the behavioural forms of marital therapy with no-treatment controls, and in all these the active treatment has been superior (Hahlweg and Jacobson 1984). Two studies have compared behavioural marital therapy with other approaches. Crowe (1978) showed that the behavioural approach was superior to a non-specific supportive approach to couple therapy, with a third, interpretative, form of therapy being intermediate in its effect. Emmelkamp *et al.* (1984) found that reciprocity-based marital therapy was equal in its effect both to communication training and a 'system-theoretic' form of therapy. This is the only study to date to have evaluated the effect of systemic marital therapy.

Thus, there is considerable evidence that the components of behavioural–systems couple therapy are effective in themselves, and it is our belief that the combination of the two approaches is more effective than either alone. We are intending to carry out various controlled studies to evaluate the components of the therapy, and we have already embarked on a trial of the negotiated timetable for couples with incompatible sexual drives compared with straightforward Masters and Johnson therapy. Another relevant and answerable question is whether, in a case of depression or similar psychiatric illness where the patient is in a relationship, couple therapy adds something both to the treatment of the acute problem and to the long-term prophylaxis against depression.

Clearly with any treatment approach such as the behavioural systems one there are many further developments which may be made in future, and no such approach should be static and unchanging. We feel that the most important criterion on which to judge a form of therapy is its perceived efficacy in changing behaviour and interaction in the couple. The same will apply to further innovations in our method, and we hope to develop techniques to resolve more difficult problems and to provide help more quickly to those couples for whom we can now already do something.

In this context it should be mentioned that there is a long waiting list at most Relate Marriage Guidance centres, and if a more rapid and effective approach to couple problems were more widely applied and accepted it should be possible to increase the numbers treated and thereby improve the service.

In the area of prevention of relationship problems this approach may have a good deal to offer. Two aspects which lend themselves particularly well to 'do-it-yourself' therapy are reciprocity negotiation and timetables. The present authors are already planning a couples' self-help guide to these two types of therapy, and if this led to only a 5 per cent drop in the number of couples seeking therapy it would be worth doing.

Clearly it would be impossible to prevent or successfully treat all relationship problems, but if it is possible to help a greater proportion of those in this kind of distress, particularly those who are in the psychiatric spectrum, much will have been achieved.

References

Azrin, N.H., Naster, B.J. and Jones, R. (1973) Reciprocity counselling: a rapid learning-based procedure for marital counselling, *Behaviour Research and Therapy* 11: 365–82.

Bancroft, J. (1989) *Human Sexuality and its Problems*, Edinburgh: Churchill Livingstone.

Bateson, G. (1971) *Steps to an Ecology of Mind*, New York: Ballantine Books.

Birchler, G.R., Weiss, R.L. and Vincent, J.P. (1975) A multi method analysis of social reinforcement exchange between mentally distressed and nondistressed spouse and stranger dyads, *Journal of Personality and Social Psychology* 31: 349–60.

Byng-Hall, J. (1985) Resolving distance conflicts, in A.S. Gurman (ed.) *Casebook of Marital Therapy*, New York: Guilford Press.

Crowe, M.J. (1978) Conjoint marital therapy: a controlled outcome study, *Psychological Medicine* 8: 623–36.

—— (1985) Marital therapy – a behavioural–systems approach, in W. Dryden (ed.) *Marital Therapy in Britain*, London: Harper & Row.

—— (1982) The treatment of marital and sexual problems. A behavioural approach, in A. Bentovim, G.G. Barnes and A. Cooklin (eds) *Family Therapy, Vol. 1*, London: Academic Press.

—— and Ridley, J. (1990) *Therapy with Couples: A Behavioural-Systems Approach to Marital and Sexual Problems*, Oxford: Blackwell Scientific Publications.

Dell, P.F. (1981) Some irreverent thoughts on paradox, *Family Process* 20: 37–51.

Emmelkamp, P., van der Helm, M., MacGillavry, D. and van Zanten, B. (1984) Marital therapy with clinically distressed couples: a comparative evaluation of system-theoretic, contingency contracting and communication skills approaches, in K. Hahlweg and N.S. Jacobson (eds) *Marital Interaction: Analysis and Modification*, New York: Guilford Press.

Falloon, I.R.H., Boyd, J.L. and McGill, C.W. (1984) *Family Care of Schizophrenia: A Problem Solving Approach to the Treatment of Mental Illness*, New York: Guilford Press.

Gottman, J., Markman, H. and Notarius, C. (1977) The topography of marital conflict: a sequential analysis of verbal and nonverbal behaviour, *Journal of Marriage and the Family* 39: 461–77.

Hahlweg, K. and Jacobson, N.S. (1984) *Marital Interaction: Analysis and Codification*, New York: Guilford Press.

Haley, J. (1976) *Problem Solving Therapy*, New York: Harper & Row.

Hawton, K. (1985) *Sex Therapy: A Practical Guide*, Oxford: Oxford Medical Publications.

Jackson, D.D. (1965) The study of the family, *Family Process* 4: 1–20.

Leff, J. and Vaughn, C. (1985) *Expressed Emotion in Families*, New York: Guilford Press.

Liberman, R.P. (1970) Behavioural approaches in family and couple therapy, *American Journal of Orthopsychiatry* 40: 106–18.

McFarlane, W.R. (1983) *Family Therapy in Schizophrenia*, New York: Guilford Press.

Mackay, D. (1985) Marital therapy: the behavioural approach, in W. Dryden (ed.) *Marital Therapy in Britain*, London: Harper & Row.

Masters, W.H. and Johnson, V.E. (1970) *Human Sexual Inadequacy*, Boston: Little, Brown & Co.

Minuchin, S. (1974) *Families and Family Therapy*, London: Tavistock Publications.

Olson, D.H., McCubbin, H.I., Barnes, H., Larsen, A., Muxen, M. and Wilson, M. (1983) *Families: What Makes Them Work*, Los Angeles: Sage Publications.

Schaap, C. and Jansen-Nawas, C. (1987) Marital interaction, affect and conflict resolution, *Sexual and Marital Therapy* 2: 35–51.

Selvini Palazzoli, M., Boscolo, L., Cecchin, G. and Prata, G. (1978) *Paradox and Counter-Paradox*, New York: Jason Aronson.

—— (1980) Hypothesising, circularity, neutrality, three guidelines for the conductor of the session, *Family Process* 19: 3–12.

Sluzki, C.E. (1978) Marital therapy from a systems perspective, in T.J. Paolino and B.S. McCrady (eds) *Marriage and Marital Therapy*, New York: Brunner/Mazel.

Stuart, R.B. (1969) Operant interpersonal treatment for marital discord, *Journal of Consulting and Clinical Psychology* 33: 675–82.

Thibault, J.W. and Kelly, H.H. (1959) *The Social Psychology of Groups*, New York: Wiley.

7

Sex therapy: an integrative model

WAGUIH R. GUIRGUIS

Theory

Historical background

Before Masters and Johnson published their landmark book, *Human Sexual Inadequacy* (1970), sex therapy was practised by isolated professionals using a very diverse assortment of methods. Physicians were using hormones to correct the supposed hormonal imbalance, surgeons used surgery to correct the alleged anatomical abnormalities behind sexual dysfunctions, while pharmacologists were busy inventing the often dreamt-of aphrodisiac. However, it was psychoanalysis which dominated the therapy scene in the first half of this century, on the unproven assumption that sexual problems are due to deep-seated psychological conflicts in early childhood. Disillusionment with the poor outcome results of such a lengthy and expensive therapy led in the 1950s and 1960s to some early attempts to use shorter, more directive therapies.

Wolpe (1958) and Lazarus (1963) used progressive muscle relaxation, and Mirowitz (1966) used hypnosis to overcome sexual anxiety. Cooper (1963) and Johnson (1965) used graduated behavioural instructions to relieve sexual dysfunctions. Semans (1956) used the 'squeeze technique' to treat premature ejaculation and Haslam (1965) was treating vaginismus by inserting vaginal dilators of various sizes to overcome the phobia of penetration. The main contribution of Masters and Johnson was to put together these fragments of clinical methods into a comprehensive programme of treatment which made a great deal of therapeutic sense (Guirguis 1991). They made, therefore, the first attempt to integrate sex therapy. However, the way Masters and Johnson described their therapy, but not necessarily the way they actually practised it, and their insistence on denying the psychotherapeutic component of their therapy, did in fact encourage the 'split' approach which dogged sex therapy in the first decade of its existence.

The 'split' approach

Masters and Johnson described their therapy as a sequence of behavioural instructions or 'exercises' that the couple performs between sessions. The sessions are used to feed back the experience gathered from these 'exercises' and to discuss any 'difficulties' the couple may encounter during these 'exercises'. They discouraged transference and countertransference, saw them as impeding therapy and denied their occurrence in their type of therapy. Some behaviourists took these views to an extreme, denying the psychotherapeutic element of sex therapy and seeing no place for the therapist–couple relationship in it. An extreme example of that was the use of instruction sheets which were handed to couples to use as 'cooking instructions', the use of mail-order packages of therapy and the publication of many self-help manuals of 'do-it-yourself' sex therapy.

As a reaction to the rising tide of the behavioural approach in sex therapy, the Balint group of family planning doctors, known later as the Institute of Psychosexual Medicine, was adopting and practising an opposite approach. They saw the doctor–patient relationship as central to their sex therapy, considered sexual problems as intrapsychic problems and avoided the use of any directive or active forms of therapy. They even excluded the sexual partner from therapy. That led to a widening of the gap between the behavioural and psychodynamic approaches, with sexual problems being classified as *either* intrapsychic and needing to be treated individually on psychodynamic lines *or* a learned behaviour which should be corrected in joint therapy using a set of homework tasks.

Another area of split was created between the physical and psychological approaches. Although Masters and Johnson's work did not develop from a psychological theory, but from an extensive physiological study, their treatment methods and the impressive success rate they claimed gave the false impression that sexual problems are psychological problems which invariably respond to simple behavioural instructions. The physical component of sexual problems was neglected for a while. Various sources claimed that 2–5 per cent only of sexual dysfunctions were due to physical causes. As a reaction to that, urologists, gynaecologists and endocrinologists were actively looking for physical causes and physical cures for sexual problems. Recently quoted figures for physical causes are as high as 40–60 per cent in the case of impotence (Guirguis 1988a). This led to another unhelpful split between the physical and psychological approaches with cases classified as *either* physical *or* psychological in origin and thus requiring *either* physical *or* psychological methods of treatment (Kellett 1990).

Another irrational split was between marital and sexual problems. Although Masters and Johnson recognize 'the relationship' as the focus of their therapy, they saw marital discord as an exclusion factor in selecting couples for therapy and as a bad prognostic factor. Sex therapists turned down couples with marital problems as unsuitable for sex therapy, or at least referred them to marriage-guidance clinics prior to, or instead of, taking them on for therapy. Marital therapists, on the other hand, saw sexual problems as only a feature of marital discord which should correct itself once the non-sexual side of the relationship improved. Couples were classified, therefore, as having *either* a marital problem for which they needed marital therapy *or* a sexual problem for which sex therapy was the answer.

The need for integration

By the end of the 1970s clinicians fully realized the futility and absurdity of the split approach. Integration, 'to complete what is imperfect by the addition of necessary parts' (*Standard Oxford English Dictionary*), was the inevitable end to a decade of wasteful split and rivalry between seemingly opposing approaches. A rational and unbiased look at the nature of sexual problems will explain why sex therapy had no choice but to integrate these therapeutic approaches into a comprehensive integrated approach. The reasons are as follows:

1 *Sexual dysfunctions are psychosomatic conditions*, with physical, psychological and relationship factors contributing in various proportions to the dysfunction. Cases of the most obvious physical origin may be largely caused by psychological or relationship problems. Equally, cases of the most obvious psychological origin could have an underlying physical cause and would only respond to physical forms of therapy (Guirguis 1988a).

   Sexual problems are not, therefore, either psychological or physical but they often are both, as the two are not mutually exclusive. Assessment should be directed to measuring the relative contribution of both factors and sex therapy should take care of both aspects.

2 *Sexual dysfunctions often operate at more than one level*, and assuming that sexual dysfunctions are not more than learned behaviours or sexual anxieties is not only over-simplistic but incorrect. Equally, assuming that all sexual dysfunctions are due to deep-seated conflicts or early childhood experiences is not only unhelpful but also unsupported, even if that may be true in some individual cases. In most cases there is more than one factor operating at more than one level and with varied degrees of significance. Assessment should be directed to the relative significance of each of these factors, and therapy should be able to move freely between the different levels depending on the level at which therapy encounters resistance.

3 *Sexual dysfunctions happen within a relationship*, and trying to separate the sexual from the non-sexual parts of the relationship is not only artificial but is often impossible. By the time the couple comes for therapy they usually have problems in both areas of the relationship. The futile exercise of trying to find out which started first, the sexual or the non-sexual problems, is only of academic value. Sexual and couple therapy cannot, therefore, be separated.

4 *Sexual dysfunctions are such a heterogeneous group of disorders*, that it will be unreasonable to claim that there is one approach or one therapeutic tool which helps all problems. The only thing sexual dysfunctions have in common is that they affect sexual function. They may, therefore, have some common features, like performance anxiety, spectating or fear of failure. Apart from that, sexual dysfunctions are so diverse that an effective therapist has to be eclectic, or 'therapeutically opportunistic' (Sager 1987), calling on as many techniques as can be mastered from as many therapeutic sources as he or she knows of.

To be able to do so the therapist has to be established in one of the major therapeutic schools, and be confident enough to deviate from that school to borrow from other schools any therapeutic tools he or she may need to achieve therapeutic success. However, eclecticism alone is not sufficient, and as Sager stressed, 'a new level of integration is required' (Sager 1987).

The era of integration and eclecticism

One of the earliest attempts to integrate the two opposing schools of psycho-therapy, psychoanalysis and behaviour therapy, was successfully made by Kaplan (1974). She saw sexual problems as operating at two different levels: the superficial or 'immediate' level, which is amenable to behavioural and educational measures, and the deep or 'remote' level which can only be dealt with by directing the therapy to a deeper level. This can only be done, accord-ing to Kaplan, by using psychoanalytic techniques either to tackle the resis-tance or to get round it (circumvention). A few years later Kaplan made another attempt to integrate physical and psychological factors in her edited book on the evaluation of sexual disorders (Kaplan 1983). The book presents an integrated model of evaluation which takes into account not only physical but also psycho-logical factors, whether they be superficial or deep. With the surge of physical methods of treatments, notably the use of intracavernous injections of vaso-active drugs to treat impotence, there have been many reminders of the need to integrate the seemingly opposing approaches: physical and psychological (Guirguis 1989; Gregoire 1990; Kellett 1990). The area where integration was most successful is integrating sexual and marital therapy. One of the earliest attempts came from Germany in 1982. Arentewicz and Schmidt (English trans-lation, 1983: vii) argue that there is no such thing as sex therapy and that 'therapy is most effective when it is integrated into a total programme for treat-ing neurotic conflict and marital distress along with the symptoms of sexual dysfunction'. From the United States came a major contribution to integrating sex and marital therapy by adding the systems perspective (Weeks and Hof 1987). The most recent and innovative attempt came from Britain. Crowe and Ridley presented in their recent book a behavioural–systems approach which can be used to help couples with relationship problems whether they present with a sexual or a marital problem (Crowe and Ridley 1990; see also Chapter 6, this volume).

Sex therapy clinics in Britain developed their own models to reflect these attempts at integration. Cooper (1986) asked sex therapists in Britain to indicate the main approach they use in their practice. Of the 144 respondents only 33 (less than 23 per cent) stated that they used only one approach in their practice, while 111 (more than 77 per cent) of them were using a modified version which incor-porated two or more approaches.

Some of these integrated eclectic models are described in detail in various publications. A representative sample includes the Edinburgh model (Bancroft 1989), the Oxford model (Hawton 1985), the St George's London model (Stanley 1981) and the Ipswich model (Guirguis 1991). The rest of this chapter describes the Ipswich model as an example and how it is applied in practice, with a full case example to illustrate the model. This account is based on the more detailed account published in another book in this series (Hooper and Dryden 1991).

Practice

The Ipswich Psychosexual Clinic was first established by the author in 1979. The approach adopted by the clinic went through repeated changes which reflected the gradual move from the 'split' to the 'integrated' approach and from 'orthodoxy' to 'eclecticism'. The present model is an integrated model which takes account of both the physical and psychological factors. It is also a dynamic model which sees sexual dysfunctions not as a static condition but a constantly changing situation, which develops over time. It emphasizes the role of maladaptive solutions, like trying too hard, not communicating or criticizing, in not only converting a difficulty into a dysfunction but also in maintaining such a dysfunction, even after the original causes are removed.

A model of causation has to give some indication as to why some people have problems and how they can be helped to overcome them. The model is summarized in Figure 7.1.

Why do some people have sexual problems?

According to the Ipswich model, sexual problems are the result of an interaction between predisposing factors, which make some people more susceptible to having sexual problems, and some precipitating factors. The interaction between these two set of factors produces the first few failures. 'Few failures' need not develop into a 'dysfunction' unless the couple get caught into the vicious circle of failure (see Figure 7.1) Once the vicious circle is established it can go on indefinitely, driven partly by its own momentum, but largely by the maladaptive ways in which the couple tries to break it. These maladaptive methods act as perpetuating factors which make the vicious circle go faster and deeper.

A brief account of these *predisposing, precipitating* and *perpetuating* factors follows.

Predisposing factors
Predisposing factors could be one or more of these four factors:

1 False beliefs and concepts, which may take one of two forms: either sexual prohibitions like 'nice girls should not do it, and if they do should not enjoy it' or 'you should not touch yourself, especially if you are married'. Or it may take the form of sexual misconceptions like 'a man should always initiate sex and do all the work' or 'if your man really loves you he should give you an orgasm every time'. These prohibitions and misconceptions predispose people to sexual dysfunctions by inhibiting the free expression of their emotional and sexual feeling. It also enforces a set of rules about the 'right' and 'wrong' ways of feeling and behaving which are based not on what is best for the couple but on what society feels most comfortable with.

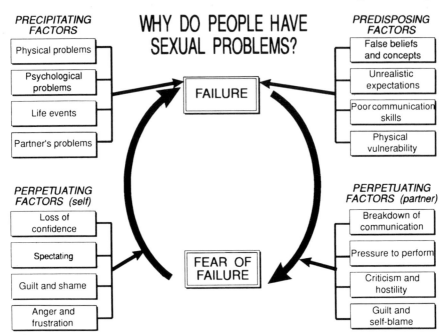

Figure 7.1 The vicious circle of failure in sexual problems

2 Unrealistic expectations are a natural product of ignorance. Being such a taboo
   subject, sex is one of the most poorly understood functions of the human body
   and is, therefore, an area where expectations are very unrealistic. These are
   some examples: 'the ultimate goal which every couple should aim for is mutual,
   simultaneous and earth-moving orgasm'; 'vaginal orgasm is better than
   clitoral orgasm and multiple orgasms are better than a single orgasm'; 'men
   can have an erection anytime if they try hard enough'; or 'a woman must
   always respond sexually if touched in the right spot, i.e. the clitoris'.
       Unrealistic expectations can lead to a predisposition to sexual dysfunctions
   by putting an enormous pressure on men and women to perform beyond what
   their body is capable of. If they do not live up to these unrealistic expectations,
   they panic and make themselves feel a failure.
3 Poor communication skills predispose couples to having sexual problems
   because sex is a form of communication. Partners who cannot even talk to each
   other should not wonder why they cannot enjoy sex together. To communicate
   effectively, the couple need to tell each other what they want, like and dislike
   about sex. They should also be able to express feelings, particularly negative
   ones like guilt, anger, hostility and frustration.
       Holding back erections, orgasms or sexual desire is one of the most power-
   ful expressions of anger in a sexual relationship. Placid, timid and overtly
   quiet men, who are frightened of their own anger, tend to use erections as a
   weapon in marital conflicts. Women who feel resentful, misused and unap-
   preciated by their husbands will naturally find it difficult to feel loving and
   sexual towards them unless these negative feelings are expressed and dealt

with. Families who pride themselves on the fact that they 'never have rows' are particularly vulnerable.

4 Physical and psychological vulnerabilities are personal weaknesses which make some individuals more susceptible. As people who suffer from peptic ulcers have a vulnerable stomach and those who have asthma have a vulnerable chest, people who have sexual problems seem to have vulnerable sex organs which react to stress by becoming dsyfunctional. Physical vulnerabilities could be constitutional – that is, the person is born with it – or it could be acquired later in life as a result of ageing, illness, trauma, drugs or surgical operations.

Psychological vulnerabilities could also be either constitutional, like a high level of arousal, or neurotic personality traits, or it could be acquired at an early stage of psychosexual development. Unresolved attachment to one of the parents may lead to either an abnormal fear of intimacy or a fear of abandonment. One of the most traumatic childhood experiences is the betrayal of trust and the early sexualization of relationships as a result of being subjected to sexual abuse as a child (Guirguis 1987).

A person or a couple who are made particularly vulnerable, by one or more of these predisposing factors, will experience a sexual failure if subjected to one or more of these precipitating factors.

Precipitating factors

These are stresses which determine *when* the predisposed person experiences the sexual difficulty and not *whether* he or she does or not. The stress could be a physical illness like diabetes or hypertension, or a psychological problem like depression, anxiety or fear of pregnancy, or it could be a life event like the loss of a spouse, loss of status, children leaving home or an extra-marital affair. The stress may also be a problem in the non-dysfunctional partner like pregnancy, menopause, traumatic surgery or even a sexual dysfunction in the partner, like reacting to premature ejaculation by losing interest in sex. Drugs, including alcohol, and major surgery can also act as precipitating factors.

Perpetuating factors

Perpetuating factors are the unsuccessful attempts to deal with sexual failure and with the fear of failing again. Far from solving the problem these attempted solutions complicate the problem even further, and the longer or harder they are attempted the more intractable the original problem becomes. The problem with these attempted solutions, which become perpetuating factors later on, is that they seem so natural and make so much common sense that the couple find it difficult to abandon them or to try something else. The perpetuating reactions come from both sides: the presenting person may start by being frightened of failing again, trying hard not to fail, watching his own performance, feeling guilty and ashamed, making an extra effort to succeed, and when all that fails he loses his confidence, thinks that he is abnormal and gets very angry and frustrated with himself or with his partner. The non-dysfunctional person may react to her partner's failure by not talking about it to avoid hurting him or by putting subtle pressure on him to try harder, accusing him of not trying hard enough, criticizing him or feeling guilty and blaming herself. The couple may even end up switching off sex completely to avoid the unpleasant feelings generated by trying and failing. That is how attempted solutions can perpetuate a problem and convert a 'failure' into a 'dysfunction'.

How to break the vicious circle?

In the Ipswich model the aim of therapy is to break the vicious circle of failure by abandoning the unsuccessful attempts and adopting a different approach. Although doing that may, in itself, break the vicious circle, in most cases the therapy is not complete unless the predisposing and precipitating factors are dealt with. In a simple non-complicated case of sexual dysfunction in partners who are physically healthy and have no personal or relationship problems the treatment is straightforward. The couple is started on the first stage of therapy by engaging in the sensate focus exercises. We suggest that the couple puts aside two or three periods of unpressurized time a week, in which they do together something physical at which they could not possibly fail. To minimize the chances of failure, we ban the achievement side of love-making like sexual intercourse and touching the genital areas. This ban eases pressures considerably. We then recommend that the couple take turns in organizing these sessions so that the responsibility for the treatment is shared between them. On the designated night they try to come home early, or put the children to bed in good time, so that they are both fresh and not tired or exhausted.

They start by doing something non-sexual first, like having a bath together, playing a game or having a small drink. They then proceed from that into a touching session in which they take turns in 'getting' pleasure. We deliberately avoid using the word 'giving' as we expect the couple from then onwards to take responsibility for their own pleasure and stop waiting for their partner to 'give' it to them. The person whose turn it is to get pleasure should ensure, therefore, that he gets pleasure by concentrating on what happens to his body, exploring different feelings from different parts, experimenting with varieties of pressures or directions and he must give feedback to his partner about what her touch is doing to him so that she can modify her touch accordingly. When he has had his turn she starts having hers and she follows the same rules. We emphasize that these exercises are not meant to turn them on, make them feel sexual or produce erections or orgasms. We even suggest that if they start to have any of these reactions that they should stop.

These seemingly simple exercises have immediate effects of easing pressure, reducing performance anxiety, redefining success as having fun rather than producing reactions, and they emphasize the joint nature of the problem. They are also a useful exercise in assertiveness and in communicating about sexual matters.

When the partners feel comfortable with non-genital touch we gradually introduce genital touch, but still follow the same principles and keep the ban on erections, orgasms and intercourse. When these forbidden reactions start to happen in spite of trying to stop them we feel then that the couple is ready to go on to experimenting with sexual intercourse. But before we lift the ban on intercourse we may have to correct some misinformation by giving sex education, modify some unhelpful attitudes and to widen the concept of 'sex' to include anything which a couple does together which gives them pleasure or makes them feel good rather than the narrow concept which equates sex with intercourse. We originally limit intercourse to the female superior position and restrict sexual movement to the slow, gentle and non-demanding movements. When they feel comfortable with restrained intercourse we encourage more demanding movements and experimenting with different positions. By the end of six to eight sessions the partners learn a great deal, their attitudes become more positive, communication improves and the sexual dysfunction is resolved. A follow-up session occurs in six weeks' time and if all is well then, the couple is given no more regular appointments but invited to telephone for an appointment if they feel the need to come back at any time in the future.

Unfortunately, very few cases follow this smooth straightforward course. Most of the cases we see encounter problems at some stage during this course. The sensate focus exercises are, in our model, rarely seen as a 'therapy' tool; their most valuable use is as a 'diagnostic' tool (Guirguis 1988a). When couples attempt the intimate exercises of the 'sensate focus', undisclosed attitudes will be uncovered, deep-seated problems in the partner or in the relationship will unfold and resistance to change will be mobilized. It is at this point in the course of therapy that the strictly behavioural approach will get stuck and reject the couple as 'not motivated enough to get better', while an integrated approach will deal with these issues as they arise and keep the therapy moving until complete resolution.

How and when to deal with underlying issues?

That depends on the stage at which these issues emerge (see Figure 7.2). Resistance and blocks could be encountered at any of the following stages.

The stage of history taking

Traumatic experiences often emerge at a later stage of therapy, but if they are severe enough to make it difficult for the couple to engage in sensate focus exercises, they may have to be dealt with at this stage of history-taking. Traumatic experiences may be a recent life event or a traumatic childhood experience. Recent life events include the loss of status, like redundancy or retirement, loss of a spouse by death or divorce, loss of femininity or fertility as after a mastectomy, hysterectomy, sterilization or menopause. These life events are dealt with by grief work, like any other case of unresolved grief. A history of sexual abuse during childhood may also emerge at this stage and should be dealt with either in individual or group therapy (for full details see Guirguis 1987). If dealing with these traumatic experiences are not enough to resolve the sexual dysfunction the couple could go on to the next stage.

The stage of physical examination

Full physical examination and routine physical investigations are not necessary in every case. But if there is a doubt, from the history, that physical or psychiatric conditions may be contributing to the problem, a full physical and mental state

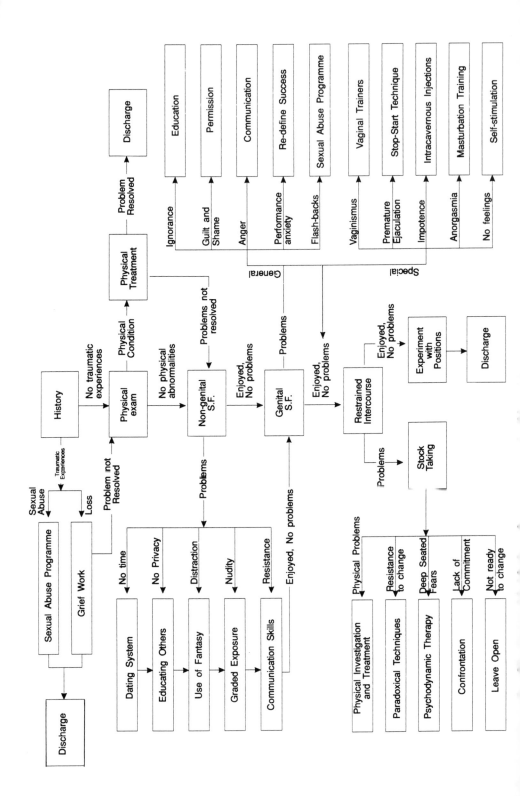

examination is undertaken. Depression has to be treated by anti-depressants, menopausal symptoms by hormone replacement, vaginal infections by the appropriate agent and osteoarthritis by anti-inflammatory drugs. One simple physical intervention which can achieve a dramatic improvement in some cases is the manipulation of drug intake. The mere cutting-down on smoking and on alcohol consumption or going on a diet to reduce excessive obesity can lead to a marked improvement. Some prescribed drugs can cause problems but others with a similar therapeutic effect do not. Beta blockers for high blood pressure can be replaced by alpha blockers or the new calcium ion antagonists which are less interfering in sexual function. Cimetidine (Tagamet), an antacid for treatment of peptic ulcers, could similarly be changed to Ranitidine (Zantac) (Guirguis 1988b).

If appropriate treatment of the physical or mental condition was not enough to resolve the sexual dysfunction, probably because the vicious circle of failure had already been established, the couple could go on to the next stage.

The stage of non-genital sensate focus
Few couples encounter problems at this stage. I discuss below some of the commonly encountered problems and how to deal with them.

'We could not find the time to do it, we were too busy' This is a common problem, and to deal with it couples need to learn the skills of time-budgeting, to give up some activities to create time for themselves and to get used to saying 'no' more often. In some cases introducing the 'dating system' can ensure that time will be made. The couple is advised to get together every Sunday night and fix two to three nights of the following week to spend together. Part of this time could be used to do the sensate focus exercises.

'We had the time but the children kept walking into the room, the telephone did not stop ringing and friends dropped in unexpectedly' When couples have a sexual problem they allow children, family and friends to have a free access to their time and privacy. To re-claim this time and privacy they need a lot of self-discipline and to re-educate children and friends to respect their need for privacy. However, an act as simple as putting a lock on the bedroom door may take two or three sessions to achieve.

'I could not get completely undressed, I felt self-conscious' Problems with nudity can be due to a very simple cause like 'the room was too cold', which can be resolved by simple measures like investing in a fan heater. It could also be due to problems in the relationship like 'I couldn't trust him, he would jump on me', which can only be resolved by working on the issue of trust and by encouraging graded exposure. Sometimes the cause may be more deep-seated, like negative attitudes towards nudity or problems of body image. The latter problems may need individual therapy using a cognitive therapy approach and specific techniques to improve body image (Guirguis 1987).

'*I could not concentrate, my mind was wandering all over the place*' This could be either an avoidance technique or a genuine difficulty in maintaining the mental link between the body and pleasure centres in the brain, a 'tuning-in' problem. The use of fantasies can be an effective way of dealing with distraction. Unfortunately, some women have difficulty in recalling a fantasy. Reading a book like *My Secret Garden* (Friday 1976) can stimulate imagination, supply material for fantasies and give permission to have and to use the sexual fantasies.

'*I hated it, felt irritated, ticklish and the whole thing seemed silly*' This response is not uncommon in couples who are 'bottling-up' unpleasant feelings like anger, hostility or resentment. These exercises are bound to bring these feelings to the surface and the couple will not be able to persevere with these intimate forms of touch unless these feelings are expressed, acknowledged and dealt with. Improving communication skills, expressing anger, handling anger and learning the art of compromise are some of the therapeutic techniques needed to deal with resistance to engage into sensate focus exercises (for details see Guirguis 1991).

Once these issues are dealt with, the couple will start to enjoy the relaxing, non-pressurized and non-demanding feelings generated by the sensate focus exercises. They may even feel tempted to break the bans. This usually means that they are ready to go on to the next stage.

The stage of genital sensate focus

Although most couples will feel excited about lifting the ban on touching genital areas, and see it as a sign that they are progressing, many of them will encounter a fresh set of problems. The problems could be general, present in any case irrespective of the presenting dysfunction, or could be specific to the presenting complaint.

Some of the general problems commonly encountered at this stage are now discussed.

Ignorance about own sexuality, partner's sexuality or sex in general Sex education using illustrated books, diagrams and three-dimensional models can be useful. *Men and Sex* (Zilbergeld 1980), *Women and Sex* (Hooper 1986), *Treat Yourself to Sex* (Brown and Faulder 1988) are a few examples. The best educational and permission-giving tool is no doubt the joint physical examination. This is not an examination to exclude physical causes but an educational exercise in which the therapist, who must be a medical practitioner, examines each partner in front of the other to reassure them about their normality and answer all the embarrassing and seemingly 'silly' questions they may have about size, shape, colour or location of their sexual organs.

Guilt and shame about masturbation, touching genital areas, enjoying being touched genitally or about discovering own sexuality To get over these feelings couples need permission from a respected parental figure to enjoy themselves, have fun, feel sexual, ask for what they want, to say 'no' sometimes and to touch themselves or allow their partner to touch them. Books like the ones mentioned above, the ease with which the therapist talks about sex and the joint physical examinations, are all permission-giving tools. Some of the negative attitudes about sexuality, masturbation or body secretions and some rigid gender-roles may have to be challenged and corrected using rational emotive or cognitive restructuring techniques.

Anger and hostility could be mobilized by the sensitive and intimate genital touch
Breakdown of communication, which may not be identified at the stage of history-taking or non-genital sensate focus, is bound to be picked up at this stage. The therapist should make it safe for the couple to communicate effectively by laying down some ground rules, teach the couple some basic communication skills and encourage them to express anger and hostility in a non-destructive way (Guirguis 1991).

Performance pressure is likely to return when the ban on touching genital areas is lifted as the performance aspects of sex like ejaculation, orgasms, erections and lubrication start to be expected Spectating, or watching own performance, is one of the features of performance pressure which, if not dealt with, could start the vicious circle of failure going again. Redefining success as having fun and feeling good rather than achieving an erection or an orgasm is one way of dealing with performance pressure. Introducing the ladder concept (Guirguis 1991), which emphasizes the widely spread spectrum of sexual arousal, highlights the pleasures enjoyed at the lower end of the spectrum and encourages playing with arousal rather than relentlessly pushing it higher and higher, can be a very useful tool at this stage. In some resistant cases paradoxical techniques like forbidding erections or banning orgasms can be effective, as trying to make a spontaneous response like erection or orgasm happen at will is impossible, while trying to stop them makes them happen when they are least expected or being actively prevented.

Sexual flashbacks from previous traumatic experience may emerge at this stage
The smell, the sound of breath, the image or the touch of an abusing person may flash back into the victim's mind, usually at the time when they start to relax and enjoy themselves. If the traumatic sexual experience, rape or sexual abuse as a child was not dealt with at an earlier stage, the victim of such experience may have to be treated individually or in group therapy to resolve the unresolved feelings about the experience. A specific technique for flashback is 'discrimination-training', a cognitive-behavioural technique in which the victim is asked to open her eyes, talk to her partner, call his name and make a request (McCarthy 1986; Guirguis 1988c).

If resolving these general problems does not improve the sexual dysfunctions, some specific techniques may have to be used to deal with the specific sexual problems. For vaginismus the graded insertion of vaginal trainers is usually used. For premature ejaculation we use the stop–start techniques. For anorgasmia in women and ejaculatory failure in men we use masturbatory techniques. For some cases of erectile failure resistant to sex therapy we may use the intracavernous injection of vasoactive drugs. For lack of desire in both sexes self-stimulation with or without fantasy may be used.

When the couple overcome both the general and the specific problems they encountered at this stage they can move on to the next.

The stage of non-demanding intercourse
When the couple enjoy the genital sensate focus exercises and the specific sexual problems, like anorgasmia or premature ejaculation, are resolved, the ban on sexual intercourse is lifted. To avoid the pressure of the demanding type of vaginal thrusting, intercourse is allowed in the female superior position first. When the couple feel comfortable with this position they can experiment with various positions. These are the difficulties which may arise at this stage:

1 Traditional gender roles and issues of power or dominance can be triggered off by the 'woman-on-top' position. Surprisingly more women object to this position than men, feeling that 'it is not right for women to be on top of men'. These issues have to be addressed in therapy using permission giving, rational-emotive therapy and exposure to the avoided situation, which in this case is the woman being on top.
2 Using positions other than the 'missionary' position, and the emphasis on variation and fun, can uncover deep-seated guilt about enjoying sex, having fun and about using sex for pleasure rather than for having children. These issues need to be dealt with either by cognitive and rational-emotive techniques or by psychodynamic psychotherapy depending on how deep-seated the guilt feeling is.
3 Recurrence of performance pressure and the feeling that now that the ban on intercourse is lifted it is expected for them to go as far as that every time. This can make the therapy slip back and needs, therefore, to be dealt with before the therapy is completed. The ladder concept can be introduced, if not introduced at an earlier stage, to stress the need to respect what the body can feel, to stop forcing sexual feelings or reactions when they are not there and to let the body react freely up to whatever level on the ladder it can reach. Redefining success as having fun and feeling good rather than having intercourse, or reaching orgasm every time, must be emphasized again at this stage.

If, in spite of all this, the problem is still not resolved and the partners are not satisfied with their sex life together, therapy must move to the next stage.

The stage of 'stock-taking'
It is our experience that couples who do well with this therapy do so in six to eight sessions. Those who do not, will not improve no matter how many more sessions they have, unless the situation is reviewed and different approaches are used. A 'stock-taking' session, in which progress so far is assessed and the outstanding problems are reviewed, is essential at this stage. These are some of the likely outcomes of this session:

1 Discovering new factors, like a physical condition which is worth investigating further or a relationship problem which needs resolving. In some cases we may discover that one of the partners is working to a hidden agenda which is different from the declared one. For example, the couple may be working with the therapist on the male partner regaining his erectile potency while the female partner is trying to keep him impotent because it suits her better. The couple should be sensitively confronted with this hidden agenda

and given the choice of working to the same agenda or stopping therapy at this stage.

2 Resistance to change, either because one of them is not ready or is not willing to change. Couples may complain bitterly about a sexual problem but they are still willing to hang on to it because of some secondary gain – 'if she becomes more interested in sex she will demand more of it and I may fail to satisfy her demands'. Fear of breaking up the relationship may be another reason for resistance, as in some cases the sexual problem may be the only thing which is keeping them together. Systems and paradoxical techniques like symptom prescription or allowing the couple to keep their problem can be useful in some cases. If these techniques fail, the couple may have to be confronted with the therapist's doubts and allowed to withdraw from therapy until they are more ready or more willing to take the risk of having a sexual relationship.

3 Deep-seated conflicts about separation, intimacy or rejection may come to the surface in the form of intense transference or countertransference with the therapist. These deep-seated fears can block therapy unless or until they are resolved in individual therapy on psychodynamic lines working mainly through dealing with transference. This could be carried out by the same therapist or by another therapist, depending on the complexity of the feelings and the experience and training of the therapist.

Case example

Jean is a 34-year-old lady in her second marriage with two children from the first marriage and none from the present. She works part time as a barmaid. Jean asked her general practitioner to refer her to a sex therapist because since she had come out of hospital six months earlier she had never reached orgasm. She did, however, come very close to it on a few occasions, but 'nothing happened'. She was very distressed about the problem and tried in her own way, and with the help of her husband, to resolve the problem, but far from resolving it they made it even worse.

The vicious circle

She started by faking orgasms: 'I did not want to let him down, I felt like a failure and was ashamed of myself'. She also told herself to 'try harder', but the harder she tried the further away orgasms seemed to be. When she could not pretend any more she broke down and told her husband. He felt very bad about it and thought that it must have been all his fault. He tried to encourage her 'come on, I am sure you can do it, if only you try a little harder', but that made her feel under pressure and more tense. He also tried to stimulate her manually and orally but that only irritated her, made her feel pressurized and even more guilty: 'he was so good about it and was doing everything to help me and I still couldn't achieve an orgasm for him'. When efforts on both sides failed they started to lose confidence and she thought that perhaps she did not love her husband any more: 'if I really love him I should be able to reach orgasm with him'. The husband felt rejected, guilty for not 'giving her an orgasm' and wondered whether his wife was still attracted to him. They never discussed these feelings together but kept them all bottled up as they did not want to hurt each other's feelings. Just before referral Jean started to lose interest in sex, made every effort to avoid it, while Steve started to have difficulty in ejaculating and that made him more frustrated and less interested in initiating sex: 'there was no point in starting when I knew that nothing was likely to happen'. They stopped making love completely in the previous two months and did see their solicitors about divorce. So a simple difficulty, 'not reaching an orgasm', became a complex and intractable problem which defied all common-sense solutions.

History-taking

Full history revealed that while Jean was in hospital for a simple operation to stop excessive bleeding during her periods, the husband suggested that it would be a good idea to get sterilized while she was under the effect of anaesthesia. Although she thought, at the time, that it was a good idea, she regretted it later on, felt cheated and pressurized by her husband to make a hasty decision about such a serious matter. She felt very angry with her husband but could not tell him because she was not sure how he would react and whether he would understand how she felt about losing fertility. She also felt that she had no right to feel angry: 'after all, I *did* agree to it, I should have said no, but I didn't'.

Another traumatic experience was recalled by Jean, but she was not sure how relevant it was. She was subjected to sexual abuse by an adult male friend of the family when she was nine. Measuring the seriousness of the incidence, using our clinical scale, she scored low on all risk factors: the incidence was not repeated, not accompanied by violence or the threat of it, was not committed by a trusted member of the family and it did not involve penetrative sex. We decided, therefore, to work with her on loss of fertility at this stage and leave the sexual abuse for a later stage, and only if it started to block the progress of therapy.

We asked Jean, in individual sessions, to write down in detail what happened prior to, during and after her admission to hospital, particularly the feelings she had about her husband. She was very reluctant to write things down as she felt that 'it will make it all look real'. We explained to her that this was exactly what she needed to do, to accept that it did happen, that it was real and final, that she is now infertile and will never be able to have children any more. She found that very difficult because it released a great deal of anger, resentment, hostility and grief: 'it is not that I will not have any more children which upsets me, but the fact that I don't have the choice'. The next two sessions were devoted to help her to get in touch with these feelings, accept them and express them in a non-damaging way.

Physical examination

At some stage Jean was wondering whether something was damaged during the operation as she had noticed a piece of skin sticking out of her vagina since.

She welcomed the opportunity of having a physical examination to check on that. Physical examination revealed no abnormalities and she was reassured about her normality. During the examination she asked if we could check whether her clitoris was in the right place, as she had a long-standing doubt that it was located very far from where intercourse took place and that 'it did not seem right' to her. Her doubts were taken seriously and she was assured about that too. She found that very useful and felt much more relaxed afterwards.

The non-genital sensate focus

The husband started to be involved from the third visit, first in the joint physical examination, which he found 'very educational', and later in the sensate focus exercises. He was reluctant at first, did not like the bans imposed on touching genital areas and thought it would all be very clinical, but he was prepared to try it. While Jean was very happy with the bans, she could see the wisdom behind them and she particularly welcomed the ban on reaching orgasm: 'thank God, I don't have to pretend or push myself any more'. They did in fact enjoy this part of the treatment very much. They enjoyed the relaxed atmosphere, started to talk more freely and to have fun together again. Steve was pleasantly surprised to discover that he enjoyed it in spite of feeling so negative at first. They were both tempted to go on to the next stage but they did not break the bans.

The genital sensate focus exercises

These exercises were introduced next with the clear proviso that allowing genital touch does not mean proceeding to orgasm or ejaculation. On the next visit they both came feeling demoralized and despondent. Steve could not ejaculate although he felt very close to it and was pleased about that, but he felt frustrated for not achieving it. He was reminded of the ban on trying to ejaculate and advised to stop when he got too close to the point of ejaculation to prevent it. Jean on the other hand did not get any feelings from her genital areas being touched, hated touching his penis and felt irritated by the whole thing. On one occasion she engineered a row to avoid having a session together. On further discussion Jean admitted that she never liked being touched genitally and was only able to cope with intercourse, during which she was able to climax easily. She had problems with having time on her own, enjoying her own company, looking after herself and in getting pleasure from her own body. There was no evidence, however, that these problems were operating at a deep level and we decided, therefore, to deal with them at a behavioural and cognitive level. We advised her to put aside two or three periods of 45 minutes to spend on her own, having a hot bath and exploring the different feelings she gets from touching different parts of her body and to write down the feelings this touching evoked in her. The next two sessions were devoted to discussing the feedback from these exercises, and this gave us the chance to correct some of the misconceptions, challenge some of the taboos about sexuality and about touching her own body, and to modify any unrealistic expectations. She started to enjoy these self-stimulation sessions and to get more feelings out of them. She managed to relax and enjoy herself for the first time without feeling guilty. Steve came back two sessions later looking pleased but rather anxious. He reported ejaculating for the first time in months but was anxious to stress that it was an accident and that he did try to stop it but could not. The therapist did not show any excitement about the news, reminded Steve of the rules and asked him to try harder to stop ejaculation. This had the paradoxical effect of producing more 'accidents', but the therapist maintained his paradoxical position by showing disapproval for not sticking to the rule, but accepting that 'you are only human, as long as you keep trying to stop it'. Jean continued to have a nice time on her own, but reported no orgasms 'by accident', but that did not bother her because she was enjoying everything else. The therapist reframed her not reaching orgasm as being co-operative and sticking to the therapy rules.

However, the joint sessions continued to be strained and irritating to Jean. The couple were confronted with the therapist's 'hunch' that this irritation was the disguised form of expressing bottled-up anger. The couple surprisingly accepted this explanation and they were prepared to deal with whatever anger they both bottled up. It took three sessions to introduce to them the basic rules of effective communication, teach them the skills of expressing as well as handling anger and to learn the art of compromise. They came to the following session looking very pleased and reported that after a good discussion, in which they both told each other for the first time how they felt, and in spite of shouting and screaming at each other at some stage, they ended up making love and breaking all the therapy rules. They had intercourse and both climaxed. The therapist expressed a mild degree of pleasure and congratulated them for communicating so effectively, but was sceptical about the maintenance of such success and not very pleased about breaking the therapy rules. He did, however, give them an excuse: 'maybe you just got carried away, but it is still very early days and you are still not ready to go as far as that'. He reinforced the bans on intercourse and on trying to reach orgasm. They tolerated these bans for a few more weeks but became increasingly more frustrated because they felt ready to move on and they accused the therapist of being too cautious and of holding them back. He then reluctantly lifted the bans, but stressed that they should not go as far as intercourse every time and should not try to climax unless they feel very close and could not stop it. They were not allowed to set out to reach orgasm or drive for it when it did not feel imminent.

Intercourse in the female superior position

This was allowed to start with. Steve was not very happy about it and Jean thought it was wrong but they were encouraged to experiment with it and they ended up enjoying it even better than the missionary position they were used to before. Steve started to ejaculate every time and Jean started to have orgasms more often and with less effort. She was able to climax six times out of ten, on average, and was very pleased about that. She did not mind when it did not happen because I did not expect it or drive for it; if it didn't happen it didn't happen, it does not matter any more, as long as I enjoy other things I feel I am getting something out of it, I don't feel cheated or used any more.

The last therapy session

The final session was used to assess progress that far and to look for any unresolved issues. They reported that things were progressively improving not only in their sexual but also in their non-sexual relationship. Jean looked at Steve and asked the therapist: 'we discussed this together and I think I need help with this problem which started when we resumed intercourse'. Since then she occasionally gets flashbacks from the sexual abuse incident which she mentioned earlier. When Steve holds her tight, she remembers what happened to her and feels Steve's hands on her body as if they are the sticky hands of the man who abused her. That brings back the fear she experienced at the time. She was particularly annoyed because the flashback usually occurred at the time when she was about to relax and enjoy herself. The therapist suggested that the next time she feels like that she should put the lights on, if it is dark, look at Steve, call his name and ask him to do something for her. Steve could also speak to her. They did not think that something as simple as that would help but they were prepared to try it. That concluded the eighth and final session, which was to be followed six weeks later by one follow-up visit.

The follow-up session

This session was spent updating the therapist on their progress and discussing how to cope with any future difficulties or minor relapses. They reported that although orgasms were happening they were not coming as often and as easily as they were before the problem started. However, the most important thing they gained from therapy was that 'orgasms did not matter as much as they did'. They also admitted that the therapy did in fact benefit the non-sexual side of the relationship far more than the sexual side. They were communicating better than they had ever done, they were having more fun together, were able to resolve their differences speedily and effectively and that their relationship was stronger and more stable than ever. Both were congratulated for their success and praised for persevering with therapy even at the times when it was difficult and stormy. No further appointments were made, but they were reminded of the skills they had learned in therapy and encouraged to use them in the future if they encountered any more problems. They were given the opportunity to ring again and make another appointment if they had any more problems which did not respond to their newly acquired skills.

Two years later

We have not heard from this couple again.

Conclusion

Sex therapy is not a separate discipline but an integrated and comprehensive approach to helping people with the heterogeneous group of disorders called collectively 'sexual dysfunctions'. Sex therapy has to integrate behavioural with psychodynamic psychotherapy, physical with psychological approaches and marital with sexual therapy. Sex therapists have to be eclectic, or 'therapeutic opportunists', calling on as many therapeutic tools as they can master. However, the whole thing has to hang together in an empirical model which should make therapeutic sense to the couple seeking help as well as to the therapist. One such model, the Ipswich model, was described in detail and a full case was quoted in order to illustrate how this model works in practice.

Acknowledgement

The author would like to thank the Medical Illustration Department at Ipswich Hospital for producing Figures 7.1 and 7.2, D. Hooper and W. Dryden (eds) and the Open University Press for permission to reproduce Figure 7.1 and to quote from the author's chapter in *Couple Therapy: A Handbook* (Hooper and Dryden 1991).

References

Arentewicz, G. and Schmidt, G. (eds) (1983) *The Treatment of Sexual Disorders*, New York: Basic Books.

Bancroft, J. (1989) *Human Sexuality and its Problems*, 2nd edn, Edinburgh: Churchill-Livingstone.

Brown, P. and Faulder, C. (1988) *Treat Yourself to Sex: A Guide to Good Loving*, London: Penguin Books.

Cooper, A.J. (1963) A case of fetishism and impotence treated by behaviour therapy, *British Journal of Psychiatry* 109: 649–52.

Cooper, G.F. (1986) *Survey of Sex Therapists in Britain*, Birmingham: Training and Consultancy Services.

Crowe, M. and Ridley, J. (1990) *Therapy with Couples*, Oxford: Blackwell Scientific Publications.

Friday, N. (1976) *My Secret Garden: Women's Sexual Fantasies*, London: Quartet.

Gregoire, A. (1990) Physical or psychological: an unhealthy splitting in theory and practice, *Sexual and Marital Therapy* 5(2): 103–4.

Guirguis, W.R. (1987) Helping women who were sexually abused as children, *British Journal of Sexual Medicine* 3: 61–2.

—— (1988a) Erectile inadequacy: a guide to diagnosis, *British Journal of Sexual Medicine* 15: 8–11.

—— (1988b) Erectile inadequacy: a guide to treatment, *British Journal of Sexual Medicine* 15: 12–18.

—— (1988c) Literature up-date: a critical review, *Sexual and Marital Therapy* 3: 125–8.

—— (1989) The use and abuse of intracavernous injection of vasoactive drugs, *British Journal of Sexual Medicine* 1: 9–11.

—— (1991) Sex therapy with couples, in D. Hooper and W. Dryden (eds) *Couple Therapy: A Handbook*, Milton Keynes and Philadelphia: Open University Press.

Haslam, M.T. (1965) The treatment of psychogenic dyspareunia by reciprocal inhibition, *British Journal of Psychiatry* 111: 280-2.

Hawton, K. (1985) *Sex Therapy: A Practical Guide*, Oxford: Oxford University Press.

Hooper, A. (1986) *Women and Sex*, London: Sheldon Press.

Hooper, D. and Dryden, W. (eds) (1991) *Couple Therapy: A Handbook*, Milton Keynes and Philadelphia: Open University Press.

Johnson, J. (1965) Prognosis of disorder of sexual potency in the male, *Journal of Psychosomatic Research* 9: 195-200.

Kaplan, H.S. (1974) *The New Sex Therapy*, New York: Brunner/Mazel.

—— (ed.) (1983) *The Evaluation of Sexual Disorders*, New York: Brunner/Mazel.

Kellett, J.M. (1990) Physical or psychological: time we bridge the divide, *Sexual and Marital Therapy* 5(2): 101-2.

Lazarus, A.A. (1963) The treatment of chronic frigidity by systematic desensitisation, *Journal of Nervous and Mental Disorders* 136: 71-9.

McCarthy, B.W. (1986) A cognitive-behavioural approach to understanding and treating sexual trauma, *Journal of Sex and Marital Therapy* 12(4): 322-9.

Masters, W.H. and Johnson, V.E. (1970) *Human Sexual Inadequacy*, London: Churchill.

Mirowitz, J. (1966) The utilization of hypnosis in psychic impotence, *British Journal of Medical Hypnosis* 17: 25-32.

Sager, C.J. (1987) Foreword, in G.R. Weeks and L. Hof (eds) *Integrating Sex and Marital Therapy*, New York: Brunner/Mazel.

Semans, J.H. (1956) Premature ejaculation: a new approach, *South Medical Journal* 49: 353-7.

Stanley, E. (1981) Principles of managing sexual problems, *British Medical Journal* 28: 1200-5.

Weeks, G.R. and Hof, L. (1987) *Integrating Sex and Marital Therapy*, New York: Brunner/Mazel.

Wolpe, J. (1958) *Psychotherapy by Reciprocal Inhibition*, Stanford: Stanford University Press.

Zilbergeld, B. (1980) *Men and Sex*, Glasgow: Collins.

8

Family therapy: evolving an integrated approach

ANDY TREACHER

Introduction

My first contribution to the 'Psychotherapy in Britain' series was written in 1984 (Treacher 1985) so there is effectively an eight-year gap between that earlier chapter and this one. It is difficult for me to estimate what has happened to my style of therapy during these years, but it is clear to me that I have developed more and more towards using an integrated model. My philosophy of therapy is very simple – since families differ widely in terms of their structures, needs and experiences, it is essential that therapists avoid forcing them on to the Procrastean bed of a single approach. The art of good therapy for me is the ability of a therapist to change her style to suit the family in therapy. This may involve changing style during a course of therapy because as a family evolves in therapy it can and does respond differently. It is equally true, I think, that the individual needs of family members must be recognized as therapy unfolds. This means that individual therapy has a crucial role to play within an integrated model. The assumption of many systems theorists is that changing the family system inevitably induces changes in individuals. If only it were that simple! It is of course true that changes in family processes can cause change in individuals but the process is not automatic – individual therapy is required to sustain such changes and enable individuals to develop sufficient identity and self-esteem to break free of the oppressive family processes that enslave them.

I am, of course, not alone in suggesting that an integrated approach is likely to be more productive than approaches that are 'pure' and really only involve one style of therapy. At the end of this chapter I include a brief bibliography of books by other workers who have developed integrated approaches. However, my own path to an integrated approach has been only partially influenced by these parallel developments. The major exception to this rule is the work of Stanton (1980) whose work on the integration of structural and strategic family therapy (to be discussed later on in this chapter) was an important influence on me.

Fortunately or unfortunately, I have developed my own idiosyncratic approach, which I suppose could be called the caddis fly (larva) approach, i.e. most forms of therapeutic technique tend to stick to me because I find something of value in most approaches.

Theoretical assumptions

As I have become increasingly experienced as a therapist I find it increasingly difficult to explain how I undertake therapy. Perhaps this is senility catching up with me but I suspect not: the truth of the matter is that as I become more experienced I tend to abandon technique more and more. Or to be more accurate, since I have at my disposal a big potting shed with lots of useful tools in it I can hopefully go to the shed and select the right tool to help the family. Or to use the metaphor more accurately, I can invite the family into the shed to look at the tools and see which ones they think will be useful. We can then try a few and see which ones are helpful and which are not in getting the job done.

For some readers I suppose this metaphor is inappropriate. Male instrumentality looms large but let me hasten to add that, first, my range of 'tools' is rather peculiar and 'untool-like' and, second, none of the work can take place unless a warm supportive therapeutic climate has been established (see Carpenter and Treacher (1989), especially Chapter 3, for an extended discussion of the importance of the therapeutic alliance in family therapy).

At a practical level this means that my therapy is much more discursive and reflective than when I was first trained. I am more and more fascinated by family members' understanding not just of their problems but what methods they think will help them change. This partly reflects the influence of the brief therapy school associated particularly with the work of Weakland (Fisch *et al.* 1982) but other family therapists have also influenced my work in this direction. The net result of these influences is that I see myself less as a source of change and see the interface between myself and the family as the real source of change. This is a big step away from my initial training. Originally I trained with Brian Cade at the Family Institute in Cardiff and like many beginning therapists I somewhat uncritically adopted the style of my first mentor. Brian was a brilliant trainer whose zest for family therapy was tremendously energizing. At the time I trained with him (1977) he was an exponent of strategic family therapy, particularly the work of Jay Haley whose book *Problem-solving Therapy* (Haley 1976) was a brilliant summary of the major features of the approach.

Simon *et al.* (1985) have offered the following definition of strategic therapy:

> This directive form of therapy is consistent with the principles of cybernetics. Family problems are seen as being the expression of dysfunctional organizational patterns such as blurred generational boundaries, the pathological formation of triangles, confusions in the family hierarchy, as well as disturbances of adaptation in the context of the family life cycle. The therapist begins by negotiating the goals of therapy with the family and then proceeds to develop a strategy for achieving these goals.

The techniques that the strategic therapist utilizes in achieving his goals have been neatly summarized by Stanton (1980: 431):

1 The utilization of tasks and directives.
2 The problem must be put in soluble form. It should be something that can be objectively agreed upon, e.g. counted, observed or measured, so that one can assess if it has actually been influenced.
3 Considerable emphasis is placed upon extra-session change.
4 Power struggles with the family are generally avoided, the tendency being to take the path of least resistance and use implicit or indirect ways of turning the family investment for positive use.
5 'Positive interpretation' . . . to the family of its symptom(s), motives and homeostatic tendencies is readily employed.
6 Paradoxial interventions are common and may be directed toward the whole family or to certain members.

The clarity of Haley's model was very appealing to me – I also enjoyed the cut and thrust of working in a team (which also utilized a one-way screen and videotaping). However, I found the strategic approach too 'cold' and clinical. The role of the therapist in front of the one-way screen was primarily as an asker of questions – the 'real' therapeutic work took place in the back-up room where the team worked frenetically to devise interventions which were then delivered to (and at?) the family by the therapist who rejoined them in the therapy room.

Curiously this approach has many of the hallmarks of the medical model, i.e. the all-powerful 'experts' devise interventions for the family members who remain passive and often mystified as to what is happening to them. The ethical problems of the approach were never discussed in my original training, so after using the model for two years or so I remained uneasy about whether I should continue to use it. Fortunately my dilemma was resolved by my encountering the work of Minuchin. He gave a workshop in Cardiff in 1978 which resulted in my undertaking a practicum at the Philadelphia Child Guidance Clinic. Minuchin's (1974) structural approach was far more appealing to me since it allowed the therapist to be much more of a protagonist in achieving change. The warmth, intensity and even passion of the approach appealed to me – the endless questioning and probing of the strategic therapist who keeps himself at a distance from the family was always a difficulty for me so I found Minuchin's invitation to be more real and engaged with families irresistible.

It is difficult to summarize briefly the richness of structural family therapy but Stanton has made a very good attempt at it:

1 The basic goal is to induce a 'more adequate family organization' of the sort that will maximize growth and potential in each of its members.
2 The thrust of the therapy is toward 'restructuring' of the system, such as establishing or loosening boundaries, differentiating enmeshed members and increasing the involvement of disengaged members.
3 The therapeutic plan is gauged against knowledge of what is 'normal' for a family at a given stage in its development, with due consideration of its cultural and socio-economic context.

4 The derived interactional change must take place within the actual session (enactment).
5 Techniques such as unbalancing . . . and intensifying . . . are part of the therapy.
6 The therapist 'joins' and accommodates to the system in a sort of blending experience but retains enough independence both to resist the family's pull and to challenge (restructure) it at various points. He thus actively uses himself as a boundary marker, intensifier and general change agent in the session.
7 Treatment is usually limited to include those members of a family who live within a household or have regular contact with the immediate family. However, this might involve grandparents living nearby, or even an employer, if the problem is work-related.
8 The practice is to bring a family to a level of 'health' or 'complexity' and then stand ready to be called in the future, if necessary. Such a model is seen to combine the advantages of short and longer term therapy.

(Stanton 1980: 429–30)

The appeal of Minuchin's approach was very strong but I did not abandon strategic working because it is possible to integrate the two methods. Stanton himself has been an important pioneer in developing this way of working but I would personally recommend interested readers to read my chapter in a previous volume in the 'Psychotherapy in Britain' series (Treacher 1988). In this chapter I work out a reasonably convincing way of integrating structural and strategic work but I have to admit that during the last four years my position has changed yet again.

In step with many other workers, notably Palazzoli *et al.* (1989) and Hoffman (1990) I have become increasingly concerned to use much more open and contractually based methods of working with families. I am increasingly sensitive to both ethical and gender issues in family therapy so that I find it increasingly difficult to utilize strategic techniques which all too often depend upon covert methods of intervention in order to achieve change (see Treacher (1987) for an extended discussion of the ethical problems mostly avoided by strategic therapists whose pragmatism often overrides other considerations).

At a practical level this means that my model of therapy is much more purely structural but I have made a conscious effort to avoid some of the chauvinist pitfalls that were present in Minuchin's original formulations. For example, respect for existing hierarchies within families – a corner-stone of the original presentation of the theory – is clearly very problematic. (Dyed-in-the-wool systems theorists see no problem because individual 'components within a system' (i.e. individual family members) are seen to have no gender and are therefore treated interchangeably.) Equally, Minuchin's tendency to confront women in therapy and protect men needs to be challenged – his explanation that he does this because women are emotionally stronger (Minuchin, personal communication) is just not convincing and avoids seeking ways of working that are more egalitarian and respectful to women (see Osborne (1983), Goldner (1985) and especially Urry (1990) for further explorations of these issues).

My abandonment of strategic work is not total – I still utilize some of the ideas of strategic work, particularly when devising tasks, but I think it is accurate to say that my approach is best characterized as a structural–transgenerational–cognitive approach. This is a very clumsy label but at least it is reasonably accurate.

Structural work has always been interested in transgenerational processes so it is not surprising that I have attempted to develop this aspect of the model. This means that I am particularly concerned to assess the extent to which unfinished business influences the maintenance of the problems that are currently troubling a family. Obviously other family members, for example the parents' parents, can be convened so that any tangles and difficulties in these relationships can be unravelled. However, experience has taught me that such convening is hazardous and can seriously disrupt the therapeutic alliance with my original clients.

For this reason I generally adopt a 'coaching' style of therapy which involves me working with an individual family member so that they can feel empowered to visit other family members with a view to resolving the tangles involved. (Of course unfinished business often involves dead family members so that I usually need to use Gestalt empty-chair techniques to enable my clients to confront these issues.) I often use adjunct therapists to help me resolve transgenerational difficulties – for example, if a woman has a difficulty in stopping her mother from interfering in her relationship with her partner then I will get a colleague to role-play the mother so that she can experiment with different ways of confronting her mother. I am also careful to pay close attention to the effects that the real-life enactment will have on the mother in question. If the unravelling of the tangle is problematic then I would encourage my client to bring her mother to a subsequent session so that I can hopefully be of more direct help to both parties.

The remaining strand of my model is a cognitive one. I personally find the work of Burns (1980) very valuable and I do not hesitate to offer my clients individual sessions to work on troublesome automatic thoughts if I feel that these are the real source of stuckness in therapy. I am particularly interested in the origins of the automatic thoughts that trouble my client and I have found that the simple question 'whose voice do you hear when you are listening in to that particular automatic thought?' is remarkably productive. Clients answer this question with a wide range of answers – 'my mother' or 'my father' or (less obviously) 'the headmaster at my primary school'. By identifying that the automatic thought belongs to somebody else (and not the client) I find I often create an important shift in the client's understanding. They now see the automatic thought as an invasion of their life – an intrusion which can now be more easily confronted and/or ignored.

Summary

My current model is essentially a structural–transgenerational–cognitive model. This may at first sight appear to be a clumsy amalgam of disparate strands but

I don't think this is true. The structural element in the model enables me to use in-session techniques to facilitate change in the here-and-now processes which maintain the family's stuckness. The transgenerational element in the model enables me to place on the agenda any unfinished business that also contributes to the maintenance of the problem. Cognitive techniques can be mobilized, particularly with individuals if they cannot sustain the changes that interactionally oriented interventions have helped initially to facilitate. An obvious example of the latter would involve individual work with a depressed husband who found that his 'depressogenic' thought processes were maintained despite considerable positive changes in his relationship with his wife.

Such an intervention, of course, contradicts one of the shibboleths of systems thinking – that interactional change inevitably produces individual change. Such a formulation is naïve and overlooks the fact that each individual in a family makes a unique contribution to the interactional pattern of the family which is predicated on their own unique learning history, set of coping responses, abilities and disabilities.

The integrative aspects of my model are not solely confined to integrating three different styles of therapy: my caddis fly approach means that I will also use techniques derived from other frameworks too. Personal construct theory, especially as utilized by Ryle (1989) and Procter (1984), is valuable to me in clarifying my thinking about family functioning. Procter's ideas about shared family constructs is useful but his emphasis on exploring the idiosyncratic nature of each family's construing is particularly valuable. I have already mentioned using Gestalt techniques in relation to blocked mourning responses, but there are other aspects of Gestalt work that are very appealing to me – for example, getting a symptom to 'speak' by seating it in a chair and getting the client to carry out a conversation with it. Structural family therapy can easily absorb psychodrama techniques, so the breadth of my model is also increased by adopting techniques derived from this approach (see Williams (1989) for an interesting attempt to integrate family systems ideas and psychodrama).

But there is another sense in which my model is integrative. Usually in the course of working with a family I will undertake a variety of different types of session. I will certainly see the family conjointly for some of the time but I will typically also undertake sessions, with individuals, sessions just with the children and sessions with the parents (or parent in the case of a single-parent family). Such an approach of course runs the risk of becoming overcomplex, but I find that carefully considered convening of different combinations of family members – for example, a father and son (rather than the more usual parents and son) – can be very valuable in creating new possibilities for families.

Practice

In this section I should, at my editor's bidding, explore how my practice flows from my theory. However, I hope you as a reader will have realized, on the basis of reading the previous section, that it is really very difficult to lay down precise rules about how theory is to be translated into practice. My original attraction to strategic work took place because I liked the clarity of Haley's problem-focused work. The initial stages of my work are problem-focused, but in working with many families I find it virtually impossible to be elegant and conceptually tight.

The middle phase of therapy for me therefore often involves a search for the most productive area in which to work. I try to find an area of competence within the family on which to build. This may well mean that for a time I choose to avoid working directly on the major presenting problem (a tactic called under-focusing). Obviously this tactic may be hazardous with some families whose customerhood is solely dependent on solving the main presenting problem, but in the majority of cases a suitable contract can be negotiated.

In textbook terms my approach is therefore decidedly inelegant but I am not repentant – I find my approach does achieve good outcomes but I suspect that many brief therapists would criticize my approach for being dilatory. It is, however, difficult for me to summarize the typical tactics that I employ, partic-ularly in middle therapy. And if I were asked the question, 'why did you choose to focus on that particular issue with that family at that time?', I could no doubt provide some sort of *post hoc* explanation, but the truth of the matter is probably that I chose the route I took for rather unconscious reasons. In other words, I am learning more and more to trust my gut feelings and allow an essentially Gestalt type of process to decide the next step in therapy.

This is perhaps an embarrassing thing to say in a book which, because of its format, invites authors to structure their chapters in very precise ways. I personally believe that textbooks run the risk of overformalizing therapy – of presenting readers with a false, scientistic rendering of the way that therapy is undertaken. I hope the way that I have presented my case-study will enable the reader to see that my therapy does have overall shape and direction but the steps along the path may at times be stumbling, and retracing is inevitable before further progress can be made.

Case illustration – the 'C' family

It is always difficult to select a case which is truly representative of a way of work-ing. The one I have selected is a very messy, inelegant case of a type not usually recorded in journals or books. Typically, only successful cases are published, hence perpetuating the myth of seamless therapy rather effortlessly undertaken. Elsewhere I have explored with my colleague, John Carpenter, many of the problems that almost inevitably crop up as family therapy gets under way (Carpenter and Treacher 1989). I will present the case in a fairly straightforward narrative way but add some further comments (see Commentary notes, p. 216) which will help the reader to understand some of the alternative methods of work-ing that my model allows me to utilize. It is best to refer to these notes while reading this section rather than reading them as though they were a separate section.

Referral information

John C (aged 15) was referred to me by a GP-attached counsellor, who was increasingly concerned that John was in need of help because of his withdrawn behaviour at secondary school. John also had problems with soiling. The referral arrived at a time when I had a trainee working with me. After due deliberation we decided that she should act as therapist for the case, and that I should act as live consultant (cf. the Smith and Kingston (1980) model of live consultancy). This model involves both workers being in the room with the family, but only one (designated the therapist) plays an active role in interviewing the family. The other worker sits back from the family in an observer-consultancy role which involves sharing ideas with the therapist but not getting involved in transactions with the family.

1st session

This proved to be a very difficult session for all of us. My trainee was confronted by a very demanding single-parent family. Mrs C was not at all happy with our family-oriented approach. The index client, John, refused to say a word, and the only mileage generated by the session came from his older brother, Paul, who was fortunately more relaxed and talkative.

Mrs C rang up my secretary shortly after the session to complain about it and to cancel the next one. Fortunately I was able to ring her back within a few minutes. Despite being very angry she was able to understand that we were genuine in our attempts to help. She agreed to a solo session so that we could hear her point of view in more detail before seeing whether we could get John to be more communicative.[1]

As a methodological aside, I should add that it was clearly a mistake to have assigned the case to my trainee. Uncommunicative teenagers are difficult enough to work with, but the added difficulty of encopresis should have alerted me to the severity of the problem we were likely to encounter during the first interview. I was caught up in the difficulty of wanting to give my trainee as much basic experience as possible, but not having suitable cases in the pipeline during the first few critical weeks of the placement.

After detailed discussion with my trainee we decided that I should reverse roles with her so that I would now become the therapist for the family. My trainee felt out of her depth and quite rightly insisted that it should be my task to recover from the bad start that we had made.

2nd Session: Mrs C solo

Since I have teenage children myself I was able to join Mrs C successfully around a whole series of issues to do with the impossibility of getting things right as a parent to teenagers. Mrs C proved to be a very thoughtful woman who understood many aspects of her son's problems. She helped to formulate the idea that John's problems probably emanated from the divorce seven years ago. Somehow, and the process was not made clear, he had become emotionally caught up in the marital breakdown. The situation was further aggravated by a family move to the Exeter area. John's father was left behind 400 miles away and so John was left in a difficult position of not being able to resolve the problem that arose at an earlier stage in the family's life cycle.

After careful discussion with Mrs C we decided that the next session should involve just John and Paul, since we all felt that the situation in which John was most likely to talk was with his brother present. Interestingly Paul had originally stayed behind with his father when his brother and mother moved south two years previously. He lived with his father for 18 months before deciding that he too wanted to move. He had a dispassionate view of his father as a rather uncommunicative, secretive man whose interest in his sons was, to say the least, very uneven. Sometimes the father made an effort to phone his sons and even made an occasional visit – at other times he seemed curiously unmotivated and took no interest in them.

3rd session

John was more communicative at this session, but despite Paul's usefulness in opening up issues, John was unable to discuss any of the issues in any depth. We suggested several alternative ways which we felt could help him, but he used his characteristic cutting-off tactics to prevent any genuine negotiation taking place. Crucially we were able to establish that he trusted nobody and was not prepared to confide in anybody.

At our debriefing after the session, we were very despondent since we felt that our experience with John was identical to that of the referrer and John's school counsellor. Both had tried to establish rapport with him, but in both cases he had put up a stone wall. Faced by this impasse we decided that we must reconvene a session with Mrs C and attempt to use her insight and resourcefulness to find a way forward. We also had very real worries on her behalf because we felt that she also had a great deal of unfinished business from the breakdown of the marriage. At times during the first session she had been very tearful and we had both felt (independently) that she was caught up in some sort of blocked mourning response. Given John's uncooperativeness we also felt that we would have to use an 'underfocusing' approach which would probably result in us not working with him directly.[2] Our working with other family members could still achieve change and hence avoid the impasse experienced by the individual counsellors who had tried to help him before.

4th session

This session involved feeding back our ideas to Mrs C on the basis that she might well be able to help us unravel the problem. It became clear to us that John was very like Mr C in his behaviour and attitudes, while Paul was more like Mrs C. It seemed likely that John was having difficulties in resolving his identity problems because he was faced with wanting to grow away from his mother and yet his father was a very nebulous figure who was not easy to identify with. Mrs C's anxieties about John further exacerbated an already tense and difficult situation.

Mrs C rightly felt aggrieved that she had been forced to take on sole responsibility for solving John's insoluble problems. Her ex-husband apparently took little interest and her attempts to get him to take a share of the responsibility came to nothing since his main way of dealing with uncomfortable issues was by avoiding them – a tactic that quite understandably goaded Mrs C into a flurry of frustrating phone calls which caused him to retreat still further.

We adopted a stance of encouraging Mrs C to see that there was very little that she could do to change the situation. John's silence was, in fact, very power-ful and the only way out of the impasse was for us to take some responsibility for the situation by seeing whether we could become honest brokers in improving communication between John and Mr C.[3] Much of the session was concerned with discussing wider issues to do with sexism, peripheral fathers and the way that a chauvinistic society always blames mothers for problems that children pro-duce. However, the final part of the session refocused on issues drawn from the first session. We explored the impact of the marriage break-up on Mrs C and in the process of tracking the details of the break-up we discovered (not to our great surprise) that there was indeed a crucial area of unfinished business. Mrs C had been very close to her father-in-law who had died suddenly just before the marriage had finally broken up. Mrs C had not been able to mourn at the time. The reasons for this were not entirely clear, but she had had to undertake an organizing role at the time of the funeral and had been caught up in a complex family tangle with her mother-in-law who had always rejected her. Mrs C was still very distressed by these events, so we decided that this would become the focus for the next session.

5th session

This session involved discussing her father-in-law and his role in the family. In fact he was a very warm, loving man who treated Mrs C like a daughter. Since she had always felt second best as far as her own parents were concerned, Mrs C naturally felt that her father-in-law's affections made up for what she had lost from her own parents. His death was therefore a double blow since she had lost a father-in-law who had been able to replace her parents. Mrs C brought her family album with her for the session and we spent some time looking through the photographs. The session was very moving – Mrs C was able to get in touch with her sense of loss but was not overwhelmed by the experience.[4]

Sessions 6–9

Mrs C returned to the sixth session after an unscheduled gap of four weeks. She was noticeably changed and revealed that she had cried daily for about a fortnight after the last session. She felt that she was now able to mourn her father-in-law, and as the days progressed she could sense herself moving on and hence getting a new perspective about his death. The agenda of the therapy moved on likewise as we made preparation with her for Mr C's visit. The impending visit of her husband placed John's future firmly on the agenda. Bravely, Mrs C was able to begin to face the fact that John might well want to rejoin his father (just as

Paul had done a few years earlier). It seemed as though Mrs C's mourning of her father-in-law had now cleared the way for her to mourn the loss of her son. We focused our attention on the other side of the coin too, insisting that John's leaving would free her to live her own life. Like most mothers she had had to give herself away for years and years – now she had the right to concentrate on her own future and her own rights to enjoy life.

Between sessions

I periodically made a number of phone calls to Mr C, gently urging him to come down since we felt no progress could be made without hearing his point of view.[5] He eventually agreed and the tempo of the therapeutic work quickened. He agreed to attend sessions as and when necessary during the week he was in the Exeter area. I undertook these sessions alone both because my trainee was unavailable and because we felt that we had needed to use the intimacy of a man-to-man discussion to explore his feelings of being overwhelmed by powerful women.

Three sessions involving Mr C

My first session with Mr C was necessarily low-key. Mr C presented himself as a shy, retiring man who had always been dominated by his allegedly overbearing wife. He was open and frank with me, admitting that his typical tactic for dealing with conflict was to bury his head in the sand. He felt he could be of help to John because he assumed that John did in fact want to go back up north and live with him. Unfortunately, Mr C was adamant that he was not prepared to meet his ex-wife, so my plan to try and undertake some minimal fence-mending came to nothing. I had hoped to help them, for example, establish some rules that would enable Mr C to phone his sons regularly without feeling beleaguered by Mrs C. Incoming phone calls were often fielded by her and used as an opportunity for her to have a go at him for failing to carry out his responsibilities as a father and hence giving him (from our point of view) a perfect excuse for being even less involved.

The second session involved both the two boys and Mr C. John was noticeably more relaxed – he had been out with his father the previous day and had obviously enjoyed his company. The session was rather meandering – Paul again was helpful in enabling issues to be tabled. John was a little more forthcoming and admitted that he preferred living in the north and that he had not settled in the south. We were able to negotiate a three-week holiday with his father so that he could test out where he would like to live; in fact he decided that he would not move (if he was going to) until July of the next year when he had completed his GCSEs.

The third session with Mr C was another solo one. We debriefed each other about the joint session and I shared my puzzlement about John's symptoms and where his future lay, inviting Mr C to take up his father's duties once more and see whether he could create an atmosphere at his home which would enable John to talk through his problems with him. Mr C saw the logic of my position and agreed to see whether he could help his son. (In fact at this stage in the therapy I was personally sceptical whether John would be able to confide in his father, but I knew that he was beginning to confide in a woman teacher at his school so we felt that we could take a fairly relaxed attitude to attempting to solve John's problems. By underfocusing on John's problems and concentrating on creating situations in which he could talk in an unpressurized way, we felt we might be able to make progress, although the pace of developments was bound to be slow.)

10th session

We had anticipated that Mr C's visit would be very disturbing to Mrs C and sure enough Mr C had just happened to return the boys home very late two nights previously. Mrs C had been very anxious about their lateness and had had words with Mr C at the doorstep. We used the session to confront Mrs C about the underlying issue – that she couldn't bear to face 'losing' John to Mr C. I pointed out that such a loss was likely to be more apparent than real – perhaps there was a tradition in the 'C' family whereby sons, on leaving home, showed their loyalty to both parents by living first with one and then the other. The session got very stormy at some points since Mrs C vented her anger at me for being a party to involving Mr C in solving John's problems. I refused to be intimidated, pointing out that she couldn't have her cake and eat it too. John clearly needed to be close to his father and she knew it – I was only keeping to our contract in attempting to achieve this closeness. By the end of the session Mrs C had calmed down and was able to accept the situation more positively. She was, in fact, very exhausted by John and needed a break.

11th session

Two weeks later (with John away with his father) Mrs C returned once again, but this time she was much more sure of herself and her future. She felt that relief of having John away and had regained a long-term perspective on life. She had done her best for him and it was now up to John to sort out his own problems. If his father could help them then so be it. We consciously switched the session away from John in order to talk about her future, her social isolation and her need to make new friends and develop a new life-style as an independent woman rather than a mother who was always forced to make sacrifices for two sons who needed to develop their independence and solve their own problems.

Serendipitously, this was the last session that my trainee could attend. She had to move on to her next placement so she was able to share ideas about moving on with Mrs C. Mrs C was able to respond well to this conversation and accepted that she had many resources and skills to draw on. She had found the trainee's contributions to the sessions valuable but fortunately was not disturbed by her leaving, partly because we had anticipated it at the previous session.[6]

12th–15th sessions

The next three sessions were fairly low-key, mainly concerned with issues raised in the 11th session, but therapy took an unexpected turn after the last of these when Paul phoned me to ask for an individual session.

A solo session with Paul

Paul was very distressed because he felt that his father's interest in John resulted in his father neglecting him. He also felt that his father was very tight financially and did not support him enough. Luckily his father was due to pay another visit to Exeter so I was able to arrange both to meet him and have a joint meeting with the two of them.

Joint sessions with Mr C and Paul

This session was largely successful. Father explained his difficult financial situation but agreed to be more supportive to Paul. Paul was able to challenge his father about his apparent greater interest in John. His father defended his position, saying that John had received more attention solely because he was visiting him for a while, and Paul was not. More importantly he was able to unfreeze during the course of the session and express his feelings towards his son. Paul was reticent and did not reciprocate very much.

Debriefing session with Paul

Paul returned for an individual session after seeing his father. He was relieved by the session, which was far more successful than he had anticipated, but we discussed once again his expectations about his father. Paul spontaneously remarked that he needed to understand the limitations of his father's position and to remember his experience of the difficulties he had when he had lived with his father. He understood that his father would always be rather distant and that he had to come to terms with this fact.

Paradoxically the joint session did not result in father's behaviour changing much towards Paul. However, Paul seemed able to realize that he and his father would probably not be closer to each other, at least for some time. By reality testing that this was so he seemed to be able to relax and not be anxious about it. I was also able to talk more broadly with Paul about men and the way that they express their emotions. I congratulated him on his ability to talk about his emotions and generally reflect upon his situation. I pointed out that most men did not develop this ability, partly because their whole conditioning told them it was sissy to do so. We reflected on his father's difficulties, which were further complicated by his being over-involved with a very demanding mother who had cast him in the role of unwilling confidant.

This was a constructive session but the session was partly eased by changes in John's behaviour. Having visited his father on two occasions he decided not to pay his father a Christmas visit, although this had been planned. (By not going it seemed Paul's feelings of jealousy dissipated.)

My overall understanding of this unexpected turn of events is admittedly fragile because I did not talk directly with John, but discussion with his mother led me to the hunch that because we had been successful in helping her to support his visits to his father he had been released from the loyalty bind to her. He had then been able to experience going back to his father (and his roots) without a sense of guilt. In going back he had found that there was less there for him than he had anticipated – the fantasy of being with his father did not measure up to the reality. In many ways, therefore, he had recapitulated Paul's experience – he too had tested out being with his father but in the end had opted for a new life in the south.

Closing sessions with Mrs C

Following the sessions centred around Paul's distress I contracted once gain to work now directly on issues reflecting Mrs C's needs. John's behaviour began to change – he was much more affectionate to his mother, and was more involved in family life. His encopresis spontaneously began to improve.

Mrs C had been able to accept my hunch that the symptom would indeed improve as changes in the family occurred but it would of course be dangerous to claim that therapy had anything directly to do with it. John was very popular with girls at his school and was obviously enjoying his popularity. Perhaps these developments were enough to change his motivation and help him abandon such a humiliating symptom which would obviously cause big difficulties as he became sexually active.

My session with Mrs C concentrated on her feelings of being stuck and upon her emotional liability. She would have a 'good' week when she felt in charge of her life, and this would then be followed by a 'bad' week when she felt out of control. It seemed to be that some cognitive-behaviour therapy self-help skills would be helpful to her so we agreed to undertake three sessions exploring David Burns's (1980) self-help manual *Feeling Good*. Only two of these sessions were completed because Mrs C found the approach antipathetic. Despite my best efforts to persuade her that the approach had value she baulked at undertaking any homework assignments. Paradoxically these sessions were unexpectedly successful because they enabled her to clarify that she was still blaming her ex-husband for much of her predicament. She was able to confront her whinging about this and to affirm that she was now in charge of her life, and despite some very obvious objective difficulties she could now make a difference to her life if she chose, particularly as both boys would foreseeably leave home in the near future.

Final sessions

An agreed final session in fact turned out to be the penultimate session. A few days before the session was held John had been very tearful and had shown signs of real distress rather than stonewalling as he usually did. Mrs C had handled him very successfully, supporting him and yet not being too intrusive.

Nevertheless she was taken aback by his comparative directness. I reframed this situation as being positive precisely because he was beginning to be able to get in touch with his emotions much more directly. I also reaffirmed my belief that she would be able to support him through his difficulties. We agreed a final session. This was much lighter than the previous one. We broadly reviewed the work we had done and agreed a telephone follow-up to be carried out by me three months later.

Telephone follow-up after three months

No major developments were reported by Mrs C. John's behaviour continued to improve and she felt she was able to detach herself more, hence enabling him to be more independent. Mr C's contacts with the family remained very infrequent but neither of the boys seemed concerned. Mrs C was actively contemplating retraining as a typist and was looking forward to a holiday without the boys.

Commentary notes

1 Convening

My attitude to convening has changed fairly recently. Instead of stressing the necessity for seeing all family members at the first session, I tend to see just the parents (or parent in the case of a single-parent family) despite working in a child guidance setting where children are index clients.

This approach owes more to a parent training type of approach rather than to structural family therapy. It carries the implicit messages 'let's see how we can puzzle out what's happening to your child (children) and see how the situation can be helped by planning joint interventions by you and talking with the children and hearing their point of view'. This approach obviously has a great advantage in enabling me to build a strong therapeutic alliance with parents who often feel very stressed and beleaguered if the first meeting is with the whole family. I subsequently like to meet with the whole family but some parents have actually opted for me not to see their children since they preferred a coaching style of therapy which involved using me for brain-storming and supportive purposes.

On reflection a mistake I made with the 'C' family was not to make a preliminary phone call to negotiate the first session. Careful explanation of the whys and wherefores of my therapeutic approach usually results in a preliminary session being agreed before the children are included. I should also add that I have just recently changed my practice with families that include teenagers. Given my own experience of poor results using a more traditional approach I now work with such families in a more structured way. Because of my age (50) I opt to meet with the parent (or parents) while my co-therapist meets with the teenagers, particularly the index client. Conjoint sessions are undertaken when the need arises; most of the therapeutic work is undertaken in parallel sessions. The advantage of this approach is that the teenagers feel heard and respected by 'their' therapist who can represent their point of view at the conjoint sessions.

My work with the parents hinges around sharing my experiences of bringing up teenagers with their experiences, but it also includes discussion of the parents' right to live their own lives and not to be continually involved in taking responsibility for teenagers who can and will take responsibility for their own futures.

This model abandons traditional family therapy and involves more of an advocacy model. In the case of the 'C' family it was not used because of Paul's level of co-operativeness.

2 Underfocusing

Underfocusing is a classic structural family therapy tactic which enables the therapist to avoid working directly on the presenting problem. This approach, if successfully negotiated, enables the therapist to escape having to 'cure' the intractable problems that are, all too often, at the centre of family life. My usual approach in negotiating *not* to work directly on the central symptom is to say that I feel that we will do better to put the symptom 'on the back-burner' until I have a better understanding of how to help the family and to ensure that the help is successful rather than going off at half-cock.

This often makes good sense to families, particularly if previous attempts to help that have focused on the problem have failed. Of course there is a minority of families who will not accept this framing – engagement has to be around the problem otherwise the therapist loses credibility. In the case of the 'C' family John's soiling problem disappeared after about nine months, reflecting, I would argue, changes that were occurring in his life and within his family.

3 The therapist is a replacement for a parent

Particularly for families involving divorce the therapist needs to be able to take on many roles. By taking responsibility for connecting John to his father I necessarily allowed Mrs C to escape from an impossible role, i.e. of acting as the 'good' mother who connects her son to an ex-husband that she couldn't stand and needs to separate from. By enabling Mrs C to take a back seat on this issue a lot of steam was taken out of the most difficult triangle in the family i.e. John–mother–ex-husband/father. Obviously, in the long term Mrs C had a responsibility not to criticize John's father and to try and achieve a negotiating stance with him. My intervention did not absolve her from these responsibilities which were returned to later on in the therapy.

4 Working with mourning

The 'forced' mourning involved in this case was in fact remarkably unforced. With other cases I have had to be much more creative in my approach. For example, with one couple whose still-born child had not been buried appropriately, I and my co-therapist Arlene Vetere organized a memorial service for the child which was held three years after the baby had died. The service involved a wide circle of relatives and friends of the family involved. Fortunately it was successful in helping the couple to complete their mourning. Sometimes I use Gestalt empty-chair techniques to help the client to get in touch with their feelings about deceased relatives. A wide range of rituals and tasks (including visiting graves or the old home of the deceased relative) can be improvised to suit the particular needs of the client or clients involved in such problems.

5 *The therapist as mediator*

In cases of this type I am usually successful in holding at least one joint meeting between ex-spouses. I meet with each spouse individually to agree suggestions for an agenda. When an agenda has been agreed by both sides I then hold a strictly time-limited session which only discusses the agreed agenda. (Further sessions follow if the agenda is not completed within the session.) This procedure makes the meeting less hazardous than an 'open' meeting which might bring up issues which are too painful to discuss. My role in such meetings is as a mediator. Often the meeting resolves the impasse because the process of opening up negotiations in a structured, yet supportive way produces knock-on effects in day-to-day life so that the conflicts involving the couple begin to resolve.

Sadly, Mr C could not face negotiating with his wife. I could find no way to change his position on this and instead took a chance on Mrs C's attitude changing sufficiently for her to be able to open up a dialogue through phone calls. By the end of therapy this had been achieved to a limited extent.

6 *Involving trainees and co-workers in therapy*

Because I work mostly solo with an occasional trainee joining me on their placement rotation I have had to learn to integrate other workers into my therapeutic work in a creative way. My original training at the Philadelphia Child Guidance Clinic introduced me to the idea of the 'adjunct' therapist who participates in sessions but does not play the major role in the therapy because of being in a training or observational role. My trainee played the role of being an observer/adjunct therapist during my work with Mrs C following the catastrophe of the first session. At times she would share ideas directly with me or talk directly to Mrs C. At other times she was an observer of the process between me and Mrs C and made comments which were helpful to us both.

I am particularly happy working in this way with a female trainee when my principal client is a woman because I feel the situation helps to disrupt the formation of both transference and countertransference relations. Such an arrangement helps to de-emphasise my importance in the process and creates an atmosphere of team work, along the lines 'let's struggle together to see whether we can come up with solutions to solve the problems that are confronting you and your family'. This is not to say that the approach doesn't have its own problems but feedback from clients has been mostly very positive.

Conclusion

The case example is representative of my current case load since approximately 75 per cent of my cases involve one-parent families who are mostly struggling with the aftermath of divorce. However, the case has some weaknesses as an illustration of integrated family therapy because it does not enable me to demonstrate all the possibilities of my approach. For example, a fair percentage of my cases do involve marital or couple work which I have, of course, not touched on in this example (see Treacher (1985) and especially Treacher (1988) for a detailed discussion of an integrated marital therapy model which draws upon several different traditions within marital therapy).

However, despite these drawbacks the case example does combine several facets of therapy which draw upon different traditions within family therapy. Much of the work undertaken was structural, i.e. the techniques used were aimed at helping Mrs C to form better boundaries between herself and her sons and her ex-husband. Central to this process was the use of a forced mourning technique which enabled Mrs C successfully to mourn for her father-in-law. This in turn enabled her to separate herself further from her ex-husband's family and to take further distance from her ex-husband. Paradoxically this effective boundary-making enabled her to begin to disentangle herself from her enmeshment with John. With us she rehearsed 'losing' him to her ex-husband but at the same time became more appreciative of her own strengths. Her strengths were validated both by me as the principal therapist but more importantly by my trainee who, as an adjunct therapist, was able to confirm and expand the therapeutic messages that I constructed around her ability to deal with life despite having to make very big adjustments (e.g. returning to her birth-place feeling defeated after divorce, coping on a very low income, and so on). Mediation was offered to both ex-partners but was unilaterally refused by Mr C. My attempt to utilize cognitive-behaviour therapy techniques was also mostly unsuccessful but my attempt to introduce Burns's methods to my client did result in her shifting her attitude to her ex-husband. She stopped using him as an excuse for her difficulties and began to focus more on how she could change her situation.

The gender issues which influenced the unfolding of the family drama were, I think, appropriately explored both with Mrs C and Paul. However, I did not feel able to raise these issues with Mr C as my therapeutic alliance with him was much more tentative, partly because the travelling distance involved in attending sessions precluded regular meetings from taking place.

It is also important to stress that the family members were seen in a combination of different types of sessions – Mrs C and the two boys, Mrs C solo, Paul solo, Mr C solo, Mr C and the two boys, Mr C and Paul, Paul and John. Although individual counselling techniques were utilized in many of these sessions, much of the therapeutic work undertaken was concerned with helping family members both to differentiate from each other and to take responsibility in contributing to the overall problem-solving that was necessary if the family members were to find a better way of relating to each other. My approach therefore interleaved conjoint and individual sessions according to the needs of the therapy as it unfolded.

It is also important to reflect upon the goals that we've not achieved in the course of therapy. I was personally very sad that we did not find a way to engage John. His major symptom did change substantially during the time therapy was undertaken but I remain quite worried about whether he will be able to find ways of communicating his distress and gaining help when he needs it. I equally have worries for Mr C, who remains isolated and lonely – often fairly suicidal. My attempts to link him to a therapist in his own area were sadly refused. Paul and Mrs C were able to make effective use of the package we offered so the therapy was not ineffective. Perhaps the story is not entirely finished because my position on follow-ups (Treacher 1989) invites me to continue working with this family. I will offer them a further follow-up in the hope that John will perhaps be ready to work on the issues which I am sure still confront him. Some therapists will disagree with me about this because they will say that there was sufficient symptomological improvement to warrant termination, but since John himself has not been able to change his coping style I feel he is still very vulnerable and it is highly probable that he will run into further difficulties.

My own largely structural-cum-transgenerational view is that both John and his father are considerably at risk in terms of their long-term mental health. They seem to have been caught in a transgenerational pattern, albeit heavily influenced by the gender structure of our society, which invites men to avoid working on the important emotional issues that they encounter. Ironically Paul, perhaps because he was close to his mother and yet not enmeshed with her, is able to deal with such issues more effectively – living proof that the interplay of societal and family factors can produce different outcomes for different family members.

Addendum

There are, of course, many other therapists who have developed integrated approaches. It may be useful for you as a reader to compare my approach with that of other therapists. The following list references work by both American and British therapists.

American sources

Boszormenyi-Nagy, I. and Ulrich, D.N. (1981) Contextual family therapy, in A.S. Gurman and D.P. Kniskern (eds) *Handbook of Family Therapy*, New York: Brunner/Mazel.

Duhl, B.S. and Duhl, F.J. (1981) Integrative family therapy, in A.S. Gurman and D.P. Kniskern (eds) *Handbook of Family Therapy*, New York: Brunner/Mazel.

Grunebaum, H. and Chasin, R. (1982) Thinking like a family therapist: a model for integrating the theories and methods of family therapy, *Journal of Marital and Family Therapy* 8: 403–16.

Sluzki, C.E. (1983) Process, structure and world views: toward an integrated view of systemic models in family therapy, *Family Process* 22: 469–76.

Stanton, M.D. (1980) An integrated structural/strategic approach to family therapy, *Journal of Marriage and Family Therapy* 7: 427–39.

British sources

Bentovim, A. and Kingston, W. (1981) Brief focal marital and family therapy, in S. Budman (ed.) *Forms of Brief Therapy*, New York: Guilford.

Crowe, M. (1985) Marital therapy: a behavioural systems approach – indications for different types of intervention, in W. Dryden (ed.) *Marital Therapy in Britain*. I. *Context and Therapeutic Approaches*, London: Harper & Row.

Skynner, R. (1981) An open-systems, group analytic approach to family therapy, in A.S. Gurman and D.P. Kniskern (eds) *Handbook of Family Therapy*, New York: Brunner/ Mazel.

Will, D. and Wrate, R. (1985) *Integrated Family Therapy – A Problem Centred Psychodynamic Approach*, London: Tavistock.

References

Burns, D. (1980) *Feeling Good*, New York: Signet.

Carpenter, J. and Treacher, A. (1989) *Problems and Solutions in Marital and Family Therapy*, Oxford: Basil Blackwell.

Fisch, R., Weakland, J.H. and Segal, L. (1982) *The Tactics of Change: Doing Therapy Briefly*, San Francisco: Jossey-Bass.

Goldner, V. (1985) Feminism and family therapy, *Family Process*, 24: 31–47.

Haley, J. (1976) *Problem-solving Therapy*, San Francisco: Jossey-Bass.

Hoffman, L. (1990) Constructing realities: an art of lenses, *Family Process* 29: 1–12.

Minuchin, S. (1974) *Families and Family Therapy*, Cambridge, Mass.: Harvard University Press.

Osborne, K. (1983) Women in families: feminist therapy and family systems, *Journal of Family Therapy* 5: 1–10.

Palazzoli, M. *et al.* (1989) *Family Games: General Models of Psychotic Processes in the Family*, New York: W.W. Norton & Co.

Procter, H. (1984) A construct approach to family therapy and systems interventions, in E. Button (ed.) *Personal Construct Theory and Mental Health*, Beckenham, Kent: Croom Helm.

Ryle, A (1989) *Cognitive Analytic Therapy: Active Participation in Change*, New York: Wiley.

Simon, F.B., Stierlin, H. and Wynne, L.C. (1985) *The Language of Family Therapy: A Systemic Vocabulary and Source Book*, New York: Family Process Press.

Smith, D. and Kingston, P. (1980) Live supervision with a one-way screen, *Journal of Family Therapy* 2: 379–87.

Stanton, M. (1980) Marital therapy from a structural/strategic viewpoint, in G.P Sholevar (ed.) *Handbook of Marriage and Marital Therapy*, Englewood Cliffs, NJ: Spectrum Publications.

Treacher, A. (1985) Working with marital partners: systems approaches, in W. Dryden (ed.) *Marital Therapy in Britain. I. Context and Therapeutic Approaches*, London: Harper & Row.

—— (1987) Family therapists are potentially damaging to families and their wider networks. Discuss, in D. Watson and S. Walrond-Skinner (eds) *Ethical Issues in Family Therapy*, London: Routledge & Kegan Paul.

—— (1988) Family therapy: an integrated approach, in E. Street and W. Dryden (eds) *Family Therapy in Britain*, Milton Keynes: Open University Press.

—— (1989) Termination in family therapy – developing a structural approach, *Journal of Family Therapy* 11: 135–47.

Urry, A. (1990) The struggle towards feminist family therapy, in R. Perelbereg and A. Miller (eds) *Gender and Power in Families*, London: Routledge.

Williams, A. (1989) *The Passionate Technique: Strategic Psychodrama with Individuals, Families and Groups*, London: Tavistock/Routledge.

Integrative encounter

JOHN ROWAN

It is in a way saying the same thing twice to talk about 'integrative encounter', because it seems to me that encounter is by its very nature integrative; but it may be as well to do so because there are several different versions of encounter, some more and some less integrative.[1]

The great authoritative text on groups by Shaffer and Galinsky says that the encounter group proper is 'an outgrowth and compendium of all the group models that preceded it' (Shaffer and Galinsky 1989: 201). This kind of group originated in the 1960s and reached its most classic development in the 1970s. It is now the most general type, and someone who has learned how to lead this type of group will find any other relatively easy. But it does require a great deal of skill from the group leader.

It is of course a humanistic group, and shares with other humanistic approaches a belief that the person is basically OK. Consequently it refuses to call people 'patients', and calls them instead participants or group members. It is also a holistic group, and shares with other holistic approaches the motto 'Go where the energy is'. This energy can be expressed on the physical level, on the emotional level, on the intellectual level or on the spiritual level. The basic rule for the leader of an encounter group is to look for the signs of some kind of energy ready to emerge.

My own belief is that the main line of development of ideas about encounter, as worked out in the 1960s and early 1970s, runs through the work of Will Schutz, Jim Elliott and Elizabeth Mintz, and it is their work which lies at the heart of this chapter, though some updating material is needed and will be added.

Theory

There are many definitions of what we mean by the term 'integrative', and some are more adequate than others. What I think is meant by the fullest and most appropriate use of this term is any approach which unifies the three basic legs on which psychotherapy stands: the regressive, the existential and the transpersonal. This is a whole-hearted definition which implies a whole-hearted approach.

By 'regressive' I mean the whole business of delving back into the past, and into the personal unconscious, to find out what went wrong there, and how it can be put right. Certain approaches specialize in this, as for example classical psychoanalysis, Kleinian analysis, the body therapies such as bioenergetics and postural integration, and directly regressive approaches such as primal integration and Primal Therapy. It seems to me that no therapy can really ignore this area. Even approaches which appear at first to ignore it do actually have to cover it, as we can see from any reasonably extended case history (e.g. Kutash and Wolf 1968: Dryden 1987).

Laing (1983) makes the point that we must also talk about recession, by which he means a move from the outer to the inner world. Going back is no use unless at the same time we are going deeper into our own experience. Regression without recession is of little use or interest.

By 'existential' I mean any approach which emphasizes the here-and-now at the expense of the past and the future, although of course all approaches have to deal perforce with past, present and future-oriented material. Also of course virtually all therapies work their most effective magic by bringing the past into the present in some way. But I am speaking here mainly of an approach which says that the most important thing to pay attention to is whatever is going on right now, either inside the client or between the present participants. Approaches which specialize in this aspect include group analysis, personal construct therapy, cognitive-behavioural therapy, Neuro-Linguistic Programming, existential analysis, person-centred therapy and Gestalt therapy. Again all therapists do very often enter this area in one way or another.

By 'transpersonal' I mean the way in which some approaches emphasize the future: the direction of the person, the higher potentials of the person, the deeper perspective given by a spiritual insight. In the terms which Assagioli (Ferrucci 1982) introduced many years ago, it has to do with the higher unconscious as distinct from the lower unconscious. These approaches emphasize the intuition and creativity of both therapist and client, and the way in which the boundary separating therapist from client can sometimes disappear, with advantage. Such approaches include Jungian analysis (Zurich and archetypal versions), psychosynthesis and transpersonal psychotherapy. Some forms of psychotherapy contrive to ignore this area, but at their peril.

A truly integrative approach, in my opinion, would deal with all three of these areas and be able to handle them, and in this way be able to cope with the whole person who comes into the consulting room or the group space.

Practice

Many of the humanistic groups manage to deal with all three of these areas, but the most coherent version is the encounter group, as developed by people like Will Schutz, Jim Elliott and Elizabeth Mintz. The encounter group manages it very naturally and with little difficulty. Let us look at each of these areas in turn.

Regression

Will Schutz has probably given the most adequate account of encounter in its full form. His book *Elements of Encounter* (Schutz 1973) gives a succinct account of the history of the development of the encounter group, and also of the principles which emerged from that history. And in his book *Joy: 20 Years Later* he writes:

> I still regard encounter as the queen of the human potential methods; the best method to experience before any other training, so that the person is clear, aware, self-determining, and ready to profit much more from any other training.
>
> (Schutz 1989: 161)

He makes it clear that encounter is not about games and exercises. There is an event called a microlab which actually is about games and exercises, but this is not an encounter group and should never be confused with it.

What happens in an encounter group is that the group produces an issue of some kind through one or more of its members, and the leader finds a way of dramatizing that issue so that it can be worked through for the benefit of the individuals who raise the issue, and the group as a whole.

There is an assumption here that this may well lead into something to do with the past, and may also lead the person deeper into their inner world. This is because of the concept of the energy cycle. This is something which gets fairly close to the Gestalt notion of a cycle of awareness (Clarkson 1989). As a need begins to be felt, energy is mobilized to deal with it, and this rises to a peak when the challenge is met; after this there is a relaxation period, when the person winds down. If, on the other hand, the challenge is never met, then the tension of mobilized energy is held in the body, and chronic body structuring may be set up in the worst cases. So in his groups, Schutz looks for the signs of held tension, and seeks to enable the person to complete the energy cycle, by dealing with the real life events which need to be dealt with. For example, a tension between two men may lead to them both carrying out an exercise suggested by the leader, and this may lead to one of them getting in touch with feelings about his father (e.g. Shaffer and Galinsky 1989: 207).

Jim Elliott (1976) has given us what is perhaps the most thorough examination of what is actually done in an encounter group, and again made clear that this is a coherent and principled approach, not in any sense a rag-bag of different techniques. Its emphases are on interpersonal communication in the here-and-now; contacting, exploring and expressing feelings; and moving towards self-directedness and self-actualization. He also emphasizes that encounter is not about games and exercises. This is such a persistent misunderstanding about the nature of encounter groups that it is understandable why he should want to do this.

He suggests that there are three types of leaders in groups: the tough leader, whom he calls familiarly 'the Pusher', who likes to see many displays of aggression and will attempt to engineer them, continually pushing and challenging people to show their anger; the tender leader, whom he calls 'the Warmie', who emphasizes acceptance and support, and likes to see positive displays of affection in their groups, with no put-downs, no discounting and no invalidation; and the self-sufficient leader, whom he calls 'the Laissez-Faire', who remains detached and remote, and does nothing but drop in the odd group interpretation. There is of course a fourth type, represented by Elliott himself, who is a genuine facilitator, not bringing with him such strong biases, and intent upon bringing out whatever is ready to come out.

Elliott says that growth is a three-stage process: first, destructuring; second, the emergence of noetic material (mental contents such as thoughts, feelings, desires and so forth); and third, integration of this material.

Destructuring always feels threatening. Indeed, for some people with shaky ego structures, it may be inadvisable. It is a process of uncovering, unfreezing, opening up, letting go of defences – there are many ways of conceptualizing it. The upshot is that something is released which was kept confined before, warded-off or disowned. Sometimes this happens as a result of life events such as rows, losses, threats, discoveries or anything else which upsets the status quo. Sometimes it happens as a direct result of something which happens in the group itself.

The material which emerges may be thoughts, feelings, impulses, images or any other kind of noetic content. It may emerge subtly or explosively, may be recognized or ignored. But in a group like this, there is every encouragement to let it be recognized and acted on. The person may feel that it is wrong to have such feelings or responses, and it is the job of the leader to give permission for them to take the stage. One of the things which may be necessary along the way is for the leader to work on the resistance to allowing such material to come forth: this may be due to 'shoulds' or to scripts which firmly forbid such expression, or to whole subpersonalities which block or impede what needs to happen.

Elliott regards feelings as very important in this. Feelings, he says, are the royal road to the noetic world. Feelings are like icebergs, with the most socially acceptable aspects visible, and the more powerful, more primitive aspects submerged out of sight.

These more primitive aspects come from our childhood. 'The little child', says Elliott, 'lives in a magical world.' When Mother is angry, that can seem like the end of the world, or proof that the child is terribly bad. Our parents have the power to make us do things, and our own feelings have magical power: our anger can kill, destroy, crush, poison or spoil our parents and the others around us. So we may fear our feelings as too dangerous, and engage in all sorts of manoeuvres to get rid of them or pretend they do not really exist.

Part of my strategy in working with feelings is to help people get deeper into the feeling iceberg. What I find when I start with a tiny 'insignificant' surface feeling is that it leads to other feelings, deeper down, that seem to occur in layers. The full expression of one layer leaves noetic space for

the next layer to emerge. Growth, then, involves work on oneself in the form
of uncovering layer after layer of feeling, until one gets to what have been
called primal feelings, such as deep rage and pain. That's where the very
earliest blocks are released and the most energy becomes liberated.

(Elliott 1976: 95)

He goes on to say that it is important in such cases to elicit the complete con-
figuration rather than have a dissociated feeling. This includes the somatic component, the imagery component and the belief component, as well as the feelings
themselves. This enables the further processing to take place which leads to real
integration with the rest of the person's life.

It can be seen here how regression and recession are very important, but they
are not the end of the road. Work still needs to be done on integrating the insights
into the person's ordinary everyday world.

A good example of this kind of work in action is to be found in Gerald Haigh's
(1968) article, too long to quote here, where a woman goes into her feelings about
her mother and resolves something very important once and for all. So again the
regressive content can be very central.

Elizabeth Mintz has told us particularly about the marathon group, which
is in a way the most complete expression of what the encounter group has to
offer. She makes the point that the power of the encounter group is related to
its simultaneous functioning as a reality experience and as a symbolic experience.
This is more implicit in the work of the other two people we have examined, but
of course equally true of their work.

She is also clear that an encounter group is not only a growth group but a
therapy group. She denies that there is any real distinction between the two, as
if the healthy were healthy and the sick were sick, and a neat line could be drawn
between the two. In an encounter group we go down into the neurotic and even
psychotic material which we all have within us. This often means regression into
the past, and recession into the inner world.

Like the others, she distinguishes between her own groups which are unstructured, and highly structured experiences which are sometimes incorrectly labelled
as encounter. If there are too many prescriptions, she says, 'the phoniness which
encounter groups seek to overcome may reappear in the guise of pretended spontaneity, false rapture and pseudointimacy' (Mintz 1972: 11). Exercises are useful
as ice-breakers, but it is better to avoid them if possible.

One thing which Mintz makes clear but the others do not, or not nearly so
clearly, is that many of the theoretical pronouncements of psychoanalysis do
come out as validated in the encounter group, and her own analytic training
was by no means irrelevant in this kind of work. So one of the classic regressive
approaches (psychoanalysis) has something to say to us here. In these ways the
Mintz account is complementary to the two accounts already given.

Existential

Let us now come on to how encounter deals with the here-and-now aspects
of the matter. First of all, of course, there is the basic question of how the

group is set up. Schutz points out that there are definite phases in the group life cycle. The first is inclusion, the second control and the third openness. Usually at the beginning of a group, the inclusion issue is at the top of the list. Then, as the group progresses, control issues come to the fore. And lastly, issues of openness emerge and have to be worked through in the group. This can easily be linked to other theories of group life cycles, such as Tuckman and Jensen (1977), with their stages of Forming, Storming, Norming, Performing and Adjourning. But Schutz himself lays particular stress upon the stage of openness and honesty:

> Honesty and openness are the key to your evolutionary growth. Being honest allows your bodymind to become a clear channel for taking in all the energy of the universe, both inside and outside your body, and to use it profitably.
>
> (Schutz 1973: 16)

This is really the classic existential approach of the encounter group, but it is interesting to see that Schutz says that it only really happens once the other issues are out of the way. In this it is perhaps reminiscent of the point which psychoanalysts sometimes make, that when the client can really free-associate the therapy is over.

Mintz has some points to make about the composition of the group. Teenagers seem to respond best in a homogeneous group, and so do psychotherapists, but everyone else does best in a heterogeneous group. Very little screening is required, but people who are too disturbed take up a disproportionate amount of time in the group, and it is better to suggest some other approach to them.

She has found that 14 people is about the most who can be handled by one leader, and that less than ten makes for a group which is too restricted in its options. At the beginning of the group she lays down certain requirements:

> that the group must function as a group at all times, without one-to-one relationships or subgrouping; that social chatter and history taking are not useful; that after the ending of the group any personal data which have been revealed are to be treated confidentially; and that any reaction which one group member has to another is to be expressed openly and directly.
>
> (Mintz 1972: 17)

She goes into the question of what the norms actually are in an encounter group. Her list is so similar to those of Schutz and Elliott that I have taken the liberty of making up my own list which is based on all three (see Table 9.1). I sometimes use this as a one-page handout to give to naïve groups, especially if they are likely to be rather rigid and intellectual: I first used it with a group of engineering students, who found the whole idea of psychology very difficult, but found these rules quite understandable.

Schutz is particularly keen to emphasize the centrality of the body in all this. Non-verbal methods are used consistently, and body movements and postures are constantly referred to. Stuck feelings are usually held in the body in some quite noticeable way, and it often makes sense to exaggerate some physical action until it reveals what was behind it. Encounter agrees with the body therapies,

Table 9.1   Integrative encounter groups: basic practice

1 *Awareness of the body*   Your body is you. It expresses your feelings, if you will let it. You can learn how you feel by going into your own body and noticing what you find there. If you suppress your own body, you will probably be willing to suppress other people – and they may pick this up. In groups like this we often get rid of chairs and tables so that interaction may take place physically as well as verbally.

2 *The here-and-now*   Talk about what you are aware of in this group at this moment. If you want to talk about the past, or about events outside the group, find ways of making them present to the group members. This can often be done by action or role-playing.

3 *Feelings*   Let reality have an emotional impact on you, especially the reality of the other group members. Let yourself feel various emotions – but if they are blocked, be aware of that too. Feel what it is like to experience whatever is happening at an emotional level.

4 *Self-disclosure*   Be open about your feelings or lack of them. Let people into your world. If you are anxious, let people know about it; if you are bored, it is OK to say so. Be as honest as you can bear to be.

5 *Taking responsibility*   Take responsibility for yourself – do what you want and need to do, not what you think the group wants you to do. If the leader suggests something, it is still your decision whether to go along with it. Be aware of what you are doing to other people by what you say and do, and take responsibility for that. Be aware of the 'I and thou' in each statement. You are not an impartial observer.

6 *Risk-taking*   If you are torn between expressing something and not expressing it, try taking a risk. Doing the thing you are most afraid of is usually a good idea in this group. You can reduce the danger of hostile statements by saying them non-evaluatively: instead of saying 'You are a cold person', say 'I feel frozen when you talk like that'. This is more likely to be true, and it makes you more real to the others.

7 *Listening*   Listening to others lets us into their worlds. But listening is not just about words – it means being aware of expressions, gestures, body positions, breathing. Allow intuition. Really be there with the other people in the group.

8 *Bridging distances*   As relationships in the group become clearer, there may be one or two members you feel very distant from – or want to be distant from. By expressing this, a quite new kind of relationship may begin to appear. Opposition and distance are just as likely to lead to growth as closeness and support.

9 *Distress*   When someone in the group is distressed, encourage them to stay with that feeling until the distress is fully worked through, or turns into some other emotion. There is a 'Red Cross nurse' in all of us who wants to stop people feeling distressed, and usually jumps in too soon. A person learns most by staying with the feeling, and going with it to its natural end, which is often a very good place.

10 *Support and confrontation*   It is good to support someone who is doing some self-disclosure, some risk-taking, some bridging of distances. It is good to confront someone who is not being honest, who is avoiding all risk-taking, who is diverting energy away from the group's real work. It is possible to do both these things with love and care.

11 *Avoidance*   Don't ask questions – make the statement which lies behind the question. Address people directly, saying 'I' rather than 'it' or 'you'. Don't say 'I feel' when you mean 'I think'. Ask yourself – 'What am I avoiding at this moment?'

12 *The saver*   Don't take any of these rules too seriously. Any set of rules can be used to put someone down – perhaps yourself.

and with Gestalt, that my body is a map of my experience and my being. Schutz writes:

> You are a unified organism. You are at the same time physical, psychological and spiritual. These levels are all manifestations of the same essence. You function best when these aspects are integrated and when you are self-aware.
>
> (Schutz 1973: 16)

This is a good statement of one of the basic beliefs of the humanistic approach which is so fundamentally committed to integration.

Once the group has commenced, the issue of self-responsibility arises, and Schutz and Elliott take rather different attitudes to this. They both agree (as does Mintz) that the removal of blocks of one kind and another is very important in the process of growth. Defences and resistances of various kinds are seen as removable in an atmosphere of encouragement. In other groups safety is seen as an important value, but Schutz does not feel that growth can ever be safe. Rather does he emphasize self-responsibility and self-determination. Indeed, he pushes this much further than most people:

> Suppose, for example, that I hold to a particular belief while I am a member of a group. To my chagrin, I find that everyone in the group disagrees with me. After a great deal of 'ratpacking' and 'coercion' and 'laying trips on me', the group 'breaks me down' and forces me to change my mind.
>
> Back home, I find I still feel as I did originally. I get angry at what has been done to me. The group has brainwashed me! It has pressured me into changing my mind. The leader irresponsibly took advantage of his authority and overwhelmed me.
>
> If I choose, I may content myself with this explanation, become an indignant critic of the 'tyranny of groups', liken my experience to brainwashing, and write a paper demanding that ethics committees suppress this alien behaviour.
>
> However, if I accept the choice principle, I will go further and recognize that *they* did not change my mind, *I* did. All they did was to say and do things. *I* interpreted what they said and did as group pressure; *I* assigned authority to the leader; *I* accepted the group's projections as applying to me. Group members may have intended that my mind may be changed, but *I* had to collude with them to make it happen.
>
> This realization helps me to gain self-insight and to profit from the experience. What is there about my lack of security, my lack of stability, my off-centeredness, my need to be accepted, that leads me to change my mind when I really do not think differently?
>
> As a result of exploring my own uncertainty, I realize the group gave me a gift. It created circumstances that I could use to discover how certain I am of my beliefs, how important it is for me to be liked, or how weak I am in what I believe.
>
> (Schutz 1989: 168)

I have given this example at length, because I believe it is so central to what Schutz is saying about self-determination, and really needs to be understood thoroughly.

Elliott, on the other hand, says that in the second or third session of a ten-session group he will ask 'Would anyone like me to push them?' One or two people usually answer 'yes', and these are the ones he will challenge and push. In other words, he believes that group pressure, to be therapeutic, requires express consent.

It is already clear, then, that encounter leaders are not all saying quite the same thing, even though there is a great deal of agreement between them. Encounter is a broad-brush approach, rather than a specific and laid-down formula.

Much of the Schutz approach is based on the leader working with individuals in the group; the other group members can participate when requested to do so, as in a group go-round (where the focal person is encouraged to say the same sentence to every member of the group in turn), or of course to gain vicarious learning from the experience of the focal person at a given time. But Elliott lays more stress on the mutual interaction of the group members. He points out that people feel much more involved with this format, and that the tangles they get into with each other represent here-and-now material for the leader to work with and untangle: the members then also learn how to deal with such tangles in their everyday lives.

> By using such a format, the encounter group leader can: 1) encourage inter-personal interactions among group members in the here-and-now; 2) elicit the feelings that accompany such interactions; 3) encourage the individual to get deeper into the feelings; 4) help the group deal with the norm-setting attempts that inevitably occur as a reaction to the expression of feelings; 5) help the group create an appropriate climate in which intensive work may be done; 6) train people in more effective ways of communicating and relating; and 7) help people grow by showing them how to disengage themselves from whatever they have become attached to and, from that new, freer position, become involved with whatever aspects of human existence they wish.
>
> (Elliott 1976: 32)

So Elliott is stressing here the value of members of the group working with each other, and we shall see later that this is a theme which has become more important as the years have gone by.

And because Elliott lays so much stress on the group interaction, he does not feel that one-to-one work with the leader is all that goes on in an encounter group. In fact, he stresses over and over again that EVERYTHING THE GROUP LEADER DOES WILL TEND TO DEPRIVE THE GROUP MEMBERS OF THE OPPORTUNITY OF DOING IT ON THEIR OWN (Elliott 1976: 112).

There are differences, then, as well as great similarities between different exponents of encounter. Let us see how these work out when we come to the next category we are examining.

Transpersonal

This is a category of working where, as Stan Grof has said, we are involved with 'experiences involving an expansion or extension of consciousness beyond the usual ego boundaries and beyond the limitations of time and/or space' (Grof 1975: 155). We feel we are getting information from we know not where. At first this sounds very unfamiliar and unusual, until we realize that virtually all therapists, counsellors and group leaders rely on their *intuition* a great deal.

Now according to the psychosynthesis school, which has done a lot of work in this area, intuition is one of the faculties of the higher unconscious. This higher unconscious, or superconscious, is a natural feature of the human mind, which does go beyond the usual ego boundaries. By giving it its proper name, we are able to work with it better and understand it more fully. Intuition, then, takes us into the realm of the transpersonal.

Let us move on to take up another, similar, point about imagination. Again, many group leaders use *imagery and fantasy*, and these too are part of the transpersonal realm. When we ask a participant to bring to mind an image of his or her inner conflict, or suggest that they imagine what their opponent might turn into, or invite them to bring to mind a certain scene, we are invoking the imaginal world, which is the realm of the transpersonal. There is a brilliant discussion of all these matters in Shorr (1983), which also gives many ways of using imagery in very spontaneous ways, and in very brief bursts.

So when Schutz tells the story of a British woman in one of his groups who was asked to become very small and go inside her own body (Shaffer and Galinsky 1989: 218), he was working in a transpersonal way. We can see from this that imagery very often involves playing with the normal limitations of time and space. (In his more recent work, Schutz (1981) explicitly uses meditation, prayer, chanting and Arica spiritual exercises.)

Elliott does not say as much as Schutz about the spiritual aspects of his work, but he does say that human beings are not just physical objects but are best characterized by such words as freedom, choice, growth, autonomy and mystery. He also refers to *creativity* and liberation (Elliott 1976: 58).

Another phenomenon noted by Elliott is the Fusion Experience, which often happens after primals and similar cathartic experiences. The whole person is involved, and seems often taken outside their ordinary world. 'Looking back on the experience, [one has] the feeling that one was outside time and space. Typical comments are "The world fell away" . . .' (Elliott 1976: 198).

Mintz does not say much about spirituality in her 1972 book, but makes up for it by a later book which is all about it. In this book she gives an example where a young man's impotence was cured, not by the usual process of therapy, but by a group ritual in which he symbolically castrated each of the other men in the group. This arose quite spontaneously in the group, and she says of the event: 'It was an enactment of a mythic ritual, a primitive ceremony, which tapped the deep levels of the collective unconscious; it was a transpersonal experience' (Mintz 1983: 153–7).

In the same book, Mintz talks of countertransference of such a kind that the group leader actually feels inside her own body the next thing which needs to happen for the participant. This links directly with the research on counter-transference mentioned by Samuels (1989) in his recent book, which again links this with the transpersonal, and with the Jungian idea of the imaginal world.

It is my strong impression that the climate has changed considerably in recent years, in the direction of more open acknowledgement of the importance of the transpersonal. It was always important in encounter, but it is only more recently that people have said so very much.

Mintz cautions that it is also possible to go too far in the direction of paying attention to the extraordinary in the group. The group leader can actually start to feel like a psychic, and can indulge in activities which are basically ego-inflating, such as telling participants what they are thinking or feeling before they are aware of it themselves. This can work the other way round too: group members can try to get close to the leader by significant anticipations of what she or he wants or needs. This is particularly likely to happen when there is a strong transference to the leader. And of course it has to be treated with caution like any other transferential phenomenon.

When this happens in a group between group members, it is almost always beneficial, however. Here it comes under the heading of what is called in psycho-drama 'tele', which is regarded as a healthy and desirable phenomenon. Two or more group members may have an uncanny awareness of one another's deepest needs and feelings. This often comes out in exercises where people have to pick up partners. If the choice is allowed to be as free as possible (e.g. asking people to stand up and mill around before choosing) people very often choose each other in an extraordinarily appropriate way.

Jung has discussed this sort of thing under the heading of synchronicity – the meaningful co-occurrence of things which can be dismissed as coincidence. But these group phenomena are so common that it is hard to dismiss them in this way, any more than one would dismiss the phenomenon of transference.

Mintz even describes at some length how these transpersonal matters can be used in supervision, but to go into that would take us too far away from the ordinary encounter group.

Certainly one of the things which has always been true is that there is in encounter a hint of extraordinary depth, which is only rarely mentioned. In an encounter group it is possible to catch a glimpse of spiritual realities which go beyond ordinary consciousness. In a recent book Anthony *et al.* (1987) have suggested that these glimpses are extremely important in opening up a sense of spiritual possibilities. They can show briefly what is possible more permanently if spiritual development is continued. The gibe which is sometimes hurled at encounter groups – that the sense of wonder which they engender is temporary and therefore false – is seen to be a crass misunderstanding of the real meaning of the experience. The breakthrough and peak experiences which come through these means – what Perls calls the mini-Satori – are not illusory, even though they are temporary. They represent what I have argued at length elsewhere are mystical experiences (Rowan 1990).

Some updating material

A good description of the encounter group is given by Shaffer and Galinsky (1989), who put it in the context of other approaches to groupwork and again make clear that it is a coherent and expressive form of groupwork, which can stand with any of its competitors in a sturdy and respectable way. They too see Schutz as central in the development of the encounter group model, and some of the comments made on him above are based on their account.

More recently, Mike Wibberley (1988) has given a stimulating outline of how encounter is progressing in Britain today. He has developed the practice of the 'rolling ongoing group', where participants join for a minimum of six weeks, and thereafter drop out any time they wish on two weeks' notice. The group will run for a year or more, and as participants drop out they create a space for someone else to come in.

There are at least three important things which have happened in groups since the early days of the encounter group.

The revolutionary turn

During the 1970s, people started to come to encounter groups who were already involved in revolutionary politics, sometimes feminism, sometimes Maoism, sometimes anarchism and so forth. These people saw the group as oppressive, led by a leader who hid his oppressive power behind a smoke-screen of techniques. For a time, perhaps five years, this was a valuable corrective and critique of the taken-for-granted position of the leader. It led to a much more aware use of power in the group, and was very valuable in that way.

But as time went on, a new phenomenon began to emerge: the experience of other group members that the challenge to the leader could itself be oppressive. The revolutionary could be just as rigid and 'heavy' as the leader. An acute observer of this scene referred to:

> the peer who, on the one hand confronts that authority but, on the other hand, makes his or her fellow group members feel just as small, intimidated and vulnerable as they had felt in front of the old, discredited authority.
> (Mann 1975: 268)

Such people were now accused of 'laying trips on people' and putting down everyone who didn't agree with them.

The equality turn

During the 1980s, the general tone of the encounter group become more equalitarian. Now it was not a question of a few revolutionaries, but rather of the ethos of the group as a whole. Leaders found they had to become more like members of the group, rather than keeping to the more formal and therapist-like role which they had formerly adopted.

This is not a simple matter, however. As has been pointed out by an influential contemporary leader:

> There is often ambivalence in the group, with some people wanting the leader to be 'one of us', and at the same time resenting him or her for not being the mythical, perfect authority who knows all the answers and is able to solve all their problems and lead them to Nirvana.
>
> (Wibberley 1988: 72)

But certainly my experience is that groups in recent years are much less likely to allow the leader to be very distinct and separate than they used to be.

I think this is a permanent change, and that the old group scene can never now return. I feel quite a pang about this, because the old methods, dominant though they often were, did work and did liberate a lot of people. The new ethos seems to me slower and less effective in the short run, though no doubt healthier in the long run.

The Alice Miller turn

Towards the end of the 1980s, the work of Alice Miller and other similar writers became widely known, and it became evident that some of the traditional moves of the encounter group leader were experienced as abusive by those who were particularly sensitive to such issues. These were mostly people who had been sexually abused in childhood, though other forms of abuse could be important too.

Angry confrontation by the leader, so common in the early groups, seems to me now to have almost disappeared because of these influences. Such anger is not perceived now as something painful although freeing, but rather as a destructive kind of abuse which repeats early patterns in an anti-therapeutic way. This kind of spontaneity of the leader is now suspect rather than holy.

Some of the issues here have been well spelt out by John Southgate and his co-workers at the Institute of Self-Analysis, which has taken on board this material in a big way. In a recent article he writes:

> In practice there are a number of generally accepted things to say or do in 'therapy' which contradict this Golden Rule [THE CHILD IS INNO-CENT]. For example: 'TAKE RESPONSIBILITY FOR YOURSELF'. This contradicts another Golden Rule [NO POISONOUS PEDAGOGY]. The inner child needs to be cared for by a caregiver or advocate and not be responsible for meeting her own needs.
>
> (Southgate 1989: 14)

Obviously there is a contradiction here between the Schutz view we noted earlier and the Alice Miller position. I think this is a very difficult issue for encounter leaders at the present time, and it will take some years before we can see clearly what the outcome is to be.

These are challenging times for all forms of psychotherapy, but it seems that encounter, because of its inherent wide-ranging flexibility, will come out as still one of the strongest and most useful forms of groupwork.

Case example

My own work in encounter started in 1970, when I went to groups at the biggest growth centre at the time, Quaesitor, which at that time was located at Avenue Road in St John's Wood. It was there that I actually went to a weekend workshop led by Will Schutz, who impressed me very much. Later I also attended groups led by Jim Elliott and Elizabeth Mintz, and met Will Schutz many times in different contexts.

What I like about encounter is the way in which it allows the practitioner to use the whole range of his or her talents, and to explore the gamut of the group's capacity for healing and discovery. I find that I can stretch my capacities to the full in following the energy of the client who is focal at a given moment.

In my own work this has happened several times, as for example where a young woman was working on her fear of men. This was in a group held in a well-organized therapy centre where I knew there were resources for dealing with anyone who might become distressed or disturbed more than usual. Also there were several experienced leaders in the group. This woman was quite clearly distressed and ready to work. The previous episode in the group's life had triggered off her own response, a memory of her own rape in terrible circumstances.

I pointed out that I was a man, and encouraged her to see in me the person she was afraid of. First of all she simply experienced her fear, trembling and crying, but quite quickly it changed into anger. She now had in front of her, as it were, the source of the fear and the support to do something about it. So she took the opportunity to attack me. I held a big cushion in front of myself, and she punched and tore at it. She put a great deal of energy into this, and it seemed to go on for a long time; in reality it was not that long, but it did go on for several minutes. She punched me from the middle of the large room well into one corner. She carried on, with the encouragement of me and the rest of the group, until she could go on no longer.

When she collapsed exhausted, I encouraged the women in the group to gather round her and support her. They held her and spoke softly to her and made much of her, demonstrating that they accepted and appreciated her, and generally enabled her to return. So far this is pure regression work, encouraging the person to go back into the past and relive an episode from it with full emotional recall, at the same time transforming it by ensuring that safety is present.

While the women were working together, I was working with the men, who gathered round to find out what their role was to be. I suggested that they line up in a row along one end of the room, and whispered to them that they should accommodate whatever happened, in the manner outlined by Al Pesso (1973) in his work. This meant going with whatever the woman did, and exaggerating its effect. They each held a big cushion in front of them, as I had. The object of an encounter group is to allow action and feelings to be expressed and explored in a therapeutic way, not for people to get physically hurt or take unnecessary risks.

When she had recovered somewhat, the women encouraged her to attack the row of men, one by one. As she beat on each one, he screamed and threw up his hands and staggered into a corner and collapsed, until one side of the room was completely covered with a row of prostrate male bodies. So far this is pure existential work, bringing an activity into the here-and-now which takes forward the insights and feelings released by the earlier regression work. The strength released by the recession into her inner feelings was now enabled to come out and be expressed publicly.

She looked around, and seemed to feel that it was not quite finished. Then she took the ritual into her own hands (or in this case, feet), and trampled all over the men, feeling more and more triumphant over them. It should perhaps be said, for those who are not familiar with encounter groups, that it is normal for people to take off their shoes in such a group, and to sit on cushions bare-footed or in socks. The protagonist then sat down between two sympathetic women, who held her while she relaxed and came back to herself.

In the discussion afterwards, she said how powerful she had felt during this episode, and the other women in the group said they had been quite inspired too. The men were quite shaken, but were impressed by what had happened and wanted to understand it for themselves.

Now to those who are familiar with Eastern mythology, the last part of this episode forcibly brings to mind the words of Arthur Avalon as he talks about the relationship between the male and female polarities in Tantric religion:

> The fully Real, therefore, has two aspects: one called Śiva, the static aspect of Consciousness, and the other called Śakti, the kinetic aspect of the same. Kālī Śakti, dark as a thundercloud, is represented standing and moving on the white inert body of Śiva. He is white as Illumination (Prakāśa). He is inert, for Pure Consciousness is without action and at rest. It is She, His Power, who moves. Dark is She here because, as Kālī, She dissolves all in darkness, that is vacuity of existence, which is the Light of Being Itself.
>
> (Avalon 1978: 42)

What we had here, in effect, was a re-enactment of a very ancient ritual, express-ing the way in which female energy is sacred and has to be respected and treated correctly by the male. We had gone right outside the boundaries of the group room, and had been in touch with archetypal forces. I do not think it is right to identify the archetypal with the transpersonal, but it is through the trans-personal that we most readily get in touch with the archetypal. Assagioli (1975) says that the collective unconscious is much more complex and broad than the higher unconscious or superconscious, and I think he was the first to make this distinction clear. In any case, in this example we had moved instantly and irrever-sibly into the transpersonal.

The next phase of the group was all around male–female relationships, and brought out some deep material affecting several people in the group who had problems in this area. Here we had moved back into the existential mode once again.

This ritual affected everyone in the group very strongly, and it seems to be a fact that the transpersonal does come across with great power when this is allowed and encouraged.

Conclusion

The advantage of the integrative approach is that it enables the practitioner to do what is appropriate in a given situation, rather than sticking to some previously worked out theory. It enables, in particular, the regressive, the existential and the transpersonal all to be given their due weight. In this way theory and practice are in a dialectical relationship, each informing the other. The theory gives rise to the practice, and the practice in turn enables the theory to be further developed.

Note

1 For example, Rogers (1970) has talked about 'basic encounter', which is not very integrative; Schutz (1973) has talked about 'open encounter', which is fully integrative; Mintz (1972) has talked about 'marathon encounter', which is also fully integrative; and Yablonsky (1965) has talked about 'Synanon encounter', which is not fully integrative.

References

Anthony, R., Ecker, B. and Wilber, K. (eds) (1987) *Spiritual Choices: The Problem of Recognizing Authentic Paths to Inner Transformation*, New York: Paragon House.

Assagioli, R. (1975) *Psychosynthesis*, London: Turnstone Books.

Avalon, A. (1978) *Shakti and Shakta*, New York: Dover.

Clarkson, P. (1989) *Gestalt Counselling in Action*, London: Sage.

Dryden, W. (ed.) (1987) *Key Cases in Psychotherapy*, London: Croom Helm.

Elliott, J. (1976) *The Theory and Practice of Encounter Group Leadership*, Berkeley: Explorations Institute.

Ferrucci, P. (1982) *What We May Be*, Wellingborough: Turnstone Press.

Grof, S. (1975) *Realms of the Human Unconscious*, New York: Viking Press.

Haigh, G. (1968) The residential basic encounter group, in H.A. Otto and J. Mann (eds) *Ways of Growth*, New York: Grossman.

Kutash, I.L. and Wolf, A. (eds) (1986) *Psychotherapists' Casebook*, San Francisco: Jossey-Bass.

Laing, R.D. (1983) *The Voice of Experience*, Harmondsworth: Penguin.

Mann, R.D. (1975) Winners, losers and the search for equality in groups, in C.L. Cooper (ed.) *Theories of Group Processes*, London: Wiley.

Mintz, E.E. (1972) *Marathon Groups: Reality and Symbol*, New York: Avon.

—— (1983) *The Psychic Thread: Paranormal and Transpersonal Aspects of Psychotherapy*, New York: Human Sciences Press.

Pesso, A. (1973) *Experience in Action: A Psychomotor Psychology*, New York: University Press.

Rogers, C.R. (1970) *On Encounter Groups*, Harmondsworth: Penguin.

Rowan, J. (1990) Spiritual experiences in counselling, *British Journal of Guidance and Counselling* 18(3): 233–49.

Samuels, A. (1989) *The Plural Psyche*, London: Routledge.

Schutz, W. (1973) *Elements of Encounter*, Big Sur: Joy Press.

—— (1981) Holistic education, in R. Corsini (ed.) *Innovative Psychotherapies*, New York: John Wiley.

Schutz, W. (1989) *Joy: 20 Years Later*, Berkeley, Calif.: Ten Speed Press.

Shaffer, J.B.P. and Galinsky, M.D. (1989) *Models of Group Therapy*, Englewood Cliffs, NJ: Prentice-Hall.

Shorr, J.E. (1983) *Psychotherapy through Imagery*, 2nd edn, New York: Thieme-Stratton.

Southgate, J. (1989) Interactive self-analysis: the successor to psychotherapy, *Journal of the Institute for Self-Analysis* 3(1): 11–16.

Tuckman, B.W. and Jensen, M.A.C. (1977) Stages of small-group development revisited, *Group and Organization Studies* 2(4): 419–27.

Wibberley, M. (1988) Encounter, in J. Rowan and W. Dryden (eds) *Innovative Therapy in Britain*, Milton Keynes: Open University Press.

Yablonsky, L. (1965) *Synanon: The Tunnel Back*, London: Macmillan.

10

Research on integrative and eclectic therapy

MICHAEL BARKHAM

Introduction

There is an increasing literature on the theory and practice of both integrative (e.g. Wachtel 1987) and eclectic (e.g. Beutler 1983; Norcross 1986) pyscho-therapies, as well as on the movement towards integration in general (Beitman et al. 1989). In addition, a considerable body of literature attests to the view that a majority of practitioners align themselves more with either an eclectic or integrative approach than with any single pure therapeutic school. Norcross et al. (1989) reviewed four surveys of the theoretical orientations of clinical psychologists carried out at intervals between 1960 and 1986 and found eclectic therapy to be designated as the primary theoretical orientation by the highest number of participants on all occasions. However, their data also showed that after an initial rise in those practitioners reporting eclectic therapy as their primary orientation from 36 per cent in 1960 to 55 per cent in 1973, there has since been a decline to 31 per cent in 1981 and 29 per cent in 1986. In a survey of counselling psychologists, Watkins et al. (1986) found by far the largest number (40 per cent) of practitioners to describe themselves as eclectic in orientation. Interestingly, both surveys commented on the small but increasingly significant number of practitioners reporting a cognitive orientation: 13 per cent (Norcross et al. 1989) and 11 per cent (Watkins et al. 1986).

However, in contrast to the plethora of interest in the *practice* and, to a lesser extent, the *theory* of integrative and eclectic pyschotherapy, *research* interest and activity in this area has been a poor relation. It has often been quoted that there are more than 250 therapeutic orientations (London 1988), each with its own particular theoretical model and specific techniques. The call for integration has come from two perspectives. First, from a theoretical stance reflecting the desire to stem the proliferation of therapies by seeking commonalities at a higher level of abstraction than technique alone; and second, from a practical stance reflect-ing a desire by practitioners to become more innovative in attempts to com-bine technical orientations in order to enhance the therapeutic impact. A third perspective, that of empirical research, is only recently gaining ground. For example, a National Institute of Mental Health (NIMH) workshop on integrative and eclectic therapies concluded with 23 recommendations for future research, many of which will be cited in this chapter (Wolfe and Goldfried 1988). Against this background, the purpose of this chapter is to review the research literature relevant to integrative and eclectic therapies, first in the international arena, and second in Britain.

During the course of the chapter, considerable emphasis will be placed on the methodological aspects of research. Whether or not research findings are valid depends greatly on issues of design, methodology and analysis. In turn, these are influenced by researchers' models of how change takes place. These components comprise researchers' skills, a parallel to practitioners' therapeutic skills. Like therapy, however, the quality of research varies considerably. In the same way that practitioners aspire to 'good' therapy, so scientists should aspire to 'good' research. Ideally, good pyschotherapy research should inform practice, but this is dependent upon (a) research being made more relevant to practitioners, and (b) a greater value being placed upon scientific methods by practitioners.

Conceptual definitions

While integration and eclecticism reflect similar clinical trends (i.e. away from pure modes of delivery), a central tenet of any research endeavour concerns specificity. The need for specificity derives from an attempt to mitigate the effects of 'uniformity myths' (Kiesler 1966) whereby equivalent findings can be attributed to a lack of differentiation. In this context, it is important to distinguish eclectic from integrative therapies. Norcross and Grencavage (1989) view *eclectic* therapy as atheoretical, pragmatic and empirical, composing a collection of divergent techniques. In effect, eclectic therapy arises from the collection of *specific* techniques which have been found to be effective in therapeutic practice. *Integration* reflects a 'commitment to a conceptual or theoretical creation beyond a technical blend of methods' (1989: 234). Accordingly, integration draws on the *common* ground across therapies and attempts to identify *higher-order constructs* which can account for change mechanisms beyond the level of any single model. By contrast, pure therapeutic orientations are based upon theoretical models which are specific to particular therapeutic orientations and do not necessarily provide an account for how change occurs within contrasting therapies. Accordingly, combinations of therapies (e.g. cognitive and behavioural orientations) do not constitute either eclectic or integrative therapies as the techniques available are restricted to the two particular orientations (and therefore not eclectic) and they do not provide a superordinate theory to account for changes across contrasting therapies (and therefore not integrative). Issues relating to conceptual definitions in eclectic and integrative therapy are pervasive in the literature (e.g. Goldfried and Wachtel 1987; Norcross and Grencavage 1989).

A framework for reviewing pyschotherapy research

In order to provide a framework for addressing the research literature relevant to integrative and eclectic therapies, two 'orthogonal' models have been adopted: the first summarizes the *pyschotherapy system*, and the second encapsulates the components of any *scientific enquiry*. The model adopted here as summarizing the pyschotherapy system has been adapted from Orlinsky and Howard's (1987) 'generic' model of psychotherapy and comprises two major levels: *outcome* (i.e. what changes occur as a result of therapy), and *process* (i.e. what happens within the therapeutic context). Not included for present purposes is the level of 'input' (i.e. the precursors of therapy). The research pertaining to both these levels can be documented according to four stages of a model summarizing the task of scientific enquiry: *theory* (i.e. a particular model or understanding of the phenomenon), *methodology* (i.e. the strategies and procedures employed to test the theory), *research findings* (i.e. the results of testing the theory) and *implications* (i.e. the consequences for theory development and/or further empirical studies).

The structure of the first part of this chapter will be to follow the model of scientific enquiry (i.e. theory, method, findings and implications) for the literature across the outcome and process levels of psychotherapy. Before doing so, however, it is worth setting the context for pyschotherapy research in general. Results from meta-analytic studies (Smith *et al.* 1980; Shapiro and Shapiro 1982; Robinson *et al.* 1990) have shown that pyschotherapy is effective. These meta-analytic studies, in which the results of other studies become the data for analysis, have incorporated hundreds of comparative studies in order to provide an overall picture of the effectiveness of pyschotherapy. The conclusion has been summarized by Lambert *et al.* (1986: 158), who stated: 'There is now little doubt . . . that psychological treatments are, overall and in general, beneficial, although it remains equally true that not everyone benefits to a satisfactory degree.' A more detailed review of the literature in these areas, together with further questions relating to psychotherapy outcome, have been addressed in greater detail elsewhere (see Barkham 1990; Goldfried, *et al.* 1990).

Psychotherapy outcome

Theory

The issue of effectiveness has naturally led to a question which has particular relevance to integrative and eclectic therapies: whether one type of therapy is superior to another. At the scientific (i.e. research) level, a major rationale for integrative and eclectic treatments would exist if it could be shown that there is relatively little difference in outcome between the wide range of therapies currently practised. Different therapies are based upon different theories as to how client change occurs. In turn, they each employ a diverse range of techniques to help clients resolve their difficulties. Given the multitude of differing techniques employed, it might be hypothesized that there would be a considerable range in their relative effectiveness: that is, different therapies based on different theories and adopting different techniques would lead to different (i.e. non-equivalent) rather than similar (i.e. equivalent) outcomes.

Methodology

Studies aimed at testing the relative effectiveness of differing therapies have comprised both comparative outcome studies and meta-analytic studies, which are able to ascertain the size of any differences found between treatments in individual studies and arrive at an overall assessment of the relative effects of different treatments. The issue of methodological sophistication is a major factor in the evaluation of comparative therapies. Accordingly, this section addresses some pertinent issues concerning the procedures employed in comparative psychotherapy outcome studies which may influence the interpretation of outcome equivalence.

One aspect concerns *statistical validity*, which refers to the sample size employed in research studies. The sample size plays a critical role in determining the ability of a study to be sufficiently sensitive to detect actual differences between particular treatment orientations should they be present. This sensitivity is based on the statistical power derived from the design of the study. In the behavioural sciences, it has been stated that the size of differences to be expected, termed effect size (ES), is likely to be medium (Cohen 1977). Kazdin and Bass (1989), in a review of the statistical power of psychotherapy outcome studies, found the mean ES in comparisons between two active treatments to be medium (i.e. ES of 0.50) whereas the mean ES in comparisons between treatment and no-treatment conditions was large (i.e. ES of 0.85). Given the same sample size, therefore, the statistical power of a design comparing two active therapeutic orientations is substantially lower than that in an equivalent treatment versus no-treatment comparison.

The following example may help to clarify this issue. Supposing a researcher devised a study comparing two active treatments (e.g. pure versus integrative), with no grounds for hypothesizing that one would be superior to the other (i.e. two-tail test), and wished to be 80 per cent certain (i.e. have a four in five chance) of detecting a medium effect-size difference, what sample size would be needed? The answer, based upon statistical tables (Cohen 1977), would be in the region of 64 clients in each treatment group (i.e. a total sample of 128 clients evenly balanced between treatments). Kazdin and Bass (1989) found more than half the studies they sampled (55 per cent) to fall short of the required statistical power (i.e. 80 per cent chance) necessary to detect a difference. However, it needs to be stressed that while a study such as this may not show differences between therapies, this does not mean that differences do not exist; there would be a 20 per cent chance that there are differences. On the other hand, if they cannot be detected using this power, then any differences which do exist between therapies are likely to be very small and therefore have limited practical or theoretical importance. In addition, studies replicating such findings using independent samples, providing they have sufficient power, will serve to substantiate this body of knowledge.

Further, if a study is to tap all the factors which may impact on treatment, a sufficiently elaborate factorial design is required to control for the hypothesized variables as well as having sufficient statistical power within each of these comparisons to be sensitive to any real differential response to treatments. Stiles *et al.* (1986) suggested that such a study would need approximately 10,000 cells, placing it well beyond the realms of practical possibility. Accordingly, it will be apparent how practical and financial constraints alone have 'favoured' the equivalence paradox.

Another major issue concerns achieving a balance between *internal validity*, in which the experimenter is able to maintain tight control over the variables of interest and thereby minimize error variance (e.g. in laboratory experiments), and *external validity*, in which the experimenter has less control over the variables but works in settings and conditions which bear a greater resemblance to the natural setting in which the phenomenon occurs (e.g. clients presenting with depression at NHS clinics). Shapiro and Shapiro (1982) concluded that the majority of studies evaluating the effectiveness of behavioural therapies contained one of the following three weaknesses: (a) they were laboratory analogues, (b) they employed student volunteers, and (c) the primary targets were non-clinical presenting problems. Accordingly, while many studies of behaviour therapy satisfied the criterion of internal validity, they did not do so for external validity.

There are also issues relating to more technical aspects of outcome research which are pertinent to the development and practice of integrative and eclectic psychotherapies. For example, if the outcomes of two diverse therapies are assessed inaccurately, spurious results may lead to invalid conclusions concerning the effectiveness of a particular active ingredient as a component to be used in the development of an eclectic therapy. Central to this task is the question of how psychotherapy outcome is measured; that is, what instrumentation should be used? Differing therapeutic approaches adopt differing targets or goals. If two therapeutic orientations are being compared and the measurement procedures 'favour' one orientation rather than another, then it raises the question of whether the comparison was 'fair' or sufficiently sensitive to the range of possible changes which might have occurred. The NIMH workshop on psychotherapy integration concluded that 'one of the great challenges in pyschotherapy integration is fostering agreement among therapists of different orientations about the meaning of change . . .' (Wolfe and Goldfried 1988: 449). They recommended that 'a typology of outcome criteria from different orientations needs to be developed. These outcome criteria need to be as specific and descriptive as possible' (1988: 449). In addition, they argued for outcome evaluations to be multi-dimensional so as to include critical variables of different pure therapies. Two stages in this process are necessary; first, the utilization of a 'core battery' of measures and, second, the use of highly specific and refined measures targeted on integrative therapy.

The first stage, the adoption of a 'core battery' of outcome measures (Waskow 1975), would have considerable merits on three counts. First, it would comprise existing (i.e. validated) measures, preferably with normative data; second, it would provide a comprehensive view of the areas of change to be evaluated (e.g. affective, cognitive, behavioural and relationships); and third, it would provide a step towards systematic cross-site collaboration in psychotherapy research. To date, however, while certain measures are used more than others, no agreed battery is currently in use. In terms of the second stage (i.e. the development of specific measures to tap integrative therapies), some measures have been developed which tap purported integrative functions between client and therapist (e.g. therapeutic focus: Goldfried, *et al*. 1989) while other measures have tended to operate at a relatively high level of abstraction (e.g. the overall state of readiness of the client to address their problems: McConnaughy *et al*. 1989).

A further issue concerns the metric used to evaluate outcome. To date, the vast majority of findings are derived from tests of statistical significance based upon differences between group means. More recently, researchers have addressed the issue of determining, in addition to statistical significance, the degree of *reliable and clinically significant* change (Jacobson and Revenstorf 1988). Congruent with this aim is the need for statistical procedures to focus on the individual client in relation to the group rather than use the group mean alone. This implies that a more specific relationship between effective treatments and individual clients can be determined. Research procedures which focus solely on differences between groups may mask important clinical differences and make research findings less relevant to practitioners.

A final issue worth raising concerns possible uncontrolled variation in treatment delivery. That is, if no differences are obtained between two contrasting therapies (e.g. cognitive versus psychodynamic), how can we be sure that this was not due to therapists within each orientation employing differing variants of their therapy, or even techniques from the other therapy and thereby generating considerable overlap and lessening the probability of finding any significant differences? This problem has been addressed recently through the implementation of two procedures: (a) manualization, and (b) treatment adherence. The manualization of therapies enables different therapists to deliver a similar brand of the treatment and is seen as an important methodological advance. We need to know that the cognitive therapy delivered by therapist A is similar to therapist B and different from psychodynamic therapists C and D. To test whether therapists are delivering a particular brand of therapy, researchers now evaluate treatment adherence; is therapist A actually delivering the therapy as advocated in the manual? However, while these procedures may help 'purify' the delivery of treatments and possibly lead to differential effects, their application to eclectic and integrative therapies is likely to be more problematic. For example, in practical terms alone a manual for technical eclecticism would be vast, while a manual for an integrative therapy may operate at too high a level of abstraction from the moment-to-moment therapeutic situation.

Research findings

The findings arising from comparisons of the relative effectiveness of contrasting pure therapies have important implications for the development of integrative and eclectic therapies. In general, the literature attests to little difference in outcome between contrasting therapeutic orientations. This finding has been referred to as one of *outcome equivalence* despite the technical diversity of contrasting therapies (Stiles *et al*. 1986). Major reviews of comparative outcome studies (e.g. Luborsky *et al*. 1975), meta-analytic studies (e.g. Smith *et al*. 1980; Shapiro and Shapiro 1982), in addition to well-designed and carefully implemented comparative outcome studies (e.g. Elkin *et al*. 1989) all conclude that the outcomes of diverse psychotherapies are *broadly* similar. This is not to say that the literature has not reported differences between treatments. For example, in a meta-analytic study of psychotherapy for depression, Robinson *et al*. (1990) found a significant effect-size advantage of 0.47 standard deviation units for cognitive over general verbal therapy. However, when researcher allegiance was partialled out, the results showed no significant advantage of any one therapeutic orientation over any other. These findings indicate the caution required and critical stance necessary before accepting the results of research studies.

Of central importance is that outcome equivalence arises from researchers seeking *main* effects: that is, addressing the question of whether treatment A is 'better' than treatment B. For example, results from a large comparative outcome trial, the NIMH Collaborative Study of Depression (Elkin *el al*. 1989), suggested that, although there were few differences between four conditions employed, more severe clients responded better in one particular group (those receiving imipramine and clinical management), and that this group showed superior improvement over the initial phase of treatment (Watkins *et al*. 1989). Accordingly, the relative effectiveness of one therapy can be a function of client severity or treatment duration. Accordingly, it is likely that *interaction* effects will be more informative and may identify conditions under which differential treatment effects may occur. The studies by Elkin *et al*. (1989) and Robinson *et al*. (1990) highlight both the necessity for testing possible contaminating effects as well as the need to recognize the complexity of actual findings (i.e. interaction effects) when compared with the simple 'is one better than the other?' question (i.e. main effect). Thus, Beutler (1989) states that our

> failure to find differential outcomes among psychotherapies may be less attributable to the fact that we study the wrong variables than to our implicit belief that all patient, setting, and treatment variables exert independent rather than interactive effects on outcome.
>
> (1989: 276)

Early research studies addressing the question of differential effectiveness did appear to suggest a superiority for behavioural therapies (Rachman and Wilson 1980). However, the purported advantage to more behavioural therapies can be attributed to methodological procedures largely related to their lack of external validity and the type of measures employed (see above). Klein *et al*. (1983) reviewed 13 studies comparing systematic desensitization (SD) with other treatments for clients presenting with phobia and found only two studies (Gelder *et al*. 1967; Gillan and Rachman 1974) which reported a superior outcome for SD over dynamic psychotherapy, and even these two studies had methodological flaws which could have accounted for the results. Indeed, the authors' own results from a comparison between SD and supportive dynamic therapy found equivalent outcomes. When studies containing seriously flawed methodologies are omitted, the outcome of psychological treatments has been summarized as follows: 'On balance, studies of better than average quality using patient populations show little advantage of behavioral over nonbehavioral methods in the treatment of affective and anxiety disorders' (Stiles *et al.* 1986: 166).

However, meta-analytic studies (Smith *et al.* 1980; Shapiro and Shapiro 1982) do not appear to have convinced all researchers of the general equivalence of comparative outcomes. While Smith *et al.* (1980) state: 'The well-controlled comparisons yielded no reliable differences in effectiveness of behavioral and verbal therapies' (1980: 125), Lazarus (1989) states that '. . . when selecting "well controlled" studies, Smith *et al.* found behaviour therapy to be significantly superior to psychodynamic and other verbal therapies' (1989: 254). It does appear that research findings are still open to differing interpretations. However, those researchers espousing the differential effectiveness of therapies need to address a range of methodological issues (e.g. researcher allegiance) as well as the relative effect size of any difference obtained. Even if one therapy were found, statistically, to be more effective with some clients in certain situations, the question remains as to the size and clinical significance (i.e. actual importance) of that difference.

Implications

The finding of broadly equivalent outcomes between contrasting therapies is of paramount importance for integrative and eclectic psychotherapies and raises the following axiomatic proposition: If there is no effective differential outcome between standard pure treatment orientations, then there is no *a priori* scientific, and consequently ethical, argument why practitioners should adopt any one mode rather than another. Further, therapists may see a number of choices. They may amalgamate differing techniques from other therapies and move towards an eclectic approach; they may seek what is common to many therapies and move towards an integrative model of therapy; or they may seek to refine and sharpen the particular techniques and procedures within their preferred therapeutic orientation in order to enhance its effectiveness.

The finding of outcome equivalence has important implications for research. If the view is that there *are* specific techniques which are more effective than others, then these become candidates for an eclectic therapy. This development would lead, logically, to two types of outcome studies: (a) those comparing the outcome of pure therapies with that of integrative or eclectic therapies, and (b) those comparing the outcome of differing variants of integrative or eclectic therapies against each other. The research literature in both these areas is virtually non-existent (although see section on Development and evaluation of integrative therapies, p. 260). Several reasons lie behind this situation.

First, as stated earlier, psychotherapy research has traditionally shadowed clinical practice, and with the reduction in funding to carry out increasingly sophisticated studies, the lack of research is understandable. However, this assumes that the best or most appropriate way to demonstrate the effectiveness of a particular treatment is by the 'controlled clinical trial' with all its ensuing costs. This view has been challenged in Stiles and Shapiro's (1989) critique of many of the assumptions underlying psychotherapy research. These authors argue that reliance on the controlled clinical trial 'constrains the process investigator to look only at established treatments, denying the possibility that newer treatments could be developed or discovered via process' (Rice and Greenberg 1984: 531). A corollary of this argument is that a research programme studying the comparative outcomes between eclectic and integrative therapies may counter the philosophy of integration by unwittingly promoting another 'horse race' (i.e. is one therapy better than another?). Rather than comparing global outcomes, a more productive focus would involve pursuing an understanding of client change (Greenberg 1986).

Second, it *could* be argued that if eclectic and integrative therapies derive from treatments which have already been shown to be both effective and broadly equivalent in their outcome, then evaluating the effectiveness of eclectic or integrative therapies may be redundant. However, this presupposes a simple 'additive' model of therapeutic components in relation to treatment outcome in which the delivery of one particular technique is unaffected by others. It also presupposes that the design which best tests integrative therapies is one in which *homo*geneous client samples are used as in traditional comparative outcome studies. However, it is likely that any greater effectiveness of integrative and eclectic therapies will derive from studies which tap a *hetero*geneous sample of clients similar to those presenting in out-patient clinical settings, enabling the greater flexibility of integrative/eclectic therapies to be realized.

Against this background, however, it does seem that any substantial refinement of a pure orientation therapy or the development of an integrative therapy ought to be tested empirically against the standard (i.e. pure) orientation from which it was developed. But the nature of the question changes from 'which therapy is better?' to 'who is better served by one or other treatment?' Indeed, the NIMH workshop (Wolfe and Goldfried 1988) concluded that pilot studies are required to compare the relative effectiveness of an integrative therapy with a pure approach in the treatment of specific clinical problems, with the aim of identifying those clients who benefit most from an integrative approach. If the refinements or new therapies are better than their predecessors (i.e. more effective or efficient), then they are likely to lead to noticeable differences in the proportions of clients attaining clinically significant improvement. If not (i.e. if outcome equivalence prevails even with heterogeneous client samples), then it could be argued that such efforts at devising more integrative treatments, while increasing practitioners' choices, have not enhanced the efficacy and effectiveness of psychotherapy.

Psychotherapy process

Theory

If the finding of outcome equivalence is valid (i.e. is not an artefact of methodological flaws), then some theoretical construct or concept has to be invoked in order to explain this finding. Probably the most powerful explanation for the broad equivalence of outcomes is the contribution of what has been termed *common* factors; that is, factors that underlie or override differences between therapies. These have often been termed 'non-specific' factors but would be more accurately construed as '*un*specified'. Currently, the term common factors acts as a conceptual umbrella for including a number of client and therapist contributions. The exact nature of these, however, needs to be specified. The term 'common factors' better reflects their role in accounting for similarities across differing therapies. Indeed, Gaston (1990) identified three differing conceptions of the therapeutic relationship which apply equally well to all common factors: (a) that they are therapeutic in and of themselves; (b) that they are prerequisites for specific techniques to be effective; and (c) that they interact with specific techniques in determining success in therapy.

In accounting for the broad similarity in outcomes, the most parsimonious argument is that if common factors are sufficiently potent in contributing to psychotherapy outcome (i.e. they equal or outweigh the unique technical contribution of differing therapies) such that effective outcome can be largely attributed to common factors, then the finding of equivalent outcome for technically differing therapies is no longer a paradox. Further, these effective components would then become elements in future eclectic therapies. However, this is not to imply that there is any single 'ideal' eclectic therapy. Alternatively, the finding of broadly equivalent outcomes could be accounted for by the equivalent effectiveness of very different therapeutic techniques (i.e. that different techniques have similar psychological impacts). This view emphasizes the hugely differing combinations of common and specific ingredients which may be effective for differing individual clients.

Methodology

The investigation of psychotherapy process lies at the heart of integrative and eclectic psychotherapies and is evidenced by attempts to determine the *active ingredients* of therapy. Wolfe and Goldfried (1988) have stated that 'process analysis can . . . stimulate theory and, eventually, can lead to the development of a genuine, integrative theory of psychotherapy' (1988: 449). Accordingly, they recommended that 'research is needed on the actual change processes that take place in psychotherapy' (1988: 449). However, as stated in the previous section on outcome, the ability of research studies to determine the relationship between process variables and outcome depends upon the validity of the procedures employed.

One obvious strategy has been to correlate a single process variable (e.g. therapist-offered interpretations) with outcome: a significant positive correlation would establish grounds for the particular process variable being an active contributor to successful outcome. However, serious problems arise from assumptions made about the linkage between process and outcome. Many of these issues have occurred through the adoption of research strategies based on the assumption that psychotherapy works in a similar way to psychopharmacology (i.e. drugs: Stiles and Shapiro 1989). For example, studies have attempted to look at the *amount* of a particular process variable assuming that the more there is of it, the better the outcome. However, it cannot be assumed that all interpretations have an equivalent impact, nor that the 'definition' of interpretation in one study is synonymous with that used in another study. In addition, ratings have usually involved *aggregates* of a particular measure across time. However, clinical experience tells us that the depth of, for example, therapist interpretations can vary considerably (Speisman 1959). The skilful therapist will deliver, for example, an interpretation *in response to* some cue from the client (i.e. client readiness). In effect, consideration needs to be taken of the *context* within which interventions are made. Accordingly, the focus on active ingredients necessitates a different research strategy from that employed in psychopharmacological research.

These, and other, inappropriate research strategies based upon the 'abuse of the drug metaphor' have seriously hindered psychotherapy process research. To date, research methodologies and the assumptions underlying them have tended to be too simplistic with the reporting of null correlations between process variables and outcome interpreted, not necessarily correctly, as meaning that process–outcome relationships do not exist. In an attempt to address this misconception, researchers have increasingly abandoned the bipartite system of process and outcome in favour of viewing therapy as a process of multiple *small outcomes*, termed 'small O', which ultimately lead to a *big outcome* (i.e. 'big O'), the traditional view of outcome.

Two approaches have recently been advocated and espoused by the NIMH workshop (Wolfe and Goldfried 1988): the analysis of significant or critical events, and task analysis. The study of significant events derives from a 'new' paradigm, termed the events paradigm, which focuses on those moments in therapy which are felt to be most helpful to clients. The procedures for carrying out this strategy are variants of Interpersonal Process Recall (IPR: Kagan 1981) and have been extensively employed by only a few psychotherapy researchers. Research based upon this procedure enables intensive investigation of particular classes of events (e.g. insight events, interpretations, perceived-empathy and so on) at specific times in therapy, thereby evaluating their contribution to subgoal outcomes, and building a comprehensive picture of the process of change across therapy. Elliott *et al.* (1987), for example, used highly intricate analyses of insight events occurring in cognitive-behavioural and relationship-oriented therapies to detail a summary model of the sequential steps in the process of insight in which the crucial step termed 'connection', where the client recognizes a meaningful pattern in his or her experience, is only one of six identified steps in the prototypical insight event.

The second strategy, task analysis (Greenberg 1984), requires the development of micro-theories for understanding mechanisms of change and identifying discrete components of the therapeutic process. This requires a cumulative process but is more appropriate than attempting to study entire theories of therapeutic change. Task analysis attempts to explicate a model of the information-processing activities which the client and therapist perform across time and which leads to the resolution of particular cognitive–affective tasks. This preliminary model can be developed by rational/theoretical speculations and then its 'goodness of fit' verified against empirical examples of psychotherapy change processes. This will be achieved by means of a cycling back and forth between the rational model and the empirical phenomenon, resulting in a final model of how change actually occurs. Task analytic procedures used by Greenberg (1984) corroborated the role of many clinically observed phenomena in the resolution of conflict (e.g. the softening in attitude of the harsh critic). In addition, task analysis suggested evidence for the specific role of the client experiencing previously disavowed feelings as well as moving from an attitude of self-criticism to one of self-acceptance. Both these procedures (i.e. IPR and task analysis) focus on the level of clinical description which is important in promoting the iterative nature between therapy processes and sub-outcomes.

Research findings

Lambert (1986) estimated that on the basis of previous reviews of research, approximately 40 per cent of improvement in psychotherapy clients was a function of spontaneous remission. Of the remaining 60 per cent, specific techniques and client expectancy effects each accounted for approximately 15 per cent, while common factors accounted for approximately 30 per cent. The overall impact of common factors has been demonstrated in the Sloane et al. (1975) study in which clients were asked at a four-month follow-up to identify those components of therapy which they found helpful. Although statements included items referring both to techniques and common factors, clients having a successful outcome, irrespective of the therapy they received (dynamic or behavioural), identified similar items: personality of the therapist, providing understanding of problems, encouragement to face problems, and helping them towards greater self-understanding. Psychotherapeutic techniques were not rated as most important. However, it is worth bearing in mind that therapeutic techniques are conceptual entitles which have salient theoretical meaning for practitioners but not necessarily for clients. This section addresses research findings concerning three domains of interest relating to common factors: client, therapist, and relationship variables.

Client variables

In considering the contribution of client factors, Stiles et al. (1986) stated that 'a major active ingredient in all psychotherapies is the client's involvement in therapy and the verbal exploration of his or her own internal frame of reference' (1986: 172). Frank (1973) identified five processes held in common by psychotherapies which relate directly to the client: (a) new cognitive and experiential learning, (b) strengthening of hope, (c) success experiences, (d) emotional arousal and (e) mitigation of social isolation. There is evidence that less specific measures, for example, client participation (O'Malley et al. 1983) or positive contributions (Marziali 1984), are related to greater therapeutic gains. A further category of client factors concerns expectancies, both prior to and during therapy. Indeed, client expectancies became a major feature of placebo control groups which, it is known, account for nearly half the effect of active treatments. Overall, however, there has been relatively little reward from efforts to link specific client behaviours with therapy outcome. Stiles et al. (1986) have stated that 'it has proved surprisingly difficult to demonstrate a convincing relationship between specific behaviors and therapy outcome' (1986: 173). Much of this can be attributed to methodological difficulties in terms of attempting to correlate single process variables with a single ultimate outcome. In addition, there are problems in interpreting process–outcome correlations because we know that client requirements and therapist responsiveness do not happen randomly but do so in a complex and mutual fashion (Stiles 1988).

Therapist variables
Therapist factors incorporate commonly offered conditions over and above the theoretically essential characteristics of a given therapy. Frank (1973) identified three processes: (a) genuinely caring about the client's welfare; (b) having ascendancy/power; and (c) acting as a mediator between the client and 'society'. The literature pertaining to the first of these (i.e. therapist-offered conditions) focuses mainly on the 'necessary and sufficient conditions' postulated by Rogers (1957): warmth, empathy and genuineness. These variables have been much researched and, although showing some promise in the 1960s, the findings of subsequent research have been equivocal largely due to shortcomings in the methodologies employed. The second process has been addressed by Bennun and Schindler (1988), in common with the behavioural focus on therapist expertise, while the third process has been examined by Orlinsky and Howard (1987) in framing the therapeutic process within a societal context.

While early work attempted to locate variables within the person of the therapist (age, sex, level of experience and so on), more recent work has addressed therapist application of technique. Goldfried (1980), for example, identified two therapeutic strategies which might be common across therapies: providing the client with corrective experiences, and offering the client direct feedback. Clients can achieve corrective experiences through different mechanisms; for example, by developing and resolving personal issues as a function of the therapeutic alliance in dynamic therapies, or by behavioural monitoring, testing and subsequent cognitive re-evaluation which occurs in cognitive-behavioural therapies. However, the evidence supporting these commonalities rests more on pooled clinical observations rather than on explicitly designed research studies.

Evidence for the primacy of therapeutic feedback has been reported by Castonguay *et al.* (1989) in a study which compared cognitive-behavioural with psychodynamic-interpersonal therapies. They found a focus on clients' actions to be significantly related to improvement while a focus on clients' self-evaluation was related to poor outcome irrespective of therapeutic orientation. This was also true across therapies for an emphasis on intrapersonal links (i.e. connections between two aspects of a client's functioning). This research on therapeutic feedback as a common strategy across therapies is continuing under the auspices of a large NIMH grant following an initial recommendation of the NIMH workshop (Wolfe and Goldfried 1988) that 'as integrative research constructs emerge and are clarified, instruments will need to be developed to assess them' (1988: 448). One such instrument involves a system of coding 'therapeutic focus' (Goldfried *et al.* 1989) in which 'feedback' is seen as a common factor in accounting for therapeutic effectiveness.

Client–therapist relationship variables

The therapeutic alliance has been described as the 'quintessential integrative variable' (Wolfe and Goldfried 1988) because '. . . competent therapists of all persuasions are able to establish a positive emotional bond and a sense of mutual collaboration with receptive clients, and this . . . relationship carries most of the therapeutic weight' (Stiles *et al.* 1986: 173). Accordingly, researchers have to espouse the broad equivalence of therapeutic outcomes as being due to the therapeutic alliance. Strupp and Hadley (1979) compared the effectiveness of analytically and experientially oriented professional therapists with college professors in order to determine the relative contribution of specific techniques versus common factors. They concluded that the positive changes experienced by clients receiving therapy from both types of therapist were 'generally attributable to the healing effects of a benign human relationship' (1979: 1135). Moreover, they deduced that therapeutic change occurred as a function of the client utilizing the relationship and the therapist employing interventions perceived by the client to reflect caring and genuine interest. They concluded that 'while the "techniques" of professional therapists did not seem to give rise to measurably superior treatment effects, these skills appeared to potentiate the natural healing processes inherent in a "good human relationship" . . .' (1979: 1136). The general weight of evidence in support of the alliance as a contributing factor has led some commentators to hold the view that the investigation of 'specific' ingredients has been misguided and that attention should be focused on the client–therapist relationship (Butler and Strupp 1986).

A significant contribution to the theoretical understanding of the therapeutic relationship has been made by Bordin (1979), who identified three components of the alliance: (a) an agreement on goals, (b) the degree of concordance regarding tasks and (c) the development of personal bonds. The model facilitates the proposition that different tasks and goals (which vary as a function of the mode of therapy) will lead to the development of different alliances. For example, it is likely that the tasks and goals comprising a cognitive-behavioural approach characterized by a didactic ethos will lead to a substantially different kind of therapeutic bond from that which develops during the course of a relationship-oriented approach focusing on the client's interpersonal difficulties in which the client–therapist relationship is used as a vehicle of change. In effect, this construction provides greater specificity to what has traditionally been labelled a common factor. These three components (i.e. tasks, goals and bonds) have been operationalized in the Working Alliance Inventory (Horvath and Greenberg 1986).

Having considered client, therapist and client–therapist relationship variables, the question remains as to how specific and common factors contribute to therapy. A current view regarding the relative contribution of common and specific factors is that an effective therapy may depend upon both types of factors – that is, upon common factors as well as specific procedures targeted for specific client problems. This view would take into account the finding of the *broadly similar* outcomes (i.e. the equivalence paradox) but also recognize that the findings are *not exactly* identical, carrying the implication that for some clients, certain therapies may be more advantageous than others. Some support for a specific factors model was found by Glass and Arnkoff (1988) in a comparison of four group therapy orientations (social skills, cognitive restructuring, problem-solving and unstructured). Significant differences obtained for the three categories of specific change, with the reported changes being consistent with the content of the programme (e.g. greater behavioural change in the social skills orientation). In particular, client explanations for the changes were congruent with the treatment orientation they had received, possibly because clients had learned a specific way of describing their own experiences within therapy. These results were, however, moderated by the finding that benefits not only generalized across orientations, but that clients in each of the structured conditions identified the role of common group process factors as being at least as important as the specific therapy content, thereby suggesting the need for an integrative model of specific and common factors.

The interaction between common and specific factors has been investigated by Jones *et al.* (1988). In their study of specific effects in psychotherapy, they found effective therapists used different techniques depending upon each client's severity level such that their interventions were probably influenced by their evaluation of clients' characterological and emotional strengths and weaknesses. They argued that specific, intentional interventions shape and define client–therapist relationships (i.e. common factors). Further, they stated that the

> notion of nonspecific factors and of related concepts such as therapeutic alliance can serve to obscure more precise hypotheses about how patient change may be set in motion by a relationship with a psychotherapist.
> (Jones *et al.* 1988: 55)

In short, the relationship between both specific and common factors and outcome is highly complex and is, most importantly, contextual.

Beutler (1983: 6) has stated that while

> there is scant evidence that one technique is better than another across a heterogeneous group of patients, some research . . . suggests that certain types of patients may be more responsive to certain techniques than they are to others.

For example, Beutler (1979) found general support for the view that insight therapies were generally superior to behavioural therapies among highly reactive clients (i.e. clients resistant to external influences). The implication is that for particular clients, a particular subset of techniques within an eclectic therapy would be applied. Consistent with this view, Beutler (1989) has recently argued for the adoption of dispositional assessment which is directed towards assessing the clients' treatment response rather than a description of their symptoms as is traditional within diagnostic assessment. In reviewing the existing literature, he derived a base rate in which 5 per cent of outcome variance could be attributed to treatment techniques *in unselected samples*. In contrast, 30 per cent of outcome variance could be accounted for by intensive client–therapist matching. However, this latter procedure is viewed as impractical. Accordingly, a compromise is reflected in the approach of technical eclectics in which selective procedural and patient matching are employed and, on the small amount of available data, likely to account for 20 per cent of outcome variance.

Implications

The argument in favour of integration has become increasingly powerful in response to the awareness that differing therapies are employing similar over-arching or metatheories of change. For example, contrary to expectations, Kerr *et al.* (1989) found therapists working in a cognitive-behavioural orientation to place greater emphasis on client *inter*personal links (i.e. between the client and others) rather than on *intra*personal links (i.e. between the client's own thoughts and feelings). This finding is consistent with a growing emphasis on interpersonal processes within cognitive therapy (e.g. Safran 1990a, b; Safran and Segal 1990). A prerequisite for improving practice will be a greater delineation of variables and the links between technique and common therapeutic processes. One fruitful area is the increasing standardization of client populations and therapist applications arising from client selection and the training of therapists in manualized therapies (i.e. specific factors) for particular client problems. Combined with this would be an awareness that there may be specific types of therapeutic alliances (i.e. common factors) which are appropriate for the multiplicity of tasks and goals within therapy.

The interface between common and specific factors is likely to be best addressed through the development of integrative models of therapy which identify the core ingredients hypothesized to contribute to outcome and suggest specific links between the components which are amenable to empirical testing (e.g. Prochaska and DiClemente 1982, 1986; Orlinsky and Howard 1987; Castonguay and Lecomte 1989; Stiles *et al.* 1990) The value of these models lies both in their ability to describe processes which transcend single therapeutic orientation and their potential for providing cogent theoretical bases for initiating research questions central to developing our understanding of the psychotherapeutic process. The model of the psychotherapy system employed as a framework in this chapter (i.e. Orlinsky and Howard's generic model) provides one framework for identifying core components of the psychotherapy process. In the generic model, the 'process' level (existing between 'input' and 'outcome') comprises five main components: (a) *therapeutic contract*, which defines the purpose and limits of the contract; (b) *therapeutic interventions*, which comprise all that is said between client and therapist; (c) *therapeutic bond*, which can be construed as the global component of the client–therapist relationship; (d) *self-relatedness*, which addresses the degree of client openness versus defensiveness; and (e) *therapeutic realizations*, which include the helpful impacts generated during the session (e.g. insights, discriminant learning and so on). In an empiricial test of the model during the early phase of therapy, Kolden and Howard (1988) found general support for the components but in particular the central role of the therapeutic bond.

Castonguay and Lecomte (1989) have suggested a trans-theoretical model of psychotherapy based on the integration of common factors. Of particular importance to the process of change are three characteristics: first, what are termed 'basic processes' which include areas of interpersonal influence, the therapeutic relationship and therapist–client involvement; second, they identify 'dimensions of the interaction' which comprise areas of communication and methods of intervention which have traditionally provided differences between contrasting therapies; and third, 'therapeutic functions', which consist of common changes which are achieved in different therapeutic approaches (e.g. increase in hope, cognitive and emotional relearning).

Prochaska and DiClemente (1982, 1986) and Stiles *et al.* (1990) have both proposed stage models which focus on the particular processes involved in the client resolving their problems. The former postulates four stages: (a) precon-templation, (b) contemplation, (c) action and (d) maintenance. The authors identify ten superordinate types of change processes (e.g. self-reevaluation, dramatic relief, helping relationships) which can be utilized in service of faci-litating client change. They suggest that the major difference between verbal and behavioural processes of change is that the former are most important in prepar-ing clients for action, while the latter becomes more important once clients have made a commitment to the action stage. Research has been carried out on the trans-theoretical model but much of it focuses on specific presenting problems of clients (e.g. smoking, alcohol abuse and weight control). By their very nature, the processes of change associated with such presenting problems may be more targeted compared with the diffuse presenting problems associated with, for example, depression.

This step-wise model has parallels with the development of an 'assimilation model' of clients' problematic experiences (Stiles *at al.* 1990). This is an *integrative* model of change in psychotherapy in which it is proposed that the assimilation of problematic experiences is a common change mechanism in all psycho-therapies. The authors claim it to be integrative in that it draws upon concepts from psychodynamic, experiential, cognitive-behavioural and personal construct theories as well as cognitive and developmental psychology. Briefly, the assi-milation model proposed eight stages through which the successful resolution of problems progresses. These eight stages, which can be construed schematic-ally as moving from left to right, are as follows: (a) warded off, (b) unwanted thoughts, (c) vague awareness, (d) problem recognition, (e) insight/understand-ing, (f) application of understanding, (g) problem solution and (h) mastery. Clearly, not all problems originate at the stage of unwanted thoughts. Equally, not all clients achieve mastery over their problems. Accordingly, the model does not prescribe that every problem has to move through each and every stage, but it does suggest that the latter stages reflect a greater resolution of a client's prob-lem. Further, the model provides an integrative framework for evaluating how differing psychotherapies work. For example, it is more likely that psycho-dynamic and relationship-oriented therapies will operate primarily in stages towards the left of the model with material which is warded off or which the client has a vague awareness of, while behavioural therapies will focus on stages towards the right of the model where problems become increasingly concretized in terms of problem solution. In addition to comparing the impact of differing therapies via the assimilation model, research can also sample change in individual clients across time.

In sum, the development of increasingly sophisticated models of therapeutic process and outcome, together with increasingly sensitive measures of both common and specific factors, hold considerable promise for future psychotherapy research in attempting to identify the effective ingredients in psychotherapeutic practice.

Integrative and eclectic research in Britain

Having reviewed the international literature, the second part of this chapter reviews past and present research on integrative and eclectic therapies in Britain. A recent survey of clinical psychologists within one health region found the highest number (32 per cent) to designate their primary theoretical orientation as eclectic, greater than the 22 per cent selecting the more traditional behavioural orientation (O'Sullivan and Dryden 1990). Although the sample was small (N = 81) and confined to one area, the percentage is broadly consistent with data reported by Norcross *et al.* (1989), as is the number (14 per cent) reporting a cognitive orientation as their primary choice. Accordingly, there is some initial evidence suggesting that preferences in theoretical orientations in Britain are not too dissimilar from those in the United States. Against this background, the work in Britain will be addressed under the four headings of scientific enquiry adopted in the first part of the chapter: (1) theory, (2) methodology, (3) research findings and (4) implications.

Theoretical contributions

As has been a constant theme throughout this chapter, there is considerably more written on the practical and theoretical aspects of integrative and eclectic therapies than on research into their processes and outcomes. Areas of commonality between behaviour therapy and psychodynamic orientations were addressed some 25 years ago by Marks and Gelder (1966), with both these eminent academics and practitioners concluding that the two orientations were complementary rather than conflicting. More recently, several writers have made contributions at the theory–practice interface (e.g. Dryden 1986, Douglas 1989). Douglas identified shortcomings arising from a pragmatic approach which simply matched behavioural techniques with behavioural problems, cognitive therapy for cognitive problems, and so on. For example, she argued that there needs to be a rationale both for the orientation adopted and level of difficulty at which the interventions occur, and also a rationale for moving from one therapeutic orientation to another. In a similar vein, Dryden (1986) has argued that an eclectic (or indeed any other) model of therapy must provide practitioners with the necessary basis for implementing appropriate interventions. He argues that a theory must be able to address specific questions which relate to the practice of 'differential therapeutics' (Frances *et al.* 1984). The areas that require specification or recognition include (a) the type of therapeutic arena (e.g. individual versus group setting), (b) the type of therapeutic alliance, in recognition that different kinds of alliances develop with different clients, (c) an account of client variation, (d) the recognition that interventions can be conceptualized at differing levels (i.e. styles, strategies and techniques) and (e) that the process of therapy changes across time. These components provide a useful framework for testing the conceptual adequacy of a model of therapy and would provide a bench-mark for evaluating the extent to which a model can comprehensively address practitioners' questions concerning the selection of therapeutic interventions.

As a precursor to integrative therapy, Ryle (1987) has proposed a model of higher mental processes based upon cognitive psychology and artificial intelligence. The model is termed the Procedural Sequence Model (PSM) and emphasizes that the mental and behavioural processes described are a way of organizing repeated actions (i.e. procedures), while the unit of observation for the therapist includes both mental and behavioural events involved in any action or sequence. This model has been used as the underlying structure in the development of an integrative cognitive-analytic therapy (CAT: Ryle 1990). Thus, Ryle argues that CAT provides 'a general account of the sequence of mental and behavioural processes involved in the carrying out of aim-directed activity' (1990:9). Research evaluating this therapy is discussed later (see section on Development and evaluation of integrative therapies, p. 260).

Methodological contributions

Paralleling the movement towards theoretical integration, there has been a *rapprochement* between research methodologies. This is required in order to seek any possible differential effectiveness between therapies and/or to further our identification of common factors which may, in turn, account for outcome equivalence. Using a single case-study as an exemplar, Agnew *et al.* (1990) employed four research strategies aimed at enhancing methodological *rapprochement*: (1) synthesizing process and outcome so that psychotherapeutic change is construed as a continuous process of therapeutic outcomes, and outcome as an on-going process within therapy; (2) recognizing heterogeneity in the therapy process over time and the need for the adoption of research methods based upon the events paradigm; (3) integrating quantitative and qualitative methods so that confidence in qualitative-descriptive studies is enhanced by quantitative-evaluative evidence; and (4) 'zeroing in' on representative cases of clinically significant change, enabling intensive study of cases which meet stringent criteria for change based upon a multidimensional assessment. The authors argue that traditional measures of process that are quantitative-evaluative can be employed as session outcome variables and that these are a function of the cumulative impacts of specific interventions over a particular session. The importance of these four strategies lies in their amenability to individual practitioners.

In addition to these integrative methodologies, there is also an increasing sophistication in single case design and analysis. This is important because the development of integrative therapies should employ this type of evaluative design to describe the therapeutic process prior to designing large-scale process–outcome studies. In addition, relatively large data sets can be accumulated through the application of clinical replication with successive single cases. Single case methodology need not only apply to small Ns but has high applicability in meeting criteria for internal validity within naturalistic settings (e.g. NHS and private practice).

Research findings

This section addresses research findings and comprises three sub-sections focusing on (a) 'desegregation' research (i.e. seeking the active ingredients of pure orientations prior to a move towards integration), (b) common factors research and (c) development and evaluation of integrative therapies.

Desegregation research

Several British writers have described the complementary use of behavioural and psychodynamic therapies (e.g. Douglas 1989; Fonagy 1989). Fonagy argued in favour of a combination of the two orientations (separate but not integrated into a higher-order theory) and felt that the ordering should be

> the addition of behavioural techniques to psychotherapy in order to enhance the symptomatic effectiveness of the latter. Dynamic therapies frequently stop short of achieving symptomatic improvements in spite of substantial progress in terms of insight and even in-therapy behaviour.
>
> (Fonagy 1989: 558)

However, theoretically, it might be expected that differential effects may obtain as a function of the treatment order. This question has been addressed in work carried out at the Social and Applied Psychology Unit in Sheffield and led by David A. Shapiro. The effects of the sequencing of contrasting therapeutic orientations was investigated in the first Sheffield Psychotherapy Project (Shapiro and Firth 1987) in which 40 professional and managerial workers received eight sessions of Prescriptive (cognitive-behavioural) therapy and eight sessions of Exploratory (relationship-oriented) therapy in a cross-over design. Consistent with the equivalence paradox, outcomes were broadly similar although there was a slight advantage to the Prescriptive therapy attributable to one of the two principal therapists (Shapiro et al. 1989). With each client receiving the two therapy orientation from the same therapist, control was achieved for the possible bias of common factors.

Because half the clients received Exploratory followed by Prescriptive therapy while the remainder received the two orientations in the opposite order, it was possible to determine the influence of sequence effects within viable eclectic packages. For example, a Prescriptive–Exploratory (PE) order may allow for immediate crises to be resolved prior to more in-depth exploration of personal issues. However, initial coping strategies may have the effect of 'shoring up' clients' defences and lead them to be defensive when in Exploratory therapy. Conversely, an Exploratory–Prescriptive (EP) order may enhance work at a deep level while feelings are relatively raw and then proceed to learn more adaptive strategies. However, some clients may be too anxious or concerned about immediate crises to be able to work effectively. When the two treatment orders were compared after the completion of treatment (i.e. after the full 16 sessions) there was no significant effect for treatment order. Shapiro and Firth (1987: 798) argued, therefore, that the 'data do not support one ordering as more favourable than the other'. However, further research employing an analysis of Personal Questionnaire (PQ) items provided some support for the EP ordering in preference to the PE order (Barkham *et al.* 1989) as the decline in severity of presenting problems during the course of therapy appeared 'smoother' in the EP treatment order, suggesting a more natural progression in the resolution of problems within this treatment order.

General issues for both clients and therapists concerning changes in therapeutic orientation within the Sheffield Project have been addressed by Firth *et al.* (1986). Given the context that clients knew at the beginning of therapy about the impending change, Firth *et al.* (1986) suggested that a clear statement at the time of the change together with a resumé of the rationale for the new treatment mode enabled the transition to occur relatively easily. They reported no difficulty by therapists in implementing the change, and found that, post-therapy, no client in the EP sequence reported anything unhelpful about the sequence. In contrast, several clients in the PE order made adverse comments about their difficulty in adjusting to the change and stated that they would have preferred the alternative sequencing of therapies (i.e. EP). The above findings suggest further support for the view that an EP ordering of therapies (i.e. psychodynamic followed by cognitive-behavioural) is more congruent with the process through which clients proceed in resolving their problematic experiences. However, both pure and eclectic approaches based on a specific ordering of therapies, in contrast to integration, place constraints on the range of techniques available to therapists in direct response to clients' needs.

Common factors research
Several researchers have investigated the role of common factors in differing settings. Llewelyn and Hume (1979) used a retrospective questionnaire method to sample the views of 37 clients receiving either psychodynamic or behavioural therapy on what they found useful in therapy. Clients reported common factors to have been more useful than the techniques specific to either orientation. Moreover, there was no difference between clients receiving behavioural or psychodynamic therapies in their ratings of the usefulness of either common, behavioural or psychodynamic techniques. In a subsequent study investigating clients' and therapists' views of therapy, Llewelyn (1988) sampled 40 therapist-client pairings, of whom 60 per cent described themselves as eclectic in orientation, with a further 15 and 10 per cent as psychodynamic and behavioural respectively. The remainder were client-centred or 'other'. During the course of therapy, the most frequently reported helpful events for clients were reassurance/ relief and problem solution which accounted for 26 per cent and 20 per cent of responses respectively. At termination, problem solution was the most common category accounting for 22 per cent of clients' responses. From the client's perspective, at least during therapy, the salience of reassurance and relief supports the central role played by common factors, although this is superseded after ending therapy by a focus on problem solution. In contrast, therapists most

frequently rated insight as the most helpful event both during (28 per cent) and after therapy (19 per cent).

In a study of clients' perceptions of curative factors, Murphy *et al.* (1984) found 'advice' and 'talking with someone interested in my problems' to be elicited by more than half the clients. Further, they found that 'receiving advice' and 'talking with someone who understands' were both moderately correlated with outcome. Bennun and Schindler (1988) investigated therapist and client factors in the behavioural treatment of 35 phobic clients, and found evidence suggesting that interpersonal variables may contribute to treatment outcome. The results showed that the more positive the participants' ratings of each other after the second session, the greater the amount of client change at the end of therapy. The authors concluded that 'Researchers and clinicians should not be too preoccupied with technique; favourable interpersonal conditions are also essential for therapeutic change' (1988: 151).

Development and evaluation of integrative therapies
Empirical studies on integrative therapies in Britain, although minimal, have followed one of two designs: single case reports and comparative outcome studies. Single case-studies on integrative therapies reflect an initial and logical progression towards describing and evaluating various integrative models. Several studies using this design have been reported on the implementation and evaluation of CAT, work initiated by Anthony Ryle and colleagues based in the Munro Clinic at the United Medical and Dental School, Guy's Hospital in London. Ryle (1980) studied 15 cases in which clients received a form of focused integrative active psychotherapy. Results suggested that clients who achieved changes in target 'dilemmas' (i.e. the narrow way in which they saw possible alternatives) also showed changes in their cognitive structure and target problems. More recently, Ryle (1982, 1990) has presented a 'formal' integration of psychoanalytic and cognitive therapy within a therapeutic model termed cognitive-analytic therapy (CAT). Using CAT, Beard *et al.* (1990) reported case-studies in which therapists working with three patients diagnosed as personality disordered used a diagrammatic rather than verbal sequential reformulation. The case descriptions suggest the general utility of this procedural variation within CAT. Case-studies of CAT have also been reported with clients presenting with poorly controlled diabetes (Milton 1989). The delivery of CAT, in which clients are seen for 12 sessions together with a three-month follow-up, is thought to be particularly appropriate for such clients although overall comparative outcome data is not yet available.

Watts (1990) has detailed the 'integration' of behavioural and interpretative methods in the treatment of a young man with an aversion to personal body hair. Following an assessment, treatment, which lasted for 36 sessions, progressed through five discrete stages: from employing direct exposure and preliminary exploratory work, through an increasingly exploratory focus, to symbolic exposure and cognitive therapy, then exploratory work, followed by intensive exposure, and finally focusing on adjustment and termination. Treatment resulted in a reduction of behavioural avoidance, and an emotional state characterized by intense relief and deep sadness, the latter being perceived as temporary (i.e.

akin to loss). This treatment shows the iterative nature of employing contrasting therapeutic orientations in service of each other.

Two studies report 'integrating' various therapeutic orientations with Gestalt therapy. Robinson (1991) provides an account of factors influencing her combining a Gestalt with a psychodynamic approach on a sample of 44 clients presenting at a university counselling service. She reports four positive indicators for Gestalt work within a psychodynamic framework: unfinished grief or strong affect which is near the surface, inner conflicts or dialogues with internalized parents, intellectualization and symptomatic body language. In effect, these become markers for implementing Gestalt techniques. Sills *et al.* (1988) report a single case-study combining both individual and family therapy, and employing Transactional Analysis, Gestalt, behavioural and bereavement counselling in the treatment of a 12-year-old girl who was severely traumatized by her mother's suicide. Treatment comprised six seventy-five minute sessions in which the focus moved from assessing the family system, to making interventions and facilitating the grieving process, to finally reintegrating the family. The use of techniques drawn from these various orientations led to the child being able to grieve naturally as a function of freeing the family system from a position where it had become 'locked'.

The three studies reported above (Sills *et al.* 1988; Watts 1990; Robinson 1991) perhaps better reflect attempts to combine rather than integrate contrasting theoretical orientations in service of resolving specific areas of psychological distress. The therapies do not derive from an overarching theoretical model of change, but rather from an astute clinical judgement as to what orientation might best facilitate movement for the client. In contrast, single intensive case-studies of an integrative therapy are being carried out by Shapiro *et al.* (in press) in which the authors have used the assimilation model (Stiles *et al.* 1990) as the guide for matching client 'requirements' with therapist 'responsiveness'. For example, by establishing the differential level of assimilation of clients' presenting problems, particular therapeutic interventions can be 'matched' with the degree of assimilation of the problematic experience. This matching is based on the assumption that a central aim of therapy is to promote clients' assimilation of their problematic experiences. The adoption of this integrative theoretical model goes some way to addressing issues raised by practitioners (e.g. Douglas 1989).

Turning to the comparative study of therapy outcomes, to date only one study has been published (Brockman *et al.* 1987). She carried out a study comparing a traditional psychoanalytic therapy based on the work of Mann (Mann and Goldman 1982) with the CAT approach. The sample comprised 18 clients receiving psychoanalytic therapy and 30 the CAT approach, with clients randomly assigned to one of 15 therapists based on their availability. Problems with randomization and differential severity levels at intake raise issues about the stringency of comparisons between these two treatment modes. Overall, however, both treatments were found to be equally effective as measured by, for example, the Beck Depression Inventory. Differences between the two groups did obtain in favour of the CAT approach on certain repertory grid-derived measures of cognitive change assessing the improvement of attitudes to the self. Accordingly, this study suggests that an integrative cognitive-analytic approach, while giving rise to broadly equivalent findings as a traditional psychoanalytic approach, does lead to an enhancement of one component of clients' personal functioning. This finding provides support for a 'weak' advantage to integrative therapies. Arguing against this would be the view that the advantage to the CAT approach was evidenced in measures which tapped the differential treatment component (i.e. cognitions), and this is no more than one would expect. The 'strong' test of whether an integrative approach is superior to a pure treatment orientation would be derived from measures which tap a central component of the presenting symptomatology (i.e. as portrayed in specific measures of, for example, depression). The Brockman *et al.* (1987) study does not support this strong test although this could be attributable to insufficient statistical power; that is, there might actually be a real difference on global outcome measures given sufficient statistical power. Further, it would be interesting to look at individual cases of successful outcome in the contrasting therapies.

Although generalizations are problematic because of the use of trainee therapists and the unequal severity levels of the two groups, a strength of the study, as Brockman *et al.* (1987) state, was its use of both normative and ideographic measures to tap change. Methodologically, this is important as it is based on the premiss that change is multidimensional. The use of either a single outcome measure, or measures tapping only a single perspective, or a single level of the change process (i.e. global versus specific, nomothetic versus ideographic, and so on) will be neither sufficiently comprehensive nor sensitive to changes which occur during therapy.

Implications

The increasing interest shown by practitioners in both integrative and eclectic therapies has led to a research focus on the personality aspects of the therapist, a possible integrative variable, rather than on specific techniques. For example, Davis *et al.* (1987) have developed a taxonomy of therapist difficulties which cuts across the distinctive techniques which are hallmarks of contrasting therapies, and have found evidence that the most common strategy employed by therapists when feeling threatened by their clients is to retreat to specific therapeutic techniques (Binns *et al.* 1989). This integrating focus on the therapist has led to a major international study of the development of psychotherapists (Orlinsky 1990).

Concluding comments

Goldfried and Safran (1986) have concluded that research has an important role to play in the achievement of the ultimate objective of

> the construction of an overarching model of the psychotherapy change process that can serve as a theoretical guide to the flexible and informed selection of psychotherapy interventions that are most appropriate to the particular situation at hand.

> (1986: 474)

In service of this aim, these authors have advocated the adoption of a *rational-empirical* approach as a superordinate research strategy to 'articulate[s] explicit guidelines for integrating the activities of theory construction and empirical research' (1986: 475). In addition, the aim of new paradigm research, as defined by Rice and Greenberg (1984), is to understand the essential mechanisms of client change:

> What is most needed in the field is the identification and specification of mechanisms of client change at a level that transcends the particular situation in which they are initially recognised and studied.
>
> (Rice and Greenberg 1984: 13–14)

It is probable that the adoption of both pluralistic and novel methodologies in psychotherapy research may enable more realistic and valid moves towards the identification of common and specific components. The approach espoused by Goldfried (1980) is to identify common *strategies*. This level of strategies lies in between the higher level of common *theories* and the lower level of common *techniques*. A major feature of these recent moves has been the recognition that our understanding of the process of psychotherapy is likely to be better understood through adopting a pluralistic research methodology rather than espousing any single methodological approach.

This chapter has detailed findings from psychotherapy research which have either a direct or indirect bearing upon the development of eclectic and integrative therapies. Researchers are still refining and retuning their methodologies in order to tap differential treatment mechanisms. On this basis, the recommendation of the NIMH workshop (Wolfe and Goldfried 1988) that 'desegregation' rather than 'integration' research is still required appears warranted, along with investigations into what 'practicing therapists of different orientations actually do' (1988: 449). Consistent with this advice is the view of London (1988) who has stated that opposing models of treatment may not need to be reconciled, joined or combined. He has argued for 'pluralism', holding the view that 'we can reasonably aspire to a common language . . . and to some common perspectives on theory and practice, but comprehensive integration may be a gratuitous quest' (London 1988: 11). We still do not know enough about how differing psychotherapies work in order to ensure that subsequent integrative therapies will benefit from process studies of pure therapeutic orientations.

With few exceptions (e.g. Brockman *et al.* 1987), there is a paucity of research comparing pure with integrative models of therapy. The original argument that the equivalence paradox favoured the move towards integration still requires testing. If a therapeutic orientation which purports to be integrative does not provide a better outcome on some criteria when compared with a pure therapeutic orientation, then the question will need to be asked whether the moves towards integration are in service of therapists' interests rather than treatment outcome. In terms of process studies, which are seen as central to the literature on integrative therapies, there is considerable debate about current assumptions underlying research methodology. In general, many have espoused the view that researchers need to adopt more complex models of the psychotherapeutic process:

It is essential to move beyond overly simplistic attempts to associate single dimensions of process with outcome and toward more complex, multi-dimensional models of change that are closer to clinical realities.

(Jones *et al.* 1988: 55)

This aim, together with planned studies of moment-to-moment therapeutic interaction as well as recurrent testing of the efficacy of therapies aspiring to the term 'integrative', may ultimately provide a more sound basis for enhancing their impact.

Acknowledgements

I would like to thank Roxane Agnew and Jan Duffy for their helpful comments on earlier drafts, and John Protraska for helpful discussions.

References

Agnew, R.M., Harper, H., Shapiro, D.A. and Barkham, M. (1990) Resolving a challenge to the therapeutic relationship: a single case study, SAPU Memo 1071 Department of Psychology, University of Sheffield.

Barkham, M. (1990) Research in individual therapy, in W. Dryden (ed.) *Individual Therapy: A Handbook*, Milton Keynes: Open University Press.

——, Shapiro, D.A. and Firth Cozens, J. (1989) Changes in personal questionnaires in Prescriptive versus Exploratory therapy, *British Journal of Clinical Psychology* 28: 97–107.

Beard, H., Marlowe, M. and Ryle, A. (1990) The management and treatment of personality disordered patients: the use of sequential diagrammatic reformulation, *British Journal of Psychiatry*, 156: 541–5

Beitman, B.D., Goldfried, M.R. and Norcross, J.C. (1989) The movement toward integrating the psychotherapies: an overview, *American Journal of Psychiatry* 146: 138–47.

Bennun, I. and Schindler, L. (1988) Therapist and patient factors in the behavioural treatment of phobic patients, *British Journal of Clinical Psychology* 27: 145–50.

Beutler, L.E. (1979) Toward specific psychological therapies for specific conditions, *Journal of Consulting and Clinical Psychology* 47: 882–92.

—— (1983) *Eclectic Psychotherapy: A Systematic Approach*, New York: Pergamon Press.

—— (1989) Differential treatment selection: the role of diagnosis in psychotherapy, *Psychotherapy* 26: 271–81.

Binns, M., Davis, J.D., Davis, M.L., Elliott, R., Francis, V.M., Kelman, J.E. and Schroder, T.A. (1989) Some correlates of therapist difficulties and coping strategies, paper presented at the 6th Annual Meeting of the Society for Psychotherapy Research (UK), Ravenscar, April.

Bordin, E.S. (1979) The generalizability of the psychoanalytic concept of the working alliance, *Psychotherapy: Theory, Research and Practice* 16: 252–60.

Brockman, B., Poynton, A., Ryle, A. and Watson, J.P. (1987) Effectiveness of time-limited therapy carried out by trainees: comparison of two methods, *British Journal of Psychiatry* 151: 602–10.

Butler, S.F. and Strupp, H.H. (1986) Specific and nonspecific factors in psychotherapy: a problematic paradigm for psychotherapy research, *Psychotherapy* 23: 30–40.

Castonguay, L.G. and Lecomte, C. (1989) The common factors in psychotherapy: what is known and what should be known, paper presented at the 5th Annual Meeting of the Society for Psychotherapy Integration, San Francisco.

———, Goldfried, M.R., Hayes, A.M. and Kerr, S. (1989) An exploratory analysis of process and outcome variables in the Sheffield Psychotherapy Project, paper presented at the 20th Annual Meeting of the Society for Psychotherapy Research, Toronto, Canada.

Cohen, J. (1977) *Statistical Power Analysis for the Behavioral Sciences*, New York: Academic Press.

Davis, J.D., Elliott, R., Davis, M.L., Binns, M., Francis, V.M., Kelman, J.E. and Schroder, T.A. (1987) Development of a taxonomy of therapist difficulties: initial report, *British Journal of Medical Psychology* 60: 109-19.

Douglas, A.R. (1989) The limits of cognitive-behaviour therapy: can it be integrated with psychodynamic therapy?, *British Journal of Psychotherapy* 5: 390-401.

Dryden, W. (1986) Eclectic psychotherapies: a critique of leading approaches, in J.C. Norcross (ed.) *Handbook of Eclectic Psychotherapy*, New York: Brunner/Mazel.

Elkin, I., Shea, M.T., Watkins, J.T., Imber, S.D., Sotsky, S.M., Collins, J.F., Glass, D.R., Pilkonis, P.A., Leber, W.R., Docherty, J.P., Fiester, S.J. and Parloff, M.B. (1989) NIMH Treatment of Depression Collaborative Research Program: general effectiveness of treatments, *Archives of General Psychiatry* 46: 971-83.

Elliott, R., Shapiro, D.A., Firth, J., Stiles, W.B., Hardy, G., Llewelyn, S.P. and Margison, F. (1987) Insight events in Prescriptive and Exploratory therapies: a Comprehensive Process Analysis, SAPU Memo 901, Department of Psychology, University of Sheffield.

Firth, J.A., Shapiro, D.A. and Parry, G. (1986) The impact of research on the practice of psychotherapy, *British Journal of Psychotherapy* 2: 169-79.

Fonagy, P. (1989) On the integration of cognitive-behaviour therapy with psychoanalysis, *British Journal of Psychotherapy* 5: 557-63.

Frances, A., Clarkin, J. and Perry, S. (1984) *Differential Therapeutics in Psychiatry*, New York: Brunner/Mazel.

Frank, J.D. (1973) *Persuasion and Healing*, 2nd edn, Baltimore: Johns Hopkins University Press.

Gaston, L. (1990) The concept of the alliance and its role in psychotherapy: theoretical and empirical considerations, *Psychotherapy* 27: 143-53.

Gelder, M.G., Marks, I.M. and Wolff, H.H. (1967) Desensitization and psychotherapy in the treatment of phobic states: a controlled enquiry, *British Journal of Psychiatry* 113: 53-73.

Gillan, P. and Rachman, S. (1974) An experimental investigation of desensitization in phobic patients, *British Journal of Psychiatry* 124: 392-401.

Glass, C. and Arnkoff, D. (1988) Common and specific factors in client descriptions of and explanations for change, *Journal of Integrative and Eclectic Psychotherapy* 7: 427-40.

Goldfried, M.R. (1980) Toward the delineation of therapeutic change principles, *American Psychologist* 35: 991-9.

——— and Safran, J.D. (1986) Future directions in psychotherapy integration, in J.C. Norcross (ed.) *Handbook of Eclectic Psychotherapy*, New York: Brunner/Mazel.

——— and Wachtel, P.L. (1987) Clinical and conceptual issues in psychotherapy integration: a dialogue, *Journal of Integrative and Eclectic Psychotherapy* 6: 131-44.

———, Greenberg, L.S. and Marmar, C. (1990) Individual psychotherapy: process and outcome, *Annual Review of Psychology* 41: 659-88.

———, Newman, C.F. and Hayes, A.M. (1989) Coding system of therapeutic focus: user's manual, unpublished manuscript, State University of New York.

Greenberg, L.S. (1984) A task analysis of intrapersonal conflict resolution, in L.N. Rice and L.S. Greenberg (eds) *Patterns of Change*, New York: Guilford Press.

——— (1986) Change process research, *Journal of Consulting and Clinical Psychology* 54: 4-9.

Horvath, A.O. and Greenberg, L.S. (1986) The development of the Working Alliance Inventory, in L.S. Greenberg and W.M. Pinsof (eds) *The Psychotherapeutic Process: A Research Handbook*, New York: Guilford Press.

Jacobson, N.S. and Revenstorf, D. (1988) Statistics for assessing the clinical significance of psychotherapy techniques: issues, problems, and new developments, *Behavioral Assessment* 10: 133–45.

Jones, E.E., Cumming, J.D. and Horowitz, M.J. (1988) Another look at the nonspecific hypothesis of therapeutic effectiveness, *Journal of Consulting and Clinical Psychology* 56: 48–55.

Kagan, N. (1981) Influencing human interaction: eighteen years with IPR, in A.K. Hess (ed.) *Psychotherapy Supervision: Theory, Research and Practice*, New York: Wiley & Sons.

Kazdin, A.E. and Bass, D. (1989) Power to detect differences between alternative treatments in comparative psychotherapy outcome research, *Journal of Consulting and Clinical Psychology* 57: 138–47.

Kerr, S., Goldfried, M.R., Hayes, A.M. and Goldsamt, L.A. (1989) Differences in therapeutic focus in an interpersonal-psychodynamic and cognitive-behavioral therapy, paper presented at the 20th Annual Meeting of the Society for Psychotherapy Research, Toronto, Canada.

Kiesler, D.J. (1966) Some myths of psychotherapy research and the search for a paradigm, *Psychological Bulletin* 65: 110–36.

Klein, D.F., Zitrin, C.M., Woerner, M.G. and Ross, D.C. (1983) Treatment of phobias: behavior therapy and supportive psychotherapy: are there any specific ingredients?, *Archives of General Psychiatry* 40: 139–45.

Kolden, G.G. and Howard, K.I. (1988) Orlinsky and Howard's 'Generic Model of Psychotherapy': an empirical examination in the early sessions of therapy, paper presented at the 19th Annual Meeting of the Society for Psychotherapy Research, Santa Fe, New Mexico.

Lambert, M.J. (1986) Implications of psychotherapy outcome for eclectic psychotherapy, in J.C. Norcross (ed.) *Handbook of Eclectic Psychotherapy*, New York: Brunner/Mazel.

——, Shapiro, D.A. and Bergin, A.E. (1986) The effectiveness of psychotherapy, in S.L. Garfield and A.E. Bergin (eds) *Handbook of Psychotherapy and Behavior Change*, 3rd edn, New York: Wiley & Sons.

Lazarus, A.A. (1989) Why I am an eclectic (not an integrationist), *British Journal of Guidance and Counselling* 17: 248–58.

Llewelyn, S.P. (1988) Psychological therapy as viewed by clients and therapists, *British Journal of Clinical Psychology* 27: 223–37.

—— and Hume, W.I. (1979) The patient's view of therapy, *British Journal of Medical Psychology* 52: 29–35.

London, P. (1988) Metamorphosis in psychotherapy: slouching towards integration, *Journal of Integrative and Eclectic Psychotherapy* 7: 3–12.

Luborsky, L., Singer, B. and Luborsky, L. (1975) Comparative studies of psychotherapy, *Archives of General Psychiatry* 32: 995–1008.

McConnaughy, E.A., DiClemente, C.C., Prochaska, J.O. and Velicer, W.F. (1989) Stages of change in psychotherapy: a follow-up report, *Psychotherapy* 26: 494–503.

Mann, J. and Goldman, R. (1982) *A Casebook in Time-limited Psychotherapy*, New York: McGraw-Hill.

Marks, I.M. and Gelder, M.G. (1966) Common ground between behaviour therapy and psychodynamic methods, *British Journal of Medical Psychology* 39: 11–23.

Marziali, E.A. (1984) Prediction of outcome of brief psychotherapy from therapist interpretive interventions, *Archives of General Psychiatry* 41: 301–4.

Milton, J. (1989) Brief psychotherapy with poorly controlled diabetics, *British Journal of Psychotherapy* 5: 532–43.

Murphy, P.H., Cramer, D. and Lillie, F.J. (1984) The relationship between curative factors perceived by patients in their psychotherapy and treatment outcome: an exploratory study, *British Journal of Medical Psychology*, 57: 187–92.

Norcross, J.C. (ed.) (1986) *Handbook of Eclectic Psychotherapy*, New York: Brunner/Mazel.

—— and Grencavage, L.M. (1989) Eclecticism and integration in counselling and psychotherapy: major themes and obstacles, *British Journal of Guidance and Counselling* 17: 227-47.

——, Prochaska, J.O. and Gallagher, K.M. (1989) Clinical psychologists in the 1980s: II. Theory, research, and practice, *Clinical Psychologist* 42: 45-53.

O'Malley, S.S., Suh, C.S. and Strupp, H.H. (1983) The Vanderbilt Psychotherapy Process Scale: a report of the scale development and process–outcome study, *Journal of Consulting and Clinical Psychology* 51: 581-6.

Orlinsky, D.E. (1990) The international study of the development of psychotherapists: conceptual organisation of the 'common core questionnaire', unpublished manuscript: Collaborative Research Network Steering Committee.

—— and Howard, K.I. (1987) A generic model of psychotherapy, *Journal of Integrative and Eclectic Psychotherapy* 6: 6-27.

O'Sullivan, K.R. and Dryden, W. (1990) A survey of clinical psychologists in the South East Thames Region: activities, role and theoretical orientation, *Clinical Psychology Forum* 29: 21-6.

Prochaska, J.O. and DiClemente, C.C. (1982) Transtheoretical therapy: toward a more integrative model of change, *Psychotherapy: Theory, Research and Practice* 19: 276-88.

—— (1986) The transtheoretical approach, in J.C. Norcross (ed.) *Handbook of Eclectic Psychotherapy*, New York: Brunner/Mazel.

Rachman, S.J. and Wilson, G.T. (1980) *The Effects of Psychological Therapy*, 2nd edn, Oxford: Pergamon Press.

Rice, L.N. and Greenberg, L.S. (eds) (1984) *Patterns of Change*, New York: Guilford.

Robinson, J. (1991) Towards a state of being able to play: integrating Gestalt concepts and methods into a psychodynamic approach to counselling, *British Journal of Guidance and Counselling* 19: 44-65.

Robinson, L.A., Berman, J.S. and Neimeyer, R.A. (1990) Psychotherapy for the treatment of depression: a comprehensive review of controlled outcome research, *Psychological Bulletin* 108: 30-49.

Rogers, C.R. (1957) The necessary and sufficient conditions of therapeutic personality change, *Journal of Consulting Psychology* 21: 95-103.

Ryle, A. (1980) Some measures of goal attainment in focussed integrated active psychotherapy: a study of fifteen cases, *British Journal of Psychiatry* 137: 475-86.

—— (1982) *Psychotherapy: A Cognitive Integration of Theory and Practice*, London: Academic Press.

—— (1987) Cognitive psychology as a common language for psychotherapy, *Journal of Integrative and Eclectic Psychotherapy* 6: 168-72.

—— (1990) *Cognitive-analytic Therapy: Active Participation in Change – A New Integration in Brief Psychotherapy*, Chichester: Wiley & Sons.

Safran, J.D. (1990a) Towards a refinement of cognitive therapy in light of interpersonal theory: I. Theory, *Clinical Psychology Review* 10: 87-105.

—— (1990b) Towards a refinement of cognitive therapy in light of interpersonal theory: II. Practice, *Clinical Psychology Review* 10: 107-21.

—— and Segal, Z.V. (1990) *Interpersonal Process in Cognitive Therapy*, New York: Basic Books.

Shapiro, D.A. and Firth, J. (1987) Prescriptive vs. exploratory psychotherapy: outcomes of the Sheffield Psychotherapy Project, *British Journal of Psychiatry* 151: 790-9.

—— and Shapiro, D. (1982) Meta-analysis of comparative outcome studies: a replication and refinement, *Psychological Bulletin* 92: 581-604.

——, Firth J.A. and Stiles, W.B. (1989) The question of therapists' differential effectiveness: a Sheffield Psychotherapy Project addendum, *British Journal of Psychiatry* 154: 383-5.

——, Barkham, M., Hardy, G.E., Reynolds, S. and Stiles, W.B. (in press) Prescriptive and exploratory therapies: toward an integration based on the assimilation model, *Journal of Psychotherapy Integration*.

Sills, C., Clarkson, P. and Evans, R. (1988) Systemic integrative psychotherapy with a young bereaved girl, *Transactional Analysis Journal* 18: 102–9.

Sloane, R.B., Staples, F.R., Cristol, A.H. and Yorkston, N.J. (1975) Short-term analytically oriented psychotherapy versus behavior therapy, *American Journal of Psychiatry* 132: 373–7.

Smith, M.L., Glass, G.V. and Miller, T.J. (1980) *The Benefits of Psychotherapy*, Baltimore: Johns Hopkins University Press.

Speisman, J.C. (1959) Depth of interpretation and verbal resistance in psychotherapy, *Journal of Consulting Psychology* 23: 93–9.

Stiles, W.B. (1988) Psychotherapy process–outcome correlations may be misleading, *Psychotherapy* 25: 27–35.

—— and Shapiro, D.A. (1989) Abuse of the drug metaphor in psychotherapy process–outcome research, *Clinical Psychology Review* 9: 521–43.

——, Shapiro, D.A. and Elliott, R. (1986) 'Are all psychotherapies equivalent?', *American Psychologist* 41: 165–80.

——, Elliott, R., Llewelyn, S.P., Firth-Cozens, J.A., Margison, F.R., Shapiro, D.A. and Hardy, G.E. (1990) Assimilation of problematic experiences by clients in psychotherapy, *Psychotherapy* 27: 411–20.

Strupp, H.H. and Hadley, S.W. (1979) Specific vs. non-specific factors in psychotherapy: a controlled study of outcome, *Archives of General Psychiatry* 36: 1125–36.

Wachtel, P. (1987) *Action and Insight*, New York: Guilford.

Waskow, I.E. (1975) Selection of a core battery, in I.E. Waskow and M.B. Parloff (eds) *Psychotherapy Change Measures*, Rockville, Md.: National Institute of Mental Health.

Watkins, C.E., Lopez, F.G., Campbell, V.L. and Himmell, C.D. (1986) Contemporary counseling psychology: results of a national survey, *Journal of Counseling Psychology* 33: 301–9.

Watkins, J.T., Leber, W.R., Imber, S.D., Collins, J.F., Elkin, I., Pilkonis, P.A., Sotsky, S.M., Shea, M.T. and Glass, D.R. (1989) NIMH Treatment of Depression Collaborative Research Program: III Temporal course of change, submitted for publication.

Watts, F.N. (1990) Aversion to personal body hair: a case study in the integration of behavioural and interpretative methods, *British Journal of Medical Psychology* 63: 335–40.

Wolfe, B.E. and Goldfried, M.R. (1988) Research on psychotherapy integration: recommendations and conclusions from an NIMH workshop, *Journal of Consulting and Clinical Psychology* 56: 448–51.

11

Systemic Integrative Psychotherapy Training

PETRŪSKA CLARKSON

Introduction

As in psychoanalysis and psychotherapy generally, there is an impressive variety of integrative psychotherapy trainings (Norcross *et al*. 1986). Models for integrative psychotherapy training can be thrown into relief in terms of two arguably opposite positions, which are (a) integration from the beginning of psychotherapy training and (b) integration after a training in one or more 'pure' forms of psychotherapy has been completed. Proponents of the first view maintain that trainees who are educated in an integrative position from the beginning are better able to develop both academically and professionally because they meet early on the required skills of intellectual questioning and tolerance for other perspectives. Proponents of the second view contend that integrative activities are the fruits of maturity and experience which can be better done if solid foundations have been built in singular approaches which emotionally provide a sense of early security and later disillusionment as the practitioner experiences the practical and theoretical limitations of any one particular system.

metanoia Psychotherapy Training Institute provides opportunities for trainees to choose either or both of these positions: (1) the study of integration as a first training in psychotherapy (the integrative psychotherapy *qualification training*) and (2) a *post-qualifying training* (the systemic integrative psychotherapy training programme). This latter programme accepts only psychotherapists who have already trained in one or more approaches to psychotherapy. It can lead to a post-graduate qualification in Systemic Integrative Psychotherapy. Thus psychotherapists who choose to train in one particular approach first can use the structure to obtain their integrative psychotherapy training later. The following account will be interspersed with verbatim comments from trainees themselves. This is a reflection of the process of the training which emphasizes the interplay between the courses as they are designed and presented and how individual course participants use, shape and influence the programmes.

A good original training in one psychotherapeutic approach can be the beginning of *stimulating* students of psychotherapy to want to know about comparisons and to understand that there is not only one way to think about human beings. It can create a hunger and curiosity for further growth and learning which continues well after qualification. When people actually have one theory on board, they can be encouraged to go back to the beginning with their increased experience, to see the fundamentals of their chosen approach with new eyes and to go back to original sources. One trainee put it as follows:

> What I found most useful was to start with one system which gave me a firm ground on which I felt secure enough to begin to build my knowledge. Although in the beginning, I learnt this system in a rigid and fixed way, as I became more familiar with it and truly understood it, I began to become interested in how other psychotherapists worked using differing approaches and how that linked, compared or contrasted with what I had learnt. So, integration became a growing edge for my own developing expertise and competence and prevented me from stagnating in one system, believing that I had 'made it' and that my training had ended. It gave me the impetus to go on growing and developing and to get what I needed.

One needs to differentiate between realistically achievable standards of consistency in integrative psychotherapy and lack of coherence reflected in inadequate intellectual/academic prowess or personal growth and developmental need. It is possibly true that a greater degree of coherence and consistency is being demanded of integrative psychotherapists than has been achieved by other psychotherapies or even psychology in general.

Three phases – awareness, accommodation and assimilation – have been identified as distinguishable phases of the change cycle in psychotherapy or the stages in learning. This model is frequently used to describe a spiralling and pulsating process of learning, individual development and collective evolution (Clarkson and Gilbert 1990). The cyclic nature of learning as an *integrative process* is emphasized in contrast to product-oriented learning in most approaches to integrative psychotherapy training. Although the phases are obviously not separable by rigid dividing lines, they can form foci for sequencing integrative psychotherapy training. They naturally overlap and there is always a dynamic interplay between them, modified by individual preferences and constraints on the one hand, and environmental/contextual encouragement/stringencies on the other. All trainees obviously do not necessarily go through them in clockwork sequence. They are more intended to alert the clinician and the trainer to differential emphases in change and learning processes over time. The specific integrative skills of learning which are encouraged are *awareness* both of their own process and the fullest possible perceptual and intuitive awareness of the client(s), *accommodation* which can range from the introjection of earlier caveat(s) to later opposing or contradictory views to *assimilation* which concerns making the acquired skills, knowledge and information an intergal part of their individual psychophysiological system. This is of course again followed by phases of increased awareness and so on as long as the psychotherapist is learning and growing.

Principles of integrative psychotherapy training

Post-modern psychotherapy and the plural psyche

Most mature, developed approaches to psychotherapy have experienced the emergence of divisions, divergent streams and even theoretical and political schisms (as more fully discussed in my Chapter 2, this volume). An appreciation of relativity within a particular system conceivably supports and encourages a more questioning attitude towards any received wisdom. Although some schools of psychotherapy and psychoanalysis expect trainees to adopt the theoretical orientations of their psychotherapist, others have recommended that it is more beneficial that psychotherapists are exposed, with respect, to different streams of thoughts and practice within their primary approach. This can enable them to consider the points of disagreement, confusion and conflict as well as identifying commonly held principles. Samuels (1985), for example, advocates training in Jungian analysis based on points of contemporary divergence and conflict, maintaining that these represent not mutually exclusive truths, but possibly simultaneously viable aspects of 'the plural psyche' (Samuels 1989). This is probably true not only in analytical psychology but across the entire spectrum of psychotherapies, such as the 70-plus organizations represented at the United Kingdom Conference for Psychotherapy or among the 7,000 psychotherapists at the 1990 Evolution for Psychotherapy Conference in Anaheim, USA.

Personal integration

The systemic integrative approach to psychotherapy integration at *metanoia* does not seek to provide one true model of integration. Rather it provides a climate in which beginning and experienced psychotherapists can draw on the different integrative models presented in order to develop their own particular models of integrative psychotherapy. Hopefully, our[1] approach also continues to change as it influences and is influenced by others. 'Integrative' in our context means 'in process'. 'Metanoia' in the original Greek means 'transformation', 'turning' or 'to change' (Clarkson 1989). As Heraclitus (Sallis and Maly 1980) pointed out more than 2,000 years ago, change is one thing you can depend on. Nothing stands still. The main sensitivity of our programme structure is *not* to discount any of people's experience but to allow them a place where they can bring it, make sense of it and integrate or relinquish what they no longer need.

The validity of different models of integration or primary orientation are not discarded – nothing is thrown out just because it is different. The essence of Systemic Integrative Psychotherapy is personal integration within which style is linked to syllabus and philosophy, while attempting to integrate all aspects of the self, including the avoided or 'shadow' parts. Our trainers encourage individuals to conceptualize what integration means and to create a model for themselves. Trainees are encouraged not to take maps for territories but to develop the capacity to *read* maps and to *make* maps. Different types of integrative models are studied – for example, the relationship model, or the seven-level model (explained in my Chapter 2 of this volume). We invite them either to use these, others or create their own. The basic principle that 'any plan, intervention or action is conceivable' is emphasized, on the condition that it is supported by a conceptual model which illustrates the thinking and value system which mirrors the personal integration of each individual psychotherapist. Experimentation is encouraged along with consistency. In such ways, creative capacites are encouraged to keep pace with critical faculties.

Questioning of philosophical underpinnings

Since all psychotherapeutic work is conceived of as being conducted within a wider systemic context of 'man's search for meaning', trainees are encouraged continually to identify and hone their own philosophy of life/humankind. This connection between healing and meaning as exemplified in Greek myths and in ancient cultures has existed since the dawn of history and can still be maintained today.

To identify their philosophy of psychotherapy, trainees are asked what psychotherapy is, what makes for change, what they do that seems to make this happen, and what the strategies or techniques are that they use that facilitate change. Next they look at the systems from which knowledge and experiences are derived. Then testing for consistency is done in debate. For instance, someone says that her model assumes that problems in the present are due to developmental deficits or traumas in the past and so she is challenged: what is the scientific base for that assumption, how can you back that up? What is the clinical evidence, what is the research evidence? If these are not relevant parameters, which are? What are the epistemological assumptions? How do you account for contradictory conceptualizations? What does it mean to make up a developmental deficit? A Socratic process of questioning is often most fitting when trainees have a great deal of knowledge at their disposal, as is found in a post-graduate training. The issue is not to prove any one theory beyond doubt because in the present state of our knowledge this is simply not possible (Popper 1959). Most theories are vulnerable to doubt and occasionally inconsistent. What can conceivably be developed is conceptual coherence, a probable base in research, a base in developmental theory and observation, reference to outcome research and a base in clinical studies and/or in philosophy. It is important to distinguish, for example, between different levels of discourse, between what is scientifically proven and what is really belief (knowledge based on clinical practice) or wisdom, and to separate these from assumptions.

> To wit, I challenge the behaviorally committed to perceive that feelings are for real and make a difference in therapeutic outcome, the psychodynamically committed to understand the power of conscious intentions, the gestaltist to understand that a moving affective experience within a session must be conceptualized and put to work between sessions, the RET committed to realize that a therapist can get more mileage out of confrontation when it is blended with empathy or relational immediacy, and the person-centered or existentially committed to consider that being 'techniquish' or gimmicky is a fault of a therapist rather than of a therapy that uses techniques, and so on.
>
> (Robertson in Beutler *et al.* 1987: 312)

Intellectual relativity

Probably the primary overarching principle of integration is a cultural bias against any adoption of a single way of integration which should be followed. It may be difficult to define what integration is and impossible to reach consensus. However, the ideological, theoretical and practical questions perhaps need to be asked and pursued with unremitting vigour by one section of the therapeutic community, while others maintain and develop positions of greater certainty. In this way the forces of homeostasis and evolution can *both* be served. A culture of integration, which can be described by means of its values, technology and attitudes, emphatically encourages the greatest diversity compatible with the greatest cohesion; the tightest possible structure compatible with the deepest and most profound process. Exposure to the explosion of information and technique in psychology, psychotherapy and other sciences is encouraged, along with an attempt to develop emotional competence in surviving or thriving on the chaos (Gleick 1988) which characterizes the state of our science (and art?) at this late stage in the twentieth century.

There is a substantial number of clinicians, theoreticians and observer commentators who think that commonalities between approaches outweigh theoretical differences between the schools (Garfield 1980, 1982). This is particularly true for more experienced clinicians who tend to resemble each other more than less experienced practitioners resemble their seniors within a particular school (Fiedler 1950). A questioning attitude ensures that as soon as convergence occurs, divergence is encouraged; and when divergence occurs, convergence is encouraged. The natural need to integrate is necessarily followed by an organismic need to de-integrate. Destructuring in human cycles needs to be followed by restructuring. Integration is not seen as a *product*, but the accomplishment of skilfulness and competency in a *process* which often spirals (if it does not actually move circularly) in a rhythmic pulsation. Such alternating frames of learning are of course done in terms of the individual training needs of each individual trainee on a particular programme. However, the trainer may instigate or facilitate the integration in similar ways as the psychotherapist instigates or facilitates integration for each individual client (who ultimately must do it for him- or herself).

The vitality of individual difference

Theories of personal learning styles are taught and trainees are encouraged to discover their particular ways and rhythms of learning. For example, some people are more visual whereas others are more auditory; some individuals are convergent in their thinking as opposed to others who are more divergent. Such polarities and differences are explored so that the individuals gain a sense of their own style and idiosyncrasies, which in the long term aids their training in integrative process. The notions of differentially specialized left and right brain hemispheres are also attended to, for example, with the emphasis being on integration of both these parts. So, an individual who is predominantly left brain will need to develop right brain capacities and, having achieved this, will hopefully integrate the two. In facilitating the above fascination with uniqueness and difference, we hope we are enabling our trainees to have many ways of diagnosing, assessing and treating clients – developing range, flexibility and imagination in psychotherapy.

The emphasis on the individuality of the training is reflected in the emphasis on the individuality of the client. In a sense, to be congruent with the integrative idea that every client is uniquely different, the training needs to model how every trainee is encouraged to grow and develop in a unique and particular way. In a sense there is no one training in integrative therapy since the training of psychotherapists at this level of sophistication is necessarily different for each trainee. Where appropriate, exceptions to regulations or structures are made in creative ways in order to encourage the participation and development of exceptional individuals. The very values of integrative psychotherapy mitigate against mass-produced training and our emphasis stresses that the integration of self precedes any training in integrative theory. The 'self' of the therapist becomes the integrating instrument and the core self the primary integrative factor so that strategies and techniques and theoretical ideas are not haphazardly acquired 'tools' but become 'blood and gesture' (Rilke 1929).

The relationship between individuals in the training group becomes another matrix for intellectual, experiential and emotional learning and experimentation concerning the management of different contrasting, complementary or overarching frames of reference. The polarities of conviction versus uncertainty *both* serve to deepen understanding of the field and challenge presuppositions as long as neither become fixed or fickle. It is viewed as vitally important to observe and to study 'pure systems' as well as to be open to the methods, approaches and values of integration. It is considered as important to have and defend strong convictions as it is essential to be willing to question and perhaps even relinquish them.

Multi-lingualism and/or common language

Psychologically we endeavour to encourage a metaphoric multilingualism so that a trainee will be able to converse about a particular client or patient in a number of psychotherapeutic languages. In the same way, as different subjective universes are postulated by different languages, people may either be initiated or engulfed into different perspectives. This can be helpful or handicapping, often depending on the temperamental proclivities of the individual trainee. What is being offered is not a predigested integration, but a framework within which (and principles of excellence according to which) experienced individual practitioners can develop, share and test their respective integrations. Multilingualism may include the ability to speak Esperanto – the metaphorical psychotherapeutic equivalent of a vernacular such as suggested by Goldfried (1982) who

> argues that to increase the likelihood of productive dialogue between therapists of different persuasions, therapists need to use a neutral language in explaining their clinical strategies, i.e. one which is free from the jargon of specific therapeutic schools.

All psychotherapists who are not entirely solipsistic in their orientations will either want to learn other languages or employ effective translators. In the USA Finzi, for example, unfortunately experienced that in several institutions: 'There was almost complete ignorance of other fields offering alternative explanations, except for sarcastic remarks aimed at caricatures distorting the other theories' (Finzi, 1987: 4).

Translation is essential for communication purposes in multinational or pan-European economic or cultural contexts. This attitude is also applied to the world of the psychotherapies. In doing this it is hoped that some sense of mutuality among differing schools of thought is experienced. When different trainers, supervisors and psychotherapists model the ability to translate and communicate we are implicitly showing goodwill in a post-modern world where there is no consensual truth any more and even the hope of this fades. However, hopefully, we are all working towards the same goal, which is health and well-being. Our languages are our personal instruments. Understanding one anothers' language is showing willingness to share and to model humility as opposed to a model that attempts to say 'we know it all'. Ultimately, however, any of these languages, useful as they may be, must be experienced in all their limitations when we as psychotherapists enter the realms of 'the language of the heart' in the healing encounter with another human being.

Integrative psychotherapy – Qualification training

Entry and course requirements

Trainees are required to have training, qualification and experience in one of the helping professions, or to hold a psychology degree. Preference is given to those students who have had some supervised client experience and who have had some experience as a client themselves.

Trainees on the course are required to be in weekly individual psychotherapy for the duration of the course and in weekly supervision over the course of the three years. It is recommended that they receive supervision from specialists in each of the three major approaches (psychoanalytic, cognitive-behavioural and humanistic-existential) but the supervision for the last year needs to be with an integrative psychotherapist. All trainees are required to have practical experience of integrative psychotherapy and appropriate placements are arranged in consultation with trainers and supervisors. Attendance is required at a monthly seminar on integrative psychotherapy (to which colleagues and other professional visitors are welcome) where they will make regular presentations. In addition, trainees can attend integrative psychotherapy research workshops. These are regular one-day research projects where experts from different schools and from integrative psychotherapy come together to study, contrast and compare, for example, video recordings of psychotherapy sessions from different approaches.

It is expected that applicants to this course will already have developed a range of basic skills and techniques. Where communication skills, listening and observation skills, verbal and non-verbal reaction patterns, assessment and psychodiagnostic skills need further refinement, this will be arranged. Close co-operation between trainers and supervisors facilitates the accomplishment of such goals.

> At a minimum, psychotherapists should become competent in the use of several behavioral methods (response cuing, contingency management, covert rehearsal, counterconditioning, etc.), procedures used to facilitate cognitive insight (e.g., free association, interpretation, confrontation), experiential therapy modes (e.g., imagery/dialogue methods for dealing with splits and feeling reflections), cognitive approaches (e.g., thought monitoring, self-instruction, practiced cognitive change, evidence gathering and evaluation), and group/interpersonal therapies (e.g., group process, family interventions).
>
> (Beutler in Norcross *et al.* 1986: 86)

Course description

The basic three-year integrative psychotherapy training course is based on a model of integration founded on psychotherapy outcome research, our own and others' clinical experience and integration of theoretical models drawn from all three major areas of thought in psychotherapy. It particularly focuses on the integrative framework of five relationship dimensions (Clarkson 1990) which spans a theoretical integration of psychoanalytic, behavioural-cognitive and humanistic-existential views of the person. Each of the five types of therapeutic relationship may be potentially available for constructive use in psychotherapy: the *Working Alliance*; the *Transferential/Countertransferential Relationship*; the *Reparative/Developmentally Needed Relationship*; the *I-You Relationship*; and the *Transpersonal Relationship*. 'These five modalities can act as an integrative framework for different traditions (or approaches) of psychotherapy notwithstanding apparently irreconcilable schisms or popular stereotypes' (Clarkson 1990: 148).

These relationships are briefly summarized in Chapter 2 on Systemic Integrative Psychotherapy in this volume. Most forms of psychotherapy recognize the importance of the relational dimension in human existence. Different approaches to psychotherapy put the emphasis on different kinds of therapeutic relationships for different reasons. Our integrative model always sees the individual in relation and considers that all five forms of relationship are potentially present in effective psychotherapy.

> How explicitly and purposefully which of these modes of psychotherapeutic relationships are used may be one of the major ways in which some approaches resemble each other more and differ most from other approaches.
>
> (Clarkson 1990: 160)

Psychotherapy can be seen as the intentional use of relationship. Research results consistently show that the choice of a particular theoretically based psychotherapeutic method appears to have little influence on the effectiveness of psychotherapy. There is growing recognition that the helping relationship is probably the most significant component in successful psychotherapy (Frank 1979; Hynan 1981). Therefore, the *metanoia* basic Integrative Psychotherapy course is built on understanding, learning and using these five identified therapeutic relationship modalities as an integrative framework. Each of the five kinds of psychotherapeutic relationship is clarified and differentiated in terms of relevant theories and practical application. The different modalities are studied and explored in terms of their suitability for different individuals at different stages of psychotherapy along with a commitment to evaluating effectiveness. This model requires that psychotherapists develop flexibility, judgement, range, skills, intuition and imagination in the appropriate use of each one of them. (Of course not all these relationships are required for all patients in all psychotherapies.)

The course is divided into twelve 30-hour modules and is schematically summarized in Figure 11.1 (This summary is *indicative* of the areas covered, and by no means exhaustive. Many authors with valuable contributions are not mentioned for reasons of space and brevity. Integration assumes a thorough ongoing study of the *fruits* of our intellectual forebears, and in the basic course, this work is led by the trainers and integrative psychotherapists who have made such study their life's work. The Systemic Integrative course to be described later provides experienced or qualified individuals with the further opportunity for developing their own model of integration because a thorough grounding in particular systems is a pre-requirement to that course for such an advanced level of integration.) Each of these modules includes theoretical integration of relevant theories, including *personality* and *developmental theory* under the particular headings, *relevant strategies, practice and coaching* in the appropriate *intervention skills* as well as *education in models and methods of evaluating* the outcomes of psychotherapy conducted in that particular field. The *process of psychotherapy over time* is built into the overall course design. *Levels, stages* and *processes of change* (as mentioned in Chapter 2 of this volume) are used as parameters. Throughout the modules, advantages, disadvantages, uses, contra-indications and caveats are explored in depth in terms of when, why and with whom (*individual differences*), or *different modalities of relationship* would be given precedence over others at particular periods in a person's psychotherapy.

A trainee comments:

> What became so apparent was that the therapeutic relationship is the core of our work and therefore that's where integration happens, i.e. within me with the other. This I saw through all the various ways of presenting diagnoses, case histories, psychotherapy design or treatment planning. At the core of it all was – how can I best be with this person to affect change? Does this mean I need to understand personality, learning skills, history, etc? We were regularly questioned, for example, how does that fit with your own conceptual model of integration? An important representation of integration was the implicit permission to be myself with my history, my temperament, my style.

Assessment and examinition
Ongoing self- and peer assessment applies throughout the course. Trainees are required to present examples of their work or make theoretical presentations at

YEAR 1	YEAR 2	YEAR 3
Module 1: Integrative Psychotherapy *Philosophy*, Values and Theory of Psychotherapy *History* of integrative psychotherapy, models of integration and commonalities between different approaches identified by *psychotherapy research*	**Module 5:** Working Alliance (2) Comparative and integrative focus on phenomena such as 'resistance', non- compliance and strategic/ systemic parameters *Theoretical Integration:* e.g. Greenson (1965), Liotti (1989), Watzlawick *et al.* (1974), Keeney (1983) *Strategies* *Intervention skills* *Assessment and Evaluation*	**Module 9:** Developmentally Needed/ Reparative Relationship (2) Comparative and integrative focus on approaches to the Self and reparative relationship *Theoretical Integration:* e.g. Winnicott (1958), Lowen (1976), Miller (1983), Boadella (1987), Balint (1968), Masterson (1985), Davanloo (1980) *Strategies* *Intervention skills* *Assessment and Evaluation*
Module 2: Person to Person Relationship (1) Comparative and integrative focus on necessary conditions, particularly empathy *Theoretical Integration:* e.g. Jaspers (1963), Rogers & Stevens (1967), Maslow (1968), May (1969), Kohut (1977) *Strategies* *Intervention skills* *Assessment and Evaluation*	**Module 6:** Transference/ Countertransference (1) Comparative and integrative focus on drives and transference phenomena *Theoretical Integration:* e.g. Freud (1977), Malan (1979), Mann (1973), Clarkson (1992) *Strategies* *Intervention skills* *Assessment and Evaluation*	**Module 10:** Person to Person Relationship (2) Comparative and integrative focus on existentialist meaning and creativity *Theoretical Integration:* e.g. Perls *et al.* (1951/1977), Polster & Polster (1973/ 1974), Laing (1965), Frankl (1964), Rank (1989), May (1975) *Strategies* *Intervention skills* *Assessment and Evaluation*
Module 3: Assessment & Change Processes From psychiatric *diagnosis* to phenomenological *description* Transformational processes from growth to change *Awareness, accommodation and assimilation*: Clarkson & Gilbert (1991)	**Module 7:** Transference/ Countertransference (2) Comparative and integrative focus on object relations and countertransference phenomena *Theoretical Integration:* e.g. Klein (1984), Fairbairn (1952), Langs (1976) *Strategies* *Intervention skills* *Assessment and Evaluation*	**Module 11:** Transpersonal Relationship (1) Comparative and integrative focus on body-mind holism and quantum dynamics in human systems *Theoretical Integration:* e.g. Reich (1972), Mindell (1984), Zohar (1990), Pierrakos (1974) *Strategies* *Intervention skills* *Assessment and Evaluation*
Module 4: Working Alliance (1) Comparative and integrative focus on ego, contracting, and cognitive behavioural approaches *Theoretical Integration:* e.g. Berne (1975), Beck & Emery (1985), Ryle (1990), Meichenbaum (1974), Lazarus (1971) *Strategies* *Intervention skills* *Assessment and Evaluation*	**Module 8:** Developmentally Needed/ Reparative Relationship (1) Comparative and integrative focus on approaches to the 'self' and the developmentally needed relationship *Theoretical Integration:* e.g. Kohut (1977), Ferenczi (1980), Fromm-Reichmann (1974), Schiff *et al.* (1975), Clarkson & Lapworth (1992), Shapiro (1988), Stern (1985) *Strategies* *Intervention skills* *Assessment and Evaluation*	**Module 12:** Transpersonal Relationship (2) Comparative and integrative focus on soul/spirit ('Self') in psychotherapy *Theoretical Integration:* e.g. Jung (1968, 1969), Assagioli (1971), G. Adler (1979) *Strategies* *Intervention skills* *Assessment and Evaluation*

Figure 11.1 Integrative psychotherapy training – qualifying course outline

seminars held regularly each year. In particular, a presentation is made at the end of each year to the student peer group. In the final year, the following are required: (a) an intensive case-study of a client; (b) a description of the psychotherapist's professional context; and (c) an oral examination where taped segments of their work are brought for discussion. Satisfactory completion of the course and the fulfilling of the above requirements, leads to a Diploma in Integrative Psychotherapy.

Systemic Integrative Psychotherapy training

Systemic Integrative Psychotherapy training is the core of the advanced, post-graduate training programme for psychotherapists who are already qualified in one or more approaches to psychotherapy or who have already completed a basic training in integrative psychotherapy. Although systems theory may or may not have formed part of such a basic training, the systemic component is much elaborated in this advanced (post-graduate) training.

Systemic Integrative Psychotherapy is currently defined as a personal, conceptual and experiential integration of values, theories, strategies and specific interventions within a psychotherapeutic relationship which is based on a systems perspective. This includes specifically systems theory which describes natural systems (e.g. von Bertalanffy 1969), as well as the systemic context of psychotherapy as a process evolving over time. It is more fully discussed in Chapter 2 on Systemic Integrative Psychotherapy in this volume.

Entry and course requirements

Experienced practising psychotherapists need a pre-initial psychotherapy training degree in psychology or a mental health qualification (social work, counselling psychology, clinical psychology or psychiatry). Entrants to the course will also already have completed a full training in one or more major approaches to psychotherapy. Appropriate exceptions are made for professionals who have accumulated comparable training hours or experience elsewhere.

One of the basic aims of this course is to further facilitate individuals to identify and formulate their own philosophies and values about who they are in the world, and the practice of psychotherapy both on an individual level as well as a collective one. Trainees become acutely aware of their responsibilities towards the profession and what this means in terms of commitment both to themselves, and the communities within which they live and work.

A broad-based *knowledge* of the field is required. Entrants who have personal *qualities* of co-operation enthusiasm and a commitment to personal growth and professional development are given priority. Non-judgemental questioning *attitudes* are highly valued as well as a desire to learn and to grow *with* other professionals. Preferred course *skills* include creative thinking, good communication, a wide and solid range of accomplished therapeutic skills ranging, for example, from transference interpretation to active imagination techniques. Where there are gaps trainees may choose to do some additional specific training or supervised experience to acquire the skills which they may want to learn.

It is important to the integrity and challenge of the course structure and process to have psychotherapists who qualified from a variety of schools of thought or practice, and who trained at *metanoia* as well as at other recognized institutes. The usual training group consists of some 12 to 16 experienced clinicians from such orientations as psychodynamic, group analytic, Transactional Analysis, Gestalt, person-centred, bioenergetics, and rational-emotive therapy. Individuals who have done a first psychotherapy training which followed integrative models from the beginning – such as the *metanoia* Integrative Psychotherapy Course, the Cognitive-analytic Therapy of Ryle (1990), Bath counselling and psychotherapy courses, the Institute for Psychotherapy and Social Studies, or the Minster Centre – also attend. This training has often also been successfully combined with or followed MSc courses in the psychology of counselling and psychotherapy, as well as MA counselling psychology programmes. This variety aids the individual's process of integration as each course participant can take the opportunity to learn how to talk across schools, find a common language and personally integrate what is felt to be experientially and practically fitting for the individual psychotherapist. The group context encourages mutual curiosities and a desire to question and learn from each other.

The intake process usually combines formal written applications followed by interviews and a group assessment procedure. In some cases an accompanying course of study, observation or experience may be arranged for students to experience an approach in 'pure' or classical form. Individuals are encouraged to attend conferences relating to many different approaches within the world of psychotherapy so that they continue to be aware of current thoughts and developing theories in the 'field'. One of the long-term aims of this training is to facilitate individuals to value the art of questioning and the concept that there is no one absolute truth. What remains important is 'awareness' of options with the outcome not being dependent on only one solution. It is our intention to teach 'the wisdom of insecurity' and humility, to have opinions and not be opinionated, to have judgements but not be judgemental. Our goal is to create a learning environment filled with the paradoxes of life, time and freedom.

> That is why I say to any beginner: Learn your theories as well as you can, but put them aside when you touch the miracle of the living soul. Not theories but your own creative individuality alone must decide.
>
> (Jung 1928: 361)

Training programme components

An individual trainee should experience a *personal psychotherapy* of the kind, intensity and duration which they intend to practise. In addition, personal exposure to individual, group, couple, family, child and systemic consultations, creative therapies and adjacent modalities can enrich the self-knowledge and applied repertoire of the psychotherapist. Psychotherapy or personal growth experiences at post-qualification phases mean that psychotherapists have usually already developed a thorough self-knowledge and developed an inner map. Seeking additional experiences can help them to gain personal insights which might have been overlooked because of their familiarity with the original modality or call into question assumptions or methods which they have begun to take for granted.

Supervision, which is an integral part of primary psychotherapy training, ideally continues for the rest of a professional's practising life. It does not stop at a licence to practise independently but finds new and more challenging scope for growth, support and development. Hopefully a psychotherapist during his or her primary training will have had one supervisor to maintain continuity over the years as well as at least one change of supervisor to complement or contrast with the primary supervisor for style and content. Depending on previous experience, the trainee integrative psychotherapist will often seek supervision from a supervisor experienced in a different approach from the original training. Such differences should be as large as can be tolerated by both parties while maintaining their integrity and coherence. Such a process can result in questioning of commonly held assumptions, concepts or ways of working which the therapists (and supervisor) may have grown used to taking for granted. Supervision should take a variety of formats over a practitioner's professional life – for example, individual, group, team or supervision with co-workers would be included.

Professional responsibilities, practice and ethics should be a constant component of any psychotherapy training. Students should know how to diagnose, assess, manage a practice and manage emergencies. This is a stage of training which involves reading and particularly an awareness of previous unconscious accommodation and assimilation. Trainees are required to make their own integration in a way that makes sense to others in a coherent and logical manner. Their understanding is demonstrated through the application of their learning to the client material, shared discussion and participation in the Integrative Psychotherapy Seminar.

Hopefully, an awareness of professional responsibilities will have been inculcated during a clinician's first psychotherapy training. Awareness of the national and international context of psychotherapy will be served by participation in the activities of professional psychotherapy associations, multi-disciplinary discussion groups, involvement in workshops and conferences of the international (SEPI) or national (BSIP) societies for integrative psychotherapy and continued professional development.

Optional additional advanced training modules in other specific approaches, particularly suitable for integrative psychotherapists or clinical or counselling psychologists, are (a) chaos theory and quantum dynamics in human systems, (b) counselling and psychotherapy in organizational contexts, (c) interventions in organizations and (d) training for trainers. A trainee writes:

> In the first year we learnt to make comparisons across systems and use other modalities focusing on different patient populations while retaining our personal integrity and striving for theoretical coherence. The trainer gave information about where we could find training in other modalities. Previous psychotherapy then becomes enlarged by, for example, a Jungian

analysis or a course of Rolfing. While we were encouraged to be experimental, we had also learnt to be more discriminating and self-protective. When such additional experiences are garnered from a position where they can be compared and contrasted, learning is actually more experiential, particularly where supported by reading the relevant literature.

Training in a specific other modality, for example, in couples work or body work can lead to the in-depth comparison and contrast of another model with their own. Experienced psychotherapists develop a secure, original knowledge base which enables them to choose additional experiences/trainings with greater discrimination. The greater the degree of their own personal, theoretical and practical integration, the more likely they are to find aspects of value without rubbishing or over-defending their original modality. Theory and practice are of course combined in the training course itself.

Course description

The syllabus for the *metanoia* Psychotherapy Institute's two-year part-time advanced course in Systemic Integrative Psychotherapy is summarily indicated in Figures 11.2 (First Year) and 11.3 (Second Year). The course is designed for psychotherapists who are interested in integration both theoretically and in practice. Students will be involved in regular reading and written work to support the training received on a modular (two- or three-day) basis.

First year: Systemic Integrative Training Programme – assessment and process
This course is designed to integrate different areas of values, theory, strategy, skills, interventions and to contextualize the personal psychotherapy integration which the author believes every clinician already does (whether they are aware of it or not). The historical development of integrating approaches in the field of psychotherapy is traced with reference to research showing commonalities across different modalities. Loose eclecticism is distinguished from systematic eclecticism, and systemic integration by comparing and contrasting various models of integration and eclecticism with their individual emphases as indicated above. A trainee comments:

> My understanding of Systemic Integrative Psychotherapy is having a conceptual model which integrates the many approaches I have studied and want to use. It is integrating theories and approaches into a coherent system rather than pulling out techniques to use, which for me is more eclectic. I see being an integrative psychotherapist integrating what I know, what I use, my values, philosophies, etc, into who I am and then being that 'I' when practising. It is using *what I know* for the client. It is being discriminative, able to differentiate and use what is appropriate within my value system.

The 'medical model' and the 'growth model' of cure or healing are thoroughly explored. The advantages and disadvantages of each are discussed and evaluated in terms of how these different models affect psychotherapy practice and reflect

MODULE†	FOCUS
1 Paradigms and Parameters of Psychotherapy Integration	History and Models of Integrative Psychotherapy Views of the Person* Strategic Parameters, e.g. Style, Field (Individual or Group), Intention or Goals*, Interventions*
2 Degrees of Freedom, Time and Context in Psychotherapy	Systems Principles* Review of Developmental Theories* Variation over Time*
3 A Multiplicity of Therapeutic Relationships	Personal Qualities of the Psychotherapist* Client/Psychotherapist Match* Five Dimensions of the Psychotherapeutic Relationship*
4 The Nature and Limits of Growth and Change	Assessment and Diagnosis* Transformational Processes* Growth, Types and Limits of Change* Management of Emergencies
5 Anticipation and Spontaneity in Psychotherapy	Normal Personality Adaptations Personality Disorders Assessment and Treatment Design from Different Theoretical Orientations
6 Boundaries With Others and Deficits of the Self	Borderline and Narcissistic Disorders
7 Trauma, Learning and Defence	Anxiety Disorders, Phobic Disorders, Compulsive Disorders
8 The Meaning of Madness	The Schizophrenias and Related Disorders
9 The Tyranny of Affect	Affective Disorders
10 Termination and Evaluation In Psychotherapy	Assessment of Outcome, Research, Self and Peer Evaluation

† Each module is the equivalent of two full days of training and is accompanied by (a) theory review based on extensive recommended reading, (b) the presentation of cases by course members, (c) participation in the Integrative Psychotherapy Seminar.

* These topics are referenced and referred to in the theory discussion in the earlier chapter on Systemic Integrative Psychotherapy (Chapter 2, this volume).

Figure 11.2 First year: Systemic Integrative Psychotherapy – assessment and process

our values. This part of the course includes teaching and discussion about short-term and long-term contracts in psychotherapy and a section on crisis intervention. Various approaches to treatment, including Supportive, Interpretive and Reconstructive approaches and their use in different contexts and with different client groups, are examined.

Central to this section of the course is a focus on the importance of the relationship in psychotherapy. This is borne out by many years of clinical experience of the centrality of the relationship in the healing process. There is also support for this in research findings (Frank 1979; Hynan 1981). Clarkson's (1990) paper entitled 'A Multiplicity of Psychotherapeutic Relationships' is used as a springboard for discussion.

The course emphasizes a clinical developmental focus in treatment planning based on contemporary modern insights into child development (Pine 1985; Stern 1985) in the context of a holistic existential framework which takes into account the client's previous life experience and current life situation. The totality of the 'field' in which a client operates (the 'gestalt' constituted by the complexity of the client's early, current and subsequent life experiences) constitutes the material for psychotherapy in a systemic integrative approach. In treatment planning it is important to hold an awareness of the family networks and the wider social and political context in which our clients conduct their lives.

The concepts of change and cure in psychotherapy are explored with reference to different types of change (Clarkson 1988). It is important for a psychotherapist to distinguish between changes that are constructive and changes that are actively destructive in their clients' lives. At this points students will review the research literature on transformational processes and the factors that make a difference in psychotherapy and discuss these in the context of their own approach to integration.

Psychotherapy is viewed in its wider social and environmental context, ranging from psychopharmacology, first aid and psychotherapeutic emergencies to ethics, to the politics of psychotherapy and the ecology of psychotherapy. This section also includes the self-management of the psychotherapist, peer and supervisory support, practice management and practice inventories, professional networks and professional responsibilities within a professional and social context both nationally and internationally.

A familiarity with different methods of psychodiagnosis is assumed or acquired. This should include in-depth review of concepts of normality as relative to historical, political or cultural contexts. A metaperspective on diagnosis is encouraged as well as a careful evaluation of the uses and abuses of diagnosis. Diagnostic approaches and tools – for example, psychometric assessment *and* phenomenological description – are equally relevant here. Psychotherapeutic assessment is approached from multiple perspectives – for example, identifying developmental fixations, self-development, a psychiatric perspective, current life functioning and rational/irrational beliefs, to mention only a few. Diagnostic ability is refined, not for its own sake, but as an aid to encourage facility and flexibility in changing frames of reference in thinking about and working with different individuals or groups in psychotherapy. The very serious objections and criticisms of diagnosis, particularly when used as a way of labelling cases instead of relating to people, are thoroughly studied in Rowan (1983).

In addition to more psychodynamic perspectives *and* on an existential suspicion of the very notion of catagorization of people, the *DSM-III-R* (*Diagnostic and Statistical Manual of Mental Disorders* of the American Psychiatric Association 1987) is sometimes used in the course as a basis for discussion and treatment planning. This diagnostic approach, carefully used, can provide a comprehensive multi-axial descriptive approach to understanding people rather than a uni-dimensional categorization of patients. It is only useful if it can be used as a tool for sharper conceptual differentiation and empathic appreciation of individuality.

Different patients with psychiatric (Axis I) disorders are dealt with in terms of differential diagnosis, psychotherapy process, treatment design and context of treatment. Different theoretical and applied approaches are drawn from within an integrative framework. These have included, for example, behaviour therapy, Transactional Analysis, Gestalt, rational-emotive therapy, existential and psychodynamic approaches to the treatment of schizophrenia, the major affective disorders and eating disorders.

All the personality disorders listed on Axis II of *DSM-III-R* are dealt with systematically. Issues addressed include: What is a 'personality disorder', a 'personality trait or quality'? Personality disorders are particularly studied in the context of historical developments from drive theory, to ego psychology through to object relations theory and so to contemporary self-theory within the psychoanalytic field as a basis for understanding or treating clients. (Jung's and the analytic concern with self, frequently neglected by commentators, is also explored in this historical context of development.) Gestalt and Jungian approaches to personality disorders are also covered, as well as specific personality disorders and treatment approaches, and special attention is paid to relevant research findings. This is studied in the context of developmental theory, for example Mahler *et al.* (1975), Pine (1985) and Stern (1985), as well as an integrative framework built from the many different views of the 'self' as these occur in the psychological literature (Clarkson and Lapworth 1992).

The role of physical disorders or conditions, as represented on Axis III, are seen as potentially relevant to the understanding or management of a client, for example a person with a neurological disorder associated with a personality disorder. The psychotherapy of the client is discussed in a holistic manner, taking into account any physical conditions that may influence the manner in which the client is presenting and the client's overall functioning. In an integrative approach, this aspect of diagnosis forms an important part of the total body-mind systemic context that the client is presenting to the psychotherapist and within which the patient lives.

The severity of the psychosocial stressors (Axis IV) to which the client has been subject in the year preceding and their current severity are assessed as they may have contributed to the development of the client's existing condition, to the recurrence of a prior problem or to the exacerbation of an already existing mental disorder (for example, divorce occurring during a major depressive episode). In order to get a full picture of a client's prior level of functioning, it is important to ascertain the stresses to which the person has been subjected in the previous year. This information assists the psychotherapist in formulating a comprehensive and integrated treatment design for the client to guide the psychotherapist's anticipation without destroying his or her spontaneity or contact in the relationship.

The client's current level of functioning is assessed as well as his or her highest level of functioning for at least a few months during the past year within their current psychosocial system. The assessment of current functioning gives the psychotherapist an idea of the current needs for psychotherapy. The highest level of functioning during the past year gives useful prognostic information for the future, particularly in terms of a client's strengths. These are discussed in the context of the integrative psychotherapist's overall strategy. This corresponds with Axis V of *DSM-III-R*.

Several modules follow which concentrate on differential diagnosis and treatment design for a variety of disorders. Whether or not the psychotherapist uses a diagnostic system, groupings around descriptive clusters, such as 'people with specific issues with boundaries' or 'self-deficits', act as an ordering principle. Since the training group is composed of experienced psychotherapists with different theoretical and clinical approaches to such clusters, they will have the opportunity to hear how others conceptualize and deal with patients similar to those in their own current practice. Thus, cross-pollination is encouraged since clinicians with different orientations are presenting their work for each other's consideration. Such proximity and familiarity breeds a curiosity to understand each other's languages and frames of references. Natural desires for affiliation versus ideological convictions often lead to fertilizing dialogue and mutual learning.

This is a year of converting and becoming stimulated by others' views and ways of working and relating to their clients and their taboos. Special attention is paid to what is understood by 'cure', termination and relevant research issues in psychotherapy. A trainee comments:

> The course taught tolerance for difference, joy in excellence, excitement in competition, striving for congruence, search for 'first nature' (e.g., temperament) and then being/living who we are. I felt challenged in learning how to detect pathology, treatment planning, etc., and just when I really had it, I was being challenged again not to pathologize but to go to a simple emphasis on contact in the relationship. That is, 'learn your theories and throw them away'. The training has been about building me up, learning to tolerate being broken down and then going back to essence to find my integration, my me-ness. This I feel/think is in the ideology of the teaching.

Second year: Systemic Integrative Training Programme – knowledge and experience

This programme is designed to facilitate integration of personal style and experiential assimilation, as well as the integration of different approaches. It involves a review of the building blocks and epistemologies of different theories combined with experiential work. This can be a revision for those students familiar with

MODULE†	FOCUS
1 Physiological Level	Review of Reich (1972), Keleman (1985), Lowen (1976), Greenberg (1975) and Wolpe (1961); Classical conditioning, Desensitization techniques, Breathing and Relaxation; the use of medication, Acupuncture, Body-posture procedures and techniques (e.g. Bioenergetics), Massage and Gestalt techniques for enhancing sensory awareness.
2 Emotional Level	Review of Winnicott (1960), Bowlby (1953), Rutter (1972), and Miller (1983); Gestalt (Greenberg & Safran 1987), Primal Therapy, Psychodrama (Greenberg 1975), Bioenergetics (Lowen 1976), Rechilding (Clarkson & Fish 1988) and Redecision work of Transactional Analysis (Goulding & Goulding, 1979), Rebirthing and Pre-natal work.
3 Nominative Level	Review of Phenomenology (e.g. Merleau-Ponty 1962), Reflective Process (Rogers 1986), NeuroLinguistic Programming/Reframing (Bandler & Grinder 1982), Renaming in Gestalt (Enright 1980) Behavioural uses of Transactional Analysis, the Naming of Ego-States (Watkins 1976, Watkins & Watkins 1986), the Naming of Personified Introjects, Empathic Attunement (Rowe & MacIsaac 1989), Jungian Archetypes (Jung 1968, 1969) or Subpersonalities (Rowan 1990).
4 Normative	Review of Cultural Influences, Feminist Approaches (Chaplin 1988), Multi-Cultural Approaches (d'Ardenne & Mahtani 1989, Rack 1982, Littlewood & Lipsedge 1982), Parent Egos (Berne 1975), Alcoholics Anonymous, Reality Therapy (Glasser 1965), Reparenting Approaches (James 1974, Osnes 1974) and the Cathexis Approach (Schiff *et al* 1975), the work of Peck (1978).
5 Rational Level	Review of Rational-Emotive Therapy practice (Ellis 1962, Dryden 1987), Decontamination of the Adult Ego State in Transactional Analysis (Berne 1975), Strengthening the Ego (Federn 1977, Weiss 1950), the Objective Ego (Fairbairn 1952).
6 Theoretical Level	Review of theories of *behaviourally oriented approaches*, e.g. RET (Ellis 1962, Dryden 1987), Cognitive-Behavioural Therapy (Dryden & Trower 1989), the work of Skinner (1953) and Beck & Emery (1985). *Psychoanalytical approaches*, e.g. Drive Theory (Freud 1973), Ego Psychology (Hartmann 1964a, b), Object Relations (Klein 1984, Fairbairn 1952) and Self-Psychology (Kohut 1977, Kernberg 1982). *Existential-Humanistic approaches*, e.g. Gestalt, Existential Analysis, Transactional Analysis, and Client-centred approach of Rogers (1986).
7 Transpersonal	Review of Jung (1968, 1969), Fox (1983), Psychosynthesis (Assagioli 1971), Zen (Fromm 1960, Clarkson 1990).

† Each of these modules is the equivalent of three full training days, spread over one academic year and each module is organized around (a) Theory Review based on extensive recommended reading, (b) Strategy and Intervention Review and (c) Personal Experiential work.

Figure 11.3   Second Year: Systemic Integrative Psychotherapy training modules – knowledge and experience

an approach and for others it can be the stimulation to read, experience and learn more about other approaches with which he or she may be less familiar. External trainers – experts in particular approaches – are invited on to the programme so that trainees begin to learn a variety of models of the person and how they each in their own way can make sense from inside the particular frame of reference. This builds tolerance on the one hand and self-questioning on the other. Within this framework students are more able to choose specific modality(ies) which they find of benefit and interest, and they experience enrichment of viable choices. A modality which suits a particular personality and style of working can be better defined and also expands the original style of working. Often, integrating knowledge or skills which are rather dissimilar can involve creative tensions which evolve in more differentiated appreciation, relativity and tolerance for polarity of theory and of psyche.

The second year of the Systemic Integrative Training Programme, sometimes called 'Body and Soul', thus focuses on each individual's personal integration of knowledge and experience. Clarkson's (1975) 'Seven-level Model' of epistemology (as discussed in Chapter 2 of this volume) provides a framework for the second year of this advanced course in Systemic Integrative Psychotherapy. The Seven-level Model is an attempt to construct a thinking tool or conceptual protractor to provide a meaningful reference framework to deal with knowledge and experience in the widest possible holistic fashion. It is a map rather than the territory; a map that assists exploration of the territory created in the face-to-face encounter of therapist and client and the life experiences brought by the client into the therapeutic arena. Its nature is that of a reference grid to be used as a guide and measure rather than a template to dictate the therapeutic journey. This model can be used as an organizing model of the various kinds of epistemology associated with different levels of psychological theory and knowledge. On the other hand it can also be used to discriminate different experiential levels. The seven levels are currently named: (1) Physiological, (2) Emotional, (3) Nominative, (4) Normative, (5) Rational, (6) Theoretical and (7) Transpersonal (see Figure 2.3 in Chapter 2, p. 62).

A trainee comments:

> Personal Models of Integration: I developed my own personal model of integration based on the integration and assimilation of theories and philosophies in psychotherapy which I have learnt in order to develop my own philosophy and way of being with myself and with my clients. The trainer facilitated a process of drawing out the commonalities in the different approaches to psychotherapy, the holding of these commonalities in the foreground and using them as a base when working with the client. With this in mind, 'fitting' the theories on the person takes precedence. I hold as the core in my model of integration the relationship between myself and the client. The process of psychotherapy therefore will focus on our relationship and holding that in the foreground, think of how it can be best furthered, used, or worked with.

These levels around which the course is currently structured provide (a) a sorting system for multiple and varied interventions at different levels; (b) a conceptual grid for facilitating the differentiation between different 'levels of discourse' in order to clarify and sharpen therapeutic strategies and (c) a check-list for the review of most major approaches to the psyche. At each level, and through all the levels, the integration of various psychotherapies is explored in terms of the compatibility of assumptions about human nature, theories of psychotherapy and specific interventions. This work is done experientially, by means of discussion, case presentation and teaching, and is supplemented by the written work required in the course. A trainee comments:

> My systemic integrative model is evolving in my struggle between form and chaos – the balance of closed and open features in the total system. Part of this process is the relation between my personal therapy and the various models which I am learning. And as my father/authority issues move towards a degree of resolution so my sense of safety in psychoanalysis diminishes. That is, I need less of their protective boundaries and can tolerate a wider spectrum of presence with the client. Theory and praxis are inseparable, like breath and the body.

Dissertation and examination

Students applying for the Diploma in Systemic Integrative Psychotherapy are required to write a dissertation which shows their own personal and professional integration both in theory and practice. Executed towards the end of the course (or even after completion of the course), students have reported the usefulness of writing as identifying, clarifying and solidifying their own method and process of integration in their work with clients.

A special section in the dissertation is used by each candidate to describe the process and development of their own learning process since the integrative approach is so much based on the ability to keep learning, assimilating, reforming and essentially being self-reflexive. A trainee comments:

> Writing the dissertation allowed for the integration of the theoretical and conceptual learning through applying it in one's own practice and testing it against the perspective of senior colleagues outside of the institute where the particular integrative training had been completed.

The dissertation is usually read and assessed by at least two academic examiners who are also practising psychotherapists. At least one of these would be external to *metanoia* Psychotherapy Training Institute. The co-operation of international colleagues, particularly from the European community universities, has proved extremely valuable on moderating standards according to international criteria.

At the end of the 2-year training, further to the dissertation, students are required to complete a case-study of a client and to sit an oral examination at which they will play taped segments of their work, one of these representing their work with their case-study client. This forms part of the process of learning to speak to colleagues and assuming co-professional status. Of the four examining board members one is internal and three are external. The external members come from a variety of theoretical orientations – for example, psychodynamic, cognitive-behaviour therapy, psychiatry, Gestalt psychotherapy and so on.

Candidates experience this examination as a collegial discussion, answering questions on the differant approaches represented. Other parameters measured are treatment direction of psychotherapy, client assessment, effectiveness of interventions, professionalism, and intuition and creativity.

Professional development and continuing education

More and more professions throughout the world have begun to establish, and in some instances insist on, re-accreditation or other measures of encouraging the continuing education and development of their senior qualified practitioners. This can be done by means of conference attendance, ongoing multi-disciplinary case discussion or supervision, writing papers or books, attending other courses, and other ways of keeping interest, challenge and motivation alive. Of course, learning and further integration finds profound stimulation from our continued engagement in the teaching, supervision, writing, and giving of workshops to our students and peers. The most crucial fulcrum, however, is constituted by the everyday struggles and joys of clinical practice where our relationships with our patients and clients remain our most stringent and challenging teachers.

Specialized training in *integrative child therapy*, *integrative group psychotherapy* and *organizational consultancy* can follow or coincide with the integrative psychotherapy training. A *training for trainees course* or *supervision diploma course* are also ways in which professionals in clinical and counselling psychology and psychotherapy can continue to develop themselves, their understandings and their skills.

One of the most underlying values is that integration is an ongoing process in a continual state of development and evolution. Fixed syllabuses or fixed 'goalposts' are intrinsically antithetical to an orientation which is by its very nature perpetually questioning its own assumptions, developing its own ideas and responding to developments in the wider field of psychotherapy, psychology and psychiatry. Psychotherapists also need to take account of the social, global and historical context within which they work. No practising psychotherapist in any country where there is injustice of privilege, opportunity or rights can afford to ignore the wider context in which they are working. This is all relevant to, and is an influence on, the process of integration whether it be clinical, political or transpersonal. Sometimes one must stop in order to catch one's breath and commit some fraction of an ongoing dynamic process to the constraints of words on paper as has been done in this chapter. But integration never stops for long. Perhaps by the time this is published, the *metanoia* programme will have evolved significantly further or differently.

Teaching, writing and research involvement are seen as essential to the continuing maintenance and development of a seriously committed practising professional. It has often been said that it is only when you teach a subject, that you really begin to know it thoroughly. This is also true of writing and research. Without the sometimes hazardous, and often lonely and unrewarding labours of researchers, organizers, editors, theoreticians and scholars of the subject, the field of psychotherapy could hardly survive with integrity. And without the enlivening dialogue of the relationship between them and their audience, psychotherapeutic evolution would become impossible.

The way forward

I close with the words of Norcross:

> I am convinced that it is premature to advance any one integrative system, just as it is inappropriate to select any one all-purpose pure-form psychotherapy system. Nor should eclectic systems be pitted against each other in a 'dogma eat dogma' or 'my dad is stronger than your dad' manner – strategies that have proven historically unproductive. Instead, these eclectic models are presented as preliminary attempts to synthesize a diverse body of knowledge and as evolving systems in need of clinical experimentation and empiricial verification. I urge students, in the integrative spirit, to take the 'best' from each model and to discern converging themes for themselves.
>
> (Norcross in Beutler *et al.* 1987: 318)

Note

1 'We' or 'our' used in this context acknowledges the independent development of Systemic Integrative Psychotherapy at *metanoia* as the result of 20 years of interdisciplinary professional collaboration with Dr Brian Dobson, Maria Gilbert and Sue Fish, as well as the contributions of our graduates and trainees.

References

Adler, G. (1979) *Dynamics of the Self*, London: Coventure (first published 1951).
American Psychiatric Association (1987) *Diagnostic and Statistical Manual of Mental Disorders*, 3rd edn revised, Washington, DC: American Psychiatric Association.
d'Ardenne, P. and Mahtani, A. (1989) *Transcultural Counselling in Action*, London: Sage.
Assagioli, R. (1971) *Psychosynthesis: A Manual of Principles and Techniques*, New York: Viking.
Balint, M. (1968) *The Basic Fault: Therapeutic Aspects of Regression*, London: Tavistock.
Bandler, R. and Grinder, J. (1982) *Reframing: Neuro-Linguistic Programming and the Transformation of Meaning*, Moab, Ut.: Real People Press.
Beck, A.T. and Emery, G. (1985) *Anxiety Disorders and Phobias: A Cognitive Perspective*, New York: Basic Books.
Berne, E. (1975) *Transactional Analysis in Psychotherapy*, London: Souvenir Press (first published 1961).
Bertalanffy, L. von (1969) The theory of open systems in physics and biology, in F.E. Emery (ed.) *Systems Thinking*, Harmondsworth: Penguin, pp. 70–85.
Beutler, L.E., Mahoney, M.J., Norcross, J.C., Prochaska, J.O., Robertson, M.H. and Sollod, R.N. (1987) Training integrative/eclectic psychotherapists II, *Journal of Integrative and Eclectic Psychotherapy* 6(3): 296–332.
Boadella, D. (1987) *Lifestreams: An Introduction to Biosynthesis*, London: Routledge.

Bowlby, J. (1953) Some pathological processes set in motion by early mother–child separation, *Journal of Mental Science* 99: 265.

Chaplin, J. (1988) *Feminist Counselling in Action*, London: Sage.

Clarkson, P. (1975) 'Seven-Level Model', paper delivered at University of Pretoria, November.

——(1988) Script cure? A diagnostic pentagon of types of therapeutic change, *Transactional Analysis Journal* 18(3): 211–19.

—— (1989) Metanoia: a process of transformation, *Transactional Analysis Journal* 19(4): 224–34.

——(1990) A multiplicity of psychotherapeutic relationships, *British Journal of Psychotherapy* 7(2): 148–63.

—— (1992) Transference and countertransference in TA, in P. Clarkson *Transactional Analysis Psychotherapy: An Integrative Approach*, London: Routledge, pp. 148–74.

—— and Fish, S. (1988) Rechilding: creating a new past in the present as a support for the future, *Transactional Analysis Journal* 18(1): 51–9 (first published in Spanish translation 1986).

—— and Gilbert, M. (1990) The training of counsellor trainers and supervisors, in W. Dryden and B. Thorne (eds) *Training and Supervision for Counselling in Action*, London: Sage, pp. 143–69.

—— and Lapworth, P. (1992) The psychology of the self in transactional analysis, in P. Clarkson *Transactional Analysis Psychotherapy: An Integrative Approach*, London: Routledge.

Davanloo, H. (ed.) (1980) *Current Trends in Short-term Dynamic Therapy*, New York: Jason Aronson.

Dryden, W. (1987) *Counselling Individuals: The Rational-Emotive Approach*, London: Taylor & Francis.

—— and Trower, P. (eds) (1989) *Cognitive Psychotherapy: Stasis and Change*, London: Cassell.

Ellis, A. (1962) *Reason and Emotion in Psychotherapy*, Secaucus, NJ: Citadel Press.

Enright, J. (1980) *Enlightening Gestalt: Waking Up from the Nightmare*, Mill Valley, Calif.: Pro-Telos.

Fairbairn, W.R.D. (1952) *Psycho-analytic Studies of the Personality*, London: Tavistock.

Federn, P. (1977) *Ego Psychology and the Psychoses*, London: Maresfield Reprints (first published 1953).

Ferenczi, S. (1980) *Further Contributions to the Theory and Technique of Psycho-Analysis*, London: Maresfield Reprints (first published 1926).

Fiedler, F.E.A. (1950) A comparison of therapeutic relationships in psychoanalytic, non-directive and Adlerian therapy, *Journal of Consulting Psychology* 14: 436–45.

Finzi, S.C. (1987) On advanced training of an eclectic kind, *Journal of Integrative and Eclectic Psychotherapy* 6(1): 3–5.

Fox, M. (1983) *Original Blessing*, Santa Fe, NM: Bear & Company.

Frank, J.D. (1979) The present status of outcome studies, *Journal of Consulting and Clinical Psychology* 47: 310–16.

Frankl, V. (1964) *Man's Search for Meaning: An Introduction to Logotherapy*, London: Hodder & Stoughton (first published 1959).

Freud, S. (1973) Introductory lectures on psychoanalysis, in A. Richards (ed.) and J. Strachey (trans.) *The Pelican Freud Library Vol. 1*, Harmondsworth: Penguin (original work published 1915–17).

—— (1977) Three essays on sexuality, in A. Richards (ed.) and J. Strachey (trans.) *The Pelican Freud Library, Vol. 7*, Harmondsworth: Penguin, pp. 33–170 (original work published 1905).

Fromm, E. (1960) *Psychoanalysis and Zen Buddhism*, London: Allen & Unwin.

Fromm-Reichmann, F. (1974) *Principles of Intensive Psychotherapy*, Chicago: University of Chicago Press (first published 1950).

Garfield, S.L. (1980) *Psychotherapy: An Eclectic Approach*, New York: Wiley.

—— (1982) Eclecticism and integration in psychotherapy, *Behavior Therapy* 13: 610-23.

Glasser, W. (1965) *Reality Therapy*, New York: Harper & Row.

Gleick, J. (1988) *Chaos: Making a New Science*, London: Heinemann.

Goldfried, M.R. (ed.) (1982) *Converging Themes in Psychotherapy: Trends In Psychodynamic, Humanistic, and Behavioral Practice*, New York: Springer.

Goulding, M.M. and Goulding, R.L. (1979) *Changing Lives through Redecision Therapy*, New York: Grove Press.

Greenberg, I.A. (ed.) (1975) *Psychodrama: Theory and Therapy*, London: Souvenir Press (first published 1974).

Greenberg, L.S. and Safran, J.D. (1987) *Emotion in Psychotherapy: The Process of Therapeutic Change*, New York: Guilford Press.

Greenson, R.R. (1965) The working alliance and the transference neuroses, *Psychoanalytic Quarterly* 34: 155-81.

Hartmann, H. (1964a) *Ego Psychology and the Problems of Adaptation*, New York: International Universities Press (first published 1939).

—— (1964b) *Essays on Ego Psychology*, New York: International Universities Press.

Hynan, M.T. (1981) On the advantages of assuming that the techniques of psychotherapy are ineffective, *Psychotherapy: Theory, Research and Practice* 18: 11-13.

James, M. (1974) Self-reparenting: theory and process, *Transactional Analysis Journal* 4(3): 32-9.

Jaspers, K. (1963) *General Psychopathology* (J. Hoenig and M.W. Hamilton, trans.), Chicago: University of Chicago Press (first published 1913).

Jung, C.G. (1928) Analytical psychology and education, in H.G. and C.F. Baynes (trans.) *Contributions to Analytical Psychology*, London: Trench Trubner, pp. 313-82.

—— (1968) Archetypes of the collective unconscious, in R.F.C. Hull (trans.) *The Collected Works, Vol. 9 Part 1*, 2nd edn, London: Routledge & Kegan Paul, pp. 3-41 (original work published 1954).

—— (1969) Psychology and religion, in R.F.C. Hull (trans.) *The Collected Works, Vol. 11*, 2nd edn, London: Routledge & Kegan Paul, pp. 3-106 (original work published 1958).

Keeney, B.P. (1983) *Aesthetics of Change*, New York: Guilford Press.

Keleman, S. (1985) *Emotional Anatomy: The Structure of Experience*, Berkeley, Calif.: Center Press.

Kernberg, O. (1982) Self, ego, affects and drives, *Journal of the American Psychoanalytic Association* 30: 893-917.

Klein, M. (1984) *Envy, Gratitude and Other Works*, London: Hogarth Press and Institute for Psychoanalysis (first published 1957).

Kohut, H. (1977) *The Restoration of the Self*, New York: International Universities Press.

Laing, R.D. (1965) *The Divided Self*, Harmondsworth: Penguin.

Langs, R. (1976) *The Bipersonal Field*, New York: Jason Aronson.

Lazarus, A. (1971) *Behavior Therapy and Beyond*, New York: McGraw-Hill.

Liotti, G. (1989) Resistance to change in cognitive psychotherapy: theoretical remarks from a constructivistic point of view, in W. Dryden and P. Trower (eds) *Cognitive Psychotherapy: Stasis and Change*, London: Cassell, pp. 28-56.

Littlewood, R. and Lipsedge, M. (1982) *Aliens and Alienists: Ethnic Minorities and Psychiatry*, Harmondsworth: Penguin.

Lowen, A. (1976) *Bioenergetics*, Harmondsworth: Penguin.

Mahler, M.S., Pine, F. and Bergman, A. (1975) *The Psychological Birth of the Human Infant*, London: Hutchinson.

Malan, D.H. (1979) *Individual Psychotherapy and the Science of Psychodynamics*, London: Butterworths.

Mann, J. (1973) *Time-limited Psychotherapy*, Cambridge, Mass.: Harvard University Press.

Maslow, A. (1968) *Towards a Psychology of Being*, 2nd edn, New York: Van Nostrand.

Masterson, J.F. (1985) *The Real Self: A Developmental, Self, and Object Relations Approach*, New York: Brunner/Mazel.

May, R. (ed.) (1969) *Existential Psychology*, New York: Random House.
—— (1975) *The Courage to Create*, New York: W.W. Norton.
Meichenbaum, D. (1974) *Cognitive Behavior Modification*, New York: Plenum.
Merleau-Ponty, M. (1962) *Phenomenology of Perception*, London: Routledge & Kegan Paul.
Miller, A. (1983) *The Drama of the Gifted Child and the Search for the True Self* (R. Ward, trans.), London: Faber & Faber.
Mindell, A. (1984) *Dreambody: The Body's Role in Revealing the Self*, London: Routledge & Kegan Paul.
Norcross, J.C. (ed.) (1986) *Handbook of Eclectic Psychotherapy*, New York: Brunner/Mazel.
Norcross, J.C., Beutler, L.E., Clarkin, J.F., DiClemente, C.C., Halgin, R.P., Frances, A., Prochaska, J.O., Robertson, M. and Suedfeld, P. (1986) Training integrative/eclectic psychotherapist, *International Journal of Eclectic Psychotherapy* 5(1): 71–94.
Osnes, R.E. (1974) Spot-reparenting, *Transactional Analysis Journal* 4(3): 40–6.
Peck, S. (1978) *The Road Less Traveled*, New York: Simon & Schuster.
Perls, F., Hefferline, R.F. and Goodman, P. (1977) *Gestalt Therapy*, New York: Bantam (first published 1951).
Pierrakos, J. (1974) *The Core of Man*, New York: Institute for the New Age.
Pine, F. (1985) *Developmental Theory and Clinical Process*, New Haven: Yale University Press.
Polster, E. and Polster, M. (1974) *Gestalt Therapy Integrated*, New York: Vintage Books (first published 1973).
Popper, K. (1959) *The Logic of Scientific Discovery*, London: Hutchinson.
Rack, P. (1982) *Race, Culture, and Mental Disorder*, London: Tavistock.
Rank, O. (1989) *Art and Artist: Creative Urge and Personality Development*, New York: W.W. Norton (first published 1932).
Reich, W. (1972) *Character Analysis*, 3rd edn, New York: Simon & Schuster.
Rilke, R.M. (1929) *Briefe an einen Jungen Dichter* [*Letters to a Young Poet*], Frankfurt am Main: Insel.
Rogers, C.R. (1986) *Client-Centred Therapy*, London: Constable.
—— and Stevens, B. (1967) *Person to Person: The Problem of the Human: A New Trend in Psychology*, Lafayette, Calif.: Real People Press.
Rowan, J. (1983) *The Reality Game: A Guide to Humanistic Counselling and Therapy*, London: Routledge & Kegan Paul.
—— (1990) *Subpersonalities: The People Inside Us*, London: Routledge.
Rowe, C.E. and MacIsaac, D.S. (1989) *Empathic Attunement: The 'Technique' of Psycho-analytic Self Psychology*, London: Jason Aronson.
Rutter, M. (1972) *Maternal Deprivation Reassessed*, Harmondsworth: Penguin.
Ryle, A. (1990) *Cognitive-analytic Therapy: Active Participation in Change*, Chichester: John Wiley.
Sallis, J. and Maly, K. (eds) (1980) *Heraclitean Fragments: A Companion Volume to the Heidegger/Fink Seminar on Heraclitus*, Alabama: University of Alabama Press.
Samuels, A. (1985) *Jung and the Post-Jungians*, London: Routledge & Kegan Paul.
—— (1989) *The Plural Psyche*, London: Routledge.
Schiff, J.L., with Schiff, A.W., Mellor, K., Schiff, E., Schiff, S., Richman, D., Fishman, J., Wolz, L., Fishman, C. and Momb, D. (1975) *Cathexis Reader: Transactional Analysis Treatment of Psychosis*, New York: Harper & Row.
Shapiro, M.K. (1988) *Second Childhood: Hypno-Play Therapy with Age-Regressed Adults*, New York: W.W. Norton.
Skinner, B.F. (1953) *Science and Human Bahavior*, New York: Macmillan.
Stern, D.N. (1985) *The Interpersonal World of the Infant*, New York: Basic Books.
Watkins, J.G. (1976) Ego states and the problem of responsibility: a psychological analysis of the Patty Hearst case, *Journal of Psychiatry and Law* Winter: 471–89.
—— and Watkins, H.H. (1986) Hypnosis, multiple personality, and ego states, in B.B. Wolman and M. Ullman (eds) *Handbook of States of Consciousness*, New York: Van Nostrand Reinhold, pp. 133–58.

Watzlawick, P., Weakland, J.H. and Fisch, R. (1974) *Change: Principles of Problem Formation and Problem Resolution*, New York: W.W. Norton.

Weiss, E. (1950) *Principles of Psychodynamics*, New York: Grune & Stratton.

Winnicott, D.W. (1958) *Collected Papers*, London: Tavistock.

—— (1960) *The Maturational Processes and the Facilitating Environment*, London: Hogarth Press.

Wolpe, J. (1961) The systematic desensitization treatment of neuroses, *Journal of Nervous and Mental Disease* 132: 189–203.

Zohar, D. (1990) *The Quantum Self*, London: Bloomsbury.

Appendix

List of articles with an integrative-eclectic theme or focus written by British authors and published in British Journals (1966-90).

1966

Crisp, A.H., Transference, symptom emergence and social repercussion in behaviour therapy: a study of 54 treated patients, *British Journal of Medical Psychology* 39: 179-96.

Marks, I.M. and Gelder, M.G., Common ground between behaviour therapy and psychodynamic methods, *British Journal of Medical Psychology* 39: 11.

1971

Marks, I., The future of the psychotherapies, *British Journal of Psychiatry* 118: 69-73.

1974

Antonouris, G., Counselling theory and practice: a first enquiry, *The Counsellor* 19: 1-3.

Lambley, P., Differential effects of psychotherapy and behavioural techniques in a case of acute obsessive compulsive disorder, *British Journal of Psychiatry* 125: 181-3.

1976

Antonouris, G., Values, counselling theory and the school counsellor, *British Journal of Guidance and Counselling* 4(2): 171-80.

1978

Kraft, T., The combined behaviour therapy-psychotherapy approach, *Projective Psychology* 23: 15-29.

Ryle, A., A common language for the psychotherapies, *British Journal of Psychiatry* 132: 585-94.

1979

Black, D., Family therapy as a setting for other treatment modalities, *Journal of Family Therapy* 1: 183-92.

Levere, R. and Kirk, M., A combined therapeutic approach in a family setting, *Journal of Family Therapy* 1: 271-80.

Llewelyn, S.P. and Hume, W.I., The patient's view of therapy, *British Journal of Medical Psychology* 42: 29-35.

Nelson-Jones, R., Goals for counselling, psychotherapy and psychological education: responsibility as an integrating concept, *British Journal of Guidance and Counselling* 7(2): 153–68.

Ryle, A., The focus in brief interpretive psychotherapy: dilemma, traps and snags as target problems, *British Journal of Psychiatry* 134: 46–54.

1980

Dryden, W., 'Eclectic' approaches in individual counselling: some pertinent issues, *The Counsellor* 3(2): 24–30.

Fontana, D., Psychology in the 1980s, *The Counsellor* 3(2): 2–10.

Llewellyn, S.P., The uses of an eclectic approach: a case study, *British Journal of Medical Psychology* 53: 145–9.

Rowan, J., Heresy-hunting in the AHP, *Self and Society* 8(1): 2–9.

Ryle, A., Some measures of goal attainment in focused integrated active psychotherapy: a study of 15 cases, *British Journal of Psychiatry* 137: 475–86.

1982

Dryden, W., Rational-emotive therapy and eclecticism, *The Counsellor* 3(5): 15–22.

Nelson-Jones, R., The counsellor as decision-maker: role treatment and responding decisions, *British Journal of Guidance and Counselling* 10(2): 113–24.

Sundborn, M., Comparison of Gestalt and Reichian schools of psychotherapy, *Self and Society* 10(5): 239–47.

1983

Davis, J.D., Slaying the psychoanalytic dragon: an integrationist's commentary on Yates, *British Journal of Clinical Psychology* 22: 133–4.

Wright, H., Wilkinson, J. and Proud, A., Success after failure; the realignment of responsibility in an integrated approach to a family with an adolescent bedwetter, *Journal of Family Therapy* 5: 189–98.

1984

Kraft, T., Injection phobia: a case study, *British Journal of Experimental and Clinical Hypnosis* 1(3): 13–18.

Ryle, A., How can we compare different psychotherapies? Why are they all effective?, *British Journal of Medical Psychology* 57: 261–4.

1985

Dyne, D., Questions of 'Training'. A contribution from a peripatetic cousin, *Free Associations* 3: 92–147.

Hinshelwood, R.D., Questions of training, *Free Associations* 2: 7–18.

Jenkins, H., Orthodoxy in family therapy practice as servant as tyrant, *Journal of Family Therapy* 7: 19–30.

Macaskill, N., Homework assignments in brief psychotherapy, *British Journal of Psychotherapy* 2(2): 134–41.

Martin, I. and Levey, A.B., Conditioning, evaluations and cognitions: an axis of integration, *Behaviour Research Therapy* 23(2): 167–75.

Nelson-Jones, R., Eclecticism, integration and comprehensiveness in counselling theory and practice, *British Journal of Guidance and Counselling* 13(2): 129–38.

Ryle, A., Cognitive theory, objective relations and the self, *British Journal of Medical Psychology* 58: 1–7.

1986

Hinshelwood, R.D., Eclecticism: the impossible project. A response to Deryk Dyne, *Free Associations* 5: 23–7.

Molnos, A., From video recordings, towards integrated thinking in brief psychotherapy. Reflections after the first European Symposium on short-term dynamic psychotherapy, Copenhagen, 7th–11th July, 1986, *British Journal of Psychotherapy* 3(2): 165–71.

Richard, B., Psychological practice and social democracy, *Free Associations* 5: 105–36.

Zigmond, D., Babel as bible? Order, chaos and creativity in psychotherapy, *British Journal of Psychotherapy* 2(4): 302–9.

1987

Bennun, I., Behavioural marital therapy: a critique and appraisal of integrated models, *Behavioural Psychotherapy* 15: 1–15.

Brockman, B., Poynton, A., Ryle, A. and Watson, J.P., Effectiveness of time-limited therapy carried out by trainees: comparison of two methods, *British Journal of Psychiatry* 151: 602–10.

1988

Coleman, E.Z., Room to grow: how divergent approaches to counselling can enrich one another, *British Journal of Guidance and Counselling* 16(1): 21–32.

Llewellyn, S.P., Psychological therapy as viewed by clients and therapists, *British Journal of Clinical Psychology* 27: 223–37.

Murgatroyd, S.J., Reversal theory and psychotherapy: a review, *Counselling Psychology Quarterly* 1(1): 57–74.

Nelson-Jones, R., Counselling psychology in Australia: some comparisons with America and Britain, *BPS Counselling Psychology Section Review* 3(2): 15–29.

—— Choice Therapy, *Counselling Psychology Quarterly* 1(1): 43–55.

Pilgrim, D., Psychotherapy in British Special Hospitals: a case of failure to thrive, *Free Associations* 11: 58–72.

1989

Coffey, D., A systematic approach to counselling training: the Ulster way, *Counselling* 70: 6–12.

Douglas, A.R., The limits of cognitive-behaviour therapy: can it be integrated with psychodynamic therapy?, *British Journal of Psychotherapy* 5(3): 390–401.

Dryden, W. and Norcross, J.C., Eclecticism and integration in counselling and psychotherapy: introduction, *British Journal of Guidance and Counselling* 17(3): 225–6.

Fonagy, P., On the integration of cognitive-behaviour theory with psychoanalysis, *British Journal of Psychotherapy* 5(4): 557–63.

Kraft, T., Working with terminally ill patients, *Proceedings of British Society of Medical and Dental Hypnosis* 6(4): 16–20.

1990

Beard, H., Marlow, M. and Ryle, A., The management and treatment of personality-disordered patients: the use of sequential diagrammatic reformulation, *British Journal of Psychiatry* 156: 541–5.

Bott, D., Epistemology: the place of systems theory in an integrated model of counselling, *Counselling* 1(1): 23–5.

Clarkson, P., A multiplicity of psychotherapeutic relationships, *British Journal of Psychotherapy* 7(2): 148–63.

Daines, B., Marital counselling: teaching an eclectic approach, *Counselling Psychology Quarterly* 3(4): 363–70.

Gregoire, A., Physical or psychological: an unhealthy splitting in theory and practice, *Sex and Marital Therapy* 5(2): 103–4.

Hornby, G., A humanistic developmental model of counselling: a psycho-educational approach, *Counselling Psychology Quarterly* 3(2): 191–203.

Kellett, J., Physical or psychological: time we bridge the divide, *Sex and Marital Therapy* 5(2): 101–2.

O'Sullivan, K.R. and Dryden, W., A survey of clinical psychologists in the South East Thames Health Region: activities, role and theoretical orientation, *Clinical Psychology Forum* 29: 21–6.

Shum, J., Counselling Psychology in Britain: status and current issues, *BPS Counselling Psychology Review* 5(1): 6–10.

Smail, D., Design for a post-behavioural clinical psychology, *Clinical Psychology Forum* 28: 2–10.

Walker, L.G. and Patten, M.I., Marriage guidance counselling II. What counsellors want to give, *British Journal of Guidance and Counselling* 18(3): 294–307.

Watts, F.N., Aversion to personal body hair: a case study in the integration of behavioural and interpretative methods, *British Journal of Medical Psychology* 63: 335–40.

Index